September 06

for Our dear friend
    Chris
with Our love

Barbara +   Clive x

A MAN ABOUT A DOG

A MAN about A DOG

Euphemisms & Other Examples
of Verbal Squeamishness

NIGEL REES

Collins

First published in 2006 by Collins
An Imprint of HarperCollins*Publishers*
77–85 Fulham Palace Road
Hammersmith
London
W6 8JB

The Collins website address is www.collins.co.uk

Collins is a registered trademark of
HarperCollins*Publishers* Ltd

12   11   10   09   08   07   06
7   6   5   4   3   2   1

Front cover images:
Man behind newspaper taken from '*The Other Book*',
Mitchell Symons © The Random House Group;
Greyhound taken from '*3,800 Early Advertising Cuts*'
© Dover Publications Ltd

A catalogue record for this book is available
from the British Library

ISBN-10: 0-00-721453-7
ISBN-13: 987-0-00-721453-2

Typeset by Rowland Phototypesetting Ltd,
Bury St Edmunds, Suffolk

Printed and bound in Great Britain by
Clays Ltd, St Ives plc

INTRODUCTION

Everyone knows what the word 'euphemism' means. It describes the process of mincing words and the tendency that most of us have towards verbal squeamishness. As my wife rather neatly put it, euphemism is the business of *not* calling a spade a spade. But if this can be generally agreed, there is plenty of scope for argument as to which words and phrases actually fall into the category.

If you accept the starting definition that a euphemism 'speaks fair' (as the word's Greek origin has it) – that it tries to break an idea gently or inoffensively to the reader or hearer – then you can list hundreds if not thousands of examples, as I have done.

Yet it is possible to extend the net too widely. In considering entries for inclusion in *A Man About a Dog*, I have asked myself whether the word or phrase has the specific function of *concealing* something of the nature and meaning of what it describes. A true euphemism holds something back. It does not come right out with it. It is, if you like, mealy-mouthed for whatever reason – taste, decency, politeness, unwillingness to offend. A euphemism says something in an intentionally indirect, obscuring or obfuscatory way.

If a word or phrase is simply an alternative or roundabout way of saying something, I do not consider it to be carrying out a euphemizory function. So, when I have found that what we have in front of us is just another name for something, especially just a slang alternative for it, then I have excluded it. Or if I have included it, then I have flagged my doubts about its standing.

To plunge right in and consider a few examples: I do not think that *prick* is really a euphemism for 'penis', because in genteel conversation or polite society – whichever yardstick you care to choose – it would stick out just as boldly ... How about *bog* for 'lavatory'? I was minded to exclude it on the grounds that it is hardly obfuscatory and, indeed, is even more ugly than the term it might be trying to replace. Nevertheless, it does seem to be avoiding the straightforward descriptive word. A borderline case, but I have let it in. Much the same difficulty occurs with another euphemism that I have included: *period* for 'menstruation' hardly disguises what is being talked about, whereas *having the decorators in* surely does. Similarly, although *bent* and *queer* are not less offensive and certainly are not more gentle than 'homosexual', they do not directly state what is being talked about – or at least they did not when first coined and long before they were taken up as badges of honour by some gay groups.

Anyway, these considerations have had to be made quite frequently during the writing of this book. All I can say is that where slang alternatives are being primarily playful rather than purposely indirect, I have *tended* to exclude them. Indeed, if I had listed all the slang words for sexual parts and activities, it would surely have unbalanced the book and to no great purpose. On the other hand, in those areas where there are many, many euphemisms – death and going to the lavatory most notably – I have included a number of terms that may not have been widely used. Indeed, some of them may be one-off coinages or have probably been restricted to one person or household. But if they struck me as unusual and entertaining, I have gone with them.

I have had no hesitation in including the language of political correctness. This has been a major new euphemizing force since the late 1980s, even though it has little to do with either modesty or politeness or good taste. PC tries to protect special interest groups from insensitive language – even if the groups themselves often couldn't care less how you talked about them. Of course, you can laugh at the excesses of PC – *femholes* and *herstory* are ludicrous – but I try to look on the positive side and would claim that it has produced a greater awareness generally of the importance of considering the effect of the words we use.

As will be obvious, there is plenty of scope for debate on the qualifications of individual words and phrases for inclusion in this book of euphemisms. Fortunately, there is a great number about which there is no doubt that they are correctly designated as such. *A Man About a Dog* could not ever be a comprehensive survey of the field. It just aims to be an exploration and an enjoyment of it.

Lastly, a word about dating: I have tried to include an indication of when individual words or phrases may first have been used euphemistically (they may have existed in other ways before this, of course). Where early citations have been found, I say 'by 1922' but this is really a very imprecise business and more often than not I have had to resort to guesswork. You will know that I am pretty uneasy when I resort to something like '19th century' or 'by the 1930s?'

I am most grateful to the many correspondents who have, over the years, alerted me to euphemisms they have encountered in their lives. These people are referred to by their name and the year in which they were in touch with me. Hence, in this regard, the coiner of the excellent term 'loophemism' (i.e. a euphemism for 'going to the lavatory') I would here acknowledge as Frank Deakin of Wilmslow (1995). My chief debt, however, is to the late Vernon Noble with whom I collaborated on *A Who's Who of Nicknames* (1985). The starting point for my collection of euphemisms – together with examples of their use – was a booklet he wrote in 1982. Entitled *Speak Softly – Euphemisms and Such*, it was published by The Centre for English Cultural Tradition and Language at the University of Sheffield. I know that Vernon would have been gratified by the way his small work was to inspire this larger effort and to provide it with so many leads. I happily dedicate *A Man About a Dog* to his memory.

NIGEL REES
London 2006

HOW TO USE THIS BOOK

The euphemisms are listed in **bold** in word-by-word order. Cross-references are in SMALL CAPITALS. Cross-references are also grouped under the appropriate theme, namely:

ACTIVITY/BEHAVIOUR ENHANCEMENT

APPEARANCE

BIRTH/PREGNANCY

BODY MATTERS

BUSINESS/EMPLOYMENT/WORKPLACE MATTERS

CONDITIONS/STATES OF AFFAIRS

CRIMINAL ACTIVITY/JUSTICE/LEGAL TERMINOLOGY/
  POLICE MATTERS

DEATH/FUNERAL MATTERS

DEFECATION

DESCRIPTIVE OF PLACES, THINGS

DEVIL

DISABILITIES

DISHONESTY/LYING

DRINKING ALCOHOL

ESTATE AGENTS' SPEAK

FATNESS

GENTILITY ENFORCEMENT

HEALTH/ILLNESS/MEDICAL CONDITIONS

HOMOSEXUALITY

HUMAN/PERSONAL CHARACTERISTICS/QUALITIES

JOB-TITLE ENHANCEMENT

LAVATORY, GOING TO THE

MARRIAGE/RELATIONSHIPS/SINGLENESS

MASTURBATION

MENSTRUATION

MENTAL MATTERS

MILITARY ENHANCEMENTS

MONEY/SELLING/TRADE

OATH CONTROL

OLD AGE

ABBREVIATIONS AND SOURCES

Apperson: G.L. Apperson, *English Proverbs and Proverbial Phrases* (1929)
Bible: The Authorized Version (1611), unless stated otherwise
DOAS: Wentworth & Flexner, *Dictionary of American Slang*, 2nd
   supplemented edn (1975)
OED2: *The Oxford English Dictionary*, 2nd edn (1989), CD-ROM version
   3.0 (2002)
Partridge/Catch Phrases: Eric Partridge, *A Dictionary of Catch Phrases*, 2nd
   edn edited by Paul Beale (1985)
Partridge/Slang: Eric Partridge, *A Dictionary of Slang and Unconventional
   English*, 8th edn edited by Paul Beale (1984)
Safire: William Safire, *Safire's Political Dictionary* (1978)
Shakespeare: The Arden Shakespeare (2nd series)

Aa

(an) abattoir A slaughterhouse. The word was imported from French in the mid-1860s. Note how the slaughter aspect is minimized by being expressed in a foreign language – though, in fact, the French derives from *abattre* meaning 'to beat, strike, cut, blow, hew or break down', which is really just as bad.

(the) abdomen The stomach, belly. A genteel, grandiloquent term, in use since the 19th century, as also **the abdominal regions**. Hardly more precise than **(the) lower abdomen** when used to describe the male genitalia. By the late 19th century. '*Fig-leaf*, an apron. In fencing, the padded shield worn over the lower abdomen and right thigh' – John S. Farmer and W.E. Henley, *Slang and Its Analogues* (1891). Hence, also **(an) abdominal protector**, a device for shielding the important male parts in sporting activities. 'Leather Professional Boxing Abdominal Protector. All Leather Construction. Rubber padding to absorb shock. Elastic Strings with lace adjustment. Meets all professional and amateur safety specs. Complete hip, groin and kidney protection. Recommended for men. Fully adjustable closure. Durable protective cup sewn inside' – US advert (2005).

– abled See DIFFERENTLY ABLED

ableism Discrimination in favour of able-bodied people and against the unfit and the disabled. The word was coined by US feminists in the early 1980s, but the notion has also been expressed (especially in the UK) through the words 'able-bodism' and 'able-bodiedism'. Given that none of these words is easy to say, it is not surprising that the concept has hardly entered into mainstream usage. 'A GLC report ... referred throughout to a new phenomenon called mysteriously "able-bodism" – a reference apparently to that malevolent majority, the fully-fit' – *The Daily Telegraph* (1 November 1984); 'The Labour Party in Haringey has come up with the "ism" to cap the lot. The latest term ... is "ableism", presumably coined to describe those sinners who discriminate in favour of able-bodied persons for jobs on building sites' – *The Daily Telegraph* (8 November 1986); 'Ableism – oppression of the differently abled, by the temporarily able' – 'Definitions', Smith College Office of Student Affairs (1990).

An example of how ableism may be unconscious: 'Even when journalists think that they are presenting positive images of disabled people, by praising them for achieving something that would be unremarkable if done by an able-bodied person, all too often this is patronizing to disabled people, and reinforces stereotypes' – The Royal Association for Disability and Rehabilitation, Briefing Note, May 1992. Sources include: *The Longman Register of New Words* (1989); *The Oxford Dictionary of New Words* (1991).

ablution facilities Washbasins, showers. 'Performing one's ablutions' can either refer to washing or going to the LAVATORY but is rather an arch archaism in the first sense and probably only a true euphemism when used in the second sense. 'Please note that campers must provide their own drinking water, as the water supplied to the ablution facilities is not ideal for drinking' – South Africa national parks advert (2005).

(in) Abraham's bosom Dead/in heaven, i.e. where the dead sleep contentedly. From Luke 16:23: 'And it came to pass, that the beggar died, and was carried by the angels into Abraham's bosom.' The phrase alludes to Abraham, first of the Hebrew patriarchs. 'The sons of Edward sleep in Abraham's bosom' – Shakespeare, *Richard III* (1592–3), IV.iii.38 – not so surprising, really, as Richard has just had them murdered. Compare **Arthur's bosom**, a malapropism from Shakespeare's *Henry V* (1599), II.iii.9. The Hostess (formerly Mistress Quickly) says of the dead Falstaff: 'Nay, sure, he's not in hell: he's in Arthur's bosom, if ever man went to Arthur's bosom.'

absence of — Lack of —. Hence, 'absence of literary skills' is a polite way of saying what backward readers and writers have. 'They are constantly overhearing ex cathedra judgments on the state of Australian women's fiction, its tendency to cheap violence and crude mockery, its unseemly passions and absence of political correctness' – *The Guardian* (16 July 1992).

abuse (1) Cruelty or maltreatment of another person. (2) Misuse of any substance. (3) Illegal or taboo use of a person or thing. As in 'alcohol abuse', 'child abuse', 'drug abuse', 'heroin abuse', 'ritual abuse', 'satanic abuse', 'solvent abuse', SUBSTANCE ABUSE. Employed in the first sense since the 1960s and in the second since the 1970s, but both constructions were especially prevalent in the 1980s. When applied with reference to drugs and other 'substances', it has always struck me as an odd way of talking about the matter. Although both alcohol and drugs can be used 'properly', the term 'substance abuse' suggests that the blame is placed on the substance rather than the user and also implies that the substance could never be used in a *proper* manner. 'Pot-smoking is widespread in spite of dire warnings about the dangers of "drug abuse" repeatedly broadcast by the armed forces radio' – *The Times* (28 May 1970); 'Child abuse occurs in all walks of life ... Doctors and lawyers, too, batter their kids' – *The New York Times* (6 January 1974); 'International Congress of Child Abuse and Neglect', held in London (September 1978); 'This is a setback for the campaign against increasing heroin abuse among the young in all parts of the country' – *The Sunday Times* (9 December 1984).

(to) abuse the bed To commit adultery. An obsolete encapsulation of 'to violate the marriage-bed' that occurs, for example, in Shakespeare, *The Merry Wives of Windsor* (1601),

II.ii.281: 'My bed shall be abused,' cries Ford on hearing of Falstaff's designs upon his wife.

AC/DC Bisexual. From the abbreviations for alternating current/direct current in electricity and simply implying 'both'. *DOAS* dates this from about 1960. 'You can also tell *Time* Magazine you're bisexual, be AC-DC in the international edition' – Kate Millett, *Flying* (1974), ch. 1.

academically subnormal Dim-witted, thick. A later variation of EDUCATIONALLY SUBNORMAL. 'Academically subnormal Old Etonians, who might once have looked forward to blameless careers as estate agents, are today pressed into profitable service as security operatives' – *The Spectator* (14 December 2004).

(an) access hole A manhole. The good feminist may also use **sewer hole / utility hole** and **utility access hole**. See also FEMHOLE. The source for this useful information is *The Nonsexist Word Finder: A Dictionary of Gender-Free Usage*, ed. Rosalie Maggio (Boston, Mass., 1988).

(an) accident (1) An unplanned pregnancy and the result of it. By the 1930s. (2) The result of a child's inability to control its defecation or urination. By the mid-20th century.

accommodation A railway carriage. Part of British railspeak since about the 1980s: 'The buffet car is situated towards the rear of the First Class accommodation.' 'If you have a First Class ticket (or the equivalent) and no First Class accommodation (or the equivalent) is available, and you travel in Standard Class accommodation (where it is provided), you may claim a refund of the difference in fare' – National Rail Conditions of Carriage (2005).

(an) accommodation unit A single place of residence, whether it be a room, a flat or a house, made to sound grand for official enumeration purposes. Jargon possibly introduced by the British Ministry of Health in the late 1940s. Sir David Maxwell-

Fyffe said in the House of Commons, 'One million "accommodation units" have been built since the war.' The term was
mocked by Winston Churchill in an election speech at Cardiff
(8 February 1950) when he sang: 'Accommodation unit sweet
accommodation unit'.

(an/the) account A/the bill. The use of this word in a
straightforward way goes back beyond the 16th century. However,
it seems to have become a genteelism for 'bill' some time in the
early 20th century. People would ask to 'settle the account' or
'settle up' in a hotel or restaurant rather than use the more blunt
four-letter word. Tony Hancock used it regarding his telephone
bill in the BBC radio show, *Hancock's Half-Hour* (26 October 1955).

(to) acquire (1) To buy. (2) To steal. 'The Americans don't
have a monopoly of circumlocution. I remember the British
civil servant who asked a government department for a book,
and was told he was "authorised to acquire the work in question
by purchase through the ordinary trade channels" – i.e. buy it' –
Harold Evans, BBC Radio 4, *A Point of View* (18 September 2005).
Circumlocution does not in itself mean that euphemism is at
work but the use here would seem to suggest that the civil servant
considered 'buy' a vulgarism.

(an) act of shame Adultery. In Shakespeare, *Othello* (1604),
V.ii.212, Othello excuses his murder of Desdemona by saying
Iago knew: 'That she with Cassio hath the act of shame a
thousand times committed'. Apart from this, **the act**, on its own,
can be used to describe SEXUAL INTERCOURSE, either in or
out of marriage, as also 'the act of love', 'the act of marriage'
and so on.

(an) activist A stirrer-up, usually on a political extreme. One
who believes in direct action or protest to advance his/her views.
Known by 1915, but an especially popular concept since the
1970s/80s. 'He had almost forgotten his role as student activist' –
Emma Lathen, *When in Greece* (1969), ch. 10; '[A] six year battle
with activists which culminated in the unsolved theft of the

remains of the owner's late mother-in-law' – *The Independent*
(24 August 2005).

activity / activities Murder and other crimes, or anything
unmentionable. Since the second half of the 20th century?
'All Volunteers have been instructed to assist the development
of purely political and democratic programmes through
exclusively peaceful means. Volunteers must not engage in any
other activities whatsoever' – IRA statement on ending its armed
campaign (29 July 2005); 'On the *Caronia*, formerly a Cunard
ship ... inspectors in July last year discovered that "cockroach
activity" had been logged by staff' – *The Times* (1 September 2005).

activity/behaviour enhancement See ABATTOIR; ABUSE;
ACTIVIST; ACTIVITY; ADJUST ONE'S DRESS; AFFIRMATIVE
ACTION; ANTISOCIAL BEHAVIOUR; APPREHEND;
APPROPRIATE TECHNOLOGY; ATTENTION DEFICIT
DISORDER; ATTITUDE PROBLEM; BACKHANDER; BEG TO
DIFFER; BELOW MEDIUM HEIGHT; BELOW STAIRS; BELOW
THE SALT; BEND/STRETCH THE RULES; BOOTLEG; BROWNIE
POINTS; CARRY THE CAN; CATCH A COLD; CHINESE
WHISPER; CLAIM RESPONSIBILITY FOR; CONDUCTING A
SURVEY; COUNTER-FACTUAL PROPOSITION; COURTESY
CALL; CUT AND PASTE JOB; DAY OF ACTION; DEEP-SIX;
DISPLACEMENT; DISPOSE OF; DISSENT; DISSIPATION;
DITCH; DOCTOR; DONATE; DRESS TO THE LEFT/RIGHT; DRY;
DUMBING DOWN; EMBROIDER; ENERGETIC DISASSEMBLY;
ESCALATE; EXPECTORATE; EYE FOR THE MAIN CHANCE;
FAIL TO WIN; FALL ON ONE'S SWORD; FLEXIBILITY;
FORBIDDEN FRUIT; GET INTO BED WITH; GET (SOMETHING)
OFF THE GROUND; GIVE/TEACH SOMEONE A LESSON;
GO AND SEE A MAN ABOUT A DOG; GO DOWN THE TUBES;
GO OUT WITHOUT ONE'S HAT ON; HANG SOMEONE OUT TO
DRY; HAVE WORDS; KEEP UP WITH THE JONESES; LAND OF
NOD; LEAK; LEAVE; LEFT-HANDED COMPLIMENT; LOOK
AFTER NUMBER ONE; MEANINGFUL DIALOGUE; MESSAGE;
MIXED REVIEWS; MONKEY BUSINESS; MOONLIGHT FLIT;
NATIONAL SERVICE; NATURAL BREAK; NATURIST; NERVE;

OBLIGE; OPTICAL ENHANCEMENT; OWN GOAL; PACK IT IN;
PAINT THE TOWN RED; PAPER THE HOUSE; PAY LIP SERVICE;
PECCADILLOES; PHOTO OPPORTUNITY; PROFESSIONAL
FOUL; PUSH THE ENVELOPE; READJUSTMENT; RUBBER-
CHICKEN CIRCUIT; RUSTICATE; SALAMI TACTICS; SEND
DOWN; SHOOT A LINE; SHOOT THE BREEZE; SHORTFALL;
SLIP INTO SOMETHING MORE COMFORTABLE; SMOKE AND
MIRRORS; SOW ONE'S WILD OATS; STROKING SESSION; TAIL
BETWEEN ONE'S LEGS; TAKE A BREAK; TAKE NO PRISONERS;
TAKE THE MICKEY; TAKE THINGS EASY; TEA AND
SYMPATHY; THIRD DEGREE; THOUGHT SHOWERS; TRIBUTE
BAND; TROUBLE; UP THE WOODEN HILL TO BEDFORDSHIRE;
WARDROBE MALFUNCTION; WELL-INFORMED SOURCE;
WHITEWASH; WRITTEN OUT OF THE SCRIPT

(to) adjust one's dress To fasten/button up/zip up one's flies.
Hence, the notices that used to be found in some men's lavatories
during, approximately, the first half of the 20th century: 'Please
adjust your dress before leaving' or 'Gentlemen will please adjust
their dress.' This last, inevitably attracted graffitoed comments:
'... others will button up their flies' and '... as a refusal often
offends'. 'Adjust' is a perfectly normal word for 'arranging' one's
clothes (and has been since the early 18th century), but here it is
euphemistic. The 'dress' is a little worrying: Arthur Marshall in
Sunny Side Up (1987) recalls querying this and other aspects of the
wording, possibly in the 1910s. An uncle promised to write to the
authorities proposing instead: 'Before leaving please engage all
trouser buttons securely and return hands to normal position.'
Winston Churchill denied (1941) having said of a long-winded
memorandum from Anthony Eden that 'as far as I can see, you
have used every cliché except "God is love" and "Please adjust
your dress before leaving".'

(an) admirer A lover – i.e. a man (usually) who, in actual fact,
doesn't simply *look* at what he fancies. Since about 1700, but one
must not jump to such dastardly conclusions: 'Yet, what her
discretion would have concealed, was discovered by her eyes,
which, in spite of all her endeavours, breathed forth complacency

and love; for her inclination was flattered by her own self-sufficiency, which imputed her admirer's silence in that particular to the hurry and perturbation of his spirits, and persuaded her that he could not possibly regard her with any other than honourable intentions' – Tobias Smollett, *The Adventures of Peregrine Pickle* (1751), ch. 75.

adult Pornographic. As in 'adult books', 'adult videos' and so on. Since the 1950s and originally in North American usage. '[Advertisement] Unusual adult photo sets. S.a.e. Free exciting offer' – *New Musical Express* (20 June 1958); 'As one child speaking to another in a *New Yorker* cartoon succinctly puts it, "Adult means 'dirty'" ... We have "adult" movies, books, and magazines' – *Verbatim* (September 1978); 'Solo Sex Machines – manufacturer of bespoke handcrafted adult furniture and equipment' – company exhibiting at Erotica 2005, London.

(an) adult male A man. This is the PC euphemism, avoiding the word 'man' – at least according to *The New York Times* style book, quoted in *The Independent* (21 July 1992). This is because, in PC, the word 'man' should never be used as inclusive of all humans. An early offender here, in more ways than one, was G.K. Chesterton, who wrote: 'Individually, men may present a more or less rational appearance, eating, sleeping and scheming. But humanity as a whole is changeful, mystical, fickle and delightful. Men are men, but Man is a woman' – *The Napoleon of Notting Hill* (1904), ch. 1. 'To include women in a word like *man* or *mankind* suggests that they don't merit their own word, that they must be content to be included in the generic *man*. Women become conditioned to borrowing men's descriptions ... work ... and even men's ideas. The result of this emphasis on men's contributions to civilization is the repetitious message that women are also-rans, second-class citizens, tag-alongs, things' – Val Dumond, *The Elements of Nonsexist Usage* (New York, 1990). 'Those resisting language reform often say that the meaning of *man* is clear: context alone allows us to distinguish between its sex-specific and its generic use. However, since the early 1970s, researchers have studied what children, high school students, and adults understand when they encounter the term *man*. Studies summarized by Wendy Martyna (1978) show that, in response to the generic *man* and *he*, women, men and children alike form mental pictures of males, thus seriously undermining the efficiency of *man* and *he* as generic terms. Further, we encounter intended sex-specific usage far more often than generic usage' – Ruth King, ed., *Talking Gender: A Guide to Nonsexist Communication* (Toronto, 1991). 'Guidelines for Factual Programmes', BBC (1989), states of 'Men': 'Usually better as "people", "staff", "workforce", "workers", "union members", "trade unionists", "employees" or a "factory employing 3,000".'

(to have an) advanced social life To have affairs and sexual relationships, perhaps in excess of the norm, whatever that may be. Late 20th century. 'A study of 1,200 families found that they fuck you up, your mum and dad, by rushing off to work [and] ... parking you with a 23-year-old Moldovan au pair with rudimentary English and an advanced social life' – *The Observer* (9 October 2005).

(a lady of) advanced years An old/elderly woman. A formula less often applied to men. Since the early 20th century. 'Darby and Joan. A jocose appellation for an attached husband and wife who are "all in all to each other", especially in advanced years and in humble life' – *OED2* definition. 'Mental Disorders of Advanced Years' – title of article in *Geriatrics* (April 1959).

adverse weather conditions Bad weather. 'Television news people here [in the US] ... never tell us about bad weather, only adverse weather conditions' – Harold Evans, BBC Radio 4, *A Point of View* (18 September 2005).

(an) adviser A military helper who might also end up as a combatant soldier. The term, in its original sense of a soldier advising or helping a foreign government, was in use by 1915, when it referred to German soldiers advising the Turkish government. The euphemistic twist came about through the controversial sending of US 'advisers' to countries in South-East

Asia during the 1950s before the Vietnam War. The term had
been used to show that the country sending the 'advisers' was
not involved directly in military action against some other power
at that time. The extent to which 'advisers' actually participated
in combat is debatable. 'If the Australian Labour Party wins the
election and the troops come home – there are only 150
"advisers" left in Vietnam – no one doubts that ANZUK would
break up' – *The Guardian* (6 September 1972).

(an) affair   A sexual relationship with a person who is not one's
usual partner. As in 'they are having an affair'. It could refer
to simple flirtation but more usually implies that SEXUAL
INTERCOURSE is taking place. Probably not before the 20th
century in this sense. 'We could carry on a backstairs affair for
weeks without saying a word about it' – Noel Coward, *Design
for Living* (1933), act I.

affirmative action   Pressing the claims of minorities and
assisting them to overcome prejudice (in getting jobs, etc.)
Of American origin, since the 1930s. 'For those who, like me,
are long-time supporters of affirmative action, the new labels
and demagoguery do little to change our view that, given the
current realities of American society, color-blindness equals
total blindness' – *The Washington Post* (16 June 1991); 'Nor do we
understand that by so mistreating our homosexual community
we will engender a backlash that will bring in the most mindless
affirmative action policies to redress their injustices' – *The Sunday
Times* (7 June 1992).

African-American   Black American, (formerly) Negro.
Since the onset of PC in the United States, African-American
has become the almost mandatory replacement for 'black' or
'Black' – though not necessarily among blacks themselves. It is
not invariably used with care. There is a story told of a (white)
American female TV reporter interviewing either Bishop
Desmond Tutu or Nelson Mandela in South Africa. She was
apparently so intent on avoiding the word 'black' that she asked
the interviewee what it felt like being an 'African-American'.

It is not totally clear why African-American has emerged in preference to **Afro-American** at the present time. Both terms have been in use in North America (and elsewhere) since the mid-19th century (there is even an 1835 example of the term **Africo-American**). Another discarded form is **Aframerican**, which H.L. Mencken was using by 1920. 'In our opinion, the true policy of the Afro-American race ... is to emigrate to Canada, the West Indies' – *Voice of the Fugitive* (Windsor, Ontario) (21 June 1853); 'She is a New Orleans Creole, her mother being an Afro-American, and her father a Louisiana Frenchman' – *Westminster Gazette* (31 May 1898); 'Many blacks ... came to see it [the African-American Institute] as a "honky" (white) conservative force' – *The Guardian* (1 May 1971); 'Upon spotting the Afro-American, the Ghanaians shouted out, "Hey, Negro!" The other ... retorted angrily, "I'm a Black Man, not a Negro. Don't call me Negro".' – *Black World* (May 1973).

Although there has been an Afro-American Studies Department at the City University, New York, the 'Afro-' version is definitely less common than it once was. Could this possibly be because the word 'Afro' has predominantly come to be associated with the bushy hairstyle of the 1960s?

Afro-Caribbean West Indian. This term has been used (mostly in Britain) to emphasize their roots but, apparently, it is resented by some actual Africans on the grounds that the West Indies nowadays have precious little to do with matters African. 'Anyone even suspected of sexism, racism, smoking or cultural imperialism (alleging that, say, Christmas is in some way "better" than an indigenous Afro-Caribbean feast) is out, out, out' – *The Sunday Telegraph* (29 December 1991); 'His [Home Office minister's] comments coincided with a report confirming that ethnic minorities – particularly Afro-Caribbeans – are less likely to benefit from schemes to keep offenders out of prison' – *The Independent* (16 September 1992).

(died) after a long illness Died of cancer (usually). Obituary code, possibly of American origin. It has been suggested that **a short illness** could indicate suicide.

afternoon men Drunkards ('afternoon', presumably because they have imbibed a liquid lunch) or because they customarily pursue other forms of sensual indulgence at this time. Rarely encountered nowadays but an interesting one. 'As if they had heard that enchanted horn of Astolpho, that English duke in Ariosto, which never sounded but all his auditors were mad, and for fear ready to make away [with] themselves ... They are a company of giddy-heads, afternoon men.' This is the final part of the quotation given by Anthony Powell as the epigraph to his novel *Afternoon Men* (1931). He gives the source as Burton's *Anatomy of Melancholy*. The only other use found of the term 'afternoon men' is from the same work. In the introductory 'Democritus to the Reader', Burton has: 'Beroaldus will have drunkards, afternoon men, and such as more than ordinarily delight in drink, to be mad.'

(an) afterthought A child (probably unplanned) who is born some time after other children in a family. Early 20th century. 'Have you ever considered the fact that I was an afterthought? ... My father was 44 when I was born. My mother was 41' – Bernard Shaw, *Misalliance* (1914), act 3.

ageful Old, geriatric. 'So why does old age get such a bad press? Even the word "old" is frowned upon by some Americans: "ageful" has now joined "follically challenged" (i.e., bald) in the hideous lexicon of political correctness' – *The Times* (22 January 1992).

(the) agent The person who plays the active role in some questionable activity. Since the 17th century. 'Buggery is now almost grown as common among our gallants as in Italy, and ... the very pages of the town begin to complain of their masters for it. But blessed be God, I do not to this day know what is the meaning of this sin, nor which is the agent nor which the patient' – Samuel Pepys, diary entry for 1 July 1663.

(have) agreed to part Are separating with a view to getting a divorce. Customary wording in announcements from such couples, both publicly and informally. 'Madame Sangeeta's own *Gharana* is in a state of collapse. Apparently her marriage has undergone irreparable damage. She has developed major differences with husband Naveed Akber Butt and they have agreed to part ways without taking public pot shots at each other' – *The Lollywood Reporter* (June 2001).

(an) air sickness container A vomit bag (in the US). Cited in Willard R. Espy, *An Almanac of Words at Play* (1975).

(an) air strike A bombing attack. By the end of the Second World War. 'The hawks favored an air strike to eliminate the Cuban missile blockade ... The doves opposed the air strikes and favored a blockade' – *Saturday Evening Post* (8 December 1962).

air support Bombing from the air to kill people. Those who are 'supported' are soldiers on the ground. The idea is not to bomb them. The first Doublespeak Award – by the (American) Committee on Public Doublespeak – in 1974 was given to a certain Colonel David H.E. Opfer, a US air attaché in Cambodia. After a bombing raid, during the invasion of Cambodia the previous year, he had admonished reporters: 'You always write it's bombing, bombing, bombing. It's not bombing! It's air support!'

Alaska sable Skunk fur. 'The Skunk yields a handsome fur, lately become fashionable, under the euphemism of "Alaska Sable"' – Elliott Coues, *Fur-bearing Animals* (1877), ch. 7.

all the way (Of sex) full penetration. By the 1920s. 'The things we found in her room! I mean it was obvious she was going all the way and her not fifteen!' – William John Burley, *To Kill a Cat* (1970), ch. 10; 'They would do as much as they could without either removing the rest of her clothes or going all the way' – Rona Jaffe, *Class Reunion* (1979), ch. 6.

(to go) along the passage To go to the LAVATORY. Curiously enough, this is where most lavatories are situated.

alternative Not in the mainstream. The basic notion is that the subject differs from the established norm (because that is regarded as dull, conventional and unsatisfactory in some way). Hence, 'alternative comedy / life-style / medicine / society / theatre' and so on. 'Alternative Press' may have been the first such usage in the UK in the late 1960s.

amber fluid / liquid / nectar Lager / beer. 'Amber fluid' and 'amber liquid' are both Australianisms acknowledged by the *Macquarie Dictionary* (1981) for beer (particularly amber-coloured lager). Nectar was the (sweet) drink of the gods, in classical mythology. Put all this together and you have the term 'amber nectar' used by Paul Hogan in 1980s TV commercials in Britain for Foster's. Earlier examples: in 1713, the *London and Country Brewer* was referring to 'the amber-coloured Malt'; 'Barrel of amber' and 'amber fluid' are terms used about beer in *Chicago Gang Wars in Pictures, X Marks the Spot* (1930); 'Amber-coloured fluid' was a term for cocktails used in the novels of the British-born writer, E. Phillips Oppenheim (1866–1946). These are not disguising but elevating euphemisms.

ambidextrous Bisexual. Wordplay combining concepts of sexuality and manual dexterity. Perhaps since the 1930s.

(an) ambient replenishment assistant A shelf-stacker in a supermarket – according to a recruitment advertisement for a Safeways supermarket in Scarborough and as told to the Plain English Campaign – reported in the *Northern Echo* (13 May 1997). Another alleged euphemism for the same job is **stock replenishment executive**.

(an) ambulance chaser An unscrupulous lawyer who touts for clients, or any opportunist who hovers around unfortunate people hoping to make money out of them or dubiously on their behalf. Of American origin, by the end of the 19th century. 'In New York City there is a style of lawyers known to the profession as "ambulance chasers", because they are on hand wherever there is a railway wreck, or a street-car collision [with] their offers of professional services' – *The Congressional Record* (24 July 1897); 'A new kind of "ambulance chaser" – who were unscrupulous lawyers who collected details of casualties as they were taken to hospital in order to persuade the person concerned to bring action for damages' – *The Guardian* (14 March 1961).

Amerindian Red Indian. The least popular of the PC euphemisms for this ethnic minority. 'Up with the Asians and Amerindians, down with the Europeans. Up the natives, down with the colonists if they are white, that is' – *The Times* (2 November 1991).

ample (Of a woman) fat. By the 1860s. 'She was already more ample than a woman of thirty-eight need be in active life' – Sarah Grand, *Babs* (1901), ch. 3; 'Tony [Lumpkin] has pledged at least his body and possibly his soul to the ample barmaid at the Three Pigeons, Bet Bouncer' – *The Washington Post* (22 March 1991); 'Stone's Onegin is as handsome and haughty as Colin Firth's Darcy, which is as it should be; [Camilla] Roberts's ample Tatyana shrinks to appropriate scale in his shadow' – *The Observer* (24 July 2005).

amply-proportioned (Of a woman) fat. Since the early 20th century? '[On an airliner] Hancock ... gets himself jammed in the aisle with the amply-proportioned air hostess (Peggy Ann Clifford). After considerable effort and argument, they free themselves' – Roger Wilmut, *Tony Hancock 'Artiste'* (1978), pt I, ch. 6.

(a/the) anatomy A/the body. Since the 16th century (Shakespeare, *Romeo and Juliet*).

anecdotage Old age. This lightens up the harsh criticism that someone is in his/her dotage – meaning they are feeble-minded and senile. The coinage is associated with Benjamin Disraeli: 'When a man fell into his anecdotage it was a sign for him to retire from the world' – *Lothair* (1870), ch. 28. Earlier, however, his father, Isaac Disraeli, had noted in his *Curiosities of Literature*

(1839): 'Among my earliest literary friends, two distinguished themselves by their anecdotical literature: James Petit Andrews, by his *Anecdotes, Ancient and Modern*, and William Seward, by his *Anecdotes of Distinguished Persons*. These volumes were favourably received, and to such a degree, that a wit of that day, and who is still a wit as well as poet, considered that we were far gone in our "Anecdotage".' The word 'anecdotage' in a less critical sense had been used by De Quincey in 1823 simply to describe anecdotes collectively.

(an) angel crossed over the bridge The person died. Recorded in Hugh Meller, *London Cemeteries* (1981), ch. 5 and possibly a one-off inscription on a gravestone.

(an) animal companion A pet. This is the PC-preferred term, presumably because the older one is thought to be condescending to animals, if not outright animalist. Hence, also, **non-human animal companion** and **household non-human animal**. I cannot believe that any of these achieved much penetration but who knows. 'A person who believes that men and women are more significant than the rabbit or mouse is liable to be accused of "Speciesism". Even the word "pet" is now frowned upon. President Bush was recently publicly corrected for using it [instead of] "animal companion"' – *The Daily Telegraph* (26 June 1991); 'Imagine the shift a children's tale would have to undergo to rid itself of all offending elements. "It's raining nonhuman animal companions," said Wendy and Melissa's father' – Beard and Cerf, *The Official Politically Correct Dictionary and Handbook* (1992).

(to) annex (1) To conquer. By the 17th century. 'The annexation of the Slovakish territory of Hungary' – *The Nation* (New York), vol. 36 (1883). (2) To steal. 'The man with a flag believed himself to have supernatural qualities and had annexed the table flag from the camp, thinking it to have supernatural power' – photo caption in Thor Heyerdahl, *Aku-Aku: The Secret of Easter Island* (1958).

anno domini Advanced or advancing age. Since the mid-19th century, if not before. 'Whenever he felt less able to do things than formerly, he used to say he was afraid "Anno Domini" was the cause' – Frederick Gale, *The Life of the Hon. Robert Gimston* (1885), ch. 16.

(an) anorak An obsessive who enthuses over some (usually) not very significant pursuit. Named after the weatherproof jacket worn, for example, by trainspotters (people who collect railway engine numbers). In British use, since the 1980s. Anoraks also worry themselves to death over the minutiae of radio comedy programmes – like precise recording dates and programme numbers. *Anorak of Fire* was the title of a heroic stage depiction of a trainspotter (1993) and written by Stephen Dinsdale.

(there's) another chance to see It's another repeat – of a TV programme. In British use, by voice-over announcers, especially, since the 1970s.

Anschluss Forced takeover or conquest. This German word for 'union, connection' was applied to the takeover of Austria by Germany in March 1938. 'The incorporation of Austria into a Greater Germany occupied the first place both in the party programme of 1920 and in the opening pages of *Mein Kampf*. The Austrian Nazis, who formed a part of the German Party under Hitler's leadership, lived and worked for the day when the *Anschluss* should take place' – Alan Bullock, *Hitler: A Study in Tyranny* (1952), ch. 6.

(to) answer the call (of nature) To go to the LAVATORY – perhaps specifically to URINATE. Known since 1761 when Laurence Sterne's *Tristram Shandy* had that someone 'hearkened to the call of nature'. Hence, jokes along the lines of 'Have you had the call?' – as in the BBC radio show *Round the Horne* (28 March 1965). 'The calls of nature are permitted and Clerical Staff may use the garden below the second gate' – *Tailor & Cutter* (1852); '"What were you up to in Causey Spinney last Monday?" ... "Call o' Nature, please, sir"' – Flora Thompson, *Lark Rise* (1939),

ch. 3; 'When I was aft obeying a call of nature ... a huge tunny
had delivered a sideways smack at my nakedness with his 160 lbs.
or so of cold fish' – Thor Heyerdahl, *The Kon-Tiki Expedition* (1950),
ch. 6; 'Call of nature "sent [Robert] Maxwell overboard" ...
He would frequently get up in the middle of the night and found
it more convenient, as a lot of men do on a boat, to relieve
themselves over the side as it was moving' – headline and text,
The Independent (21 October 1995). There is also the variant, **to
answer a certain requirement of nature**. The **call of the great
outdoors** may also be used in the same way. Originally the phrase
'great outdoors' was used simply to describe 'great open space'
(by 1932).

(an) anti-personnel bomb   A bomb designed to kill people
(not just to be 'against' them) and as opposed to one intended to
destroy buildings. By 1939. 'These are anti-personnel weapons,
like a home-made grenade, and the effect would be to tear
through flesh causing terrible, lethal injuries' – *The Independent*
(28 July 2005).

antisocial behaviour   Bad and/or criminal behaviour. The
word 'antisocial' has been in use since the 18th century. 'Despite
the antisocial behavior related to alcohol consumption, piano
bars are still governed by a certain civility' – *The Washington Post*
(11 August 1991). The term has enjoyed a second coming with
the coining of the British legal term 'antisocial behaviour order'
or 'ASBO' in 1999. This is a court order obtainable by local
councils aimed at restricting individuals identified as trouble-
makers.

any   Extramarital sex (usually), as in the question, 'Are you
getting any?' Mid-20th-century origin? But in this citation it
is extended to include marital sex – or, rather, the absence of
it: 'Are You Getting Any? Your Post-baby Sex Life. Why your
post-baby sex life may be a few rolls in the hay short of its
former self. By Brandie Weikle' – article in *Today's Parent*
(March 2005).

appearance See AU NATUREL; DIFFERENTLY HEIGHTED;
DIFFERENTLY HIRSUTE; FIVE O'CLOCK SHADOW;
FOLLICALLY CHALLENGED; FUGLY; FULL-FRONTAL; HAIR
LOSS; HAIR-DISADVANTAGED; HIGH COLOUR; HOMELY;
MUTTON DRESSED AS LAMB; NO OIL PAINTING; NOT A
PRETTY SIGHT; NOT MUCH TO LOOK AT; ORTHODONTICALLY
CHALLENGED; RUBENESQUE; SARTORIALLY CHALLENGED;
SENSIBLE SHOES; SHAPELY; SILVER; SLENDER; SNOWING
DOWN SOUTH; STATE OF NATURE; SYLPH-LIKE; THIN ON
TOP; UNDRAPED; UNPREPOSSESSING; UNSIGHTLY; VITAL
STATISTICS

(an) appearance engineer A hairdresser. In the US, anyway,
by the mid-1950s, according to *The Lyttelton Hart-Davis Letters*, vol. 1
(1978) – for 23 February 1956.

appearance money Payment improperly made to an amateur
sportsman/woman for participating in an event. Known by 1977.
'Essentially a euphemism for expenses which are offered to
technically "amateur" athletes to lend their presence and thus
status to a particular event' – *Event* (9 October 1981).

appeasement Avoidance of war or other threat by making
concessions and (usually) by landing other people in it. It was
the name given to the policy of conciliation and concession
towards Nazi Germany, around 1938. The word had been used
in this context since the end of the First World War. On
14 February 1920, Winston Churchill said in a speech: 'I am, and
have always been since the firing stopped on November 11, 1918,
for a policy of peace, real peace and appeasement.' The word may
have become fixed in the language following a letter to *The Times*
(4 May 1934) from the 11th Marquess of Lothian: 'The only
lasting solution is that Europe should gradually find its way to
an internal equilibrium and a limitation of armaments by
political appeasement.'

(an) appendage A penis. Literally something that hangs or
dangles. You get the picture? Since the late 19th century?

(a/an) (surgical) appliance A truss (for a rupture) – though the euphemism is so vague it conceivably might be a deaf aid or an elastic stocking or a wooden leg. 'Surgical Appliance Industries (SAI) got its start in 1893, having been founded as the Ohio Truss Company (OTC), by Joel Adams and his son-in-law Isaac Pease' – online company history (2005).

(an) appointment A job. 20th century? 'Frances Cairncross, Management Editor of *The Economist* and Chair of the Economic and Social Research Council, took up her appointment as Rector of Exeter College on 1 October 2004' – University of Oxford Annual Review 2003–4.

(to) apprehend To arrest. Elevated language in police-speak, when giving evidence in court. Used in this way since the 16th century. *PC Trubshawe* (Arthur Mullard): 'I was proceeding along Bond Street in an easterly direction ... whereupon we apprehended him and took him into custard ... y' – BBC TV *Hancock's Half-Hour* (2 December 1957).

(to) appropriate To steal. Probably since the 16th century. 'Whatever the ladies of his family required ... he would appropriate to them' – Daniel Defoe, *The History and Remarkable Life of Colonel Jacque* (1722).

appropriate What the controllers of political correctness consider to be in line with their prescriptions. Hence, for example, 'inappropriately directed laughter' refers to jokes about women, gays or ethnics. 'The University of Connecticut ... sought to ban "inappropriately directed laughter, inconsiderate jokes ... and conspicuous exclusions (of others) from conversations." The University of Michigan published material warning students that they could be brought up on charges of laughing at ethnic jokes, questioning the equal ability of men and women to perform certain tasks or excluding an individual from a dorm party because of his sexual orientation' – *The Washington Post* (17 March 1991).

appropriate technology Torture. This may have been a one-off use but like the previous entry it employs 'appropriate' to mean what the speaker wants to get away with. 'In the House of Assembly, Harare's Commons, he called it "appropriate technology", a euphemism for electric shock treatment that drew appreciative nods from his colleagues' – *The Daily Telegraph* (September 1983).

(an) approved school A penal institute for young criminals (or young people needing protection). In British use since 1932. 'The effect of the change of name from "Reformatory" and "Industrial" to "Approved Schools" cannot be exaggerated. No youth is ashamed of having been in an approved school' – *The Times* (7 December 1938).

(an) armed conflict A war. Used when the speaker is trying to play down the nature of the activity – or it may just be that a war has not been officially declared. 'We are not at war with Egypt. We are in an armed conflict; that is the phrase I have used. There has been no declaration of war' – Sir Anthony Eden, speaking in the House of Commons (1 November 1956) about Britain's response to the Egyptian take-over of the Suez Canal. The prime minister seemed curiously punctilious about his words.

(the) armed struggle Murder and mayhem in pursuit of Irish reunification. This was the Irish Republican Army's phrase of choice in its public pronouncements during the second coming of the TROUBLES from 1969 to 1998. Has also been used in an attempt to dignify other terrorist, guerrilla or revolutionary activities elsewhere in the world. 'The lengthy IRA statement insisted the armed struggle was valid, and referred to the violence of the 1960s and 70s as "pogroms" against the Catholic community' – *The Guardian* (28 July 2005).

armour Contraceptive sheath. Now obsolete and rather quaint. 'I felt carnal inclinations raging through my frame. I determined to gratify them. I went to St James's Park and ... picked up a whore. For the first time I did engage in armour, which I found but dull satisfaction' – James Boswell, diary entry for 25 March 1763; 'At bottom of the Haymarket I picked up a strong, jolly young damsel, and taking her under the arm I conducted her to Westminster Bridge, and then in armour complete did I engage her upon this noble edifice' – 10 May 1763; 'We went down a lane to a snug place, and I took out my armour, but she begged that I might not put it on, as the sport was much pleasanter without it, and as she was quite safe. I was so rash as to trust her, and had a very agreeable congress' – 17 May 1763.

(in the) arms of Jesus Dead. Much used in memorial inscriptions and notices. 'Safe in the Arms of Jesus' is the title of a Moody and Sankey type chorus (1868), words by F.J. Crosby. 'Safe in the arms of Jesus. (Inserted by her loving husband)' – an In Memoriam notice from the Calcutta *Statesman* in the 1930s. 'In loving memory of our grandson Peter / Safe in the arms of Jesus / From Grandma, Aunties and Uncles' – an In Memoriam notice that 'might have been expressed better', quoted in J.B. Morrell, *The Biography of the Common Man of the City of York* (1948). 'Safe in the arms of the Lord' is another version that features in In Memoriam notices.

(to) arouse To cause sexual excitement. 'A ... lustful male [advances] purposefully on a naked female ... The man's pink, thinly painted flesh is outlined in red, the colour of arousal' – Hilary Spurling, *Matisse the Master* (2005), ch. 1.

(the) arrangements The LAVATORY. 'Can you tell me where the arrangements are?' Since the early 20th century?

art / artistic Sexually titillating. As in 'art movies' or 'artistic photographs'. Perhaps since the 1950s. The movies may not actually be sexually explicit – and are simply from foreign sources or made in an arty, non-mainstream, manner – but the term 'art' acts as a come-on. Hence, also, 'artistic poses', a very 1950s phrase for nude photographs. 'Here is a selection of glamour and artistic figure photographs of attractive sensual models in artistic

poses and settings. Some images may be interpreted as erotic' –
online showcase for Karl Brandt Photo Art Artistic Figure
Photography (2005).

(an) article A chamber pot. Sometimes **bedroom article** or
night article. Short for 'an article of furniture'. 'Pitcher and
night article (on the floor, separate)' – James Joyce, *Ulysses* (1922).

(an) artificial aid to vision Binoculars. By the mid-20th
century. 'The Windmill [was] the famous "nude show" theatre
where the naked girls had to stand stock-still by order of the Lord
Chamberlain's Office, and "artificial aids to vision" were not
permitted' – Roger Wilmut, *Tony Hancock 'Artiste'* (1978), pt I, ch. I.

as well as can be expected Ill but not actually dying. By the
18th century. 'Often, medical staff, when asked, will describe
a patient who isn't in a bad state as "doing as well as can be
expected" if he or she is your relative. The irony comes in that
someone who is doing well wouldn't be in the hospital' –
BBC h2g2 website (6 November 2005).

(an) Asian-American An Oriental in the US. This expression
is PC preferred because the older word was not chosen by the
'oppressed' people themselves but by 'other' people, namely,
Europeans. '[David Henry Hwang] grins suddenly, and the smile
lights up his face like a schoolboy. "I remember my first play,
FOB (standing for Fresh Off the Boat, about recently arrived
Chinese immigrants to America) was staged at the Asian-
American house at Stanford and then afterwards I had to have a
"self-criticism", a session so that the community could comment
on the work' – *The Times* (17 March 1989).

asleep See FALL ASLEEP

(an) assignation A meeting of lovers at which SEXUAL
INTERCOURSE is on the agenda. Since the 17th century. By 1870,
'assignation house' had become an American term for a brothel.

assistance See NATIONAL ASSISTANCE

at His/Her Majesty's pleasure Indefinitely. In English
law when a convicted criminal is being sentenced, a fixed term
of imprisonment may not be handed down for a number of
reasons (madness, age etc.). Rather curiously, because the law is
conducted in the sovereign's name, he or she is deemed to enjoy
this state of affairs. Sometimes the phrase is used rather loosely
to suggest that a person is simply in prison. In the 17th century,
the dissolvability of Parliament was also said to be 'at His
Majesty's pleasure'. Hence, *Pleasure at Her Majesty's*, the playful title
of a charity show when televised (December 1976). It had been
staged not in a prison but at Her Majesty's Theatre in London.

at it Engaged in SEXUAL INTERCOURSE. Since the early 17th
century. As in 'to be at it all night' or 'at it like rabbits'. One of
the several applications of IT meaning 'sex'. 'Five times a night!
Are you thinking what I'm thinking? It's hardly surprising that
our prime minister [Tony Blair] feels tired all the time and
needs his eight hours' "sleep" if he's going at it all night like a
jack rabbit and has been in the grip of this habit for fully quarter
of a century' – *The Sunday Times* (8 May 2005).

at rest Dead. Another popular graveyard inscription. Compare
the term GARDEN OF REMEMBRANCE / REST. 'Here lies the
body of Mary, wife of John Jones of this parish. Here lies the
body of Martha, wife of John Jones of this parish. Here lies
the body of Jane, wife of John Jones of this parish. John
Jones. At rest' – adjacent epitaphs that used to be quoted by
Lt Commander D. Gill Jones in his talk 'A quiet hour among
the dead' (mid-20th century).

(an) athlete A sexually vigorous male (usually) or one who is
skilled in the exercise of SEXUAL INTERCOURSE. By the 1930s.
'Who can blame all guys out there seeking something to help them
in the sack? Some women have come to expect a sexual athlete in
bed. So what's a mildly neurotic guy to do other than pop a pill?'
– *Chicago Tribune* (6 November 2005).

(an) athletic supporter A jockstrap (or the small garment that keeps a male athlete's genitalia neat, tidy and protected). Both name and euphemism may have arisen at the same time. By 1897 in the US. President Truman wrote to a music critic who had criticized his daughter's singing (6 December 1950): 'I have just read your lousy review buried in the back pages ... Some day I hope to meet you. When that happens, you'll need a new nose, a lot of beefsteak for black eyes, and perhaps a supporter below.'

(an) attendance centre A non-residential institution for young criminals. In the UK, since 1948. As part of their sentence, they may have to 'attend' for a certain number of hours each week for instruction and training. 'An Attendance Centre Order sentences a young person to attend an Attendance Centre. Attendance Centres are normally run by the police. The regime typically involves discipline, physical training and social skills. The order can last up to 36 hours depending on the age of the offender and the seriousness of the offence' – Youth Justice Board website (2005).

(an) attention deficit disorder Idleness, naughtiness / stupidity in children. They were first said to have this highfalutin condition in the US during the 1980s. 'CHADD: A national non-profit organization representing children and adults with attention-deficit/hyperactivity disorder (AD/HD). CHADD works to improve the lives ...' website (US) (2005).

(an) attitude problem Truculence, hostility, usually among young people. Probably of American origin and known there by 1977.

(to) attract / come to the attention of the police To commit illegal acts on a regular basis. Since 1900. 'Thomas Hamilton, aged 43, a disgraced former Scout master whose behaviour had attracted the attention of the police, turned one of his four guns on himself after killing or injuring all but one of a class of 29 five- and six-year-olds at Dunblane primary school,

25

near Stirling' – *The Guardian* (14 March 1996). See also KNOWN TO
THE POLICE.

attributes   (Of a woman) breasts. 20th century. 'I'm a fan of
Jessica Biel. I've never seen her on that goodie-goodie TV show
called "7th Heaven", but became more than aware of her
remarkable "attributes" when she decided to bare some skin in
one of those Maxim-style mags while shooting that series, in
order to showcase her "range"' – joblo.com (26 November
2004).

au naturel   Naked. Originally the phrase was applied to
anything in its natural state – not least food cooked plainly
(by 1815) or not at all. The euphemism for 'naked' is said to
be an American borrowing from the French, however there
is this British example: 'You would have preferred ankles
au naturel?' – Mrs Humphrey Ward, *The Marriage of William Ashe*
(1905), ch. 10.

(to go and see one's) aunt   To go to the LAVATORY – as in
'I'm going to pay a visit to my aunt'. Probably 'the aunt' has been
so described since the mid-19th century. 'As I was the youngest
of six children (and the only boy) I was often surprised by the
affection shown to their relations by various friends of my elder
sisters. "Just going to see my aunt" was an expression I must
have heard hundreds of times in my youth' – R.W. Tincombe,
Norfolk (1996).

Aunt Flo is visiting   Menstruation. By the 1950s, also in the
US. There is an awful pun involved here.

auto-erotic habits / practices   Masturbation. 'Auto-erotism'
was defined by Havelock Ellis in *Alienist and Neurologist* (April 1898)
as 'The phenomena of spontaneous sexual emotion generated
in the absence of an external stimulus proceeding, directly or
indirectly, from another person'. 'Auto-erotic indulgences may
quickly become an addiction' – Arthur Koestler, *Invisible Writing*
(1954). The use of the term came to popular attention in 1994

when the British MP Stephen Milligan died while performing 'auto-erotic asphyxiation' (self-strangling while masturbating).

auto-euthanasia Suicide. Late 20th century. A lesser-known use 'euthanasia' (from the Greek for 'death'), more usually applied to bringing about the death of *another* person.

(to) avail oneself of the facilities To go to the LAVATORY. 'I have been attending the [Glastonbury] festival since 1997 and have had to avail myself of the facilities provided for disabled festival goers' – efestivals.co.uk website (23 May 2004). See also FACILITY.

available Sexually willing (of a woman). 20th century.

Bb

B. / b. Bastard, bitch, bloody, bugger. The most-used abbreviation? Sometimes printed 'b——'. Hence, a 'b.f.' is a 'bloody fool' and 'b. off' stands for 'bugger off'. 'The poor b—— is in "stir" (prison)' – Henry Mayhew, *London Labour and the London Poor* (1851), ch. 1; 'I'd have moved those Irish b's seven times to hell' – D.H. Lawrence, letter (17 November 1925); 'The children heard no bad language beyond an occasional "B——" or "d——", for their mother was greatly respected and the merest hint of anything stronger was hushed' – Flora Thompson, *Lark Rise* (1939), ch. 3.

(the) baby blues Post-natal depression. Known by the 1980s but perhaps not widely taken up. 'People often confuse the baby blues with postpartum depression (PPD) because they have common symptoms. So how do you know whether you're going through the baby blues or a real depression?' – HealthyPlace.com (2004).

(a) bachelor girl A young spinster. Anything to avoid the doom-laden official term. Known since the 1890s. *The Bachelor Girl in London* – title of a novel by G.E. Mitton (1898). 'The term "old maid" is now seldom or never heard; the expression "bachelor girl" has taken its place' – *The Queen* Magazine (10 November 1906).

(the) back passage The anus or arsehole. Possibly originating in doctor–patient-speak. Hence: 'Woman to friend on Nottingham bus: "Oh, yes, I've felt ever so much better since they painted my back-passage spring green"' – included in BBC Radio *Quote... Unquote* (26 May 1982); 'Dr David Starkey, a historian who was once described by the late Russell Harty as "an expert in the back passages of history"' – in the same show (13 June 1995).

(a) backhander A bribe – from the way money might be placed discreetly in a hand held behind the back and waiting for it. Originally, a 'blow with the back of the hand', this figurative term emerged in the mid-19th century. 'It seems that Gorgeous George has finally been awarded £150,000 in libel damages from the *Daily Telegraph* over claims he received a backhander from Saddam Hussein's regime in Iraq' – hodgers.com (2 December 2004).

(the) backside The buttocks. This is from an early telling of the Robin Hood legend (about 1500): 'With an arrowe so broad, He shott him into the backe-syde.'

backward Up the anus, sexually. By the 17th century. 'And so to Mrs Martin and there did what je voudrais avec her, both devante and backward, which is also muy bon plazer' – Samuel Pepys, diary entry for 4 June 1666. I suppose a more modern rendering would be **up the back**.

backward children Of low intelligence, if not mentally handicapped. Known as such by the first half of the 20th century. *The Education of Backward Children* – title of a Board of Education pamphlet, published by HMSO (1937), subtitled *With special reference to children who are backward because they are dull*.

(with the) balance of one's mind disturbed Suffering from temporary insanity. A legal term used at inquests, where the dead person may have committed suicide and relatives want a veil to be drawn over this fact. 'As a train pulled into the station, the 63-year-old [Peter Llewellyn Davies] threw himself into its path, to the horror of onlookers. A coroner's jury ruled he had killed himself "while the balance of his mind was disturbed". A tragic end to the boy who found growing up so hard' – mirror.co.uk (28 October 2004).

balls (1) Testicles. By the 14th century. (2) Courage. The following citation marks the development of the second meaning from the first: 'You say a man's got no brain, when he's a fool … And when he's got none of that spunky wild bit of a man in him, you say he's got no balls. When he's sort of tame' – D.H. Lawrence, *Lady Chatterley's Lover* (1928), ch. 14.

bally Bloody. In use by 1885. 'I've been in this bally country for five years' – G.W. Steevens, *With Kitchener to Khartum* (1898).

(a) banana skin A cause of upset or humiliation. This figurative use by 1900. 'Treading upon Life's banana skins' – P.G. Wodehouse, *Right Ho, Jeeves!* (1934), ch. 1; '[Lord Whitelaw] was recently asked whether he thought Mrs Thatcher would face any more banana skins. He boomed out cheerfully, "I think there will be banana skins as long as there are bananas"' – *The Observer* (22 April 1984).

(a) bar assistant / attendant / lady A barmaid. 20th century. The search for a less pejorative term is ongoing: compare VICTUALLER'S ASSISTANT.

(he's) bar sinister He's a bastard. From heraldry, referring to the two parallel lines on a family escutcheon (from the sinister chief to the dexter base point) denoting bastardy. Also **bend sinister**.

(a) Barclays A wank (male masturbation), from rhyming slang Barclays Bank/wank. *Partridge/Slang* suggests a 1930s starting date. Became popular when people found several instances of its use in *The Kenneth Williams Diaries* (1993) – for example, in his entry for 12 August 1976: 'Quite the barclays before bed. Masturbatory success is the result of imaginative conceit.'

(to) bash / flog the bishop To masturbate. *Partridge/Slang* dates
this from the late 19th century and suggests it derives from the
resemblance between the penis and a chess bishop or a bishop
in ecclesiastical mitre. It was unfortunate, therefore, that Labour
MPs should have accused the Conservative minister, John Selwyn
Gummer MP, of 'bishop-bashing' when he was involved in
criticisms of various Anglican bishops in March 1988. To SHAKE
HANDS WITH THE BISHOP means, however, 'to URINATE'.

(a) basket case (1) A mental or physical cripple. (2) A totally
ruined enterprise. Either way, it seems to be an American
term and *OED2*'s earliest citation is from the *U.S. Official Bulletin*
(28 March 1919) in the aftermath of the First World War: 'The
Surgeon General of the Army ... denies ... that there is any
foundation for the stories that have been circulated ... of the
existence of "basket cases" in our hospitals.' Indeed, another
definition of the term is 'a soldier who has lost all four limbs' –
thus, presumably, requiring transportation in something like
a basket. To complicate matters, Stuart Berg Flexner in *I Hear
America Talking* (1976) describes this as being originally *British* Army
slang. It has been suggested, probably misguidedly, that the
association with mental disability comes from the fact that basket-
weaving is an activity sometimes carried out in mental hospitals.
Another suggestion is that the basket referred to is that from
which charitable support is doled out. The second meaning was
established by about 1973 and is still frequently used in business
journalism when describing doomed ventures: 'On a continent
that is full of economic basket cases, the small, landlocked nation
is virtually debt free' – *Newsweek* (11 January 1982). Here, one
might guess that the original phrase has been hijacked and the
implication changed. What the writer is now referring to is
something that is so useless that it is fit only to be thrown into
a waste-paper basket.

(a/the) bathroom A/the LAVATORY. On the assumption,
originally, that the whole contains the part. The principal
American euphemism for this thing. Since the late 19th century?
'Julian wanted to go to the bathroom after the dinner party stood

up, and on his way to the men's locker room he had to pass
Mrs Gorman's table' – John O'Hara, *Appointment in Samarra* (1934),
ch. 4; 'An unfortunate amount of the humour in other British
programmes tends to centre around the bathroom' – *The Listener*
(22 February 1968).

(a/the) bathroom utensil A chamber pot (itself a
euphemistic term, of course). Sometimes **bedroom utensil**.
'There once was a young man called Stencil / Whose prick was as
sharp as a pencil. / He punctured an actress, / Two sheets and a
mattress, / And dented the bedroom utensil' – Anon. limerick
current in the early 1980s.

(to have) bats in the belfry To be harmlessly insane, mad,
batty. This expression conveys the idea that a person behaves in
a wildly disturbed manner, like bats disturbed by the ringing of
bells. Stephen Graham wrote in *London Nights* (1925): 'There is a
set of jokes which are the common property of all the comedians.
You may hear them as easily in Leicester Square as in Mile End
Road. It strikes the unwonted visitor to the Pavilion as very
original when Stanley Lupino says of some one: "He has bats in
the belfry." It is not always grasped that the expression belongs
to the music hall at large.' Attempts have been made to derive
'batty', in particular, from the name of William Battie (1704–76),
author of a *Treatise on Madness*, though this seems a little harsh,
given that he was the psychiatrist and not the patient. On the
other hand, there was a Fitzherbert Batty, barrister of Spanish
Town, Jamaica, who made news when he was certified insane in
London in 1839. The names of these two gentlemen merely, and
coincidentally, reinforce the 'bats in the belfry' idea – but there
do not seem to be any examples of either expression found
before 1900.

battle fatigue Cowardice. Mid-20th century. 'A successor to
the "shell shock" of World War I, battle fatigue denoted the
psychophysiological state of Anglo-American soldiers in World
War II who were no longer able to function in combat. Like shell
shock, battle fatigue was a term used by troops but considered

suspicious by medics and brass hats. Early campaigns extinguished official belief that psychological screening would eliminate recruits who might become mentally unhinged by the prospect of being blown up or crippled' – Cowley and Parker, eds, *Reader's Companion to Military History* (1996).

(to make / play the) beast with two backs To have SEXUAL INTERCOURSE. Somewhat archaic, dating from Iago's comment: 'I am one, sir, that come to tell you, your daughter, and the Moor, are now making the beast with two backs' – Shakespeare, *Othello* (1604), I.i.115. Rabelais had earlier had *faire la bête à deux dos*. Probably, **to make the beast** became the more commonly used euphemism. 'The beast that has two backs at midnight' – James Joyce, *Ulysses* (1922).

beastliness Male masturbation. Originally it referred to heterosexual SEXUAL INTERCOURSE, but then became more narrowly applied to male homosexual goings-on and then, finally, to single-handed activity. Or, at least, this is so if Robert Baden-Powell is anything to go by. In *Scouting for Boys* (first published 1908), he wrote: 'It is called in our schools "beastliness", and this is about the best name for it … should it become a habit it quickly destroys both health and spirits; he becomes feeble in body and mind, and often ends in a lunatic asylum.'

(to) beat one's meat To masturbate (males only). Of American origin, possibly by the late 19th century. 'Oh, it's so neat to beat your meat while sitting on the toilet seat' – from a traditional rhyme.

(a) beauty cake A bar of soap (in the US). Cited in Willard R. Espy, *An Almanac of Words at Play* (1975).

(the) beaver Female genitalia, particularly the pubic-hair covering. Since the 1920s? From the beaver's thick dark-brown fur. Hence, the term 'beaver shot' given to a photograph in pornography featuring 'a well-haired pudendum'. Earlier, the

word 'beaver' had been applied, non-euphemistically, to a beard.
This may date from the Middle Ages when the beaver was that
part of a soldier's helmet which lay around the chin as a face-
guard (the vizor was the bit brought down from the forehead).
In Shakespeare's *Hamlet* (1600–1), I.ii.228, the Prince asks:
'Then saw you not his face?' (that of his father's ghost). Horatio
replies: 'O yes, my lord, he wore his beaver up.'

(to) be no more To be dead. Possibly originating with the
Dane's: 'To die – to sleep, / No more' – Shakespeare, *Hamlet*
(1600–1), III.i.60. Whatever the case, it became one of the roll-
call of euphemisms in the *Monty Python's Flying Circus* 'Dead Parrot'
sketch, first shown on BBC TV (7 December 1969). A man
(named Praline in the script) who has just bought a parrot that
turns out to be dead, registers a complaint with the pet shop
owner in these words: 'This parrot is no more. It's ceased to be.
It's expired. It's gone to meet its maker. This is a late parrot ...'

(to go to) bed with someone To have SEXUAL
INTERCOURSE with someone. As old as time. 'How much less
awful the man would be ... if only he sometimes lost his temper
... or went to bed with his secretary' – Aldous Huxley, *Time Must
Have a Stop* (1945), ch. 4. '"If you go to bed with a man, he won't
marry you," she used to say. "Every girl knows that"' – John
Wain, *Strike Father Dead* (1962), ch. 6. Hence, also, the verb **to
bed**, usually what a man does to a woman. 'His wooing that
would thoroughly woo her, wed her and bed her' – Shakespeare,
The Taming of the Shrew (1592–3), I.i.1144; 'I have wedded her, not
bedded her' – *All's Well That Ends Well* (1603), III.ii.20.

bedroom Relating to sexual activity. By the 1920s. Hence,
bedroom eyes etc. 'It has also been described as a bedroom farce
set in a living room' – *Time* Magazine (6 July 1953); 'Italians are
bedroom-eyed gigolos' – Mary Chamberlin, *Dear Friends and Darling
Romans* (1959), ch. 4.

(to have) been To have just gone to the LAVATORY – probably
simply to URINATE. Since the 19th century?

beer and sandwiches at No. 10 Political appeasement of a trade union in British industrial disputes. An encapsulation of the informal (and often eleventh-hour) style of negotiation held at senior level (and quite often at the prime minister's residence, No. 10 Downing Street) between trade unionists and politicians to avert threatened strikes and stoppages. These occasions only really took place under the Labour administrations of Harold Wilson (1964–70, 1974–6). Nothing like it was known under Margaret Thatcher, who seldom, if ever, conversed with union leaders, let alone offered them any form of hospitality. Some called it a pragmatic approach; others viewed it less favourably. Phillip Whitehead (a one-time Labour MP) was quoted in *The Independent* (25 April 1988) as having said of Wilson that he 'bought the hours with beer and sandwiches at No. 10 and the years with Royal Commissions'. Compare 'coffee and Danish at the White House' – an expression from the Carter administration for the breakfasts of coffee and Danish pastries offered by the president to Congressional leaders and others to win them over.

(to) beg to differ To quarrel, to disagree. By the 1940s in the US. There was a BBC radio programme called *We Beg To Differ* – 'a lively discussion on subjects upon which the sexes may disagree' – from 1949 until the late 1960s.

behaviour enhancement See ACTIVITY

(the) behind The buttocks. By the 18th century. 'Go and do my bidding – tell him he lies, and kick his behind in my name!' – King George IV, quoted in the *Saturday Review* (8 February 1862).

below medium height Shorter than average. Since the 19th century, if this citation is anything to go by: 'The Nootkas are of less than medium height ... but rather strongly built' – H.H. Bancroft, *The Native Races of Pacific States* (1875), pt 1, ch. 3.

below stairs In the kitchen or servants' hall, i.e. where a domestic servant is to be found. Since the 16th century. 'Why, shall I always keep below stairs?' – says Margaret in Shakespeare, *Much Ado About Nothing* (1598), V.ii.10.

below the salt Inferior socially. In the Middle Ages it was the custom to station a large salt-cellar in the middle of a dining table. Hence, those above it (on the host's side) were more honoured guests than those below it. Euphemistically used since the 16th century. 'Though of Tory sentiments, she by no means approved of those feudal times when the chaplain was placed below the salt' – James Payn, *The Luck of the Darrells* (1885), ch. 37.

(to) bend / stretch the rules To act illegally. By the mid-20th century. 'Trying to get other members of the European Community to "bend the rules" so that exports can be resumed' – *The Times* (2 November 1973); 'He bent over backwards to be straight in all his dealings ... He wouldn't stretch the rules' – Oliver Jacks, *Autumn Heroes* (1977), ch. 2.

benefit State aid paid to the poor and otherwise needy. Since the late 19th century and particularly since the National Insurance Act of 1911. Hence 'maternity / medical / sickness / unemployment benefit'. A recipient could claim to be 'on the benefit'. 'Incapacity Benefit is paid at three rates, starting at just £55.90, rising at the six-month point and then rising to £74.15 after a claimant has been on the benefit for a year. With additional allowances, the average payment is £84.51 a week' – *The Socialist* (12 February 2005).

bent Homosexual (chiefly of a male). Since the mid-20th century. Presumably, as with 'bent' meaning 'crooked' (in the criminal sense), because one deviates from the norm. 'No one cares if you're boy, or girl, or bent, or versatile, or what you are' – Colin MacInnes, *Absolute Beginners* (1959). Sometimes self-applied as a badge of honour. Hence, *Bent* – the title of a play by Martin Sherman (filmed UK/US/Japan 1996) about Nazi homophobia.

(a) bereavement A death. As in 'We've had a bereavement in the family' and said to avoid mention of the d-word. 'The delay, which halted jury selection for a week, came on the heels of a week-long adjournment because of a bereavement in the family of the chief defence lawyer' – *The Irish Times* (16 February 2005).

(a) bestseller Merely a phenomenon wished-for by a publisher. It is not necessarily connected to an impressive number of copies sold. In fact, many books are so described before they have even been put in shops with a view to being sold. Since the 1880s, in a straightforward descriptive sense, in the US. A euphemism chiefly notable for its lack of any precise meaning by the 1970s. 'He [John F. Kennedy] is the author of *Profiles of Courage*, a prize-winning and best-selling work of pop history' – *The Economist* (20 June 1959).

(to) betray To seduce. 'When lovely woman stoops to folly / And finds too late that men betray' – Oliver Goldsmith, *The Vicar of Wakefield* (1766), ch. 29; 'Years before she had been betrayed by a man and had sworn she would never marry until she had brought up the boy she had had by him' – Flora Thompson, *Lark Rise* (1939), ch. 3. Also, in modern use, to be sexually unfaithful to one's marriage partner by sleeping with a third party.

(to be) between shows To be in involuntary unemployment (of actors). For non-actors, it would be **between jobs**. Since the mid-20th century? '"Are you on holiday?" ... "Resting, to use a theatrical term. Between jobs"' – Reginald Hill, *Another Death in Venice* (1976).

(to be) between the sheets To be engaged in SEXUAL INTERCOURSE. Since the 17th century. 'Section A [of the intelligence agency even] make a study of the kind of greens [green vegetables] the big shots go in for. Sometimes we know more about what these people are like between the sheets than they do themselves' – Cyril Connolly, *Bond Strikes Camp* (1963), ch. 3.

(the great) beyond Death, the afterlife. Since the 19th century. 'Each is yearning for the Great Beyond, which attests our immortality' – Edward Bulwer-Lytton, *Rienzi, the Last of the Tribunes* (1835), ch. 10.

big (1) Pregnant. As in 'big with child'. Since the 16th century. 'Their women bygg with childe' – Hosea 13:16, in Coverdale's translation (1535). (2) Fat, obese.

(the) big C Cancer. Anything to avoid saying this particular c-word. Of American origin, since the 1960s. 'John Wayne ... accepted the news with true grit. "I've licked the Big C before," he said' – *Time* Magazine (29 January 1979).

(a) big girl An ugly and sexually unattractive young woman. 20th century.

(a) big girl's blouse A sissy, a man who is not as manly as he might be. Since the 1960s? A rather odd expression, possibly of Welsh origin, and suggesting what an effeminate football or rugby player might wear instead of a proper jersey. Could it have something to do with the wobbliness of the image conjured up? Miller and Nown, eds, *Street Talk: The Language of Coronation Street* (1986) states that it 'describes an adult male who has a low pain threshold. When trying to remove a splinter someone might say: "Hold still you big girl's blouse. It won't hurt".' Confirming its mostly North country use, the phrase has also been associated with the British comedienne Hylda Baker (1908–86) in the form 'You big girl's blouse', probably in the situation comedy *Nearest and Dearest* (ITV 1968–73). From *The Guardian* (20 December 1986) – about a nativity play: 'The house is utterly still (except where Balthazar is trying to screw the spout of his frankincense pot into Melchior's ear, to even things up for being called a big girl's blouse on the way in from the dressing room).' From *The Herald* (Glasgow) (20 October 1994): 'His acid-tongued father [Prince Philip] might be reinforced in his view of him as a big girl's blouse, but Prince Charles is actually a big boy now. His children, locked away in the posh equivalent of care, are not.'

From *The Sunday Times* (6 November 1994): 'Men, quite naturally,
are equally unwilling to accept paternity leave, because of the fear
that this will mark them for ever as a great big girl's blouse.'

big-boned Fat. Though, of course, it is rather what's on the
bone that makes the person fat. 'No big-bon'd men fram'd of the
Cyclops' size' – Shakespeare, *Titus Andronicus* (1588), IV.iii.46; 'To
understand why firm resolve is not necessarily virtuous, you have
only to imagine some of the Great Resolutions of History ... Eve:
"Stupid man, I'm not fat, just big-boned. From now on, I'll eat
what I bloody well like"' – *The Independent* (31 December 1994).

(a) biggie A pile of excrement – mostly in children's use. Known
by 1953. 'He's a bit erratic where he does his biggies, now he's a
grown up parrot' – Angus Wilson, *No Laughing Matter* (1967), ch. 2.
Sometimes **bigs** or **big jobs** or a **big one**.

bijou Small. In CAMP parlance, as in 'a bijou whingette' (from,
say, the 1960s) and especially in estate-agent-speak, as in 'bijou
residence' (known since 1904). 'An apartment so tiny that an
auctioneer would have been justified in terming it "bijou"' –
Arnold Bennett, *The Card* (1911), ch. 2.

(the) birds and the bees Matters relating to sexual
reproduction. Since the 19th century? From the way such matters
would be tactfully explained to children by describing the habits
of birds, bees and other creatures. 'Birds do it, bees do it / Even
educated fleas do it / Let's do it, let's fall in love' – Cole Porter,
song, 'Let's Do It, Let's Fall in Love', *Paris* (1928).

birth/pregnancy See AFTERTHOUGHT; BAR SINISTER;
BORN ON THE WRONG SIDE OF THE BLANKET; BRING
INTO THE WORLD; BROUGHT TO BED; BUN IN THE OVEN;
BUNDLE OF JOY; CAUGHT; CERTAIN STATE; CHILDFREE;
CLUB; CONDITION; CONFINEMENT; DELIVERY; DOUBTFUL
PARENTAGE; ENCEINTE; FACTS OF LIFE; EXPECTANT/
EXPECTING; FAMILY PLANNING; FAMILY WAY; GET INTO
TROUBLE; GIFT FROM GOD; GOOSEBERRY BUSH; HAPPY

EVENT; ILLEGITIMATE; IN THE CLUB; INFERTILE; LITTLE
STRANGER; LOVE CHILD; MAKE A SLIP; MISTAKE; NATURAL
CHILD; NEAR HER HOUR; OFFSPRING OF UNMARRIED
PARENTS; PATTER OF TINY FEET; PREGGERS; STERILE;
STORK HAS COME; SUB-FERTILITY PROBLEM; TERMINATION
OF PREGNANCY; THAT WAY; TIME; TROUBLE; UP THE SPOUT;
WITH CHILD

birth control   Contraception. Since the early 20th century.
'The Birth Control League' – heading in *The Woman Rebel* (June
1914); 'It's a tiff likely to be repeated between men and women
everywhere: Who should be responsible for birth control?
For making safe love?' – *The Washington Post* (9 March 1992).

birth name   Maiden name – which is a totally unacceptable
concept for the PC, implying as it does that all unmarried women
are virgins (which is probably not the case). Val Dumond, *The
Elements of Nonsexist Usage* (New York, 1990) provides the PC term.
'Most published sources refer to John Wayne's birth name as
Marion Michael Morrison. Wayne's birth certificate, however,
gives his original name as Marion Robert Morrison' –
Encyclopaedia Britannica (2005).

(in one's) birthday suit   Naked (i.e. what you were born in).
By 1809. 'Movie great Tony Curtis is celebrating his upcoming
80th birthday by baring all in the pages of the new Vanity Fair
magazine' – Contactmusic.com (16 May 2005).

(a) bit of a rogue   A scoundrel. By 1833. 'The problem is that
Mr Agha, like almost every other governor in Afghanistan, is a
bit of a rogue. Taxes do not all go to central government. His
own militia are better paid than government soldiers ... but it's
no secret in Kabul that the governor is a loose cannon' – Robert
Fisk in *The Independent* (9 August 2002).

(to) bite / kick / lick the dust   To die. *OED2* finds 'bite'
in 1856. 'Kick the dust' is nicely illustrated by a passage from
Thoreau's *Walden* (1854): 'I was present at the auction of a

deacon's effects ... after lying half a century in his garret and other dust holes ... When a man dies he kicks the dust.' Psalm 72:9 has: 'They that dwell in the wilderness shall bow before him; and his enemies shall lick the dust' – though this is suggesting humiliation rather than death.

(the) black economy The sector that provides goods and services illegally, without paying tax. Also **underground economy**. Both known by the 1970s. 'With pot and porn outstripping corn, America's black economy is flying high. Illegal migrants provide the muscle for US black market' – headline in *The Guardian* (2 May 2003).

(the) black market The illegal dealing in rationed or restricted goods. By the 1930s. 'Iran received designs from the nuclear black market run by a Pakistani scientist showing how to cast highly radioactive uranium into a form that could be used to build the core of an atomic bomb, diplomats said Friday' – *The Guardian* (18 November 2005).

black-coated workers Prunes as laxatives. This term, of earlier origin, was popularized from 1941 onwards in an early-morning BBC programme *The Kitchen Front* by the 'Radio Doctor', Charles (later Lord) Hill. He noted in his autobiography *Both Sides of the Hill* (1964): 'I remember calling on the Principal Medical Officer of the Board of Education ... At the end of the interview this shy and solemn man diffidently suggested that the prune was a black-coated worker and that this phrase might be useful to me. It was.' Earlier, the diarist MP Chips Channon was using the phrase in a literal sense concerning the clerical and professional class when he wrote (8 April 1937): 'The subject was "Widows and Orphans", the Old Age Pensions Bill, a measure which affects Southend and its black-coated workers' – *Chips: The Diaries of Sir Henry Channon*, ed. Robert Rhodes James (1967).

bleeding BLOODY (as a mild oath). Since the mid-19th century. 'Costermongers have lately substituted the participle "bleeding" for the adjective. "My bleeding barrow" is the latest phrase in vogue' – *The Athenaeum* (24 July 1858).

(a) blessed / happy release A death seen as a benefit to those who remain – particularly where the dead person has been a burden through ill health. Since the 19th century. 'Her going to be with the Lord came as a blessed release from suffering but her absence will be keenly felt by all who knew her' – *Mennonite Weekly Review* (22 September 1955); 'Chris died peacefully and gently in April 2003, a happy release after a long and dreadful illness' – Keele Alumni Web (June 2005).

blinking BLOODY (as a mild oath). Since the 19th century. Hence, its use in the abusive term 'blinking idiot'. This, however, was coined in *The Merchant of Venice* (1596), II.ix.54 when the Prince of Arragon opens the silver casket and exclaims: 'What's here? the portrait of a blinking idiot / Presenting me a schedule.' This, however, is probably a more literal suggestion of an idiot whose eyes blink as a token of his madness.

bloody By our lady (as an oath) – though not if you believe *OED2*: 'There is no ground for the notion that "bloody", offensive as from associations it now is to ears polite, contains any profane allusion or has connexion with the oath "'s blood!"'

(to) blow away To kill (with a gun). The image obviously refers to the body being thrown backward by the force of the shot. By the 18th century, apparently. 'I ordered ... the artillery officers to prepare to blow them away' – *The Monthly Review*, No. 55 (1776).

(a) blow job Cunnilingus or fellatio, but usually the latter. Since the 1940s? Because blowing is what it looks as though the AGENT is doing. 'Dear Dr. Bob: Can you please answer one irrelevant question? ... Does a blow job from a gay guy feel any different from a blow job from a straight dude?' – TheBody.com (14 November 2005).

(to) blow off To fart. 20th century. But almost as bad as the original expression. 'Sunday saw the premiere of *Thunderpants*, a film about a boy who has problems in the wind department – he can't stop blowing-off! – CBBC Newsround Online (12 May 2002).

blue Erotic, obscene. As in 'blue jokes', 'blue movies'. The association of blue with obscenity goes back a long way, perhaps to 17th-century New England, as Vernon Noble suggested in *Nicknames* (1976): 'Puritan magistrates promulgated what were known as "blue laws" (was it because they were printed in blue?) to enforce church attendance and moral standards, especially in New Haven, Connecticut. In England, the first Monday before Lent used to be called "blue Monday" because workmen spent it in dissipation.'

Hence, however, the euphemistic expression **(to) blue pencil**, meaning 'to censor'. In the BBC wartime radio series *Garrison Theatre* (first broadcast 1939), Jack Warner as 'Private Warner' helped further popularize this well-established synonym (*OED2*'s first citation is an American one from 1888). In reading blue-pencilled letters from his brother at the Front, expletives were deleted ('not blue pencil likely!') and Warner's actual mother boasted that 'My John with his blue-pencil gag has stopped the whole nation from swearing.' In his autobiography, Warner recalled a constable giving evidence at a London police court about stopping Mr Warner, a lorry driver. The magistrate inquired, 'Did he ask what the blue pencil you wanted?' 'No, sir,' replied the constable, 'this was a different Mr Warner ...' It is said that when the Lord Chamberlain exercised powers of censorship over the British stage (until 1968), his emendations to scripts were, indeed, marked with a blue pencil.

(the) bodily functions Defecation and urination (to be precise). In medical use since the mid-19th century. 'His bodily functions became a means both of communication and of punishing his parents. By then, toilet talk had seeped into almost every conversation. Not only was it getting tiresome to listen to,

it was becoming embarrassing when it happened in public' –
bcparent.com (November 2005).

body harassment (Of one's own body) self-indulgence. 'Not
far behind racism and sexual harassment on the charge sheet
of political correctness comes "body harassment" … The sins
against the Holy Ghost of PC are smoking, drinking too much
(or indeed at all), eating too much (or any cholesterol) and,
as a recent addition, engaging in unsafe sex' – *The Daily Telegraph*
(14 July 1992).

body matters See BLOW OFF; BODY ODOUR/B.O.; BREAK
WIND; BRONX CHEER; BIRTHDAY SUIT; BUFF; LET OFF;
PERSPIRE; PROFOUNDLY DEAF; RASPBERRY; SEEING
DIFFICULTIES; UNSEEING PERSON; VISUALLY IMPAIRED
INDIVIDUAL

body odour / B.O. Sweat smell. This politely worded but
worrying concept was used to promote Lifebuoy soap, initially
in the US, and was current by 1933. In early American radio
jingles, the initials 'B.O.' were sung *basso profundo*, emphasizing
the horror of the offence: 'Singing in the bathtub, singing for
joy, / Living a life of Lifebuoy – / Can't help singing, 'cos I know
/ That Lifebuoy really stops B.O.' In 1960s UK, TV adverts
showed pairs of male or female friends out on a spree, intending
to attract partners. When one of the pair was seen to have a
problem, the other whispered helpfully, 'B.O.'. 'We proceed
to the state dining-room … By dinner time the smell of BO is
detectable, and no one has thought of letting some fresh air in'
– James Lees-Milne, *Through Wood and Dale* (1998), diary entry for
2 August 1975.

body parts See PARTS OF THE BODY

(a/the) bog A/the LAVATORY. Since the 18th century. For
obvious reasons. Really just another slang term but, especially
when pronounced *boge* (known since the 1960s), it does have
a euphemistic quality. 'Every decision counts and you know

that you can't afford to take time off to smell the roses. More importantly, you can't take time to go to the bog – even if your bladder feels like its the size of a medicine ball and filled with hot gravel – because that would be your biggest mistake' – theregister.co.uk (18 November 2005).

Bohemian Disorderly, of loose morals, flouting accepted standards of behaviour, arty. At first, the term 'Bohemian' was applied to gypsies because they were thought to come from Bohemia (in what is now the Czech Republic) or, at least, because the first to come to France had passed through Bohemia. The connection between the irregular life of gypsies and that of artists is just about understandable – they are on the margins of society. Hence, the 'Bohemian life' came to describe life as lived by artists and writers, often poverty-stricken and amoral. Puccini's opera *La Bohème* (1896) was based on Henry Murger's novel *Scènes de la vie de Bohème* (1847), set in the Latin Quarter of Paris.

bonny Fat, plump (albeit healthily). And not just about babies or in Scotland. 'The bonny housemaid begins to repair the disordered drum-room' – Henry Fielding, *Tom Jones* (1749), bk 9, ch. 9.

(a) bonus A tip for services rendered among business employees; a bribe. Either way it denotes remuneration over and above what is normally due. It is paid to encourage performance. 'British capitalism is now a huge financial parasite, providing services for those sectors of the world that are creating productive wealth. In 2003, the world's financial markets went up sharply after three hard years. That helped all the parasitic sectors of capitalism, like the City of London, the banks and the consultants, to boom. Huge bonuses in the City were paid out after Xmas and the property boom resumed' – marxist.com (28 April 2004).

boobs Breasts. A slang word that is now humorously euphemistic. Mid-20th century. Has been said to derive from late Latin *bubo*, a swelling, though from 'booby', a fool, may be more likely. 'If people insist on talking about her [Barbara Windsor's] boobs, she would rather they called them boobs, which is a way-out word ... rather than breasts' – *Daily Mirror* (27 August 1968).

bootleg Illicit, counterfeit. From American, in the mid-19th century. Originally applied to the illegal selling of liquor, in more recent times this term has been applied to such things as records and DVDs and means 'counterfeit'. The word arose in the American Far West when illegal liquor sales were made to Indians on reservations. The thin bottles of alcohol are said to have been concealed in the vendor's long boots. 'There is almost as big a market for bootleg disk records as there is for bootlegged books' – *Variety* (10 April 1929).

born on the wrong side of the blanket Born out of wedlock, ILLEGITIMATE. Since the 18th century. Perhaps deriving from the rural custom of allowing a courting couple to lie in bed with a bolster between them. 'An old friend of mine not quite the right side of the blanket as they say' – Daisy Ashford, *The Young Visiters* (1919), ch. 5.

(to) borrow To steal. A possible Biblical origin is in Exodus 12:35, when the children of Israel followed Moses' instruction, 'borrowed of the Egyptians jewels of silver and jewels of gold, and raiment' and took them into the desert. It is doubtful whether the Israelites had any intention of returning them. 'Even Kevin Costner's happy, smiling "politically correct" version of Robin Hood looks austere in comparison with the nationalistic bravura of Edward, the quickfingers who borrowed the Gulf War Plan computer. Ed's personal message to our Defence chiefs began in classic style, "I am a common thief, but I am patriotic and love my country"' – *The Guardian* (29 June 1991).

bosom(s) Breast(s). Since the 19th century – whence comes the story of such delicacy of feeling that a guest might be invited to have 'a slice of chicken bosom' rather than 'a slice of chicken breast'. 'It was my fate to sit opposite to a fine turkey, and I asked my partner if I should have the pleasure of helping her to a piece of the breast. She looked at me very indignantly, and said, "Curse your impudence, sar, I wonder where you larn manners. Sar, I take a lily turkey *bosom*, if you please"' – Captain Marryat, *Peter Simple* (1856). 'I ask you, what sort of an inflated woman is that? She's got bosom, bosom and still more bosom. I bet every inch of her chest is worth its weight in gold' – Shelagh Delaney, *A Taste of Honey* (1958), act 1, scene 2; 'She gave him a quick glimpse of fine bosoms as she bent to the door of the icebox' – Ian Fleming, *The Man with the Golden Gun* (1965), ch. 5; 'Many men told me, in no uncertain terms, they didn't like big bosoms ... I can't stand the word boobs – not too keen on bosom, either. I've always called mine: "snokes"' – Madeline Smith, quoted in the *Daily Mirror* (15 September 1976).

(to) bother   (1) To approach sexually in or out of wedlock, especially when the bothered party is unwilling. Since the early 20th century? (2) To impose one's help on the poor. Since the early 19th century. In her diary for 20 February 1839 (published after her death in *The Girlhood of Queen Victoria*, vol 2), Victoria quotes Lord Melbourne, the prime minister, thus: 'Walter Scott said, "Why do you bother the poor? leave them alone"; don't you think there's a great deal of truth in that?' 'Bothering the poor' was to become a notable Victorian activity, evoked by Charles Dickens in Mrs Jellyby and Mrs Pardiggle in *Bleak House* (1851).

(the) bottie / botty / bottom / b.t.m.   The buttocks, arse. Since the 18th century. On 20 April 1781, Samuel Johnson remarked, 'The woman had a bottom of good sense.' In the *Life*, Boswell comments, 'The word *bottom* thus introduced, was so ludicrous when contrasted with his gravity, that most of us could not forbear tittering and laughing.' Johnson did not take kindly to this and demanded, 'Where's the merriment? ... I say the *woman* was *fundamentally* sensible.' Boswell adds: 'We all sat composed as at a funeral.' 'Like a wellwhipped childs botty' – James Joyce, *Ulysses* (1922).

(the) bottle / bottle (1) Alcohol – as in 'he took to the bottle'.
(2) Courage. 'Milk's gotta lotta bottle' was a slogan promoting
milk consumption in Britain in about 1982. Milk comes in
bottles, of course, but why was the word 'bottle' used to denote
courage or guts in this major attempt to get rid of milk's wimpish
image? Actually, the word 'bottle' has been used in this sense
since the late 1940s at least. To 'bottle out' consequently means
to shrink from, e.g. in *Private Eye* (17 December 1982): 'Cowed by
the thought of six-figure legal bills and years in the courts, the
Dirty Digger has "bottled out" of a confrontation with Sir Jams.'

One suggestion is that 'bottle' acquired the meaning through
rhyming slang: either 'bottle and glass' = class (said to date from
the 1920s); 'bottle and glass' = arse; or, 'bottle of beer' = fear.
But the reason for the leap from 'class/arse' to 'courage', and
from 'fear' to 'guts', is not clear, though it has been explained
that 'arse' is what you would void your bowels through in an
alarming situation. And 'class' is what a boxer has. If he loses it,
he has 'lost his bottle'.

Other clues? Much earlier, in *Swell's Night Guide* (1846), there
was: 'She thought it would be no bottle 'cos her rival could go in a
buster', where 'no bottle' = 'no good'. In a play by Frank Norman
(1958), there occurs the line: 'What's the matter, Frank? Your
bottle fallen out?' There is also an old-established brewers,
Courage Ltd, whose products can, of course, be had in bottles.

The way forward for the 1982 advertising use was probably
prepared by the ITV series *Minder*, which introduced much South
London slang to a more general audience.

(a) bowel movement Defecation. Possibly of biblical origin,
if you can understand this: 'My beloved put his hand in by the
hole of the door, and my bowels were moved for him' – Song
of Solomon, 5:4. Otherwise: '*Movement* ... the act of evacuating
the bowels; as well as the matter resulting therefrom' – *Lexicon of
Medicine and Allied Sciences* (1891). In 1996, I was told this anecdote:
Martita Hunt was rehearsing a TV play. At the end of one day's
rehearsals, the PA announced the next day's calls. 'Miss Hunt,
you're called at 9.45.' 'Quite impossible,' she replied. 'Why's
that?' 'Because my bowels don't move until 10.15.' Accordingly,

an actor who was working with her, relates that in his house the phrases 'Just off to see Martita' or 'Martita's decided to play the matinee after all' were long current euphemisms in regular use.

(a/the) box (1) A device protecting the male genitals against sporting injuries. Compare LUNCHBOX. (2) Television. A superior and slightly passé term for a TV set (having earlier been applied to wirelesses and gramophones), and one of several derogatory epithets which were applied during the medium's rise to mass popularity in the 1940s and 50s. 'The risks of obesity and diabetes also increased with every additional two hours spent sitting down at work – though these were much smaller than the risks from watching the box for the same length of time' – BBC News online (22 April 2003).

(a) boyfriend A male extramarital sexual partner (heterosexual or homosexual). 'Pansies only use pubs for picking up boy friends' – John Braine, *Room at the Top* (1957), ch. 30.

(the) boys in blue The police. Originally, 'gentlemen in blue' in the 19th century (from the colour of their uniforms). 'You must now begin to think seriously about handcuffs and prison, and men in blue' – Walter Besant, *All Sorts and Conditions of Men* (1882), ch. 43. Also applied to sailors and American Federal troops. Of a TV show: '[It] was also noticeably friendlier towards the boys in blue than it might have been had it been made for Britain alone, which suggests that we are in Pan European aren't-our-policemen-wonderful country' – *The Sunday Times* (13 November 1988).

(a) bracket A class. As in 'the lower, middle or higher income bracket', where divisions of people into classes is being avoided. Since the 1880s. 'They were both from the same social bracket' – Michael Innes, *Appleby Plays Chicken* (1956), ch. 5.

Brahms and Liszt Drunk. From rhyming slang, Lizst/pissed. Untypically, the whole phrase is used and not just the first word. Since the 1970s in the UK. Originally, it was **Mozart and Liszt,**

which was known by the mid-1960s. Neither phrase would seem to be part of traditional Cockney rhyming slang but later inventions.

(a) bread-and-butter letter A routine letter of thanks (suggesting obligation rather than genuine thanks). Originally an American term and known by 1900. 'Please *never* write me bread-and-butter letters' – Noel Streatfeild, *Tops and Bottoms* (1933), ch. 24; '*Bread-and-Butter.* After spending a night in someone else's house, however sincerely you may have said thank you when you left, you should still write a thank-you letter' – Sarah Fraser, *The Pan Book of Etiquette and Good Manners* (1962).

(to) break wind To fart (or belch). Since the 16th century. 'As she sat on the ass, she broke wind, and Caleb said, "What did you mean by that?" She replied, "I want to ask a favour of you."' – Judges 1:14 (*New English Bible*, 1970); 'Evidently, when [Rex Harrison] broke wind on stage, there was no mistaking the fact. It was about as inaudible as a stage whisper ... A substantial portion of Harrison's obituary in *The Independent* [3 June 1990] was devoted to this unfortunate failing' – *The Guinness Book of Modern Humorous Anecdotes* (1994).

(to) breathe one's last To die. Since the 16th century. 'Ah, Warwick! Montague hath breath'd his last' – Shakespeare, *King Henry VI Part 3* (1590–1), V.ii.40; '[An engraving] made twenty years after Washington died and more than a decade after Martha, his wife, had breathed her last' – *The Guardian* (23 April 1976).

brewer's droop Temporary impotence caused by an intake of alcohol. Said to be of Australian origin in the 1970s. 'As with many drugs, alcohol is particularly problematic in the "performance department", as the term "brewer's droop" would suggest. Information from the Centre for Education and Information on Drugs and Alcohol (CEIDA) suggests that it's common for guys who are long-term, heavy drinkers to report a reduction in their libido or sex drive. It's also quite common for heavy drinkers to have difficulties in getting and maintaining a hard-on' – afao.org.au (23 November 2005).

(a) brick / few bricks short of a load Of low intelligence, not very clever. One of many phrases used to describe mental shortcomings, or 'a deficiency in the marbles' department' of someone who is 'not all there' and has either 'a screw loose' or 'a bit missing'. Other versions of the 'short of' formula (all from the second half of the 20th century) include:

> a couple of bales shy of a full trailer load
> a couple of ha'pennies short of a shilling
> a few vouchers short of a pop-up toaster
> got off two stops short of Cincinnati
> not quite enough coupons for the coffee percolator and matching
>   set of cups
> one apple short of a full load
> one can short of a six-pack
> one card short of a full deck
> one grape short of a bunch
> one pork pie / two sandwiches short of a picnic
> tuppence short of a shilling
> two ants short of a picnic
> two sticks short of a bundle.

More venerable euphemisms for the same thing would include that a person is:

> dumb as a sack of hammers
> eleven pence half-penny
> fifty cards in the pack
> the lift / elevator doesn't go to the top floor / all the way up
> the light's on, but no one's in
> ninepence to the shilling
> not playing with a full deck
> not the full shilling
> only sixpence in the shilling
> operating on cruise control

> rowing with one oar in the water
> the stairs do not reach all the way to the attic.

See also under MENTAL MATTERS

(a) bride's attendant A bridesmaid. The PC American term, known by 1993. About as flattering as FLIGHT ATTENDANT. 'The matron of honor, Stephanie Lawton of Leetonia, and the bride's attendant, Stacey Sevacko of Columbiana, wore apple-colored gowns. Her other attendant was her brother, Josh Gaston of New Waterford. Flower girl was Harlie Derrick of East Palestine' – *The Vindicator* (Youngstown, Ohio) (13 November 2005).

(to) bring into the world To give birth. Since the 16th century. 'Thy mother's womb / that brought thee to this world' – Shakespeare, *Coriolanus* (1608), V.iii.125.

(to) bring to account / book To punish, bring criminal charges against. By 1804. 'In the mid-1970s there was a kidnapper and murderer in the English Midlands whom the popular press dubbed "The Black Panther". When he was eventually brought to book, a Radio 4 newsreader ... told an astonished nation: "At Oxford Crown Court today, the jury has been told that Donald Neilsen denied being the Pink Panther."' – *The Guinness Book of Modern Humorous Anecdotes* (1994).

Bristols The female breasts. Rhyming slang provides this word, the origin of which is otherwise far from obvious. The rhyme is Bristol Cities/titties – a use more or less restricted to the UK and since the 1950s. As Paul Beale suggests in his revision of *Partridge/Slang*, the football team Bristol City probably only gets invoked because of the initial similarity of the words 'Bristol' and 'breasts'. 'The main point (or should it be points?) of this programme is Miss Barbara Windsor's bristols which are ... well-developed' – *The Observer* (2 February 1969).

broad in the beam Fat, specifically with wide hips or buttocks. Since the early 20th century. '"I'm too broad around the beam." "What do you mean?" ... "My hips, silly ... I've got wide hips"' – Ian Cross, *The Backward Sex* (1960), ch. 1.

broadminded Tolerant if not enthusiastically forward in sexual matters. Since the 19th century. 'I am looking for broadminded girls above 18 years, interested in making a quick buck and having a good time in the bargain. I shoot fashion photography and erotic home movies for private viewing overseas only, in a safe and relaxed environment. Discretion required and assured' – arienter.com (18 February 2003).

(a) Broadmoor patient A criminal lunatic. From the name of the institution founded in the Berkshire village of Broadmoor in 1863. An Act of Parliament in 1948 declared: 'The expression "criminal lunatic" shall cease to be used; and there shall be substituted for it wherever it occurs in any enactment the expression "Broadmoor patient".' 'A Broadmoor patient with "extremely disruptive behaviour" is to be moved to a mainstream prison because his personality disorder is said to be "unbeatable". Philip Bradley, 35, threatened to slit the throat of his nurse. He has been in secure hospitals for almost 20 years. A judge at Reading crown court agreed that he be sentenced to two years in a mainstream jail, at his own request and that of the doctors at the high-security hospital' – *Mental Health Nursing* (July 2003).

(with a) broken accent Foreign-sounding. '"Harold," said she, speaking English with a broken accent. "I could not stay away longer. It is so lonely up there with only – Oh, my God, it is Paul!" These last words were in Greek' – Arthur Conan Doyle, *The Greek Interpreter* (1893).

(a) broken home A home in which either the mother or father is absent through separation or divorce. Since the early 19th century. 'There can be no doubt that a broken home can badly affect a child' – *The Listener* (25 September 1958).

(a) Bronx cheer A fart, actual or simulated by blowing against
the hand. *DOAS* suggests that this form of criticism (known by
1929) originated at the National Theater in the Bronx, New York
City, although the Yankee baseball stadium is also in the same
area. The UK equivalent is **to blow a raspberry**, from rhyming
slang, 'raspberry tart/fart'.

(to be) brought to bed To give birth (of a mother). By the
14th century. 'The Queene ... being brought to bed of a
daughter' – Lord Herbert, *The Life and Reigne of King Henry VIII* (1649).

brownie points Anticipated reward for calculated behaviour.
Originating in American business or the military, and certainly
recorded before 1963, this has nothing to do with Brownies, the
junior branch of the Girl Guides, and the points they might or
might not gain for doing their 'good deed for the day'. Oh no!
This has a scatological origin, not unconnected with brown-
nosing, brown-tonguing, arse-licking and other unsavoury
methods of sucking up to someone important. Note also the
American term 'Brownie', an award for doing something *wrong*.
According to *DOAS*, 'I got a pair of Brownies for that one' (1942)
refers to a system of disciplinary demerits on the railroads. The
name was derived from the inventor of the system, a Mr Brown.

budget Cheap and nasty, low-budget. Presumably the idea
behind the word is that you will not be charged for something
more than you – being a person of limited means – have budgeted
for. By the 1950s. 'EasyJet, the budget airline, delivered a 21.9
per cent rise in May passenger numbers to 2.55 million. It filled
84.1 per cent of its seats, a 3 percentage point improvement on
last year' – *The Times* (8 June 2005).

(in the) buff Naked. This seems to derive from the buff-
coloured leather shorts down to which people in the services
were sometimes stripped. Although strictly speaking they were
not naked, the term was extended to apply to those who were
completely so. An English regiment has been known as 'The
Buffs' for over three hundred years – not because it goes naked

but because of the colour of its uniform. 'Buffy the Vampire
Slayer Sarah Michelle Gellar has vowed never to appear in the
buff on screen' – tonight.co.za (25 November 2005).

(it's) Buggins' turn (more correctly **Buggins's turn**) Reason
given for a job appointment – through order of seniority or
time-serving rather than ability. The name Buggins is used
because it sounds suitably dull and humdrum ('Joseph Buggins,
Esq. J.P. for the borough' appears in G.W.E. Russell's *Collections
and Recollections* (1898). Trollope gives the name to a civil servant
in *Framley Parsonage* (1861). The similar sounding 'Muggins', self-
applied to a foolish person, goes back to 1855, at least.) The
earliest recorded use of the phrase 'Buggins's turn' is by Admiral
Fisher, later First Sea Lord, in a letter of 1901. Later, in a letter
of 1917 (printed in his *Memories*, 1919), Fisher wrote: 'Some
day the Empire will go down because it is Buggins's turn.' It is
impossible to say whether Fisher coined the phrase, though he
always spoke and wrote in a colourful fashion.

But what do people with the name Buggins think of it? In
February 1986, a Mr Geoffrey Buggins was reported to be
threatening legal action over a cartoon that had appeared in the
London *Evening Standard*. It showed the husband of Margaret
Thatcher looking through the New Year's Honours List and
asking, 'What did Buggins do to get an MBE?' She replies: 'He
thought up all those excuses for not giving one to Bob Geldof'
(the pop star and fund raiser who only later received an
Honorary KBE). The real-life Mr Buggins (who had been
awarded an MBE for services to export in 1969), said from his
home near Lisbon, Portugal: 'I am taking this action because I
want to protect the name of Buggins and also on behalf of the
Muddles, Winterbottoms and the Sillitoes of this world.' The
editor of the *Standard* said: 'We had no idea there was a Mr
Buggins who had the MBE. I feel sorry for his predicament, but
if we are to delete Buggins's turn from the English language
perhaps he could suggest an alternative.'

(the) bum 'The buttocks, the part on which we sit' – Dr
Johnson's definition. Since the 14th century. The simplest origin

for this old word would seem to be from 'bottom', but this is clearly ruled out by *OED2* which fancies some 'echoic' source (i.e. one imitating a sound). Hence, bum would seem to come from the 'bump' which a person makes as he or she sits down. *Does My Bum Look Big In This?* – title of book (1999) by Arabella Weir, after her catchphrase trying on clothes in a shop, in BBC TV, *The Fast Show*.

bum-fodder / bumpf / bumph LAVATORY paper. Hence the title of Alexander Brome's ballad *Bumm-foder: or waste-paper proper to wipe the nations rump with* (1660?). The one-word form known since 1889. Also applied to onerous paperwork containing (perhaps tiresome) details, instructions etc. 'If you'll give me your address, I'll send you all the bumf.'

(to have a) bun in the oven To be pregnant. By the mid-20th century. 'Who's got a bun in the oven? Who's got a cake in the stove?' – sung in Shelagh Delaney, *A Taste of Honey* (1958), act 2, scene 1.

(a) bundle of joy / love A baby. Possibly Victorian in origin. Now journalese, possibly to obscure the fact that there has been a struggle to conceive. 'They're considering [the names] Sean and Preston, but want to wait until the weekend – when they take their 6lb 11oz bundle of joy home – before deciding for sure' – starmagazine.com (21 November 2005).

(a) bunny A male homosexual who takes the more timid female role. Possibly by the 1940s. Hence, presumably, 'Bunnies *can* (and *will*) go to France', written by the British politician Jeremy Thorpe to Norman Scott (in a letter dated 13 February 1961). Scott, a former male model, spread rumours that the two of them had had a homosexual affair. In a bid to defuse the situation (in about 1976), Thorpe allowed publication of a letter which ended as above. Scott explained the 'bunnies' as referring to Scott as a frightened rabbit – this was how Thorpe had described him on the night he had seduced Scott. The saying became part of the folklore surrounding the scandal. Whether this euphemism was current by 1961 is not clear (*Partridge/Slang* does not have it).

The word can, of course, also be applied to a girl, though this is hardly a euphemism.

business/employment/workplace matters See
AMBULANCE CHASER; APPEARANCE MONEY; BETWEEN
SHOWS; BONUS; BUGGINS'S TURN; CHALLENGING; CHINESE
WALL; CONFERENCE; CORPORATE ENTERTAINMENT;
CREATIVE TENSION; DISPUTE; EMPLOYMENT EXCHANGE;
EXPRESSION OF TRADE UNION SOLIDARITY; GO SLOW; IN-
STORE WASTAGE; INCENTIVE (BONUS); INDUSTRIAL ACTION;
INDUSTRIAL RELATIONS; INVOLUNTARILY-LEISURED; JOB
CENTRE; MEETING; OUTSOURCING; PAYING GUEST; PRICE
SPIRAL; RESTING; SANCTIONS; SPANISH PRACTICES;
TASKFORCE; TRADE UNION MEMBER; UNOFFICIAL ACTION;
UNWAGED; WHISTLE-BLOWER; WITHDRAWAL OF GOODWILL;
WITHDRAWAL OF LABOUR; WORK TO RULE

business SEXUAL INTERCOURSE. Known since the 17th century. So, the late 20th-century expression 'to do the business' can mean, among other things, 'to be engaged in the sexual act', especially where a prostitute is involved and payment is made. 'Why do nice men go whoring? ... There was, I thought, lurking in all this, a slight distaste both for male weakness and for "doing the business"' – *The Sunday Times* (2 November 1986).

(a) business executive Anyone who earns his/her living. By the 1970s. 'Before the [1939–45] war a spade used to be called a spade – often brutally so ... But today a man who sells second-hand socks from a market [has become] a business executive' – George Mikes, *How To Be Decadent* (1977).

(the) bust A woman's breasts taken as a single unit. Since the late 19th century. 'Beautiful model offers her services. Anything considered. Bust 40. Waist 20. Hips 37' – Monica Dickens, *The Heart of London* (1961), ch. 1.

buxom   Fat (of women). Since the 16th century – usually with an implication that she is quite healthy-looking with it. Usually coupled with 'wench'.

(to) buy it   To be killed or severely wounded, in military parlance. Since the 19th century, though especially popular since the Second World War. '*He bought it*, he was shot down' – Hunt and Pringle, *Service Slang* (1943).

Cc

called hence / home / called to a better country / better state / better world / higher service / into the presence of the King himself Dead. Some of several grandiloquent epitaphic phrases, because life after death will be in a better place than life on earth. Since the 18th century? 'SACRED TO THE MEMORY OF / SIR ISAAC POCOCK KNIGHT / LATE OF THIS PARISH, / WHO WAS SUDDENLY CALLED FROM THE WORLD TO A BETTER STATE, / WHILST ON THE THAMES, NEAR HIS OWN HOUSE, / OCTOBER 8TH IN THE YEAR OF OUR LORD 1810' – inscription in Holy Trinity Church, Cookham-on-Thames; 'We thank God for the example and ministry of those still alive and the many others who have been called to a higher service on another shore' – Out Island Internet Abacom Ltd (4 November 1997); 'Called into the presence of the King himself' is recorded in Hugh Meller, *London Cemeteries* (1981), ch. 5, but may just be a one-off inscription on a gravestone. See also JOIN THE CHOIR INVISIBLE.

calling / visiting cards Animal dung/droppings when found (usually) in the domestic environment. '[Prospective bidders at the sale of Land's End were warned about] a few thousand seagulls squatting all over the place and spattering every available rock with their smudgy white calling cards' – *The Observer* (27 September 1981).

(a) calorie counter A fat person who is trying to lose weight. Since the 1980s? From the name given to the device designed to help people do this, as in: 'I will send you a copy of our Do-It-Yourself diet planner and a calorie counter, so that you can organise a diet to suit your needs' – *Homes & Gardens* (September 1971).

camp Homosexual. However, the word is used to refer to anyone, male or female, who ostentatiously, exaggeratedly, self-consciously, somewhat vulgarly and theatrically flaunts himself or herself, without necessarily being homosexual. It is probably derived from CAMP FOLLOWER and entered popular speech in the 1960s, although its origin is older. 'Alfred has a new word he uses rather a lot, which is "camp". He uses it mainly when he is talking about the opera. He says it's got nothing to do with Boy Scouts but just means anything outrageous, or over the top – camp in fact! He thinks Basil's new tie is camp' – Joan Wyndham, *Love Lessons* (1985), diary entry supposedly for 27 April 1940.

(a) camp follower A prostitute. Male and female ones used to trail along behind the military and thus literally 'followed the camp' or were followers in the camp. By the early 19th century. Hence, *Colonel's Lady & Camp-follower: The Story of Women in the Crimean War* – the title of a book (1970) by Piers Compton.

(a) canine control officer A dogcatcher (in the US). Cited in Willard R. Espy, *An Almanac of Words at Play* (1975).

capital punishment Judicial hanging, execution. Since the 16th century. 'Capitall (or deadly) punishment is done sundry wayes' – William Lambarde, *Eirenarcha: or the Office of the Justices of Peace* (1581–8).

(a) captain An airline pilot. By the 1970s? 'This is your Captain speaking ... ' 'Before the [1939–45] war a spade used to be called a spade – often brutally so ... But today the pilot of a plane [has become] a captain' – George Mikes, *How To Be Decadent* (1977).

(the) captain is at home Menstruation. Supposedly because of the red uniforms once worn by British soldiers. Also **the cardinal is at home**, because of the colour of a cardinal's hat.

(to be given your) cards To be sacked. From the name 'cards' given to an employee's documents (including national insurance card) that an employer holds and then gives back when employment is terminated, for whatever reason. In British use only, since the 1920s, at least. 'Wouldn't surprise me to know he'd helped himself from the till, and that's why they gave him his cards' – Anthony Gilbert, *Death Against the Clock* (1958).

care in the community Release of patients from mental hospitals so that they might, supposedly, be looked after better by the world at large. A cost-saving policy introduced after the 1950s/60s by successive British governments with predictably catastrophic results. 'By the 1980s people were already becoming wary of care in the community after a series of killings by people with mental health problems' – BBC News online (29 July 1998).

careful with one's money Miserly. Since about 1900? 'Bowden's former employers were owned for nearly that entire time by the late Marge Schott, notorious for being, let's say, careful with her money. Bowden tells stories about Schott bringing in the leftover donuts she bought for the media, and selling them to employees at marked-up prices' – *The Washington Post* (1 April 2005).

carnal To do with sex – although the word means only 'fleshly' or 'of the body'. One of the earliest uses of the word in conjunction with 'knowynge' dates from 1450 – now more usually rendered as **carnal knowledge**, meaning SEXUAL INTERCOURSE or, at least, sexual intimacy. 'If any person carnally knows, without the use of force, a child thirteen years of age or older but under fifteen years of age, such person shall be guilty of a Class 4 felony ... For the purposes of this section, (i) a child under the age of thirteen years shall not be considered a consenting child and (ii) "carnal knowledge" includes the acts of sexual intercourse, cunnilingus, fellatio, anallingus, anal intercourse, and animate and inanimate object sexual penetration' – legislation in the State of Virginia (1950–93).

(to) carry a torch for someone To express unreciprocated admiration or love for someone – the torch representing the flame of love. American origin by 1927. 'Tingle Alley harbors warm feelings for [Norman] Mailer as for a summer in the mid 1960s he carried a torch for my mother. (My words, not hers.) They were both living in Provincetown, and she believes that the only reason he noticed her was that she looked uncannily like the girl on the cover of his then-latest book, *An American Dream*' – tinglealley.com (28 September 2004).

(to) carry the can To bear responsibility, take the blame, become a scapegoat. This is possibly a military term, referring to the duties of the man chosen to get beer for a group. He would have to carry a container of beer to the group and then carry it back when it was empty. Some consider it to be precisely naval in origin; no example before 1936. Alternatively, it could refer to the man who had to remove 'night soil' from earth closets – literally, carrying the can – and leave an empty can in its place. Or then again, it could have to do with the 'custom of miners carrying explosives to the coal face in a tin can (hence everyone's reluctance to "carry the can")' – *Street Talk: The Language of Coronation Street* (1986).

carryings-on Questionable proceedings, sexual shenanigans. Since the 17th century. 'They were rather shocked by their old neighbour of 89 marrying ... "He has been carrying on for years. She was his secretary in the South African War"' – James Lees-Milne, *Ancient as the Hills* (1997) – diary entry for 6 March 1974.

(to) cash / hand in one's checks / chips To die. After the final procedure in a game of cards when one cashes, passes or sends in one's checks – the counters representing actual money staked. In the US originally, from around the middle of the 19th century. 'Beneath this tree lies the body of J.O. ... who handed in his checks on the 7th December, 1850' – Bret Harte, *Outcasts Poker Flat* (1870).

(to have a) cash-flow problem To be insolvent, albeit temporarily. The concept of 'cash flow', as the flow of money into or out of a business (and taken as a measure of its profitability or otherwise) has been known since the mid-20th century. 'Mr. Wilks, never a big spender, didn't have to modify his lifestyle much. "I had a cash-flow problem right after Enron, but I briefly changed the payment schedule on my mortgage just during the transition," he says' – *The Wall Street Journal* online (17 November 2005).

(a) casket A coffin. Of American origin – and still chiefly in American usage – since 1849. 'Chambers' caskets are just fine, / Made of sandalwood and pine; / When your loved one has to go, / Dial Columbus 390' – advertising jingle (to the tune of 'Rock of Ages') quoted in Jessica Mitford, *The American Way of Death* (1963).

(the) casting couch The granting of sexual favours in return for work, a tradition especially followed in American theatre and films. H.L. Mencken defined the term in *The American Language* (1948) as 'the divan in a casting-director's office'. 'In the old days ... the only way anyone got anywhere in this business was by way of the casting couch' – *Sunday Express* (27 January 1963).

(a) casual relationship A short-term sexual relationship, perhaps even a ONE-NIGHT STAND. Second half of the 20th century. 'In the Darwin Magistrates Court, Beverley Allan, Murdoch's former girlfriend, described the man she began a relationship with in Broome in October 2000 ... Ms Allan said they had a casual relationship and would not see each other on any set day. She described the relationship as very one-sided on her part' – ABC Northern Territory online (1 June 2004).

(to become a) casualty To be killed (in war, battle). By 1844. 'In spite of more than a hundred casualties, the advance never checked for an instant' – Winston Churchill, *London to Ladysmith* (1900).

(to) catch a cold To suffer from the repercussions of an action or event. Since the 19th century. 'When Paris sneezes, Europe catches cold' – a comment attributed to Prince Metternich, the Austrian statesman, in about 1830. Another form is: 'When France has a cold, all Europe sneezes.' Since the Second World War it has also been used to mean 'to contract gonorrhoea'.

Caucasian White (skin colour). A balancing euphemism when 'black' went out of fashion and was replaced by 'African-American' in the 1970s/80s. 'Caucasian' had been a name given to the Indo-European 'white' race of mankind by the anthropologist J.F. Blumenbach (1800). He said the race derived from the region of the Caucasus. '[In the US] It is becoming offensive to use the term "white" to refer to the species the police define as caucasians ... Instead of white, you are now advised to say "non-African-American" or "non-American-Indian". At the worst, "European-American" is acceptable' – *The Times* (6 November 1990).

caught Pregnant. By 1858 (when it was used by Queen Victoria). 'Very often it happens that you get "caught", and you know what you feared might come has really begun' – Marie Stopes, *A Letter to Working Mothers* (1919). Hence, informal expressions such as 'she caught her foot in the blanket'. 'Owing to a "mistake", Bernadette was probably "caught". She was beginning to "show"' – *The New Yorker* (12 January 1957).

caught short Forced to URINATE or DEFECATE at an inconvenient place and moment. 'Our headmaster told us that any boy caught short should if absolutely necessary wee into an empty milk bottle' – *Daily Mail* (30 May 1983).

(to) cease to be To die. One of the roll-call of euphemisms in *Monty Python's Flying Circus* 'Dead Parrot' sketch, first shown on BBC

TV (7 December 1969). A man (named Praline in the script) who has just bought a parrot that turns out to be dead, registers a complaint with the pet shop owner in these words: 'This parrot is no more. It's ceased to be. It's expired. It's gone to meet its maker. This is a late parrot ...'

(a) ceiling An upper limit to a salary, wages or prices. By 1934 and possibly of American origin. 'The ceiling for the grade is ...' 'The price of cocoa reached its ceiling.'

(to) celebrate To get drunk – perhaps in a more joyous fashion than otherwise. By the 1930s.

(a) celebrity (1) A person who has appeared in the media for longer than thirty seconds. (2) An otherwise ordinary person who has appeared in a TV show with the word *Celebrity* in the title. Noted in Britain from, say, 2000. (3) An entertainer who is 'known' simply because he does what he does in front of an audience. It could be argued that the term is more of a misnomer than a euphemism but the way it is currently used often involves an element of JOB-TITLE ENHANCEMENT.

cellulite Body fat – especially the lumpy form that appears on the hips and thighs of women. American *Vogue* (15 April 1968) told its readers that this word had just crossed the Atlantic from Europe. 'Joujou lay back on the bed, having her cellulite massaged away' – Shirley Conran, *Lace* (1982), ch. 37.

(in) cement shoes / overshoes Murdered and hidden. From the practice (chiefly American) of gangsters disposing of their opponents in cement work or encasing them in cement and dropping them in the river. From the 1960s onwards? Also **cement kimono / overcoat**. '"We're not going to be intimidated by some little kid's book. That wizard's going to be wearing cement shoes by the end of the summer" – Mario Puzo's editor, Jonathan Karp, on the final Godfather tome's battle with the next Harry Potter book' – salon.com (3 May 2000).

(the) centre portion   The middle. 'The buffet car is situated towards the centre portion of the train' – announcement on British Rail (June 1992).

(with) cerebral palsy / with spastic paralysis   A spastic. The need for a euphemism has been pressing because the word 'spastic' became much used as a pejorative term for 'a jerk, a giddy person, a blunderer' by the 1970s. Spasticity relates to conditions which involve muscle spasms. Slang use of the word 'spastic' in a derogatory sense, meaning 'uncoordinated' or just plain 'stupid', drew forth from an editor of *OED2*, a rare initialled note: 'Although current for some fifteen years or more, it is generally condemned as a tasteless expression, and is not common in print – R.W.B[urchfield].' In Britain, the Spastics Society was caught in the crossfire over PC nomenclature while working under a questionable banner. While apparently not wishing to interfere with an established name in order to suit current fashion, the Society encouraged references to 'people with cerebral palsy' rather than 'spastics'. In the mid-1990s, the society changed its name to Scope. 'Some diseases and disabilities are regarded by the general population with particular dread, so that the terms used to describe them have become stigmatizing and insulting and should always be avoided. Do not use spastic or mongol, instead refer to people as having cerebral palsy or Down's syndrome' – Briefing note, The Royal Association for Disability and Rehabilitation (May 1992).

(of a) certain age   Old – or at least middle-aged; at any rate, no longer young. Most commonly encountered in the phrase 'a woman of a certain age' where one is trying not to be too specific. This is undoubtedly derived from the French expression '*une femme d'une certaine âge*', denoting a mature woman of, say, between forty and sixty. By the 18th century. 'She was not old, nor young, not at the years / Which certain people call a *certain age*, / Which yet the most uncertain age appears' – Byron, *Beppo* (1817), verse 22; 'A lady of a "certain age", which means / Certainly aged' – *Don Juan* (1822), canto 6, verse 69; '"It's too ridiculous!" exclaimed a spinster of an uncertain age' – Charles Dickens, *Sketches by Boz*

(1835), 'The Four Sisters'; 'Maiden ladies of a certain age should have visiting cards of their own' – from a book of etiquette (1888); 'Is voluntary work simply the means by which women of a certain age and class salve their social consciences, an inefficient way to plug gaps that should be filled by the Government?' – *The Guardian* (2 January 1992).

(in a) certain / delicate / interesting condition / state
Pregnant. 'Interesting state' by 1748 (Smollett); 'It is extremely painful to me to trouble you on this subject, while in your present delicate state' – letter from D.G. Rossetti to his sister-in-law who was about to give birth to twins, quoted in Stanley Weintraub, *Four Rossettis* (1978); 'Interesting condition' by 1928; '"Syphilis" had always been described as "a certain disease", just as an attempt at rape had been described as "a certain suggestion", and the result of the rape on the lady was described as leaving her in "a certain condition"' – Beverley Nichols, *The Sweet and Twenties* (1958), ch. 8.

(a) certain disease Syphilis. Also FOUL DISEASE for the same thing (19th century). See the foregoing.

certain substances Drugs. A police euphemism for drugs, chiefly used in the UK where restrictions are placed on the reporting of criminal activity before a charge has been made. Starting in the 1960s, newspapers would report raids on pop stars' houses and conclude: 'Certain substances were taken away for analysis.' From the episode of BBC TV's *Monty Python's Flying Circus* broadcast on 16 November 1969: *Policeman*: 'I must warn you, sir, that outside I have police dog Josephine, who is not only armed, and trained to sniff out certain substances, but is also a junkie.'

(a) certain suggestion An attempted rape. See the previous entries.

chair / chairperson Chairman. Probably the best-known achievement of political correctness. The non-sexist term for a

chairman or chairwoman was introduced by 1976 and has had a
mixed reception, though it has demonstrated rather more staying
power than one might have expected. As *The Oxford Dictionary of New
Words* (1991) pointed out, reference to the 'chair' in this context
is of long-established usage. 'Chairperson' (which may actually
have been introduced *before* 'chair') has never really caught on,
except in a consciously mocking way, though it sometimes
surfaces. As with the invention of 'Ms', the attempt at removing
gender, in this case from 'chairman', has resulted in an oddity.
Addressing someone as 'chair' is still faintly ludicrous. Declared
Baroness Sear in 1988: 'I can't bear being called Chair. Whatever
I am, I am not a piece of furniture.' Moreover, it is based on
the mistaken premise that the 'man' in 'chairman' denotes
masculinity. On the contrary, it merely reflects membership of
the human race. Of course, this is what feminists object to in
the first place: 'man' does, after all, contain the notion of
masculinity.

'Madam Chairman' would seem to be an acceptable
compromise. It is a touch pompous and formal but, given the
context, that shouldn't really bother anyone. 'A group of women
psychologists thanked the board for using the word "chairperson"
rather than "chairman"' – *Science News* (11 September 1971); 'She
has annoyed the Black Sections by refusing to resign as chair
of the party black advisory committee' – *Tribune* (12 September
1986); 'To detractors from the film and TV camps who demand
to know why women need their own industry organisation at all,
Women in Film chairperson Brenda Reid has only one answer:
"You see, the boys already have their own organisation. It's called
the British Film Industry"' – *The Guardian* (12 December 1991).
Another method of dealing with the matter is provided in the
BBC's 'Guidelines for Factual Programmes' (1989): 'One of the
most difficult. Best to overcome the problem by turning the
sentence round: Jane Smith, who chairs the council's policy
committee.' The Guide also adds: 'Chairperson is acceptable if
it does not needlessly arrest attention' – some qualification.

− challenged A suffix designed to convey a personal problem or
disadvantage in a more positive light. Originating in the US, the

first such coinage would appear to have been PHYSICALLY
CHALLENGED in the 'disabled' sense. Actual PC ' – challenged'
coinages are now far out-numbered by jocular inventions. It is
difficult to distinguish between the two types. Among the many
suggested in Britain and the US have been:

aesthetically challenged	= ugly
aurally challenged	= deaf, hard of hearing
cerebrally challenged	= stupid
cerebro-genitally challenged	= being a dickhead
chronologically challenged	= old
constitutionally challenged	= under a dictatorship
cosmetically challenged	= ugly
ethnically challenged	= Jewish
financially challenged	= broke
gynaecologically challenged	= menstruating
horizontally challenged	= fat
ideologically challenged	= a political 'don't know'
intellectually challenged	= stupid
linguistically challenged	= dumb, speechless, with speaking difficulties, unable to speak foreign languages
metabolically challenged	= dead
morally challenged	= criminal
odorously challenged	= smelly
optically challenged	= partially sighted or blind
orthographically challenged	= unable to spell
paternally and socially challenged	= illegitimate
quantitively challenged	= fat
trichologically challenged	= bald
university-challenged	= attending a polytechnic or a 'new university' that was formerly a polytechnic
verbally challenged	= with speech impediment
visually challenged	= ugly; partly sighted or blind

See also FOLLICALLY / FOLLICULARLY CHALLENGED,
HUMOROUSLY CHALLENGED, HYGIENICALLY

CHALLENGED, ORTHODONTICALLY CHALLENGED and
VERTICALLY CHALLENGED below. Sources for this list
include: *The Washington Post* (4 August 1991); Beard and Cerf, *The
Official Politically Correct Dictionary and Handbook* (1992); *The Independent*
(25 and 30 June 1992); *The Times* (28 June 1992).

challenging Loss-making, difficult, problematical – in business
terms. Second half of the 20th century. 'Boston-based Fast
Company, a magazine for the new economy, said it has laid off 10
employees to deal with an advertising slowdown in the publishing
industry ... He cited the "challenging year for all business media"
in the company's decision to institute layoffs' – *Boston Business
Journal* (25 June 2001).

(a) chamber A prison. 'The ancient Athenians used to cover
up the ugliness of things with auspicious and kindly terms,
giving them polite and endearing names. Thus they called
harlots "companions," taxes "contributions," and the prison a
"chamber"' – Plutarch, *Lives*, 'Solon', Sect.15. Obviously now
obsolete.

(the) change (of life) The menopause. By 1834. '"I have felt
this strange restlessness for about a year now," she wrote to
Victor Gollancz [1951], "I wonder if this is the change of life?
But isn't forty-five a bit young?"' – Margaret Forster, *Daphne du
Maurier* (1993), ch. 16; *The Change: Women, Ageing and the Menopause* –
title of book (1991) by Germaine Greer.

(a) chapel of ease A LAVATORY. A chapel of ease was originally
a 16th-century term for a chapel built for the, er, convenience of
worshippers who lived a long way from a parish church. But this
term was jokingly re-interpreted as though the 'ease' in question
referred to what resulted from the BODILY FUNCTIONS.
Probably by the late 18th century.

(a) chapel of rest A mortuary. Possibly of American origin
but one of the few such funerary terms to have made it across the
Atlantic. 'From "undertaker" tout court to "funeral parlor" to

"funeral home" to "chapel" has been the linguistic progression' –
Jessica Mitford, *The American Way of Death* (1963).

(a) charlady A charwoman. The status enhancement is all too
apparent – **charworker** was, it seems, the American PC usage
of choice, though whether it really caught on, one doubts. 'West
Berliners may use them to pay their East Berlin hair dressers,
tailors, and charladies' – *The Times* (18 February 1959).

Charley's / Charlie's dead A woman's slip or petticoat is
showing below the hem of her dress. Known by the 1940s at least.
Could it be that it looks like a flag flying at half-mast because
Charlie is dead?

charm-free Boring, unpleasant. Late 20th century. 'Whether
the spivvy and charm-free Charlie Spencer is an improvement
on Charles Osborne, only *The Daily Telegraph*'s dwindling number
of readers will be able to judge, but the concept that crass
reviewers can be fired by editors who get round to reading
their bilge is heart-warming indeed' – rcubednews.com
(5 April 2002).

charms Female breasts. Since the 18th century? As in 'she
flashed her charms'.

cheeks Buttocks. Since 1600. 'My mother-in-law told of a
phrase overheard on a bus in Huddersfield, spoken by a portly
woman to her equally portly husband who in true Northern
fashion had got on the bus first. As they sat together, she said:
"Move over, Daddy, I've only got one cheek on"' – *Eavesdroppings*
(1981).

(a/your) cheque is in the post Shut up and stop bothering
me – a form of words used to a person requesting overdue
payment. As such, it is customary not to believe this response.
Used as a running gag in *Q8*, a Spike Milligan BBC TV comedy
series in 1979. 'The American Henry Beard's *Latin for All Occasions*
(Angus & Robertson, £5.99) provides us with vital expressions

such as ... "your cheque is in the post" (perscriptio in manibus tabellariorum est) ...' – *The Times* (30 November 1991).

(her) chest A female's breasts. 'I ask you, what sort of an inflated woman is that? She's got bosom, bosom and still more bosom. I bet every inch of her chest is worth its weight in gold' – Shelagh Delaney, *A Taste of Honey* (1958), act 1, scene 2; 'The belle of the baths was up to her ... well, up to her chest in it' – photo caption in the *Sunday Mirror* (16 May 1976).

childfree Childless (by choice). Used by a writer in *The Listener* and deplored by another correspondent as 'an exceedingly nasty neologism' (3 March 1977).

(a) Chinese wall An artificial division in a financial institution (or other large business organization) supposedly preventing the exchange of sensitive information which otherwise might lead to charges of conflict of interest. Became current in the 1980s. 'A dozen leading Japanese commercial banks asked the government to knock holes in the Chinese wall between banking and securities business' – *The Economist* (12 April 1986).

(a) Chinese whisper Inaccurate gossip. The term derives from 'Chinese whispers', the name of a children's party game. Seated in a circle, the children whisper a message to each other until it arrives back at the person who started, usually with the meaning changed out of all recognition. An alternative name for the game is 'Russian Scandal', which *OED2* finds in 1873 (or 'Russian Gossip' or 'Russian Rumour(s)'). Presumably, Chinese and Russian are mentioned because of their exotic 19th-century connotations, the difficulty of both languages, and because the process of whispering might sound reminiscent of both the languages when spoken. 'The words "Air Red, Air Red" had become confused as they were passed down the line, and by the time they reached the end had been changed to "Galtieri dead, Galtieri dead" ... It was later pointed out that a message had been similarly misjudged in an earlier war. "Send reinforcements, the regiment is going to advance" had been received as "Send three and four pence, the regiment is going to a dance"' – McGowan and Hands, *Don't Cry for Me, Sergeant-Major* (1983) (about the Falklands war).

(the) choir invisible See JOIN THE CHOIR INVISIBLE

(the) chosen people Jews, Hebrews. 'The Chosen People of God', in full, derives from the Old Testament. 'I give waters in the wilderness, and rivers in the desert, to give drink to my people, my chosen. This people have I formed for myself; they shall show forth my praise' – Isaiah 43:19.

chubby Fat. Seemingly less pejorative. Usually applied to children. Since the 18th century.

(to) chunder To be sick. An Australian word of uncertain origin, according to the *Macquarie Dictionary* (1981). According to the *Dictionary of Australian Quotations* (1984), 'Barry Humphries states that, to the best of his knowledge, he introduced the words "chunder" and "chundrous" to the Australian language [by 1964 at least]. Previously "chunder" was known to him only as a piece of Geelong Grammar School slang.' But this ignores the fact that 'chunda' appears in Nevil Shute's novel *A Town Like Alice* (1950).

The usual derivation concerns the cry 'Watch under!' by those about to be sick over the side of a ship, made to those on lower decks. *Partridge/Slang* has that it is rhyming slang for Chunder Loo ('spew'), from Chunder Loo of Akin Foo, 'a cartoon figure in a long-running series of advertisements for Cobra boot polish in the *Bulletin* [Australia] from 8 April 1909'.

(a) circular file A wastepaper basket. Of American origin, by the 1940s? 'I'd rewrite and redistribute a new plan with every new input. Days later (when everyone was happy), I showed my plan to the Powers That Be (who threw it in the circular file, but that's another story)' – TechSoup.org (25 July 2002).

(a) civic amenity site A rubbish dump, tip. Possibly following the Civic Amenities Act of Parliament (1967). A 'Recycling and

Waste Centre' (which is euphemistic enough) at Alkerton,
Oxfordshire, was so dubbed (1990s). The term may also have
been used to describe a cemetery run by a local authority.

(to) claim responsibility for To admit guilt. Journalistic
use, particularly when reporting bombing outrages perpetrated
by the Irish Republican Army, 1970s/80s. 'A communiqué
signed by the Symbionese Liberation Army claimed responsibility
for the attack' – *Black Panther* (19 January 1974); 'Just as one was
wondering who would "claim responsibility" for spoiling the
Headingley wicket – Saór Eire, the Women's Liberation Army –
up popped the Campaign to Free George Davis' – *The Times*
(20 August 1975).

(of) classic proportions Fat (of a woman). 20th century.
'Mosley's novel features a Chandler-esque plot complete with
a femme-fatale of classic proportions: "She was of medium
height with a more or less normal frame, but somewhere in the
mix there must have been a Teutonic Valkyrie because she had
the figure of a Norse fertility goddess ... All in all she was a
Poindexter built like Jayne Mansfield"' – journals.aol.com
(18 October 2005).

cleansing personnel Garbage collectors/road-sweepers.
Second half of the 20th century. 'All streets in the borough are
visited by our street cleansing personnel on a weekly basis for
litter-picking and other cleansing tasks' – stockton.gov.uk
(19 November 2005).

(to be) clearing one's desk To be anticipating one's
dismissal or resignation from office or actually going through
with either of these. Used especially of British and American
government ministers and officials. 'The day did not start well.
After only a dozen minutes there was a moment that created
the image of Wigley clearing his desk and collecting his P45
in the sad manner of football executions' – *The Daily Telegraph*
(14 November 2004).

(a) cleavage The divide between a woman's breasts when visible in her clothing. By the 1940s. 'I was foolish enough to wear the sort of dress which showed vistas of cleavage' – *TV Times* (10 October 1958).

(a) client A patient of Britain's National Health Service. By 1993. This might appear to be because of the new cost-conscious environment but is rather intended to convey that the client is an active participant who goes to a doctor or specialist with a problem and is not simply a passive sufferer or victim. Hence, there are now 'in-clients' and 'out-clients', at least as far as many social workers, counsellors and psychiatric workers are concerned. The term is also used to describe the 'patient' of a psychotherapist and also, for example, to describe an ex-prisoner in relation to a probation officer. 'Just remember that you and the client aren't "friends" ... For heaven's sake, don't sleep with a client of either sex' – John Mortimer, *Quite Honestly* (2005), ch. 1.

(a) client of the correctional system A prisoner. American PC term for such an unfortunate person, by 1992. Also **guest in a correctional facility / institution**. 'Strunk and White complain, in their admirable *The Elements of Style*, "Why must jails, hospitals, schools suddenly become 'facilities'?" Because when the authorities decided as a cosmetic exercise that jails would be *correctional facilities*, the newspapers tamely followed suit, that's why' – Keith Waterhouse, *Waterhouse on Newspaper Style* (1989).

(a) climax A sexual orgasm. By 1918. 'Sexual intercourse may be pleasurable to and sought for by women who do not experience a climax' – quoted in Alastair Heron, *Towards a Quaker View of Sex* (1963).

(a) cloakroom A LAVATORY. Sometimes just **cloaks**. 'There are Cloak Rooms at all the Principal Stations' – *G.W.R. Time-tables* (July 1884); 'Daphne's always first out of breakfast and straight into the girls' downstairs cloaks. No one would have noticed only she took a book and read in there' – Polly Hobson, *Titty's Dead*

(1968), ch. 5; 'Overheard in a SW1 café – a foreign gentleman, well-versed in the English use of euphemisms, asked a harassed waitress for "the cloakroom". She replied: "We 'aven't got one, you'll have to use the 'atstand"' – included in my book *Eavesdroppings* (1981).

close / close-fisted Mean, stingy. By the 17th century. 'Only about half a dozen men held aloof from the [drinking] circle and those were ... suspected of being "close wi' their ha'pence"' – Flora Thompson, *Lark Rise* (1939), ch. 3.

(to) close one's eyes To die. 'Ye vales and hills, whose beauty hither drew / The poet's steps, and fixed him here, on you / His eyes have closed!' – words by William Wordsworth on the monument to the poet Robert Southey (1774–1843) in St Kentigern's Church, Crosthwaite, Keswick, Cumbria.

(a) closet A LAVATORY – but not in US usage where the word means merely a cupboard or small room. Hence, 'to come out of the closet' meaning 'to admit one's homosexuality' carries no lavatorial implications but merely suggests that the person has come out of a place of privacy or concealment. The Empire Hotel, Bath (opened 1901), had lavatory bowls with the slogan 'The Closet of the Century' written around the rim.

(in the) club Pregnant. Known since the 1930s. Hence, 'She's joined the club!', especially when the woman in question is unmarried. The club referred to – with a far from exclusive membership – was known in the 19th century as the 'Pudding' or 'Pudden Club' (where 'pudden' was seminal fluid). This latter expression has also been used to describe a girl's first menstrual period.

(a) cockerel A cock. Anything to avoid a sexual word, though technically a 'cockerel' is a young cock. It is said that in the 1930s the Hollywood Hays Code forbade the use of the word 'cock', as in 'weathercock', and so it had to be rendered as 'weather-rooster'.

(to send a) coded message To say something indirectly and not in the literal sense. Journalistic and political use by the 1990s. 'Political speeches described as coded are ... not speeches in code but euphemisms designed to express disagreeable sentiments about something or somebody in terms less distasteful and more face-saving to the somebody in question than the blunt statement of fact would be' – *The Times* (31 December 1981); 'Mr Davis yesterday warned the party against choosing a leader because he shared Tony Blair's presentational skills. "Anybody who tries to replicate that, people will say 'it's just another politician'," he told the BBC, in what will be widely seen as a coded attack on Mr Cameron' – *Financial Times* (10 October 2005).

coffee with milk White coffee. The PC term, by 1993. Hence, **coffee without milk** refers to black coffee and spares the blushes of the possibly black person who is going to have to serve it.

cohabitation Unmarried people living together. The big word, seeking to obscure the situation, has been in use since the 16th century. 'The Methodists have agreed a new statement about sex, marriage and the family, replacing a document dating from 1939. But it manifestly coasted over some of the trickier contemporary sexual issues. Younger speakers in the debate lamented the inadequacy of its treatment of the immorality of cohabitation' – *The Times* (11 July 1992).

(a) collaborative pianist A piano accompanist. Lest this job description be taken to suggest that accompanists are in a secondary, subsidiary and submissive position, we have this substitution found on the wilder shores of PC. 'It was disheartening to learn from the programme-book that in America Miss Garrett is a "leading teacher" of "collaborative pianists" ... Throttled submission is not collaboration. Must Americans have another generation of keyboard-doormats?' – *The Economist* (16 June 1992).

collateral damage The incidental deaths and injuries sustained by people, usually civilians, who get in the way of military operations. By 1989. 'In working to fashion a coalition or trying to persuade Congress, the public, the U.N., or other countries to support an action, the National Command Authorities must not dumb down what is needed by promising not to do things (i.e., not to use ground forces, not to bomb below 20,000 feet, not to risk U.S. lives, not to permit collateral damage, not to bomb during Ramadan, etc.)' – US Defense Secretary Donald H. Rumsfeld, 'Guidelines to be Considered When Committing U.S. Forces' (March 2001); 'General Myers admitted: "In some cases, we hit those targets knowing there would be a chance of collateral damage." It was "unfortunate" that "we had to make these choices"' – *The Independent* (17 November 2005).

(a) coloured (man / gentleman) An Asian or African person. UK usage has bumped along in the wake of US custom in recent decades. Jennifer Wayne in her reminiscences *The Purple Dress* (1979), about her broadcasting work in the Second World War, notes: 'The BBC had a formidable list of forbidden words or expressions: "nigger" was banned; so was "black", you had to say "coloured".' And 'coloured' it remained – also for African and Asian immigrants to Britain – until the change of heart spearheaded by the switch to 'black', in the US, during the 1960s. Yet even in 1976, *The Guardian* was still writing this (4 May): 'The children of coloured immigrants are commonly regarded as being at the bottom of the heap as far as educational achievement and job prospects are concerned.' In the same paper a black reporter wrote about his experiences when interviewing people: 'There is always that little pause while they decide whether to be direct and say black or use the euphemistic coloured. And, typically, they can never decide...' Now largely superseded.

combat fatigue Nervous collapse (among troops). By the 1940s, especially in the US.

(to) come To have an orgasm (male or female), in particular for the male to ejaculate semen. By the 18th century (though much older as **come off**). 'And when I'd come and really finished, then she'd start on her own account' – D.H. Lawrence, *Lady Chatterley's*

Lover (1928), ch. 14. As for **come together**, this has more to do with uniting for SEXUAL INTERCOURSE than for enjoying simultaneous orgasm. 'When as his mother Mary was espoused to Joseph, before they came together, she was found with child of the Holy Ghost' – Matthew 1:18.

(a) comfort break A pause during which the participants in some activity may URINATE. From the genteel American **comfort station**, meaning a public LAVATORY, which has been in use since 1900. '9:00am Begin day one of cycle. Destination: Brighton, East Sussex 11:00am Comfort break and refreshments 1:00pm Stop at Hargate Forest, Tunbridge Wells for lunch 2:00pm Set off after lunch 4:00pm Comfort break and refreshments' – woodland-trust.org.uk (27 September 2005).

comfortable Not at death's door. Standard hospital-speak when announcing a patient's condition after some accident or emergency. 'Four other officers were injured in the raid, one of whom remained in hospital last night. His condition was described as "comfortable"' – *The Scotsman* (16 January 2003).

comfortably off Rich, prosperous. By the mid-19th century. 'I'm too comfortably off to worry much about anything' – Compton Mackenzie, *Sinister Street* (1914), pt 2, ch. 3.

(to) commandeer To steal. Using the military word makes it sound so much more proper. 'We never use such words as steal, or "collar", "pinch", or "shake": the fashion is to say he "commandeers" it' – Rudyard Kipling, quoted in J. Ralph, *War's Brighter Side* (1900), ch. 9.

(a) commercial traveller A travelling SALES REPRESENTATIVE. By about 1800.

(a) commission agent A bookmaker. In its straightforward sense of a person who transacts business on another's behalf in return for a percentage, the term has been in use since the early

19th century. The status-enhancing use was told to me by the daughter of one, on the day of the General Election in 1997.

(to) commit To install a person in a mental institution. 'He was committed as a schizophrenic suffering from somatic delusions ... In 1976, he escaped and showed up at his mother's house. He was returned to the hospital, ending up at Beverly Manor, a facility for mental patients, where he earned the nickname "Dracula"' – crimelibrary.com (29 November 2005).

(to) commit a nuisance To URINATE in public. Notices appeared with the warning 'Commit no Nuisance', according to *Harper's Magazine* (UK; December 1863).

(the) committal The burial of a dead body or its despatch for cremation. By the mid-19th century. 'The funeral service will be held on Monday July 25th 11:00am at Saint Paul's Church in Manchester. A graveside service of committal will follow in the Saint Columbans Cemetery in Arlington where Erald will be laid to rest along side her husband' – imanchester.net (Vermont) (25 July 2005).

(a) commode A portable LAVATORY. By 1850 – before this a commode was simply a chest of drawers (in which it would have been hard to install a UTENSIL). '"You'll find the commode in that corner," her auntie had said, and the commode turned out to be a kind of throne with carpeted steps and a lid which opened' – Flora Thompson, *Lark Rise to Candleford* (1945), ch. 21. A **night commode** is that even more portable LAVATORY – a **chamber pot** (an equally euphemistic term, of course).

commodious Roomy, spacious – usually referring to accommodation, especially in estate agents' literature. By about 1800. 'This luxurious 3-room apartment with the double glazing windows facing the picturesque green yard has an undoubtedly advantageous location right on Nevsky Prospect, St. Petersburg's main commercial and shopping street. Situated on the 2nd floor of a 4-storey building just a few minutes walk from

Mayakovskaya metro station, this commodious apartment comprises 2 bedrooms' – saint-petersburg-apartments.com (2005).

(a) common law wife A mistress, unmarried partner. The concept does not actually exist in English law but some of those involved like to use the term. By about 1900. 'A former Dagestani politician who raised minks and dabbled in boxing was found dead in his Moscow apartment along with his common-law wife' – *The Moscow Times* (21 April 2005).

(a) community nursing officer A district nurse in the UK, also in the US.

(a) companion A person with whom you cohabit extra-maritally. 'The ancient Athenians used to cover up the ugliness of things with auspicious and kindly terms, giving them polite and endearing names. Thus they called harlots "companions," taxes "contributions," and the prison a "chamber"' – Plutarch, *Lives*, 'Solon', Sect. 15. In modern parlance, a **constant companion** is a person, usually female, with whom a public figure is thought to be having a liaison and probably regular sex. This last, by 1984. 'The film – which he starred in with another young unknown, Daria Halprin – reflected its director's high hopes of making a definitive statement about the malaise of American youth ... After shooting the film Frechette returned to Fort Hill, reportedly with Miss Halprin, who had become his constant companion' – *The Boston Globe* (3 September 1973).

company Lice – as in the query, 'Have you got company?'

(a) company director A person in a court of law who is thus described because he does not obviously earn his living legitimately. Usually, he is thus either a crook or 'just anybody'. '"Company director" and "model" are useful euphemisms for those who appear in dubious court cases' – *The Observer* (3 November 1963); 'When I became chairman of Lazards last year I was able to put down my occupation as "merchant banker" instead of the less reputable "company director"' – *The Times Review of Industry* (October 1966).

(a) company representative A spokesman. Another attempt to find a PC way of describing such a person. The BBC 'Guidelines for Factual Programmes' (1989) also recommended referring to a 'company statement' instead, if appropriate. 'MySQL at the end of January is expected to release a beta version of its MySQL 5.0 open source database, which is to feature enterprise-level functionality such as stored procedures and triggers, according to a company representative' – infoworld.com (4 January 2005).

compassion fatigue Meanness. A reluctance to contribute further to charities and good causes because of the many demands made upon one's compassion. A coinage of the 1980s when numerous fundraising events such as Live Aid for famine relief led to instances of public withdrawal from giving. Originally used in the US regarding refugee appeals. Derived from 'metal fatigue'. 'Geldof, the Irish rock musician who conceived the event [Live Aid] and spearheaded its hasty implementation, said that he "wanted to get this done before compassion fatigue set in"' – *The New York Times* (22 September 1985); 'What the refugee workers call "compassion fatigue" has set in. Back in the 1970s, when the boat people were on the front page, the world was eager to help. But now the boat people are old news' – *The Listener* (29 October 1987).

(a) complaint An ailment, disorder, indisposition. Since about 1700. 'How careful Lord Beaconsfield was, in the great days of his political struggles, to flatter every one who came within his reach. To the same effect is the story that when he was accosted by any one who claimed acquaintance but whose face he had forgotten he always used to enquire, in a tone of affectionate solicitude, "And how is the old complaint?"' – G.W.E. Russell, *Collections and Recollections* (1898), ch. 24.

complimentary   Included in the price – and not usually very impressive. Hence, a 'complimentary breakfast' on an airline is probably no more than a roll and coffee. You would expect to find a 'complimentary towel' in a hotel, anyway. And a 'complimentary shoe wipe' is only there because the hotel does not provide a proper shoe-cleaning service anymore. Pointed out in Hastings Hotels newsletter (December 1997). 'Signature Club Suites include: Two person jacuzzi / Complimentary high speed internet / King size bed / Complimentary bottled water, coffee and tea' – deltahotels.com (Regina, Saskatchewan) (2005).

(a) concentration camp   A prison for the containment of political opponents and other folk you don't like. Originally coined as the term by the British for the places where non-combatants in the South African War (1899–1902) were 'concentrated' together, so they would not aid the combatants. Taken to even greater euphemistic heights in Nazi Germany during the Second World War.

condition   (1) Illness. 'He had a chronic heart condition.' (2) Pregnancy. Hence, 'a woman in your condition' is not going to be exhibited at a dog show but is going to have a baby. Perhaps both since the early 20th century. 'So Joseph took Mary, and they travelled on foot and on donkey. But when they arrived at Bethlehem it was teeming with people! It was also the Sabbath Day, and not easy to find anywhere to stay. Mary was tired as any woman in her condition would be. Every Inn they went to was already full. There was certainly no privacy for a woman who might go into labour at any time' – christmasarchives.com (2005).

conditions/states of affairs   See ADVERSE WEATHER CONDITIONS; ALTERNATIVE; BANANA SKIN; BRACKET; CEILING; CODED MESSAGE; DEFERRED SUCCESS; DURATION; EMERGENCY; ENTHUSIASM; EXCLUSIVE; FACILITY; GENDER; HAPPENING; HOPE/PROMISE OF RAIN; HORLICKS; IN-DEPTH COVERAGE; INCLEMENT WEATHER; INCOMPLETE SUCCESS; LAND OF THE LIVING; MEDAL SHOWING; NOT A MILLION

MILES FROM; NOT AT HOME; NOT AVAILABLE FOR
COMMENT; NOT LONG FOR THIS WORLD; NOT ROCKET
SCIENCE; NUTRITIONAL SHORTFALL; ODIFEROUS; OFF-
COLOUR; ON THE CARPET; ONE OF US; OUT OF CONTEXT;
OVER THERE; OVER-AVAILABILITY; PAST ITS SELL-BY DATE;
PEAR-SHAPED; PERMISSIVE SOCIETY; PRE-OWNED;
PRESSURE OF WORK; PRESTIGIOUS; PRIVILEGED; PRO-
CHOICE; PROMISE OF RAIN; RECEIVE PUNISHMENT;
SCARBOROUGH WARNING; SOCIAL GROUP; STAR IN THE
EAST; UNSEASONABLE WEATHER; WHITE ELEPHANT

conducting a survey Trying to sell you something while
pretending to be collecting information. In the world of opinion
pollsters this is known as 'sugging' – 'selling under the guise
of ...' (this expression known by 1991).

(in) conference Unwilling to talk on the telephone rather than
actually unable to do so. A secretary might say: 'Oh, he is unable
to talk to you now because he is in conference.' A 20th century
porky. 'You may get a message on arriving saying "Call me when
you are rested". This really means give me some peace. If you
should be mad enough to call him, his Secretary (the darling girl)
will say that he's in conference. On the other hand she may say,
"I'll see if he's here, or if he's in the building." This means she'll
put you through, but she doesn't want you to think that he's too
eager' – on-cue.org.uk (after Frederic Raphael) (2005).

confinement Childbirth. The dating of its introduction may
be found in a memorandum written by Lady Susan O'Brien
(1745–1823) on 'changes between 1760-1818': 'Language has
always been changing, & it has been said, as morals grow worse
language grows more refined. No one can say "breeding" or
"with child" or "lying in," without being thought indelicate.
"In the family way" & "confinement" have taken their place.'

(a) confirmed bachelor A homosexual male, NOT THE
MARRYING KIND. In the straightforward sense of a man who
resolutely remains single, in use since the mid-19th century.

In the modern sense, perhaps since the 1960s. Mostly
journalistic use. 'Storey had many valued and devoted women
friends, but he was, to use a euphemism once favoured
by obituarists, "a confirmed bachelor"' – *The Independent*
(15 November 2005).

conjugal relations / rights Sex within marriage. Probably
both by the 18th century. 'Muslim wives can claim conjugal
rights: a Muslim wife whose husband neglects his family,
including his conjugal duties as a spouse, can apply to the
Syariah Court for him to return home and discharge his
obligations and responsibilities accordingly' – *Malaysia Daily Express*
(28 September 2003). Also **connubial bliss / pleasure** for the
same thing, although these may also be used to refer to sexual
pleasure outside marriage. 'It is true that many Moors, especially
learned men, divorce their wives when they get old, feeling the
women an embarrassment to them, and no wonder, when we
consider these poor creatures have no education, and, in their
old age, neither afford connubial pleasure nor society to their
husbands' – James Richardson, *Travels in Morocco* (1859), ch. 10.

conked out (1) Not working (of machinery, particularly a
motor car) – since the First World War. (2) Dead (of a person) –
since the Second World War. The actor John Le Mesurier
arranged for his own death notice to appear in *The Times* when
appropriate. It duly appeared on 16 November 1983, in the
form: 'John Le Mesurier wishes it to be known that he conked
out on November 15th. He sadly misses family and friends.'

consensual non-monogamy Adultery, swapping sex
partners. A joke coinage from *The New York Times* (22 March 1991).

(a) consenting adult A homosexual. This curious locution
came about in the *Report of the Committee on Homosexual Offences &
Prostitution* (1956): 'We accordingly recommend that homosexual
behaviour between consenting adults in private should no longer
be a criminal offence.'

(to) consider one's position To contemplate resigning.
In British parliamentary usage, if a minister is being called upon
to resign, he is urged to 'consider his position'. 20th century?
On 9 November 2005, Michael Howard, the Conservative
leader, said: 'Mr Blair's authority has been diminished almost to
vanishing point [after a parliamentary defeat]. This vote shows
he is no longer able to carry his own party with him – he must
now consider his position.'

(a) consultant (1) A sacked executive who is trying to find
something else to do with his time. (2) A salesperson – for
example, demonstrating beauty products in a department
store. Both enhancements date from the late 20th century.
'Meanwhile, consultants were being hired at great expense to
tell jobcentre managers "to put plants in offices to boost the
morale of staff battered by cuts", claimed Mr Sertwotka' –
SocietyGuardian.co.uk (14 September 2005); 'If you would like
to learn more about hand massage, ask a beauty consultant' –
neobeauty.com (2005).

(a) consumer A housewife – a preferable term, at least
according to the BBC 'Guidelines for Factual Programmes'
(1989). 'The medical profession has woken up to the individual
needs of the childbearing people and given over some control
to the consumer' – lifepassages.net (2005).

(to) consummate a relationship To complete marriage
(or a relationship) by SEXUAL INTERCOURSE. 'Your maieste …
maie … contract and consummat matrimonie wyth any woman'
– an Act of Parliament (1540) in the reign of King Henry VIII.
'What I love about royal books is how their authors know
everything. I mean simply everything. Christopher Wilson, for
example, knows exactly when Prince Charles and Camilla Shand
(as she then was) first consummated their relationship. He even
knows the time, for God's sake, though he is coy about the
date, allowing only that it was sometime in 1972' – *The Observer*
(7 August 1994).

consumption Tuberculosis of the lungs. 'Consumption' is here used in the sense of 'wasting away'. Since the 17th century but very much the great 19th century complaint. '*La Traviata* is based on a play about the real life of the Parisian courtesan Alphonsine Plessis, better known as Marie Duplessis, who died of consumption in 1847. The opera was first performed in 1853' – *Yale Bulletin and Calendar* (3 March 1997).

continent See INCONTINENT

(a) contribution A tax. 'The ancient Athenians used to cover up the ugliness of things with auspicious and kindly terms, giving them polite and endearing names. Thus they called harlots "companions," taxes "contributions," and the prison a "chamber"' – Plutarch, *Lives*, 'Solon', Sect. 15.

controlled substances Illegal drugs/narcotics. After the American 'Controlled Substances Act' of the 1960s. The control came, of course, from the law enforcers rather than the users ... 'This first novel by a Southern judge features a Southern judge, who logs overtime as cuckold, bribe taker, treasure hunter and devoted tester of controlled substances but by the end has become a guy worth knowing' – *The New York Times* (3 December 2000).

(a public) convenience A public LAVATORY. Probably since the 19th century, though clear citations are lacking. Definitely by the 1930s. 'Reminiscent of Hugh Grant's shocking decision to withdraw from a brilliant acting career, George Michael of Wham! and public convenience fame has decided to end it all. His brilliant singing career, that is' – entertainmentcomplex/blognation/us (17 February 2005).

convenience foods Packaged meals, usually for simple heating up. From the US, by the 1960s. Unfortunately reminding one of the previous entry. 'Whether it's Smash Instant Mash to go with a main meal, HP Baked Beans on toast for a heart warming snack or HP Bob the Builder pasta shapes for the kids, Premier's range

of convenience foods offers something for everyone. You'll find
at least one of our brands in most kitchens, ready to be called
upon when you want good food, fast' – premierfoods.co.uk
(2005).

conventional weapons Old-fashioned (non-nuclear) ways of
killing you. Since the 1950s. 'The U.S. military has used poison
gas and other non-conventional weapons against civilians in
Fallujah, eyewitnesses report ... "Poisonous gases have been used
in Fallujah," 35-year-old trader from Fallujah, Abu Hammad
told IPS. "They used everything – tanks, artillery, infantry,
poison gas. Fallujah has been bombed to the ground"' –
commondreams.org (1 December 2005).

(to have a) conversation about sex and travel To tell
someone to 'fuck off'. According to *Brewer's Politics* (1995 edn):
'On the margins of a Commons committee debating charges for
dental examinations, the Government whip David Lightbown
had two short, sharp words for the Tory backbencher Jerry Hayes
for pointing out that Mrs Thatcher had committed the party
not to introduce them. Asked what the words were, Hayes said:
"We had a conversation about sex and travel".'

convivial Drunk (but not unpleasantly so). Since the late 19th
century? 'There being so little opportunity for social intercourse
with the gentler sex, the sterner element should not be too
severely censured if they sought diversion of a lower order. And
if our stag parties were a bit convivial, they would probably
compare favorably in that regard with the swell club dinners in
the cities' – Noah Smithwick, *The Evolution of a State or Recollections of
Old Texas Days* (1900), ch. 5.

(to) copulate To have SEXUAL INTERCOURSE. Since the 17th
century but now having an unpleasantly zoological air. 'Thus
ended my intrigue with the fair Louisa, which I flattered myself
so much with, and from which I expected at least a winter's safe
copulation' – James Boswell, diary entry for 20 January 1763.

corporal punishment Judicial birching or flogging. 'Judicial corporal punishment' was the term used in the Isle of Man where this form of punishment was retained. Originally, in the 16th century, 'corporal punishment' referred to any form that involved the body, including death and mutilation, but in the 19th century, the term was limited to the infliction of pain by this method.

corporate entertainment / hospitality Bribery, attempting to achieve goodwill by treating clients. By the 1980s. 'Mintel's latest report on Corporate Hospitality provides detailed insight into the current state of the industry and future prospects for businesses involved. Large companies in the UK can draw on a wide range of venues, caterers, activity specialists and hospitality consultants to organise their lavish days out for prized customers' – reports.mintel.com (June 2004).

(a) corporation A fat stomach. 'Sirrah! my corporation is made up of good wholesome English fat' – Tobias Smollett, *The Adventures of Ferdinand Count Fathom* (1753), ch. 1.

correct See POLITICALLY CORRECT

correctional See CLIENT OF THE CORRECTIONAL SYSTEM

cot death Death of a baby. By the late 1960s. '"Cot death" relates to children not known to be ill ... who die unexpectedly' – *The Guardian* (11 May 1970).

(a) couch potato A TV addict. The pejorative term for an addictive, uncritical (and possibly fat) viewer of trash television. Said to have been coined in the late 1970s by Tom Iacino in Southern California. *Sunday Today* was only getting round to explaining the word to British readers on 27 July 1986. But why potato? Is it because of the shape of a fat person slouched on a couch? Or does it allude to the consumption of potato crisps, or to behaviour like that of a 'vegetable'? It has been argued that the phrase may be a complicated pun on the phrase 'boob-tube'

(US slang for TV, not an article of clothing) and 'tuber', meaning a root vegetable.

(a) council member An alderman, in British local government. The PC way of avoiding a 'man' word. By 1993.

(a) counter-factual proposition A lie. This joke coinage from *The New York Times* (22 March 1991) has probably more to do with the art of bureaucratic euphemism than with mainstream political correctness.

(a) courtesan A prostitute. A dignified term derived from an Italian 15th-century word that simply meant a courtier and then, in its female form, a woman who plied her trade at court. Edward Sharpham, writing in 1607, probably got the distinction right with 'Your whore is for euery rascall, but your Curtizan is for your Courtier.' *The Oxford Dictionary of Quotations* (4th edn, 1992) rather quaintly described Mandy Rice-Davies of Profumo Affair fame as a 'courtesan', before changing this description to 'model and showgirl' in its next edition.

courtesy Free of charge but included somewhere in the price. As in the 'courtesy bus' that takes ticket-holders from one airport terminal to another or the 'courtesy car' that insurers lay on when a car is being repaired after an accident. Since the 1960s and of American origin.

(a) courtesy call An attempt to sell you a further product or service under the guise of inquiring whether you are satisfied with what you have purchased earlier. Something that has blighted our lives since the early 1990s. Originally a courtesy call was not something imposed on you over the telephone but a visit in person to show respect to another person or institution.

(to) cover To mate. A stallion does this with a mare and what an elaborate procedure it can be to get the covers into position. Since the 16th century.

(to) cover one's feet To go to the LAVATORY. A translation
of the Hebrew euphemism, as found in the King James Bible at
1 Samuel 24:3: 'And Saul went in to cover his feet.' David was
hiding from Saul in a cave when in came Saul to evacuate his
bowels. Presumably the notion was that by crouching, the upper
body literally covered his feet. Or perhaps it means that his robe
does this when in the crouching position. Most modern versions
of the Bible say 'to relieve himself'. The Revised Authorized
Version (1982) has: 'Saul went in to attend to his needs.'
The Living Bible (Illinois, 1971) has, memorably: 'Saul went in to a
cave to *go to the bathroom.*'

(she's) covering the waterfront She is menstruating. In
The Wise Wound (1978) by Penelope Shuttle and Peter Redgrove this
is listed among the many slang expressions for menstruation.

(to) cream (in) one's jeans (Of a male) to ejaculate in his
jeans involuntarily, as an indication of sexual excitement; or
figuratively just to be excited. By the 1960s/70s? 'When faced
with the reality of two women in the same bed, he finished the
race before these women even had their shirts off. Needless to
say, upon finding out that he had creamed his jeans before they
were unzipped, both women involved decided he was a totally
unnecessary part of the equation' – sparechangemagazine.com
(2000).

creative accountancy / accounting Ingenious manipulation
of accounts that may or may not actually be illegal; dishonest
bookkeeping (or that which flies close to the wind). An early
example of the phrase occurs in the film The Producers (US 1968):
'It's simply a matter of creative accounting. Let's assume for a
moment that you are a dishonest man ... It's very easy. You
simply raise more money than you need.' The film's subject is
such accountancy applied to the world of the theatrical angel.

creative tension Fractious relations between people in
business or the arts that, nevertheless, may generate positive
results. By the 1980s? 'Los Angeles Opera's artistic director,

Edgar Baitzel, praises [Gottfried Helnwein's] work but
acknowledges that there was more creative tension than usual
during the Rosenkavalier production process. "Sometimes we
really had to stop him and say, 'No, that's it. No, we cannot.'
We all love him here, but it was not an easy job. He's just not
used to compromise or working with a creative team. This
is artistic energy – you can't predict it'" – *Los Angeles Times*
(18 June 2005).

(a/the) credibility gap The difference between what is
claimed as fact and what is actually fact. The euphemism dates
from the time in the Vietnam War when, despite claims to the
contrary by the Johnson administration, an escalation in US
participation was taking place. 'Dilemma in "Credibility Gap"'
was the headline over a report on the matter in *The Washington Post*
(13 May 1965) and may have been the phrase's first outing.

**criminal activity/justice/legal terminology/police
matters** See ATTENDANCE CENTRE; APPROVED SCHOOL;
AT HIS/HER MAJESTY'S PLEASURE; ATTRACT/COME TO THE
ATTENTION OF THE POLICE; BALANCE OF ONE'S MIND
DISTURBED; BLACK ECONOMY; BLACK MARKET; BRING TO
ACCOUNT/BOOK; CAPITAL PUNISHMENT; CHAMBER; CLIENT
OF THE CORRECTIONAL SYSTEM; CORPORAL PUNISHMENT;
CRIMINAL ASSAULT; CUSTODIAL SENTENCE; CUSTODY
SUITE; DETAIN; DIMINISHED RESPONSIBILITY; DOMESTIC;
ENJOY HIS/HER MAJESTY'S HOSPITALITY; FORM; FOUL PLAY;
GENTLEMAN; GENTLEMAN OF FORTUNE; GENTLEMAN OF
THE ROAD; GO UP THE RIVER; GROSS INDECENCY; GUEST
OF HIS/HER MAJESTY; HELP THE POLICE; HOUSE OF
CORRECTION/DETENTION; INCIDENT; INDECENT ASSAULT;
INDECENT EXPOSURE; INMATE; INSIDE; INTERFERE WITH;
IRREGULARITIES; JOYRIDING; JUVENILE DELINQUENT;
KANGAROO COURT; KNOWN TO THE POLICE; LABOUR CAMP;
LAW; LAW ENFORCEMENT OFFICER; MISSIONARY WORK IN
AFRICA; MOLEST; NECKTIE PARTY; NON-TRADITIONAL
SHOPPER; OFFENDER; PERSONAL VIOLENCE; PLOD;
POPULAR JUSTICE; PORRIDGE; PREVENTIVE DETENTION;

PRISON OFFICER; PROTECTIVE CUSTODY; PUT AWAY;
REFORMATORY; SEXUAL ASSAULT; SMOKING GUN; TAKE
INTO CUSTODY; TICKET; TIME; TRANSPORTATION;
TROUBLE; UNDER THE COUNTER; UNDERWORLD;
UNLAWFUL; UPSTATE; VICE

(a) criminal assault An assault on a female, stopping short
of actual rape. Basically, an assault is just a menacing action or
word. This legal term takes the matter a stage further.

(to) cross the floor To change political allegiance in the
British parliament, which could literally involve moving across
the floor of the House of Commons or the House of Lords to
where the receiving party is seated. 'The Right Honourable
and Learned Gentleman has twice crossed the floor of this
house, each time leaving behind a trail of slime' – David Lloyd
George on Sir John Simon (1930s). 'It is easy for an individual
to move through those insensible gradations from left to right,
but the act of crossing the floor is one that requires serious
consideration. I am well informed on the matter, for I have
accomplished that difficult process not only once, but twice' –
Winston S. Churchill, speech in House of Commons (10 July
1935). Sir Hartley Shawcross, a former Labour minister, moved
to the right in 1957 and resigned his seat (without actually
joining another party in the Commons). For his pains, he was
dubbed 'Sir Shortly Floorcross' by 'Taper' (Bernard Levin) in
The Spectator.

(to) cross the Styx See under PASS AWAY

(the) crown jewels The male genitalia. Either because of their
pendulous nature or because of their supposed high value to the
possessor. Known simply as **the jewels** in the 18th century. The
variations have been known only since perhaps the 1960s. 'You
all know who you are and you're about as funny as a kick in the
crown jewels' – *The Guardian* (1 July 2004). Compare FAMILY
JEWELS.

(a bit / piece of) crumpet A sexually desirable woman.
By the 1930s. 'He's gone off with his bit of crumpet' – Shelagh
Delaney, *A Taste of Honey* (1959), act 2, scene 2. Frank Muir
famously talked of the British broadcaster Joan Bakewell as 'the
thinking man's crumpet'. This was in the 1960s.

(a) crush An infatuation – usually sexually based. It often
occurs between members of the same sex and when they are at
school together. Of American origin, by the late 19th century.
'It is common to make fun of schoolboy and schoolgirl "pashes"
[passions] and "crushes"' – Victor Gollancz, *My Dear Timothy*
(1952).

culturally different From an ETHNIC MINORITY , i.e. an
immigrant. The arrival of this term was signalled in *The Times*
(28 June 1992) but it cannot be said to have caught on in a
big way.

(the) curse Menstruation. Possibly derived from 'the curse
of Eve'. Not recorded before the 1930s, apparently. 'She is
thrilled because she finally got her boyfriend to the altar. She
goes around saying, "I'm the naughty, naughty nurse who never
has the curse"!' – Joan Wyndham, *Love Lessons* (1985), diary entry
for 1 February 1940; 'Mama is very distressed because Gertrude
is due to have the curse the very day of her wedding, which
could not be arranged otherwise because her young man has
to take his leave when he is given it. Mama says the curse will
come precisely at 11.55 a.m. that day, that it always comes
regular as clockwork with strong, healthy girls, a thing I never
knew before and can scarcely credit' – James Lees-Milne,
Ancestral Voices (1975), diary entry for 7 April 1942; 'The attitude
that regards menstruation as divinely ordained and yet
unmentionable leads to the intensification of the female revolt
against it, which can be traced in all the common words for it,
like the *curse*' – Germaine Greer, *The Female Eunuch* (1970).
See also PERIOD.

(a) cuspidor A spittoon. Since the late 18th century. From the Portuguese *cuspidor*, spitter.

(given a) custodial sentence Sent to prison, rather than fined or made to do community service. First found in the US in the early 1950s.

(a) custody suite A police cell. British use – following its coinage in the Police and Criminal Evidence Bill of January 1986.

(a) customer A passenger. Noticed in particular on British railways by 1992. This makes it clear precisely why the passenger is there – to make money for the business rather than to be transported. 'After taking over SAS in August 1981 in the midst of the airline recession Carlzon set about a dramatic reorganisation of the company aimed at improving service and making SAS the "businessman's airline". Customers rather than aircraft were established as the company's major asset, and staff were schooled to serve the customer' – *Financial Times* (15 September 1986).

(a) customer operations leader A SENIOR CONDUCTOR (formerly railway train guard). Alleged by Alan Bennett on ITV, *The South Bank Show* (9 October 2005).

customer resistance Refusal to pay high prices in shops or for services. Known in Britain by 1982. 'Colin Haddow, leader of the North Norfolk Conservative group, said: "I am concerned that we are killing the goose that lays the golden egg. We have upped and upped the car parking income and we are getting to the point of meeting customer resistance," he said' – *Eastern Daily Press* (7 June 2004).

(a) cut and paste job A piece of journalism that is cobbled together from bits and pieces of the writings of others. Originally, the article would have been assembled from pieces of paper cut out of the other work. The term probably gave rise to the name of the word-processing procedure of selecting portions of text and then slotting them in elsewhere in the computer-generated work. I first heard the term in 1968. A well-known food-writer was commenting on a slipshod book on whisky that a rival had written. Or perhaps it was oysters. Well, never mind.

D d

(a) daily (woman) A charwoman. 'In my youth there were charwomen but the "daily" is a new invention' – Dorothy C. Peel, *Life's Enchanted Cup* (1933), ch. 19.

(a) dalliance A flirtation or perhaps brief affair. Since the 14th century. But note this usage: '"Measured, fair, balanced, just." That's Bill Cosby's take (expressed, via his attorney) on today's 26-month prison sentence handed down to Autumn Jackson, the convicted extortionist who forced the beloved entertainer to admit to a decades-old dalliance with her mother in court' – eonline.com (12 December 1997).

damaged goods A woman who has spoiled her reputation by losing her virginity, having liaisons and generally wrecking her unsulliedness and, probably, marriage prospects. By the early 1900s. Alluding to the unsaleability of literally damaged goods in a market or shop. 'Donald Farfrae [in Thomas Hardy's *The Mayor of Casterbridge*] is not aware when he marries her that Lucetta is damaged goods' – included in *Essays in Criticism*, vol. 2 (1952).

daring Sexually provocative, possibly obscene – as in pictures, photographs etc. Noted by 1982. 'Early in her career, she posed for some very daring shots that she wound up using as 8x10s and autographing. In these, she is wearing only a blue nightshirt and panties, showing off most of her great legs all the way up to her buns' – tvmoms.com (2005).

dark Of non-white ancestry. The term **darky** for a black / black man (known by the 1840s) is now considered an unacceptable usage. Similarly, **a dark gentleman** is no longer used to describe an Indian (from the subcontinent).

darn Damn – as adjective or expletive. An attempt to ameliorate an expletive in the US, originally. Noah Webster noted it in 1789. 'Too darn hot' – title of song in the Cole Porter musical *Kiss Me Kate* (Broadway, 1948).

dash(ed) Damn(ed) – as adjective or expletive. Sometimes printed 'd——'. 'But dash it, Lady Nelly, what do make thee paint thy vace all over we rud ochre zoo?' – Thomas Morton, *Speed the Plough* (1800), act 2, scene 2; 'Dashed if I know' – Charles Dickens, *Our Mutual Friend* (1865), 2, ch. 8.

(a) day of action A day of inaction. An odd coinage, from British trades-union-speak of the 1970s/80s. Compare INDUSTRIAL ACTION. This was an official term for a strike or protest when no one did any work – for example, the TUC's on 14 May 1980. 'Strikes or "days of action" are planned for later this month by workers in social-security offices, France Telecom, the state gas and electricity monopolies, the postal service and Air Inter. Renault, Bull, and Thomson CSF are also threatened with further industrial action' – *The Independent* (10 May 1995).

(to be) dealing with pockets of resistance To be impeded in one's (military) advance. Familiar from communiqués in the Second World War. 'Full aid to liberated Europe ... must wait not only until the German army is beaten, but until pockets of resistance have been wiped out' – *Daily Express* (12 April 1945).

(the) dear departed The dead. By the early 19th century, following on from simply **the departed** of the previous century. 'Barely enough to ... enable me to live so as not to disgrace the memory of the dear departed' – Jane Austen, *Mansfield Park* (1814), ch. 3.

(a) Dear John A letter from a woman to a man informing him that she is breaking off their relationship. Its origins are said to lie in US and Canadian armed forces slang of the Second World War when faithless girls back home had to find a way to admit they were carrying on with or maybe had become pregnant by other men. It subsequently became the name of a letter informing a man that he had given the woman VD – perhaps even AIDS – or generally to a letter breaking bad news of any sort of partnership disintegrating. Known by 1945. 'Peter had gone to war in love with a girl named Elizabeth Schofield ... He had received a "Dear John" letter from Elizabeth, telling him she was married' – Judson Philips, *Laughter Trap* (1964), pt I, ch. 2.

death/funeral matters See ABRAHAM'S BOSOM; AFTER A LONG ILLNESS; ANGEL CROSSED OVER THE BRIDGE; ARMS OF JESUS; AT REST; AUTO-EUTHANASIA; BE NO MORE; BEREAVEMENT; GREAT BEYOND; BITE THE DUST; BLESSED/HAPPY RELEASE; BREATHE ONE'S LAST; BUY IT; CALLED HENCE; CASH/HAND IN ONE'S CHECKS; CASKET; CEASE TO BE; CEMENT SHOES; CHAPEL OF REST; CLOSE ONE'S EYES; COMMITTAL; CONKED OUT; COT DEATH; DEAR DEPARTED; DECEASED; DEPART THIS LIFE; DESTROY; DISPOSE OF; ENTER INTO REST; ETERNAL LIFE; EVERLASTING LIFE; EXECUTE; EXPIRE; FAINTED AWAY IN THIS VALE OF TEARS; FALL ASLEEP; FALLEN; FLORAL TRIBUTE; FLOWERS; FUNERAL HOME/PARLOUR; GARDEN OF REMEMBRANCE/REST; GATHERED TO ONE'S FATHERS; GAVE THEIR LIVES; GO; GO BEFORE; GONE BEFORE; GO FORTH/BE PROMOTED TO HIGHER SERVICE; GO TO A BETTER PLACE; GO TO MEET ONE'S MAKER; GO TO ONE'S DEATH; GO WEST; GOD'S ACRE; GONE FOR A BURTON; GONE TO ONE'S ETERNAL REST; GOOD CAREER MOVE; GREAT MAJORITY; GRIM REAPER; HALLOWED GROUND/SOIL; HAND IN ONE'S DINNER-PAIL; HANG UP ONE'S HAT; HAPPY HUNTING GROUND; HEAVEN; HEREAFTER; HIDDEN IN THE EARTH; HOSPICE; INTERMENT; JOIN THE CHOIR INVISIBLE; KICK THE BUCKET; LAID IN EARTH; LAID TO REST; LAST RESTING

PLACE; LEAVE THIS WORLD; LEAVE ONE'S CHAIR VACANT;
LEAVE THE BUILDING; LET GO; LIFE DRAWING TO A CLOSE;
LIKE A CRUEL UNTIMELY FROST; LIQUIDATE; LOSE; LOSE
ONE'S LIFE; LOVED ONE; MEET WITH AN ACCIDENT;
MEMORIAL GARDEN; MERCY KILLING; MORTICIAN;
NARROW BED; NEGATIVE CARE OUTCOME; NO LONGER
LIVING; NUMBER IS UP; OBSEQUIES; ONE FOOT IN THE
GRAVE; OTHER SIDE; PACK IT IN; PASS AWAY; PASS INTO
THE KEEPING; PAY LAST RESPECTS TO; PAY NATURE'S DEBT;
PEACE IN HEAVEN; PLAY THE HARP; POP OFF; POP ONE'S
CLOGS; PREDECEASE; PUSHING UP THE DAISIES; PUT AWAY;
REMAINS; REMOVE; REST IN PEACE; RESTING PLACE; SELF-
INFLICTED DEATH; SERVICE OF THANKSGIVING; SHORN
CROWN; SHUFFLE OFF; SINK; SLUMBER CHAMBER;
SUPREME PENALTY/SACRIFICE; TERMINATE WITH EXTREME
PREJUDICE; THOUGH HIS BODY IS UNDER HATCHES; TIME;
TURN ONE'S FACE TO THE WALL; TURN ONE'S TOES UP;
UNDISCOVERED COUNTRY; UNLAWFUL OR ARBITRARY
DEPRIVATION OF LIFE; VOLUNTARY DEATH; WAGES OF SIN;
WAY OF ALL FLESH; WIPE OUT; WITH JESUS

(the) deceased The dead person. Specifically used in matters
of law but also possibly the most common euphemism for this
thing generally. Originally, the Latin *decessus* [decease] was used
as a euphemism for *mors* [death]. 'Q. The father of a Baptist
friend has died, and I'm going to the viewing. As a Jew, I'm
apprehensive about looking at the deceased. Would it be rude
just to offer condolences to the mourners? – J.M., Charleston,
S.C.' – Beliefnet.com (2005).

deceptively spacious Not really as small as it looks. Estate
agents' language, noted in the 1980s. 'Deceptively Spacious
Family House in Gourin, with a Very Large Rear Garden.
An extremely spacious family house, originally two properties,
situated just off the centre of Gourin and with the benefit of
an extremely large garden, unusual for a property in the Town
Centre' – french-property.com (2005).

(a) décolletage A woman's breasts or cleavage. Originally, the revealing of her neck and shoulders by the low cut of her bodice. By the 1890s.

(a) dedicated weight-watcher A fat person (usually female). Noted by 1982.

(to) deep-six To dispose of evidence by chucking it in the river. The expression is of American nautical origin – from men who took soundings. When they said 'by the deep six', they meant six fathoms (11 m or 36 ft). In naval circles, 'to deep-six' equally means 'to jettison overboard'. An extension to this meaning in jive and jazz use since the 1940s where 'the deep six' means 'the grave'. During Watergate, former presidential counsel John Dean told of a conversation he had had with another Nixon henchman, John Ehrlichman: 'He told me to shred the documents and "deep-six" the briefcase. I asked him what he meant by "deep-six". He leaned back in his chair and said, "You drive across the river on your way home tonight, don't you? Well, when you cross over the bridge ... just toss the briefcase into the river."' (Ehrlichman, before going to prison, denied this conversation ever took place.)

(to) defecate To shit. By the mid-18th century. 'A New Jersey man was arrested for a string of burglaries. "He defecated in at least four residences," said a prosecutor. "When he was taken into custody, he also defecated, and that was in his pants"' – *The Trentonian*, quoted in *Harper's Magazine* (2005).

defecation See BIGGIE; BODILY FUNCTIONS; BOWEL MOVEMENT; CALLING/VISITING CARDS; CAUGHT SHORT; DEMANDS OF NATURE; DROPPINGS; EVACUATE; FOUL; HAVE A MOTION; LITTLE JOBS; MANURE; MOTION; NATURAL FUNCTIONS; NIGHT SOIL; OPEN ONE'S BOWELS; REGULAR; RELIEVE ONESELF; STOOL; TRADEMARK; WASTE; WHOOPSIE; and under LAVATORY

(a) defective train A broken-down train – noted especially on the London Underground, by 2000. 'There's a saying round these parts. My translation skills are not up to speed with the impenetrable argot of the locals, but it goes something like this: "Eastbound passengers, your next Circle Line train will arrive in approximately 12 minutes. This is due to a defective train at Edgware Road." That eloquent, evocative little phrase tells us so much about this place and the simple folk who eke out a living here' – eclecticboogaloo.typepad.com (1 February 2005).

defence equipment Armaments. 'Ground-to-air missiles were on the "shopping list" of defence equipment taken to Moscow by the Secretary-General of the External Affairs Ministry' – *The Times* (21 February 1963). 'Today we call providers of the means of making war or suppressing insurrection not arms manufacturers but manufacturers of defence equipment' – Basil Collier, *Arms and the Men* (1980). Compare the change of name when Britain's War Office, Air Ministry and Admiralty were amalgamated as the Ministry of Defence in 1964.

deferred success Failure. 'The word "fail" should be deleted from the school vocabulary and replaced with the term "deferred success", according to members of the Professional Association of Teachers. Being told they were a failure can put children off education for the rest of their lives, they said. The idea will be put forward by two members at the union's annual conference in Buxton, Derbyshire, next week' – *The Independent* (20 July 2005).

(to) deflower To part a female from her virginity. By the 14th century. Compare Air 6 from John Gay, *The Beggar's Opera* (1728): 'Virgins are like the fair flower in its lustre ... / But, when once plucked, 'tis no longer alluring, / To Covent Garden [the market as well as a place notorious for prostitutes] 'tis sent (as yet sweet), / There fades, and shrinks, and grows past all enduring, / Rots, stinks, and dies, and is trod under feet'; 'Associated with the growing heterosexual awareness of high-school students are such words as *cherry*, which in appropriate contexts takes on the familiar slang meaning "hymen", while a *cherry-buster*, logically, is "a professional deflowerer"' – *American Speech*, vol. 39 (1964).

delayed Late (of transport). Noted in connection with British railways in 1992.

delivery Childbirth. Since the 16th century. 'The news is every day expected from Vienna of the Great Duchess's delivery; if it be a boy, here will be all sorts of balls, masquerades, operas, and illuminations' – letter from Thomas Gray in Bologna (9 December 1739).

(the) demands of nature The urge to URINATE or DEFECATE.

(a) dementia care home An old folks' madhouse. One was seen, so described, at Kineton, Warwickshire (2005).

democratic Anti-democratic. In the 20th century, Communist states almost invariably described themselves as 'democratic', even if they were totalitarian dictatorships. Hence, East Germany was known as the German Democratic Republic while West Germany was known as the Federal German Republic. And there was no difference between them?

demonstrators A mob. Used in this sense by 1870.

dentures False teeth. A genteelism by 1874. Not everyone fell for it, however: 'The husband was a teetotaller, there was no other woman, and the conduct complained of was that he had drifted into the habit of winding up every meal by taking out his false teeth and hurling them at his wife' – Conan Doyle, *The Adventures of Sherlock Holmes* (1892), 'A Case of Identity'.

(to) depart this life To die. Perhaps the most frequently used of gravestone euphemisms. By 1728. 'In Memory of JANE AUSTEN youngest daughter of the late Revd GEORGE

AUSTEN, formerly Rector of Steventon in this County, she departed this Life on the 18th of July, 1817, aged 41, after a long illness supported with the patience and the hopes of a Christian' – from the slab on her grave in the north aisle of the nave of Winchester Cathedral.

deprived people The poor. 'When I first came to live in America I was struck by how "the poor" had vanished – vanished from the American lexicon. I discovered they were constantly being rescued by euphemism. First they became needy, then deprived, then underprivileged or disadvantaged. In the politically correct 90s they were economically challenged, or referred to as though they had been admitted to some exclusive club: they were now members of a differentiated income group. A character in a Jules Feiffer cartoon [1965] once remarked that while he still didn't have a dime, he sure had acquired a fine vocabulary' – Harold Evans, BBC Radio 4, *A Point of View* (18 September 2005). Compare the use of the term 'deprived children' to describe children who lack the basics of a proper home life, parental affection and so on – since the 1940s.

(the) derrière The buttocks, arse. From the French for 'behind' and in English by 1774. Hence the joke in '*Quand je regarde mon derrière, je vois qu'il est divisé en deux parties* [When I look at my backside, I see that it is divided into two parts]', an alleged remark attributed to Winston S. Churchill, in a speech in Paris just after the Second World War. He meant to tell his audience that, looking back, he saw his career divided into two distinct and separate periods. So what he meant by his 'derrière' was not his backside but his past.

descriptive of places, things See ABLUTION FACILITIES; ACCOMMODATION; ACCOMMODATION UNIT; ALASKA SABLE; APPLIANCE; ARTICLE; ARTIFICIAL AID TO VISION; ATHLETIC SUPPORTER; BATHROOM UTENSIL; BEAUTY CAKE; BESTSELLER; BOX; BREAD AND BUTTER LETTER; BROKEN HOME; CENTRE PORTION; CERTAIN SUBSTANCES; CHARLEY'S DEAD; CIRCULAR FILE; CIVIC AMENITY SITE;

CONTROLLED SUBSTANCES; CONVENIENCE FOODS;
CUSPIDOR; DEAR JOHN; DOMICILE; DOWN BELOW;
EFFLUENT; FAMILY; FOUNDATION GARMENTS; GAZUNDER;
GRAIN-CONSUMING UNITS; GUEST HOUSE; HAIR-PIECE;
HOME ENTERTAINMENT CENTRE; HOME PLAQUE REMOVAL
INSTRUMENT; INNER-CITY AREA; LEISURE CENTRE;
LIFE PRESERVER; LITTLE SOMETHING; LITTLE VISITOR;
LIVING CURIOSITY; LOCALIZED CAPACITY DEFICIENCY;
MOBILE HOME; MOLOTOV COCKTAIL; MOOD ENHANCER;
MOTHER'S LITTLE HELPER; NETHER GARMENTS; NEVER-
NEVER; NIGHT HOSTEL; NIGHTSTICK; NON-AVAILABLE;
NORTH BRITAIN; NOSE JOB; ODIFEROUS; OTHER PLACE;
PARK HOME; PLOUGHMAN'S LUNCH; PRECIPITATION;
PRESENTATION; PUFFBACK; RECEPTION CENTRE;
RECREATIONAL FACILITY; REFUSE; RUG; SHAM; STATE
ROOM; SUB-STANDARD HOUSING; TOUPEE; TWILIGHT
HOUSING; TWILIGHT ZONE; UNDERFASHIONS;
UNDERSTAINS; UNDEVELOPED AREAS; UNMENTIONABLES;
WEED; WELFARE HOME; WHATNOT; WORD FROM OUR
SPONSOR; YOU-KNOW-WHAT

(to) deselect To dismiss an incumbent (politician, usually), though obviously the person must have been selected in the first place. American in origin and known there by 1968. 'He has named the MPs in an attempt to persuade them to join the SDP before they are "deselected" by their constituency parties' – *The Daily Telegraph* (5 October 1984).

designer – Expensive but supposedly having a cachet. Of American origin and beginning with 'designer scarves' in the mid-1960s, this prefix went on to be applied to almost anything by the end of the 1980s, whether a designer was involved or not. 'Designer labels' helped to distinguish jeans, sheets, pillowcases, whatever – or, rather, helped push up the price. 'Designer stubble' was the exception. It meant 'fashionably unshaven'. 'Small wonder Perrier is called Designer Water. My local wine bar has the cheek to charge 70p a glass' – *The Times* (4 September 1984).

(to have) designs on Intending to seduce. Since the early 20th century? 'After the death of Emma's wealthy father some years ago, she was sent to live with her uncle and cousin, the former of whom had designs on her body and the latter, the pious and evil Miriam, had designs on her fortune' – review of romance novel at likesbooks.com (2005).

(a) despatch room facilitator A post-room helper. A coinage alleged by Susie Dent in *Fanboys and Overdogs: The Language Report* (2005).

(a) destination manager A travel agent. Reported in 2005. 'The Lake County Convention & Visitors Bureau will be the destination manager of the northwest Indiana visitor industry through accountable communications, innovative customer services, and advocacy in cultural/special event entertainment, outdoor recreation and gaming experiences benefiting visitors, businesses and residents' – alllake.org (Indiana) (2003).

(to) destroy To kill domestic animals, noxious pests etc. Since about 1700. 'A spokeswoman for the RSPCA, which had the dog destroyed, said: "We don't usually get involved in these sort of situations as dangerous dogs are the police's area, but we were called in to help by them"' – workingpitbull.com/UK (2003–4).

(to) detain To arrest, imprison. Presumably the impulse behind this euphemism is not to imply guilt. Since the 15th century but in the euphemistic way since the 19th. '"Beg your pardon, sir," said the constable … "I shall be obliged to detain you till this business is settled"' – Mary E. Braddon, *Flower and Weed* (1884). Hence, similarly, the use of the term **detention** for custody. 'I was following the morality of the Youth Detention Centre and strictly confining myself to robbing from the rich without necessarily having to give to the poor' – John Mortimer, *Quite Honestly* (2005), ch. 16.

(a) deterrent capability A nuclear bomb. By the 1950s? Hence, also, all the talk of **the deterrent** in the 1950s/60s and

the ultimate deterrent. 'Rockefeller's plea for "all the money it takes" to ensure the United States "the deterrent capability of a massive and superior second strike"' – *The Guardian* (27 July 1960).

detoxification Sobering up. 'People with a serious drink problem may be detained in the "detoxification centres" for 10 days while they receive medical treatment' – *The Daily Telegraph* (2 March 1971).

(to) detrain To get off a train. Noted in the *Northern Echo* (10 August 1993).

(the) deuce The devil, as in such expressions as 'the deuce to pay', 'what the deuce?' In use by the start of the 18th century.

developing countries Undeveloped/underdeveloped countries. In fairly wide usage from 1964. A similar sleight of hand may be detected in the use of **development areas** to mean run-down or distressed areas – this since 1948. 'The closure of a legal loophole which lets Europe dump toxic waste on developing countries as "recyclable" material has created a profitable new crime: waste smuggling' – *Independent on Sunday* (1 January 1995).

(a) deviant A homosexual (usually male) but also, by the 1970s, applied to any misfit you deplore, as in **social deviant**. 'Miss Navratilova is extraordinarily rich and famous and can, therefore, do pretty much as she likes. However, it is alarming when such prominent people do such silly things, because they only encourage deviant behaviour in other, more impressionable people' – *Daily Mail* (23 June 1994).

(a) device A hydrogen or nuclear bomb, since the 1950s. 'It's a greater threat than a planted nuclear device' – John Gardner, *Dancing Dodo* (1978), ch. 39.

devil See DEUCE; PRINCE OF DARKNESS; and under OLD NICK.

(as queer as) Dick's hatband   Queer – but not necessarily
in the homosexual sense. Tony Brisby, Staffordshire, recalled
(1992): 'A sentence used by my grandmother was, "He's as queer
as Dick's hatband – it went round twice and then didn't meet."
I have absolutely no idea what she meant.' Marjorie M. Rawicz,
Nottinghamshire, remembered (1993): 'As a young person in the
Twenties, I remember my Mother (Derbyshire with Yorkshire
roots) saying "You're as funny as Dick's hat band" when either
my sister or I was being contrary and difficult. I heard no more
of this expression until the late Sixties when a Miss Emily White
(from Cheshire) told me that *her* Mother finished the quote –
"Funny as Dick's hatband – it went twice round and then would
not tie".'

   David Scott, Cumbria (1994), remembered his grandmother
saying in the 1930s – if things didn't work out: 'That's like Dick's
hatband – it went round twice and still didn't fit!' Dorothy Hoyle,
Lincolnshire, added that, in her family, it was always 'as *black* as
Dick's hatband' when something was very dirty. Mrs J.M.H.
Wright, West Yorkshire, countered with: 'The correct version –
"as *near* as Dick's hatband" – makes the saying self-explanatory, at
least to a Yorkshire person. "Near" in Yorkshire speech as well
as meaning "close to" also means "mean or stingy with money".
Thus the person referred to is as "near" with money as Dick's
hatband is "near" to Dick's head.' 'A botched-up job done with
insufficient materials was "like Dick's hat-band that went half-
way round and tucked"' – according to Flora Thompson,
Lark Rise, ch. 3 (1939).

   So, lots of variations. *OED2* gives the phrase thus: 'as queer
(tight, odd, etc.) as Dick's (or Nick's) hatband', and adds: 'Dick
or Nick was probably some local character or half-wit, whose
droll sayings were repeated.' *Partridge/Slang* describes it as 'an
intensive tag of chameleonic sense and problematic origin' and
dates the phrase from the mid-18th to the early 19th century,
finds a Cheshire phrase 'all my eye and Dick's hatband', and also
a version that went, 'as queer as Dick's hatband, that went nine
times round and wouldn't meet.' In Grose's *Dictionary of the Vulgar
Tongue* (1796), Partridge found the definition: 'I am as queer as
Dick's hatband; that is, out of spirits, or don't know what ails

me.' A 'Newcastle form *c.* 1850' is the 'nine times round and wouldn't meet', just given.

But who was Dick, if anybody? *Brewer's Dictionary of Phrase and Fable* (1989) was confident that it knew the answer: Richard Cromwell (1626–1712), who succeeded Oliver, his father, as Lord Protector in 1658 and did not make a very good job of it. Hence, *Brewer's Dictionary of Phrase and Fable* (1989) believed, 'Dick's hatband' was his 'crown', as in the following expressions: *Dick's hatband was made of sand* ('his regal honours were a "rope of sand"'), *as queer as Dick's hatband* ('few things have been more ridiculous than the exaltation and abdication of Oliver's son') and *as tight as Dick's hatband* ('the crown was too tight for him to wear with safety').

Compare what Harry Richardson, Surrey, remembered *his* grandmother (1870–1956) used to say in answer to a child's curiosity: '"You are as queer as a Norwegian fiddle"... I saw the artefact many years later. It has two frets!'

To sum up: that 'Dick's hatband' is a euphemism for 'homosexuality' is unfounded. This meaning has merely been extrapolated from 'as queer as'.

(a) differentiated income group   The poor. 'When I first came to live in America I was struck by how "the poor" had vanished – vanished from the American lexicon. I discovered they were constantly being rescued by euphemism. First they became needy, then deprived, then underprivileged or disadvantaged. In the politically correct 90s they were economically challenged, or referred to as though they had been admitted to some exclusive club: they were now members of a differentiated income group' – Harold Evans, BBC Radio 4, *A Point of View* (18 September 2005).

differently abled   Disabled. This PC euphemism was introduced in the US at the beginning of the 1980s as a kinder, more positive way of regarding and describing disability. Also **uniquely abled**. 'Disabled, handicapped, differently-abled, physically or mentally challenged, women with disabilities – this is more than a mere discourse in semantics and a matter of personal preference' – Debra Connors, *With the Power of Each Breath*

(1985); 'In a valiant effort to find a kinder term than handicapped, the Democratic National Committee has coined differently abled. The committee itself shows signs of being differently abled in the use of English' – *The Los Angeles Times* (9 April 1985); 'Terms such as "physically challenged", "differently abled", and "special" crop up occasionally, usually in an attempt to side-step the stigma of disability, but such phrases are not widely used nor much liked by disabled people generally. An accurate and unpatronising approach need not compromise plain language. There is little value in using words and phrases which tip-toe around the subject' – 'Guide to the Representation of People with Disabilities in Programmes', BBC (1990); '"Differently abled is a term created to underline the concept that differently abled individuals are just that, not less or inferior in any way" … Well, many people with handicaps surely do develop different abilities, but that is not what makes them a category. They lack something other people possess, and while that is not a reason to oppress them, it does violence to logic and language to pretend otherwise' – *Newsweek* (14 January 1991); '"Majorism", they say, is a euphemism for someone who has got no "ism" and thus bears the same relationship to "Thatcherism" as "differently abled" does to "able". Many of us prefer to describe a "Majorite" as "differently Thatchered" or "Thatcherically challenged"' – *The Daily Telegraph* (25 August 1993).

differently advantaged Poor. A quintessentially PC euphemism, cited in Beard and Cerf, *The Official Politically Correct Dictionary and Handbook* (1992).

differently heighted Small. A PC euphemism suggested in *The Times* (28 June 1992).

differently hirsute Bald/balding. A suggested PC coinage from 1991/2.

differently interesting Boring. Source: Beard and Cerf, *The Official Politically Correct Dictionary and Handbook* (1992).

differently pleasured Sado-masochistic. A joke coinage from *The New York Times* (July 1992), but almost certainly more seriously intended when earlier employed by Julia Penelope in *Speaking Freely* (New York, 1990).

differently sized / differently weighted Fat. Suggested PC coinages from 1991/2. 'American women are discovering that it's OK to be fat or if you wish to be politically correct, "differently sized"' – *The Times* (13 April 1992); 'Players must examine a range of prejudices such as sizeism (towards fat, or rather "differently weighted" people)' – *The Times* (30 June 1992).

difficulty / hesitancy of speech Stammer, stutter or other vocal deficiency. 'Lord Hartwell, though obviously shy and coping with a slight hesitancy of speech' – *Pillars of Society*, BBC Radio 4 (20 February 1986).

diminished responsibility Mental disturbance. A legal concept since the 1950s. 'Found Not Guilty of murdering the girl but Guilty of manslaughter on the grounds of his diminished responsibility' – *The Times* (6 February 1963); 'A mother who killed her 36-year-old Down syndrome son by suffocating him with a plastic bag was spared jail yesterday when a judge said she had been subjected to unbearable pressure ... [She] denied murdering her son but pleaded guilty ... to his manslaughter on the grounds of diminished responsibility' – *The Independent* (3 November 2005).

(a) diplomatic cold / illness A (usually) made-up excuse for non-attendance at an event you seek to avoid or a reason given to cover some other awkwardness. 'Foreign Secretary Jack Straw, on his ignorance of French views that New Labour's addiction to the free market is "the new communism": "I have the lurgy. This is why I'm so ill-informed." He looked sprightly enough, but maybe this is a diplomatic illness' – *The Mirror* (25 March 2005).

direct mail Advertising junk mail. Since the 1930s – and no more direct than ordinary mail.

disabilities See DIFFERENTLY ABLED; DIFFICULTY/
HESITANCY OF SPEECH; OTHERLY ABLED; PEOPLE WITH
DIFFERING ABILITIES; PHYSICALLY CHALLENGED;
PHYSICALLY DIFFERENT; and also under POLITICAL
CORRECTNESS

disadvantaged children Bad children. In the view of social
workers who blame upbringing and environment. *Teaching
Disadvantaged Children in the Preschool* – title of book by Carl Bereiter
and Siegfried Engelmann (1966).

disadvantaged people Poor people. 'This mannered
ungraciousness towards disadvantaged people' – H.G. Wells,
An Experiment in Autobiography (1934), bk 2, ch. 8; 'When I first came
to live in America I was struck by how "the poor" had vanished –
vanished from the American lexicon. I discovered they were
constantly being rescued by euphemism. First they became needy,
then deprived, then underprivileged or disadvantaged' – Harold
Evans, BBC Radio 4, *A Point of View* (18 September 2005).

(to) discuss Ugandan affairs To have SEXUAL
INTERCOURSE. In *Private Eye* No. 293 (9 March 1973), a gossip
item launched this euphemism: 'I can reveal that the expression
"Talking about Uganda" has acquired a new meaning. I first
heard it myself at a fashionable party given recently by media-
people Neal and Corinna Ascherson. As I was sipping my
Campari on the ground floor I was informed by my charming
hostess that I was missing out on a meaningful confrontation
upstairs where a former cabinet colleague of President Obote
was "talking about Uganda". Eager, as ever, to learn the latest
news from the Dark Continent I rushed upstairs to discover
the dusky statesman "talking about Uganda" in a highly
compromising manner to vivacious former features editor,
Mary Kenny … I understand that "Long John" and Miss
Kenny both rang up later to ascertain each other's names.'
Later, 'discussing Ugandan affairs' and references to 'Ugandan
discussions' or 'Ugandan practices' came to be used – though
probably not far beyond the readership of *Private Eye*.

In a letter to *The Times* (13 September 1983), Corinna Ascherson (now signing herself Corinna Adam) identified the coiner of the phrase as the poet and critic James Fenton. She also claimed that the phrase had been included in '*The Oxford Dictionary of Slang*', whatever that might have been. It is not in *Partridge/Slang*. Richard Ingrams (editor of *Private Eye* at the time) added an interesting footnote in *The Observer* (2 April 1989), that the original Ugandan was 'a one-legged former Minister in President Obote's Government. When the *New Statesman* found out that the *Eye* was going to refer to the incident, representations were made to the effect that the Minister, on the run from Obote, would be in danger if identified. The detail of the wooden leg was therefore omitted, but the expression passed into the language.'

As a further, er, footnote, Nicholas Wollaston wrote to *The Observer* (9 April 1989) and pointed out that the one-legged performer *wasn't* on the run from President Obote but 'the much-loved chairman of the Uganda Electricity Board, also of the Uganda Red Cross, and an exile for seven years from the tyranny of Idi Amin. When he died in 1986, it was reported that 10,000 people attended his funeral ... and a memorial service at St Martin-in-the-Fields was packed with his friends, among them several who remembered their discussions on Uganda with him, the artificial limb notwithstanding, with much pleasure.'

It is mistakenly believed in some quarters that the euphemism originally applied to the Ugandan Foreign Minister, Princess Elizabeth of Toro, who was said to have had sex in a lavatory at Orly airport. For this she was sacked from her post by President Idi Amin in November 1974, though she successfully obtained substantial libel damages from newspapers that had made this allegation. Obviously, the date shows that this story went round *after* the one involving the one-legged Ugandan gentleman.

disempowered Powerless. In certain New Age and feminist discussions, it is mandatory to speak of being disempowered rather than being powerless. The logic behind this would seem to be that everyone possesses an innate power which cannot be taken away. So it is impossible to be powerless. However, circumstances or the behaviour of others may prevent you from using your power. Hence, 'I feel disempowered by you' is a useful PC phrase to throw around, even if the meaning is really, 'I don't know what to do in this situation' and 'It's all your fault'. Hence, 'empowerment', as a way of describing an important process, is also very PC. '[Sandra Bernhard] explains her dancing about in a G-string ... as a gesture of empowerment. "It's like, taking control of your own sexuality – and a kind of 'fuck you' to everybody who tells women to do stuff like that. It's saying, 'This is a statement, controlled by me'"' – *The Independent on Sunday* (31 August 1992).

dishonesty/lying   See CREDIBILITY GAP; DIPLOMATIC COLD/ILLNESS; ECONOMICAL WITH THE TRUTH; FABRICATION; FIB; FIDDLING THE BOOKS; INOPERATIVE; PORK PIES; PREVARICATION; SPANISH PRACTICES; SPEAK WITH FORKED TONGUE; STORIES; TALL STORY; TERMINOLOGICAL INEXACTITUDE; UNDER REVIEW

(the) dismal trade   Undertaking. By 1926 at least

dismissal   See SACKING

(a) disorderly house   A brothel. By 1700. 'Q. What Sort of a House does he keep? A. He keeps a disorderly House. Q. What do you know of his keeping a disorderly House, between June and September? A. 'I have gone my Rounds that way several Times, between June and September; I have called in between two and three in the Morning, and I never went in, but I found a Company of Women, and sometimes Men with them; and have taken them up sometimes, and carried them to the Watch-house, and they have been committed to the Workhouse; I was going by one Day this Month, and there was a Man at the Door, who said, he had been robbed in the Prisoner's House; that he had picked up a Woman of the Town, or the Woman had picked him up, and that he had lost 18 d. and his Handkerchief' – transcript of trial at Old Bailey (12 October 1743).

displacement Exorcism. A term introduced by religious bodies in the 1970s following adverse publicity arising from certain attempts to drive out evil spirits. 'I have never really been involved in anything like this before. I think we would call it a displacement service now, rather than an exorcism; that has become a very emotive word over the last few years' – priest quoted in the *Stockport Advertiser* (13 April 1978).

disposable income Money. Specifically, the money actually available for savings and investments. Probably of American origin and known in the US since 1948.

(to) dispose of (1) To sell. (2) To kill. Hence, in sense (2), **disposal** – the getting rid of somebody (and especially the body afterwards).

(an industrial) dispute A strike. Very much part of journalistic and trades union parlance in the 1960s and 70s. The irritation caused by this euphemism was compounded when broadcasters and officials insisted upon putting the accent on the first syllable of 'dispute' rather than the second. 'It was a local scrap over an extra few minutes on work schedules. Then 105 people went on strike and lost their jobs. Why did they take such a stand? And what can a bus drivers' dispute in Chelmsford tell us about the future of the trade unions?' – *The Guardian* (29 April 1995).

dissent Criticizing or arguing with the umpire or referee in sport. This word for disagreement covered a multitude of sins, ranging from verbal objections to rude gestures and was brought into popular use around 1975. It was a press euphemism quickly taken up by sporting organizations. 'George Best was sent off yesterday in his seventh game since returning to British soccer ... And off went Best, booked two weeks ago for dissent' – *Sunday Mirror* (3 October 1976); '[John Snow, the fast bowler] has been severely reprimanded and cautioned as to his future conduct by his county, Sussex ... The Sussex committee stated that Snow had apologised to Cec Pepper, the umpire, for showing dissent when given out lbw' – another newspaper (in about 1976).

dissipation Wasting away of the moral and physical self through indulgence in pleasures. By the 18th century. 'He died young, worn out by dissipation' – Sir William Gregory, *Autobiography* (1894), ch. 5; 'Edgar Allan Poe / (Who "died of dissipation", said the notes). / "And what is dissipation, please, Miss Long?"' – John Betjeman, *Summoned By Bells* (1960), ch. 3.

(to) ditch To abandon/discard/forsake/jilt. Mostly of a person with whom one has been romantically linked. Probably of American origin in this sense, dating from the 1920s and derived in turn from the original use of the verb for throwing an illicit traveller off a railroad train. In this case the person so treated might literally end up in a ditch.

(to) do (a) number one / two To go the LAVATORY , in nursery talk – 'one', to URINATE, 'two', to DEFECATE. By 1900. 'Our juniors have an interest in the Old English word for faeces. They use it a lot – the ones from polite homes do, I mean homes that talk of No. 2 and "going to the House of Commons"' – A.S. Neill, *That Dreadful School* (1937), ch. 7; 'This little ginger [kitten] is going to do a number one if we're not careful' – Angus Wilson, *No Laughing Matter* (1967), ch. 2; 'When I had done Number two, you always washed them out yourself before sending them to the diaper service' – Mary McCarthy, *Birds of America* (1971); 'Red, white, and blue, / Dirty kangaroo, / Sitting on the dustbin / Doing his "Number Two"' – rhyme quoted in Iona and Peter Opie, *The Lore and Language of Schoolchildren* (1977).

(to) do one's business To go the LAVATORY. Eventually this expression was relegated to nursery conversation. '[Came to Greenwich] and there Mrs. Clerke and my wife and I on shore to an ale-house for them to do their business' – Samuel Pepys, diary entry for 6 July 1664.

(to) doctor To castrate (mostly of cats and dogs). By 1900.

(a) dog warden A dog catcher. Reporting the appointment of an ex-police officer to this task, the *Civic Review* (Stockport) for November 1978, explained: 'He doesn't want to be regarded as just a dog catcher. As a dog lover he sees his job as one of educator rather than apprehender.'

(a) domestic (1) A servant in the home. 'Did some purely personal demons hound her to the point where she went to work as a domestic (she claimed she was doing research for a book) and ended up in a welfare home?' – *The Washington Post* (31 January 1992). (2) A quarrel/row/argument in the home (British police usage).

(a) domestic assistant / help A cleaning woman, charlady, charwoman. '——— help' by 1895.

(a) domestic engineer A housewife. A good try but this never really caught on, except perhaps in the US. From the 1980s?

(a) domestician A domestic servant. 'Read in the *Times* about some proposal to abolish the phrase "domestic servant", and substitute "domestician." What nonsense! An undertaker has the same ghastly function whether you call him that or a "mortician"' – James Agate, *Ego 3* (1938), diary entry for 1 February 1937.

(a) domicile A home, where you live (in the US). Cited in Willard R. Espy, *An Almanac of Words at Play* (1975).

(a) Don Juan A male flirt or philanderer. From the name of the legendary Spanish nobleman whose life was dramatized in *El burlador de Sevilla* (1630) by Gabriel Téllez and in many subsequent plays and poems, not least Byron's epic of 1819–24. The euphemism entered English shortly after this, for example in Thackeray's *Vanity Fair* (1847), ch. 22: 'Don't trifle with her affections, you Don Juan!' However, in the same book, Thackeray, possibly influenced by the Mozart/Da Ponte opera *Don Giovanni* (1787), also uses the Italian form: 'That Osborne's a devil of a fellow ... and since he's been home, they say he's a regular Don Giovanni, by Jove' (ch. 13).

(to) donate To give. A euphemism of pomposity, but also used where 'give' might sound condescending. 'PC restaurant: Serves veggie dishes. Donates leftovers to a food bank or shelter' – *The Washington Post* (2 July 1991).

donor fatigue Meanness in charitable donations. From the 1980s, following COMPASSION FATIGUE. 'The amount of donations for the deadly earthquake in Pakistan and flooding in Central America have come in at a slower pace than for other recent calamities, officials say. Two major disasters during the past year – Hurricane Katrina and the Indian Ocean tsunami – have sapped funding for other causes and contributed to what experts call "donor fatigue" among governments that finance the United Nations' efforts and individual givers who support private agencies' – *The Washington Post* (17 October 2005).

(of) doubtful parentage Bastard. '[John Major realizes that] members of his Cabinet are of doubtful parentage' – John Smith, speech to Labour Party Conference, Brighton (October 1993). (The Prime Minister had been overheard describing his opponents as 'bastards'.)

(a) dove A peace-seeking statesman or politician, an appeaser or pacifist. The opposite of this is HAWK for an aggressor. The terms are used to denote those for and against tough military action. The term 'war hawk' was coined by Thomas Jefferson in 1798. A dove traditionally has been a symbol of peace – perhaps since Noah sent one to see if the waters had abated and it returned with an olive leaf (Genesis 8:8–11). The modern division into hawks and doves, much used during the Vietnam War of the 1960s, dates from the Cuban missile crisis of 1962. 'The hawks favored an air strike to eliminate the Cuban missile blockade ... The doves opposed the air strikes and favored a blockade' – *The Saturday Evening Post* (8 December 1962).

down among the dead men   Dead drunk – where you would be down among the empty bottles and underneath the table. Also among the fallen skittles/nine pins. The phrase occurs in an English folk song/drinking song: 'Come let's drink it while we have breath / For there's no drinking after death / And he that will his health deny, / Down, down, down, down / Down among the dead men let him lie.' The words are said to be by John Dyer, an English poet (1699–1757). The music was notably arranged by Ralph Vaughan Williams. The phrase occurs in Cuthbert Bede, *The Adventures of Mr Verdant Green* (1853–7). Hence, also, *Down Among the Dead Men*, the title of a science-fantasy novel (1993) by Simon R. Green. *Down Among the Z-Men* was the title of a film (UK 1952) featuring all the original members of the BBC radio *Goon Show*.

down below   (1) Hell. (2) The genitalia of either sex. Since the mid-19th century.

(to go) down (on) / down south   To pleasure the sexual parts of another with the mouth. Because of the placing of the geographical location on maps. Of American origin, by 1916. 'Not all men have their down side ... while I was happy to give him lip service, it soon became obvious that he was deliberately avoiding taking the downtown bus ... [another lover] begged to head South' – *The Independent* (23 August 2005).

(to be) down on one's luck   To be impecunious. 'The Chevalier was ... to use his own picturesque expression ... "down on his luck"' – William Thackeray, *Pendennis* (1849), ch. 56.

Down's syndrome   Mongolism. The term 'mongolism' had been used to describe a medical condition since before 1900. *OED2* contains a definition of mongolism that clearly indicates where offence might lie: 'Congenital form of mental deficiency ... marked by numerous signs, including short stature, short thick hands and feet, a large tongue, a flat face with features somewhat similar to those of Mongolians ...' The change of name followed a conscious campaign. A letter to *The Lancet* (8 April 1961), signed by G. Allen and others, contributed to the move: 'Some of the undersigned are inclined to replace the term "mongolism" by such designations as "Langdon-Down anomaly", or "Down's syndrome or anomaly" or "congenital acromicria".' Later, *The Lancet* noted (21 October 1961): 'Our contributors prefer Down's syndrome to mongolism because they believe that the term "mongolism" has misleading racial connotations and is hurtful to many parents' (let alone Mongolians, one might think).

The condition was thus named after J.L.H. Down (1828–96), an English physician who first described the genetic disorder in 1866, and the name-change was quite rapidly adopted by most people, though even now some hesitate slightly before using the newer expression. They are probably more fully aware that they should not say 'mongolism' than why they should invoke the name of a man called Down.

Accordingly, people are said thus to be 'with Down's syndrome' or to be 'Down's syndrome patients' or simply 'Down's people' – but *not*, of course, to be a non-PC 'Down's syndrome *sufferer*'. 'In 1963 Magdalene Wilkins took her infant daughter, Jane, to the John Radcliffe Hospital in Oxford to see a consultant paediatrician ... She took one look at Jane and said, "Oh well, you've got a mongol baby"'; 'Evidently they have difficulty placing Down's people in work round here' – *The Independent* (28 August 1992); 'A mother who killed her 36-year-old Down syndrome son by suffocating him with a plastic bag was spared jail yesterday when a judge said she had been subjected to unbearable pressure' – *The Independent* (3 November 2005).

(to) drain one's lizard / snake To URINATE. 20th century. In one of his novels, Simon Raven attributed this loophemism to an army sergeant in the form: 'He's gone to drain his snake.' Hence, also, **to drain off** for the same operation, since the 19th century.

(to) dress to the left / right To allow the male genitals to dangle down the left or right fork of a pair of trousers. Bespoke tailors used to inquire of customers what their preference was – certainly by the 1960s – but heaven knows whether they still do.

It is alleged that 'dressing to the left' also became a euphemism for 'homosexual'. 'John Morgan on Carnaby Street ... "We are 'dressing' in the middle this year, man" a pop singer explains' – *The Guardian* (18 March 1966).

(to have) drink taken / a drop taken To be drunk, intoxicated. 'How easy it was to know a gentleman even when he has a drop taken' – James Joyce, *Dubliners* (1914).

drinking alcohol See AFTERNOON MEN; AMBER FLUID; BOTTLE; BRAHMS AND LISZT; BREWER'S DROOP; CELEBRATE; CONVIVIAL; DETOXIFICATION; DOWN AMONG THE DEAD MEN; DRINK/DROP TAKEN; EBULLIENT; ELEVATED; ENJOYS A DRINK; FEEL NO PAIN; FEELING THE EFFECTS OF THE MORNING AFTER; FRESHEN A DRINK; FUDDLED/BEFUDDLED; HAIR OF THE DOG; HALF-SEAS-OVER; HAPPY; HIGH; ILL; IN DRINK; INEBRIATED; LEAD IN ONE'S PENCIL; LIKE A DRINK; LIQUID LUNCH; LITTLE WEAKNESS; MELLOW; MERRY; MOTHER'S RUIN; NOGGIN; ON THE TILES; ON THE WAGON; ONE FOR THE ROAD; ONE OVER THE EIGHT; ONE TOO MANY; OVER THE LIMIT; PIXILATED; PLEDGE; SALOON; SHEETS IN THE WIND; SNIFTER/SNORT; SUN IS OVER THE YARDARM; TIGHT; TINCTURE; TIPPLE; TIRED AND EMOTIONAL; UNDER THE WEATHER; UNWELL; WIDE-EYED AND LEGLESS

droit de seigneur The imagined 'right' of a man to force a woman to go to bed with him, as perhaps a boss might do with a secretary. The general assumption is that this 'right' dates from the days when medieval barons would claim first go at the newly-wedded daughters of their vassals – under the so-called *ius primae noctis* [law of the first night]. In the play *Le Mariage de Figaro* (1784) by Beaumarchais, the Count has just renounced this right and is beginning to regret it. In March 1988, it was reported that Dr Wilhelm Schmidt-Bleibtreu of Bonn had looked into the matter very thoroughly and discovered there was never any such legal right and that reliable records of it ever happening were rare. He concluded that the whole thing was really a male fantasy – and it was exclusively men who had used the phrase – though he did not rule out the possibility that sex of the kind *had* taken place between lords and new brides in one or two cases, legally or otherwise. 'There was also something called the *jus primae noctis*, which would probably not be mentioned in a textbook for children. It was the law by which every capitalist had the right to sleep with any woman working in one of his factories' – George Orwell, *Nineteen Eighty-Four* (1949), pt 1, ch. 7.

droppings Animal dung. Since 1596. 'Japanese priests have scored only a partial victory in their attempts to stop a sweet being sold as "snot from the nose of the Great Buddha" ... Another famous Nara sweet is called "deer droppings"' – *Sunday Herald* (16 May 2004).

(to) dry To forget one's lines (in acting). Since the 1880s, at least.

due to a production error Because somebody made a cock-up. Standard newspaper excuse, as in *The Independent* (7 February 1997).

dumbing down Reprehensible simplification. This nicely alliterative phrase was apparently coined to describe a tendency in the American education system in about 1986, as the first citation explains. The usage spread to Britain, most notably with regard to radio programming in 1997. 'America's knowledge vacuum is largely caused by what has been called the "dumbing down" of school curricula and textbooks over recent years. Books have been made bland and easy, partly in an effort to appease militant interest groups, partly because the act of reading is given more importance than the matter that is read, partly in the name of "social relevance" (whatever that is)' – *The Economist* (19 September 1987); 'The BBC is about to axe 30 programmes on Radio 4 as part of the most significant shake-up in the network's history. The changes have already prompted critics to accuse the corporation of "dumbing down" large swathes of its output' – *The Sunday Times* (13 July 1997).

(the) duration The time taken for something to finish, originally a war. By 1916.

(to do one's) duty To go to the LAVATORY. Presumably because a child used to be required to 'perform' this duty every day. By the 1930s. 'The child ... never defecates or urinates; he ... does his "duty"' – Isaac Goldberg, *The Wonder of Words* (1938), ch. 6.

Ee

(to take an) early bath To be sent off the playing field early, for disciplinary reasons, most commonly in football. For British TV viewers, this phrase is inseparably linked to the Rugby League commentator Eddie Waring (1909–86). He broadcast commentaries, in his distinctive and highly imitable voice, for twenty years before he retired in 1981. This is the same as the American expression **to send someone to the showers**, in baseball or football, when a player is sent off early.

earnest Homosexual. Some claim that this was a Victorian code-word for 'gay' and that is why Oscar Wilde entitled his play *The Importance of Being Earnest*. Accordingly, the title is not just a double pun, as we had always believed, but a triple one. But evidence is slender for this increasingly popular myth. Christopher Hitchens mentioned it in his book *Unacknowledged Legislation* (2001). At about the same time, reviewing a revival at the Savoy Theatre, the critic at *The Daily Telegraph*, Charles Spencer, said: 'For those of a detective disposition, the comedy can indeed be read as a coded account of Wilde's sexuality. The very word "earnest" was Victorian slang for homo-sexual, and the whole concept of "Bunburying" suggests the necessarily double life of those of unorthodox tastes in late 19th-century society.'
    But then came this blast from the actor Sir Donald Sinden in *The Times* (2 February 2001): 'Sir, In the 1940s I was privileged to talk, at considerable length, about the first production in 1895 of Oscar Wilde's *The Importance of Being Earnest* with three of

the original participants: Irene Vanburgh, the first Gwendolen; Allan Aynesworth, the first Algy; and Lord Alfred Douglas, who was in Worthing with Wilde when he wrote the play and was present at the first night at the St James's Theatre. Although they had ample opportunity, at no time did any of them even hint that Earnest was a synonym for homosexual. The first time I heard it mentioned was in the 1980s and I immediately consulted Sir John Gielgud whose own performance of John Worthing in the same play was legendary and whose knowledge of theatrical lore was encyclopaedic. He replied in his ringing tones: "No-No! Nonsense, absolute nonsense: I would have known." Now we have Sir Richard Eyre in his otherwise excellent BBC television series about the history of the theatre repeating this ridiculous canard and adding, preposterously, that Cecily was a synonym for a "rentboy". I am emboldened to write this because only last week a theatre critic (not your own), in reviewing the latest production of *The Importance*, stated that the word "earnest" was Victorian slang for homosexual. The rot is setting in and, if unchecked, will doubtless be regurgitated in countless PhD theses.'

(an) earth closet A non-flushing lavatory that uses earth to hide the smell, as opposed to a water-closet. By 1870. 'It was not even an earth closet; but merely a deep pit with a seat over it, the half-yearly emptyings of which caused every door and window in the vicinity to be sealed' – Flora Thompson, *Lark Rise* (1939), ch. 1.

(the) earth moves for one One has an orgasm. Famously in the query posed by one participant to another after sexual intercourse, 'Did the earth move for you?' Now only jokingly alluded to, this appears to have originated as 'Did thee feel the earth move?' in Ernest Hemingway's novel *For Whom the Bell Tolls* (1940). It is not uttered in the 1943 film version, however. Headline from *The Sport* (22 February 1989): 'SPORT SEXCLUSIVE ON A BONK THAT WILL MAKE THE EARTH MOVE'.

earthy Bawdy. Compare the biblical phrase 'of the earth, earthy' (I Corinthians 15:47). 'Japanese priests have scored only a partial victory in their attempts to stop a sweet being sold as "snot from the nose of the Great Buddha" … Local media have suggested that the sweet is popular because people in western Japan have an earthy sense of humour, which other Japanese often find coarse. Another famous Nara sweet is called "deer droppings"' – *Sunday Herald* (16 May 2004).

easy Immoral (of a woman). See WOMAN OF EASY VIRTUE

(an) eating disorder Anorexia nervosa or bulimia. Avoiding being explicit about these supposedly common modern conditions. Since the 1980s/90s. 'Part of the reason for its acceptance as a genuine problem to be dealt with has been the growing number of celebrities the world over who have admitted to having, at some point in their lives, been a victim of an eating disorder. The Princess of Wales, the late Diana Spencer, was among its sufferers – her biographer wrote poignantly of her tendency to binge eat and then vomit out repeatedly as a way to deal with the unhappiness in her life' – psychology4all.com (2001).

ebullient Drunk. 'Yeltsin Goes With The Grain In Kansas; "We Can Learn From Your Experience," Ebullient Russian Tells Crowd' – headline in *The Washington Post* (19 June 1992).

(to be) economical with the truth To lie, to dissemble. On 18 November 1986, the British Cabinet Secretary, Sir Robert Armstrong, was being cross-examined in the Supreme Court of New South Wales. The British Government was attempting to prevent publication in Australia of a book about MI5, the British Secret Service. Defence counsel Malcolm Turnbull asked Sir Robert about the contents of a letter he had written that had been intended to convey a misleading impression. 'What's a "misleading impression"?' inquired Turnbull. 'A sort of bent untruth?' Sir Robert replied: 'It is perhaps being economical with the truth.' This explanation was greeted with derision not only in the court but in the world beyond, and it looked as though a new euphemism for lying had been coined.

In fact, Sir Robert had prefaced his remark with 'As one person said ...' and, when the court apparently found cause for laughter in what he said, added: 'It is not very original, I'm afraid.' In March 1988, (by now) Lord Armstrong said in a TV interview that he had no regrets about using the phrase. And he said again, it was not his own, indeed, but Edmund Burke's. The reference was to Burke's *Two Letters on Proposals for Peace* (1796): 'Falsehood and delusion are allowed in no case whatsoever. But, as in the exercise of all the virtues, there is an economy of truth.'

Other uses that have been uncovered include, working backwards: the Earl of Dalkeith MP had referred to Harold Wilson's post-devaluation broadcast in a House of Commons question (4 July 1968): 'Would he openly admit that he either made a gross miscalculation, misled the people, or at least had been over-economical with the truth?' Dr E.H.H. Green, writing to *The Guardian* on 4 February 1987, said he had found a note penned by Sir William Strang, later to become head of the Foreign Office, in February 1942. Describing the character of the exiled Czech President Benes, Strang had written: 'Dr Benes's methods are exasperating; he is a master of representation and ... he is apt to be economical with the truth.' Mark Twain wrote 'Truth is the most valuable thing we have. Let us economize it' – *Following the Equator* (1897).

The notion thus appears to have been a familiar one, especially in the British Civil Service, for a very long time. Samuel Pepys apparently used the precise phrase in his evidence before the Brooke House Committee in its examination of the Navy Board in 1669–70.

(the) economically abused / disadvantaged / exploited

The poor. Sources include: *The Sunday Telegraph* (27 October 1991); Beard and Cerf, *The Official Politically Correct Dictionary and Handbook* (1992). 'When I first came to live in America I was struck by how "the poor" had vanished – vanished from the American lexicon. I discovered they were constantly being rescued by euphemism. First they became needy, then deprived, then underprivileged or disadvantaged. In the politically correct 90s they were economically challenged' – Harold Evans, BBC Radio 4, *A Point of View* (18 September 2005).

(the) economically inactive The unemployed. Late 20th century. 'The main groups classed as economically inactive are those looking after the family and home, students and those who are long-term sick or disabled' – statistics.gov.uk (17 November 2004).

economy Cheap. As in economy airlines/class/ motors etc. Established in this sense by 1821. Specifically with regard to travel, by the mid-20th century. 'Scheduled operations ... First ... Tourist ... Economy' – *World Air Transport Statistics* (1959).

ecdysiast Stripper. A neologism offered by H.L Mencken to an American stripper who asked for his help in finding a more respectable word for her art. In a letter of 5 April 1940, he explained its derivation from the Greek: 'It might be a good idea to relate strip-teasing in some way ... to the associated zoological phenomenon of molting [moulting] ... A resort to the scientific name for molting, which is *ecdysis*, produces *ecdysiast*.' One hardly finds it catching on but a few brave souls gave it a try. 'Is it possible for a nightclub to lose money with famed Ecdysiast Sherry Britton stripping to bugle beads and pearls?' – *Time* Magazine (7 July 1958).

(an) education welfare manager A truancy officer. Since the 1990s. 'If your child's absence from school is unacceptable and fails to improve, despite involvement from the school and Education Welfare Officer, you will be sent an official warning letter pointing out your legal responsibilities to ensure the regular attendance at school of your child. You may also be invited to a meeting at the Civic Centre with the Education Welfare Manager who will explain the consequences of poor school attendance' – bromley.gov.uk (2005).

educational / educationally subnormal / E.S.N.   Dunce.
Known by 1953. This euphemism was in turn replaced – see
LEARNING DIFFICULTIES.

(an) educator   A teacher. An upgrading popularized in the US
since the 1960s, though the word had been used in a very general
sense since the 17th century. Often used when a person's precise
educational role is being left vague or is unknown. 'A few
educators fear universities themselves are becoming "politically
correct," mandating a single response to very complicated and
personal issues' – *The Washington Post* (23 September 1991);
'Thomas Arnold ... English historian and educator; headmaster
of Rugby School' – *Collins Dictionary of Quotations* (1995).

effeminate   (Male) homosexual. Mid-20th century onwards.
'[My uncle] seemed to me to be mildly effeminate and sexless.
I knew that he was supposed to have had some sort of accident
in the military, and that it involved a drunk doctor and an
unnecessary operation, which resulted in his having a regular
check from Uncle Sam and absolutely no prospects of marriage'
– epud.net (8 August 2005).

effluent   Stinking sewage discharge. Since the mid-19th century.
Often preceded by the word 'industrial' since the mid-20th
century.

(an) elder statesman   A retired politician who is past it. Since
the 1930s. Derived from the Japanese *Genro*, a group of retired
politicians who gave informal advice to the Emperor. Hence,
T.S. Eliot's play *The Elder Statesman* (1959). Sometimes now applied
to senior people in other professions who are respectfully being
described as past it. 'Professor Tawney is the elder statesman of
English economic history' – *The Observer* (19 October 1958); 'I say
this in the utmost affection ... he has passed from rising hope to
elder statesman without any intervening period whatsoever' –
Michael Foot on David Steel, speech in the House of Commons
(28 March 1979).

elderly Old. Hence, 'an elderly gentleman' is a gentle way of describing 'an old man'. 'The older houses were relics of pre-enclosure days and were still occupied by descendants of the original squatters, themselves at that time elderly people' – Flora Thompson, *Lark Rise* (1939), ch. 1; 'The novel rarely seems comfortable being talked about on the box: it is invited into the studio rather as an elderly maiden aunt is ushered into a cocktail party' – *The Independent* (28 October 1994).

(I have had an) elegant sufficiency I'm full. When declining an offer of more food, many people often say, 'No, thank you, I have had an *excellent* sufficiency'. Some say, rather, 'I have had an *ample* sufficiency' – as in the second episode of the TV *Forsyte Saga* (1967), but neither of these is quite right. Paul Beale's *Concise Dictionary of Slang and Unconventional English* (1989) has the correct form, rather, as 'an *elegant* sufficiency ... Jocular indication, mocking lower-middle-class gentility, that one has had enough to eat or drink, as "I've had an elegant sufficiency, ta!" since *c.* 1950.' In truth, 'elegant sufficiency' is the commoner of the three versions. In 1998, Mary B. Maggs, Conwy, drew my attention to the fact that it is, after all, a quotation: 'My paternal grandmother, who died in 1956 aged almost ninety, would not, I think, have acquired anything that was possibly slang – she tended to model herself on Queen Mary and made a very creditable job of it. I remember it from the 1930s. Later I traced it to James Thomson, *The Seasons* (1746), "Spring": "An elegant sufficiency, content, / Retirement, rural quiet, friendship, books".'

The basic euphemism has been expanded and taken on a life of its own. 'I once heard two elderly ladies trying to piece together a much longer version of this, which went something like "I have had an elegant sufficiency of the appetising comestibles which you in your gracious hospitality so generously have provided", but I doubt if that is an accurate version as the only thing they could agree on was that it ended, "In other words – I'm full!"' – Sylvia Dowling, Lancashire (1998).

Indeed, there are other jokey and verbose variations. 'From Wakefield in the 1890s, an aunt would say: "I've had quantum sufficio, an elegant sufficiency, and if I have any more I shall bust"' – Miss D.F. Rayner, Surrey (1999). 'My mother would say: "I have had an elegant sufficiency. Any more would be an abundant superfluity"' – Lorna Cooper, Oxshott (1999). 'It has been suggested that "Ma'am, I've had elegant sufficiency. Any more would be an indulgence of my exasperated appetite" was what Lord Palmerston replied to Queen Victoria' – Deirdre Lewis, London W11 (2000). 'My mother used to say: "I have had an excellent sufficiency and any more would be superfluous to my palate"' – S.A.F., East Sussex (2000). 'My Welsh grandmother always said on finishing a meal, "I have had an eloquent sufficiency, more would be superfluity, and render that obnoxious of that which I have already partaken"' – Helen van Oostayen-Thomas (2003). 'I've had an elegant sufficiency of the delicacy and any more would be superfluous to my already satiated appetite' – Valerie Pate, Shropshire (2003). 'I've had an elegant sufficiency, enough to suit my delicacy. Any more and I'd bust!' – (family of) Geoffrey Sparling, Cheshire (2003). 'I've had an egligent [*sic*] sufficiency and it would be presumption on my part to partake of any mair, as I'm full [to rhyme with Hull]' – (father of) Douglas Keown, Scotland (2003). 'Adequacy is sufficiency, thank you. Any more would be an over-indulgence of my already exasperated appetite' – source mislaid (2005). 'Thank you, I have had an elegant sufficiency. A little more would be a great indulgence to an exaggerated appetite. Gastronomical satiety admonishes me that I have arrived at the utmost state of deglutition consistent with dietetic integrity' – (grandfather of) Dr Peter Borrows, Buckinghamshire (2005).

Further variations: 'I've had a sufficiency of every excellent delicacy' – The Revd F.R. Dowson, West Sussex (2005); 'Ample sufficiency of plentitude' – (father of) Pat Murphy, Lancashire (2005); 'On the subject of strange family sayings, my late father would say after a meal either that he had had "an *ample* sufficiency" or "that's enough, no more, as it's not so sweet now as it was before"' – John Harrison, East Sussex (1995). 'My father (Jack Silver) when asked if he had enough to eat frequently replied, "Elephants and fishes eggs". When pressed, he explained it served for "an elegant sufficiency"' – Marion Ellis, Lincolnshire (1996).

elevated Slightly intoxicated. By 1827.

(to) emasculate To castrate. An equally long-established word (17th century) but a little longer and perhaps a little more obscure.

(an) embonpoint A fat stomach, a potbelly. From the French *en bon point* [in good condition], since the mid-18th century. 'A form decidedly inclined to embonpoint' – Charlotte Brontë, *Shirley* (1849), ch. 11.

(an) embrace A sexual caress or stimulation. As probably indicated in the Song of Solomon, 2:6 – 'His left hand is under my head, and his right hand doth embrace me' – and as Samuel Pepys used the word in his diary (entry for 25 October 1668) when he recorded that Mrs Pepys's maid, Deborah Willet, combed his hair and there was trouble because 'My wife, coming up suddenly, did find me imbracing the girl con my hand sub su coats; and endeed, I was with my main in her cunny.'

(to) embroider To exaggerate. Since the 17th century.

(an/the) emergency / (a/the) state of emergency (1) War. (2) An unpleasant, surprise event requiring action, possibly the suspending of a country's constitution. The reason for using the euphemism is because the enemy is not a 'proper' one or because there is a state of denial going regarding the true nature of the conflict. (1) since the early 19th century; (2) since the mid-20th century. 'The rebels ... had penetrated into Pennsylvania, and Philadelphia was threatened. This period was called the "Emergency"' – C.G. Leland, *Memoirs* (1893); 'He has declared a state of emergency to suppress a strike of African railway workers' – *The Spectator* (17 January 1958); 'The Malayan Emergency of 1948–1960 is regarded as a successful counter-insurgency campaign; yet, when the state of emergency was finally revoked, insurgent groups still remained at large in the jungle along the frontier with Thailand' – *Harvard International Review* (Summer 2001).

emergent (Of nations, countries) poor and uncivilized. Since the 1950s. 'Each of the "emergent" territories in Africa has different problems, to which each must find its own best solution' – *The Daily Telegraph* (13 January 1960).

employment See BUSINESS

(an) employment exchange A labour exchange. 'Labour exchange' seems first to have been coined in the US in the second half of the 19th century and was adopted in Britain soon after. 'Employment exchange' came along early in the 20th century to deal with the needs of the upper end of the market. *The Lancet* (11 September 1909) spoke of 'An employment exchange for university undergraduates'.

enceinte Pregnant. Using the French word for the condition does perhaps soften the blow. Since the 17th century. In French, of course, it is not a euphemism: *'Maman, je suis enceinte' / 'C'est épouvantable!'* [dreadful, appalling] – dialogue from the film *Les Parapluies de Cherbourg* (France/West Germany 1964).

(an) energetic disassembly An explosion. As in the Three Mile Island incident in 1979.

(an) English person An Englishman. According to Val Dumond's *The Elements of Nonsexist Usage* (New York, 1990), this is the correct PC euphemism. However, we still have not seen the title of R.F. Delderfield's novel changed to *God is an English Person*.

(to) enjoy His / Her Majesty's hospitality To be in prison. Compare AT HIS/HER MAJESTY'S PLEASURE.

enjoys a drink / is partial to a drink Drinks a lot / gets drunk. 'The tabloids have created a character who is in and out of marital trouble and very partial to a drink or two' – *The Observer* (4 September 2005).

(an) enslaved person A slave. At least, according to a report entitled 'One Nation; Many Peoples: a Declaration of Cultural Independence' issued by the New York State Board of Education (June 1991). Presumably this is because a slave is just a slave, but an 'enslaved person' has been brought to this condition by an oppressor. In addition, the new term draws attention to the *person* as much as to the condition. Source: *The Independent* (8 July 1991).

(to) enter into rest To die. Since the 16th century. 'It is a far, far better thing that I do than I have ever done; it is a far, far better rest that I go to, than I have ever known' – Charles Dickens, *A Tale of Two Cities* (1859), bk 3, ch. 15.

enthusiasm Religious hysteria. A euphemism of which John Wesley was very fond in his diaries, correspondence and journal to describe the reaction of congregations to his (and his colleagues') sermons on death, hell and damnation. Many of them shouted, screamed, writhed on the ground, fell down in fits, jumped about, had convulsions and sometimes visions. Generally speaking he was not averse to these manifestations.

enthusiastic Fat. 'It's like that *Tatler* code from the 1950s and 1960s. In picture captions of debutantes, "enthusiastic" meant "fat"' – *The Independent* (19 July 2005).

(an) erection An enlargement of erectile tissue, usually the penis, signifying sexual arousal. Since the 16th century. Nothing to do with sheds or other buildings that you might put up. 'They had proceeded thus gropingly two or three miles further when on a sudden Clare became conscious of some vast erection in his front' – Thomas Hardy, *Tess of the D'Urbervilles* (1891), ch. 58 (it was Stonehenge); 'We were so poor that if we woke up on Christmas day without an erection, we had nothing to play with' – Frank McCourt, *Angela's Ashes* (1996).

erotica Pornography (originally the written sort). Since the 1960s. From the late 1990s, *Erotica* has been the name given to a fair at the London Olympia, selling sex toys and fashions.

(to) escalate To increase or develop in stages. An American contribution which has either the euphemistic tendency to hide the real significance (in regard to prices, for example) or to dramatize the meaning. Escalators can, of course, go up or down, but in this case the direction is always up. Specifically the phrase has been much used since the late 1950s in connection with the development from conventional to nuclear warfare. 'The possibility of local wars "escalating into all-out atomic wars"' – *Manchester Guardian* (12 November 1959).

estate agents' speak See BIJOU; COMMODIOUS; DECEPTIVELY SPACIOUS; MODERN CONVENIENCES; OFFERING ENORMOUS POTENTIAL FOR IMPROVEMENT; ORIGINAL FEATURES; SEMI-DETACHED

eternal life Death – or, at least, what comes after mortal life, for believers. The phrase originates in the New Testament, for example in Romans 6:23, St Paul speaking: 'For the wages of sin is death; but the gift of God is eternal life through Jesus Christ our Lord.' In the same way, EVERLASTING LIFE and **eternal rest** are also used as euphemisms.

ethically different Corrupt. A joke coinage from *The New York Times* (July 1992).

ethically disorient(at)ed Dishonest. A coinage reported in Hugh Rawson, *A Dictionary of Euphemism and Other Doubletalk* (1981).

ethnic Neither Christian nor Jewish and so probably not white of skin either. Now used with utter looseness. It may simply mean 'non-European' or 'foreign'. Accordingly, **ethnic minority** became the key PC phrase for minorities belonging to a particular race or 'differentiated from the rest of the community by racial origins and cultural background' – *OED2*. As 'ethnic minority group', the term had been known in the US since the early 1950s. In the UK, since the 1960s, the phrase was used to refer to immigrants generally – appropriately so, as 'ethnic' has an interesting etymology, from the Greek *ethnos* (nation) and

ethnikos (heathen). Similarly, 'ethnic origin' came to be used as a
way of avoiding the word 'race' with its connotations of prejudice
and discrimination. 'Alan [Clark] was in the news, disagreeing
with the latest edict enjoining firms to employ more blacks. Alan
quite rightly argues that businesses to flourish must employ the
best staff irrespective of ethnic considerations' – James Lees-
Milne, *Beneath a Waning Moon* (2003), diary entry for 15 October
1985; 'Is there not something politically correct about the graffito
I saw sprayed on a north London wall this week: Ethnics out?' –
The Guardian (9 November 1991).

ethnic cleansing Removal of people from the territory they
occupy, verging on the genocidal. A horrifying term that emerged
from the Balkan conflicts of the 1990s. A translation of a Serbo-
Croat phrase, it referred to the forced removal of Muslims from
Serbian territory.

ethnic origin Race. The euphemism is used, presumably
because 'race' may be taken to suggest discrimination between
coloured and white people, or prejudice therefrom.

(the) Eumenides The Furies in Greek mythology.
'Eumenides' translates as 'the kindly ones' whereas what they
were was 'avenging'. 'The euphemism of calling the Furies in the
Eumenidies' – E.B. Tylor, *The Early History of Man* (1865), ch. 6.

(to) evacuate To DEFECATE – i.e. evacuate the bowels. By the
16th century.

(the) evening of one's days Old age. The closing or declining
period of a person's life has been so described since the 17th
century. 'The king of Great Britain has arrived at the evening of
his days' – P.B. Shelley, *An Address to the Irish People* (1812).

(an) eventide home A home for elderly people or geriatrics,
an old folks' home. Originally one run by the Salvation Army.
Known by 1918.

everlasting life What you are encouraged to anticipate after death. From the religious concept that is referred to once in the Old Testament – 'And many of them that sleep in the dust of the earth shall awake, some to everlasting life, and some to shame and everlasting contempt' – Daniel 12:2, but rather more times in the New Testament, for example: '[Jesus said] Verily, verily, I say unto you, he that believeth on me hath everlasting life' – John 6:47.

(to) excess To make redundant – because someone is 'in excess of requirements'. Mostly American use since the 1970s. 'The thousands of [New York] policemen, firemen … haven't been "fired". They have been, in an already classic euphemism, "excessed out"' – *The Listener* (27 May 1976).

(to) exclude To expel (from school or university). Second half of the 20th century. 'You can't expel anybody these days, you exclude them' – Baroness Phillips on BBC radio *Any Questions* (17 March 1978).

exclusive (1) (Noun) a newspaper story/serialization that is *not* exclusive but which the editors wish you to believe is. 'Otis gets a prison visit: Exclusive: Owner fighting to save dog from death sentence is allowed a 30-minute encounter – "He knew me, but it was heartbreaking to see him in such a state"' – *Daily Mail* (19 August 1994). (2) (Adjective) expensive – as in 'exclusive hotel/restaurant' etc.

(to ask to be) excused To seek permission to go to the LAVATORY. Principally in school-speak, by the 1940s/50s. 'Please, Miss, may I be excused?' 'When one of the men asked to be excused to go to the men's room, Mrs [Dorothy] Parker softly explained, as if pleading for pity for a flustered young man. "He really needs to telephone, but he's too embarrassed to say so"' – John Keats, *You Might As Well Live* (1970), ch. 5.

(to) execute To murder. Properly, 'execute' should only be used meaning 'to inflict capital punishment' on a person who has been sentenced to death by a court of justice but there has been a creeping misuse of the word to dignify gangland killings and such. Presumably the aim is to suggest that the killing is not casual or random but is planned and carefully carried out.

(an) executive A boss, a manager, any businessman. Although the effect of this euphemism is to elevate or dignify the person, the real motivation is to avoid offending 'businesswomen'. Source: BBC 'Guidelines for Factual Programmes' (1989).

executive action Assassination. This obscuring euphemism was used by the American CIA in a report on Israeli intelligence activities, reported in *The Observer* (7 February 1982). Hence, *Executive Action* – a film about the assassination of President Kennedy (US 1973).

(to) exercise the ferret To have SEXUAL INTERCOURSE. Recorded by 1985. Robert Burchfield in *The English Language* (1985) mentions 'to exercise the armadillo' as a memorable piece of Australian slang spotted in the 1970s.

(an) exotic dancer A stripper (or similar). Originally in American use, from the 1950s. 'The League of Exotic Dancers ... a group within the American Guild of Variety Artists' – *Evening Sun* (Baltimore) (19 July 1955).

expectant / expecting Pregnant. The full phrase 'expectant mother' (and, indeed, '—— father') has been known since the late 19th century.

(to) expectorate To spit. Did this word appear on warning notices at one time? If it did, it was probably not understood by potential offenders. I find that the Belmont Community Players, an American group who stage old melodramas, put this line on their playbills: 'Do not expectorate on the floor! Do not stand on the chairs! Do not rush the stage before the curtain drops!' (2005).

experienced Sexually experienced. Even if one has only had it the once – that is sufficient to qualify.

experientially enhanced Old. A joke coinage from the PC boom of the early 1990s.

(to) expire To die. Softening the reality with its gentle allusion to breathing the last breath. Since the beginnings of the English language. In Poets' Corner, Westminster Abbey, Byron is remembered by a slab bearing his lines from *Childe Harold's Pilgrimage* (1818), canto 4, st. 137: 'But there is that within me which shall tire / Torture and time, and breathe when I expire.'

(an) expletive / expletive deleted Euphemism for any swear word. Derived from the American way of indicating that an obscenity or blasphemous remark has been left out of a printed document. The phrase became general elsewhere during Watergate upon the release of transcripts of conversations between President Nixon and his aides – published as *The White House Transcripts* (1974). The documents also used 'expletive removed', 'adjective omitted', 'characterization omitted'. British practice had been to rely on **** (asterisks) or ... (dots) or —— (dashes) for sensitive deletions. Note this from a 1937 *Time* Magazine review of Hemingway's *To Have and Have Not*: 'No matter how a man alone ain't got no bloody (Obscenity deleted) chance.' For a while after Watergate people even exclaimed 'Expletive deleted!' instead of swearing. 'Nick Dear's boisterously idiomatic and theatrical version helps too, except for one thing: it bristles with expletives and some of those darling four-letter words that the British theatre fell in love with in the 1960s' – *The Sunday Times* (10 May 1992).

explicit Openly sexual. Since the 1970s, this word has acted as a titillating enticement to consumers of magazines and films portraying nudity or sexual activity. Hence, the come-on label 'contains explicit material'. 'There are, my expert friend said, still some prohibitions ... in the cinema – including what he calls "explicit penetration"' – Hansard, House of Lords (21 April 1971).

(an) expression of trade union solidarity A mob. This word is considered objectionable when referring to an unruly crowd, as of violent pickets during a strike. Hence, the euphemism employed during the days of union clashes in the Britain of the 1970s/80s.

(an) exterminating engineer An exterminator of pests and vermin. Of American origin. Second half of the 20th century.

extra-curricular activities / functions Extramarital sex. Derived from the term for anything undertaken outside a course of study. 'He's dumb enough to think that Lucy won't catch on to the extracurricular functions of that busty secretary' – Lesley Charteris, *The Queen's Awards* (1951), ch. 4.

extramarital relations Adultery. 'We, however, wish to appeal to reason, and we must therefore employ dull neutral phrases, such as "extra-marital sexual relations"' – Bertrand Russell, *Marriage and Morals* (1929), ch. 5.

extraordinary rendition The practice of taking terror suspects to be interrogated in countries where torture is employed to this end, when it is illegal in the US. An obscene euphemism, believed to have been invented to obfuscate the Clinton administration's response after the bombings of US embassies in Kenya and Tanzania in 1998. It became known widely in late 2005 when MPs questioned the British government over whether it had allowed planes to land in the UK when they were transporting prisoners on such missions. 'Congressman Markey has taken a stand. "Extraordinary rendition is the 800lb gorilla in our foreign and military policy-making that nobody wants to talk about. It involves our country out-sourcing interrogations to countries that are known to practise torture, something that erodes America's moral credibility," he said. It is up to his fellow Democrats to support him' – *The Guardian* (28 July 2004).

(the) extremities Feet/legs. It was not considered ladylike in mid-Victorian middle-class society to name parts of the body other than the head, except within the confines of the family. A delicacy had to be observed, especially in mixed company. Ladies were not acknowledged to have legs (these were rarely seen outside the bedroom, anyway) and as feet were attached to them, glimpsed beneath the skirt or the side-saddle riding habit, they too were subject to discretion. Miss Matty, going through old letters, found one from her grandmother 'with some practical remarks on the desirability of keeping warm the extremities of infants', in Mrs Gaskell, *Cranford* (1853).

(to have an) eye for the main chance To be selfish, to think only of oneself. By 1902.

Ff

(the) f-word Fuck. At one time totally taboo in public and in polite private conversation, this word has shed much of its horror since the 1960s. Nevertheless, it is still used guardedly in much of the media and a suitable compromise is struck when it is referred to by this euphemism. Probably in use no earlier than the 1990s, as also 'the c-word' for the still largely taboo 'cunt'.

(a) fabrication A lie. As ever, the longer word softens the shorter. Since the 18th century. 'The ad copy is just the sort that puts people's free-speech convictions to flight: vile, straight-faced fabrications about "the good news of Holocaust Revisionism" in full-page ads submitted recently to a wide range of college newspapers' – *The Washington Post* (21 December 1991).

(a) facilitator Someone who does something. In relation to people, this would seem to be late-20th century job enhancement and of probable American origin. See DESPATCH ROOM FACILITATOR.

(a) facility A lavatory – but also anything useful. Probably an outcrop of American grandiose verbosity. Hence, a kettle becomes a 'tea-making facility'. 'Strunk and White complain, in their admirable *The Elements of Style*, "Why must jails, hospitals, schools suddenly become 'facilities'?" Because when the authorities decided as a cosmetic exercise that jails would be

correctional facilities, the newspapers tamely followed suit, that's why'
– Keith Waterhouse, *Waterhouse on Newspaper Style* (1989); 'Then
Lipton, worried about its dependence on a few foreign suppliers,
established the Charleston plantation as a research facility' –
The Economist (31 August 1991); 'He was returned to the hospital,
ending up at Beverly Manor, a facility for mental patients,
where he earned the nickname "Dracula"' – crimelibrary.com
(29 November 2005). Compare AVAIL ONESELF OF THE
FACILITIES.

(a) fact-finding mission An expenses-paid junket.
Principally in political usage. 'As allegations of ethical lapses
continued to swirl around Rep. Tom DeLay (R-Texas), the
House Majority Leader lashed out at his critics today, insisting
that a 2002 trip his family took to Disneyland was a "top-secret
fact-finding mission." The all-expenses-paid trip, during which
Rep. DeLay and his family rode the Matterhorn no fewer than
35 times, was a clandestine mission to find weapons of mass
destruction believed to be hidden inside Space Mountain,
the congressman said today' – from a humour column in *People's
Weekly World Newspaper* (14 April 2005).

factors of peace Nuclear weapons (in the US). Cited in Willard
R. Espy, *An Almanac of Words at Play* (1975).

(the) facts of life Knowledge and understanding of human
reproduction and sexual functions. Since the 19th century,
originally referring to the brute reality of existence. 'The tone of
all the speeches at the meeting emphasized the need of teaching
boys and girls the essential facts of life, so as to equip them for
the momentous time when they choose life partners' – *MacLean's
Magazine* (June 1913).

(to) fail to win To lose. Although latterly this euphemism
has been elevated to an ideology in educational circles (see
DEFERRED SUCCESS), it has long been around to alleviate lack
of success in sporting circles.

(he/she) fainted away in this vale of tears He/she died.
An 1896 example was found at Brompton Cemetery and
recorded in Hugh Meller, *London Cemeteries* (1981), ch. 5.

fairly well-to-do Rich, prosperous. Since the 19th century.

(to) fall asleep To die. 'Asleep' is very commonly to be found
as a graveyardism for 'dead' and has been since the 13th century
at least. The root of the euphemism is most famously expressed
in Shakespeare, *Hamlet* (1600–01), III.i.60: 'To die – to sleep,
/ No more; and by a sleep to say we end / The heart-ache and
the thousand natural shocks / That flesh is heir to: 'tis a
consummation / Devoutly to be wish'd. To die, to sleep; / To
sleep, perchance to dream – ay, there's the rub: / For in that
sleep of death what dreams may come / When we have shuffled
off this mortal coil, / Must give us pause.' 'Here lies the Body
/ of JOHN EVELYN Esq. / [who] fell asleep ye 27th day / of
February 1705/6 being ye 86th Year / of his age in a full hope of
glorious / resurrection thro' faith in Jesus Christ' – tomb in the
Evelyn Chapel of St John's Church, Wotton, Surrey. 'REVD.
CHARLES LUTWIDGE DODGSON / (LEWIS
CARROLL) / FELL ASLEEP JAN 14 1898 / AGED 65
YEARS ...' – part of the gravestone of the author of *Alice's
Adventures in Wonderland* (1965), to be found in Guildford Cemetery,
Surrey. 'The euphemism ["he fell asleep"] partakes of the nature
of metaphor' – Beattie, *Moral Science* (1793); 'In affectionate
memory of Edith Mary Spencer Gray ... who fell asleep on May
8, 1930' – In Memoriam notice in *The Times* (8 May 1945).
   An elaboration of this, coupled with the ARMS OF JESUS trope
is **(to) fall asleep in (the arms of) Jesus / in the Lord.**

(to) fall on one's sword To kill oneself or, figuratively, to
accept responsibility for some action and resign from office.
After the practice of the ancients, especially the Romans, who
literally took their own lives when they had suffered a defeat of
some kind. The expression became popular in the late 20th
century. 'President Bush's US Supreme Court nominee abruptly
withdrew her candidacy yesterday ... The White House insisted

that Ms Miers, a loyalist clearly willing to fall on her sword to protect the President, had not been pushed into the decision' – *The Times* (28 October 2005).

(the) fallen The dead – or, more precisely, those killed in battle. By the 18th century but especially during and after the First World War. *For the Fallen and Other Poems* – title of collection (1917) by Laurence Binyon.

fallen off the back of a lorry Stolen (goods). From the traditional explanation given by a man suspected of stealing something and who is challenged to say how and where he obtained it. British use since the 1950s? Now also used as an example of a weak excuse about anything. 'When speaking of this type of shady merchandise, the Brits like to say, "It fell off the back of a lorry." In Harwin's case, it would be more accurate to say this stuff fell overboard from a container ship – most of it's made in China, and most of the stores are run by often-cranky Chinese women' – houstonpress.com (29 September 2005).

(a) fallen woman A woman caught in extramarital sex, a prostitute. In the first sense since the 17th century, since Victorian times in the second.

family Non-sexual, the opposite of ADULT. The essence of this term can be found in the title of Thomas Bowdler's *The Family Shakespeare* (1818), a ten-volume edition of the dramatist's works with all the dirty bits left out (or, as he put it, those words 'which cannot be read aloud in a family'). However, the euphemistic use really dates only from the second half of the 20th century. '*The School for Scandal* might be described as a Restoration comedy ... without the impudent indecencies, and so entirely suitable for family entertainment' – J.B. Priestley, *Literature and Western Man* (1960), ch. 7; 'Much of the output [is] unsuitable for "family viewing"' – *The Guardian* (22 July 1960).

(a) family butcher A butcher. To lessen, it was hoped, any
lingering association with the brutalities of the slaughterhouse.
Originally, however, the aim was simply to distinguish between
a butcher who supplied households and one who catered for
the army and navy. 'As one of the few remaining local family
butchers, we are proud to offer a quality of service which is
becoming rare amongst larger butcher shops' – R. Wisby, Family
Butcher (Lincolnshire) (2000).

(the) family jewels The testicles or the whole 'male sexual
apparatus'. *Partridge/Slang* finds this in services use in the Second
World War and probably earlier, back to the 1920s. Also a
'jocular CIA phrase for its own most embarrassing secrets',
according to *Safire* (1978). Director of Central Intelligence
William Colby reflecting on his predecessor's attempts to unearth
CIA activities which were outside its charter, noted in his book
Honorable Men (1978): 'They were promptly dubbed by a wag the
"family jewels"; I referred to them as "our skeletons in the
closet".' Compare CROWN JEWELS.

family name Maiden name. The concept of a maiden is totally
unacceptable to the PC, implying as it does that all unmarried
women are virgins (which is probably not the case). Sources
include: Val Dumond, *The Elements of Nonsexist Usage* (New York,
1990); *Sunday Telegraph* (8 March 1992.)

family planning Contraception. The euphemistic phrase was
probably coined as early as 1914 by Mrs Margaret Stranger, the
American 'Women's Lib' pioneer.

(in the) family way Pregnant. Known by 1796 as 'being in ...'
and by 1898, 'to put in ...' The dating of its introduction can
be found in a memorandum written by Lady Susan O'Brien
(1745–1823) on 'changes between 1760–1818': 'Language has
always been changing, & it has been said, as morals grow worse
language grows more refined. No one can say "breeding" or
"with child" or "lying in," without being thought indelicate.
"In the family way" & "confinement" have taken their place.'

The Family Way was the title of a film (UK 1966) based on the play *All in Good Time* by Bill Naughton (which was rather about the family than pregnancy ...).

Fanny Adams See SWEET FANNY ADAMS

Farmer Giles Piles/haemorrhoids. Since the 1950s, possibly Australian in origin. Rhyming slang based on Farmer Giles, the personification of the (British) country farmer, possibly named after the subject of Robert Bloomfield's poem *The Farmer's Boy* (1800) (although he is a labourer rather than a farmer). Coincidentally or not, Isaac Bickerstaff in *The Maid of the Mill* (1765) has: 'I am determined farmer Giles shall not stay a moment on my estate, after next quarter day.'

fast Lacking in self-restraint, of loose morals (usually of a woman). Hence, *The Fast Lady* – title of a film (UK 1962), though actually she was a motorcar, a Bentley.

fat cats Moneyed and probably complacent people. Originally, the term was popularized by Frank R. Kent of the *Baltimore Sun* in his 1928 book *Political Behavior* to describe major contributors to political campaign funds. 'I've always wondered why the Democrats call supporters of the Republican party "fat cats" but their own contributors are called "public spirited philanthropists"' – attributed to Ronald Reagan.

(to suffer a) fate worse than death (For a woman) to lose one's virginity / to be raped / to have an unwanted pregnancy. This is an expression dating from the days when such dishonour for a woman would, indeed, have seemed so. In John Cleland's *Memoirs of a Woman of Pleasure* (1748–9), Fanny Hill talks of a 'dread of worse than death'. Thomas Morell's libretto for Handel's oratorio *Theodora* (1749), act 1, has this exchange: *Septimius*: 'Death is not yet thy doom, / But worse than death to such a virtuous mind; / Lady, these guards are ordered to convey / You to the vile place, / As a prostitute to devote your charms.' *Theodora*: 'Oh worse than death indeed!' In *The Trumpet-Major* (1882), Thomas

147

Hardy reproduces what purports to be a document headed 'Address to All Ranks and Descriptions of Englishmen' dating from the time of Napoleonic invasion scares: 'You will find your best Recompense,' it concludes, ' ... in having protected your Wives and Children from death, or worse than Death, which will follow the Success of such Inveterate Foes.' Now used jokingly of any situation one might wish to avoid. 'You are fully aware that should the evil spread ... Bertram Wooster will be faced with the fate that is worse than death – viz. marriage' – P.G. Wodehouse, *The Mating Season* (1949), ch. 12.

fatness See AMPLE; AMPLY PROPORTIONED; BIG; BIG-BONED; BONNY; BROAD IN THE BEAM; BUXOM; CALORIE COUNTER; CELLULITE; CHUBBY; CLASSIC PROPORTIONS; CORPORATION; DEDICATED WEIGHT-WATCHER; DIFFERENTLY SIZED; EMBONPOINT; ENTHUSIASTIC; FINE FIGURE OF A WOMAN; FULL IN THE FACE; FULL-FIGURED; GENEROUSLY CUT; GENEROUSLY PROPORTIONED; HEAVILY BUILT; LARGER THAN AVERAGE; MIDDLE-AGED SPREAD; OBESE; OUTSIZE(D); OVER-SHAPELY; PERSON OF SIZE; PERSON OF SUBSTANCE; PERSON WITH AN ALTERNATIVE BODY IMAGE; PLUMP; PORTLY; PUTTING ON WEIGHT; ROUNDED STOMACH; SPARE TYRE; STOMACH; STOUT; VOLUPTUOUS; WELL-BUILT; WELL-ENDOWED; WITH A MATURE FIGURE

(to) feel (up) To excite sexually with the hands and fingers. By the 1930s. 'They say a man is as old as the woman he feels. In that case I'm eighty-five' – Groucho Marx, *The Secret Word Is Groucho* (1976).

(to) feel no pain To be insensibly drunk. By the 1940s. 'I feel no pain' was a common refrain of Major Denis Bloodnok in *The Goon Show* (on BBC radio 1951–61), though this usually did not refer to his drinking activities.

feeling the effects of the morning after With a hangover. By 1884. 'In addition to being a prevention remedy, tomato juice contains fructose, a type of sugar that helps your body metabolize alcohol more quickly. This is probably why the morning-after Bloody Mary seems to work' – health911.com (20 December 2002).

(a) fellow traveller A communist sympathizer who is not actually a member of the Party. By 1936. 'Few destinations left for Scots fellow travellers' – headline in *The Sunday Times* (12 July 1992).

female / feminine hygiene / physiology Pertaining to menstruation. 20th-century usage. See also PERSONAL HYGIENE.

female identified / oriented Lesbian. PC terms from the 1990s.

(a) femhole Manhole. What the good feminist says, should he or she ever have occasion to draw attention to such a thing. The word was coined by Bina Goldfield in *The Efemcipated English Handbook* (1983), but should only be used in moments of extreme protest. **Personhole** is much more straight down the middle. Other terms include 'sewer/utility/access hole' and 'utility access hole'. Sources include: Rosalie Maggio, *The Nonsexist Word Finder: A Dictionary of Gender-Free Usage* (Boston, Mass., 1988).

(a) feminine complaint An illness or medical condition that only affects mature women, usually gynaecological. 20th century.

femstruate Menstruate. Always used in preference to a word that contains the most unfortunate 'men' intrusion. 'Femstruate' is another of Bina Goldfield's coinages from *The Efemcipated English Handbook* (1983) and it is regretted that no gender-free substitute has been found for this word. Rosalie Maggio, however, in *The Nonsexist Word Finder* (1988) is quite happy with 'menses/menstrual', labelling the words 'non-sexist', as 'menses' is merely Latin for 'months'.

festivities of a luminary nature Christmas lights – as reported by the Plain English Campaign – *Northern Echo* (13 May 1997).

(a) fib A lie. One little word for another little word, but more gentle. From 'fible-fable' – nonsense. Mainly used about a trivial falsehood rather than a big lie. Since the early 17th century.

fiddling the books Deception, dishonesty. As in accountancy. 'Fiddle' in this sense since the early 17th century.

(a) fifth columnist A traitor within your own ranks or an infiltrator in the enemy's. Since the 1930s. Coinage of the term *la quinta columna* [the fifth column] is usually ascribed to Emilio Mola, the Spanish Nationalist general (1887–1937). In October 1936, during the Spanish Civil War, Mola was besieging the Republican-held city of Madrid with four columns. He was asked in a broadcast whether this was sufficient to capture the city and he replied that he was relying on the support of the *quinta columna* [the fifth column], which was already hiding inside the city and which sympathized with his side. It was also the title of Ernest Hemingway's only play (1938).

Some doubt has been cast on the ascription to Mola. Lance Haward noted (1996) that in the *Daily Express* of 27 October 1936, Moscow Radio was quoted as having attributed the phrase to General Franco. In the *Daily Mail* of 7 November, the Guardia Civile in Madrid, disaffected from the Republican cause, was being referred to as 'General Franco's now famous "Fifth Column".' In Hugh Thomas, *The Spanish Civil War* (1961), it is reported that the expression has been found in *Mundo Obrero* (3 October 1936) and that Lord St Oswald had used the term several weeks earlier in a report to the *Daily Telegraph*. Even earlier, in 1870, when Bismarck's armies invaded France, the French author Prosper Mérimée wrote to the Spanish mother of the French Empress: '*Malheureusement, alors même que l'invasion serait victorieusement repoussée, le danger ne serait pas encore conjuré. Il y a la quatrième armée de M. de Bismarck, et celle-là est à Paris.*' This 'fourth army', he suggests, is the foolish *Corps législatif*. As this Mérimée letter was first published in 1930, it might have been known to whoever coined 'fifth column' in 1936 – *Lettres de Prosper Mérimée à Madame de Montijo* (1995), vol. 2.

(a/the) final solution Genocide. *Endlösung* was the chillingly euphemistic name given to Adolf Hitler's plan to exterminate the Jews of Europe and was used by Nazi officials from the summer of 1941 onwards to disguise the enormity of what they intended. A directive (drafted by Adolf Eichmann) was sent by Hermann Goering to Reinhard Heydrich on 31 July 1941: 'Submit to me as soon as possible a draft showing … measures already taken for the execution of the intended final solution of the Jewish question.' Gerald Reitlinger in *The Final Solution* (1953) says that the choice of phrase was probably, though not certainly, Hitler's own. Before then it had been used in a non-specific way to cover other possibilities – like emigration, for example. It is estimated that the 'final solution' led to the deaths of up to six million Jews.

(a) fine figure of a woman A large woman. By the mid-18th century. 'Here I saw a *Femme Fatale* who was a fine figure of a woman' – George Bernard Shaw, in letter of 19 August 1912.

(a) firefighter A fireman. A mandatory substitution for the PC. 'The overwhelming majority are male but fire-fighters and fire crews will usually do the job' – BBC 'Guidelines for Factual Programmes' (1989).

first name Christian name. In 1967, I was present when a TV producer asked Dr Goldberg, the Chief Rabbi of Manchester, what his Christian name was. To his credit, Dr Goldberg replied with a smile, 'My Christian name is Selwyn.' 'Polemic like this is highly readable, but the bulk of the book consists of interviews with characters identified by first name only' – *The Sunday Times* (27 March 1988).

(the) fishing fleet Name given to girls who went out to India in search of husbands during the days of the British Raj. If they were unsuccessful they were known as 'Returned Empties'.

(it) fits where it touches (Of clothing) loose or ill-fitting. *Partridge/Catch Phrases* has 'they fit where they touch' as applied originally to loose-fitting trousers (with a 1932 citation) and, since the 1960s, to suggestively tight clothes, especially trousers.

(a/the) five o'clock shadow Stubbly beard growth that occurs in some dark-haired men towards the end of the day. This euphemism would appear to have originated in adverts for Gem Razors and Blades in the US before the Second World War. A 1937 advert added: 'That unsightly beard growth which appears prematurely at about 5 pm looks bad.' The most noted sufferer was Richard Nixon, who may have lost the TV debates in his US presidential race against John F. Kennedy in 1960 as a result. In his *Memoirs* (1978), Nixon wrote: 'Kennedy arrived ... looking tanned, rested and fit. My television adviser, Ted Rodgers, recommended that I use television make-up, but unwisely I refused, permitting only a little "beard stick" on my perpetual five o'clock shadow.'

(the) fleshy part of the thigh The buttocks. 'The Lift, or Buttock, is the Fleshy part of the Thigh of a Cow or Ox' – Randle Holme, *The Academy of Armory* (1688), ch. 3.

flexibility The abandonment of principle in pursuit of expediency. More or less since the 17th century.

(a) flier / flyer An airman or airwoman. Although it deals with the 'man' element, this has never really caught on. Even less than 'aviator', indeed.

(a) flight attendant An air steward/stewardess. Since the 1960s?

(a) fling An extramarital sexual relationship. Since the second half of the 20th century. 'The FA's director of public affairs tried to broker a deal with the *News of the World* to expose Ms Alam's relationship with Mr Eriksson if the paper would keep her

six-month fling with Mr Palios out of the public eye' –
The Independent (10 September 2005).

flipping Fucking, as in the mild oath 'flippin' eck' (where ''eck'
means 'hell'). Since about 1920. The euphemistic nature of this
word was soon overlooked by most people and an expression like
'flippin' kids' could become the catchphrase of Tony Hancock
on the BBC radio show *Educating Archie* in 1951.

(a) floral tribute A wreath at a funeral. Replacing the rather
dismal connotations of 'wreath'. Little known before the mid-
20th century. 'There is also a Flower Pavilion with a purpose-
built display area for floral tributes' – greenwich.gov.uk (2005).

flowers (1) A wreath or bunch at a funeral. 20th century.
'Where a call is made for "family flowers only" or "**no flowers
by request**" you might like to consider sending what we call
"sympathy flowers for the house"' – giftservice.co.uk (2005).
(2) Menstruation – or **monthly flowers**, a very old expression.

(a) flueologist A chimney sweep. A brave but failed attempt to
enhance the status of this trade. 'A chimney sweep has been given
a Royal Warrant for cleaning out Her Majesty's chimney pots ...
Mr Giddings, who calls himself the Queen's flueologist, was
recommended by other contractors working for the Royal
household' – ananova.com (2004).

follically / follicularly challenged Bald/balding. 'Even
the word "old" is frowned upon by some Americans: "ageful"
has now joined "follically challenged" (ie, bald) in the hideous
lexicon of political correctness' – *The Times* (22 January 1992).

for goodness sake 'For God's sake' rendered as a mild oath.
It was originally used as a literal appeal and occurs twice in
Shakespeare, *King Henry VIII* – Prologue, line 23 and III.i.159 –
the earliest citations known (1612).

for your convenience For *our* convenience. Members of
theatre audiences and maybe even travellers are invited to 'check
your bags – for your convenience'. Well, not really. The pleasure
is all theirs because that way they manage to run a tidy ship. Cited
in Ricks and Michaels (eds), *The State of the Language* (1991).

(eating / stealing / tasting) forbidden fruit Partaking of
something unlawful but desirable, as when Eve tempted Adam.
Since the early 17th century.

(to have) form To have a criminal conviction or a police
record. Since the 1950s. 'You can get at least a five ... for getting
captured with a shooter if you've got a bit of form behind you' –
Frank Norman, *Bang to Rights* (1958), ch. 3.

forward Impudent or rude to the point of objection. Since the
16th century. 'The favouritest young for'ard huzzy of a servant
gal as ever come into a house' – Charles Dickens, *Martin Chuzzlewit*
(1844), ch. 40.

(to) foul To DEFECATE where you shouldn't – most usually
applied to dogs. Since the 18th century. 'He *walks* as if he had
fouled his small-clothes, and *looks* as if he smelt it' – Christopher
Smart (1722–71), quoted in *Facetiae Cantabrigienses*, some kind of
19th-century Cambridge University rag.

foul disease *See* CERTAIN DISEASE

foul play Murder. A long established legal term for a
treacherous or violent deed. Hence, the police habit of saying,
on the discovery of a body that appears to have died naturally,
'foul play is not suspected'. The phrase is used in more than one
Shakespeare play, notably *Hamlet* (1600–1), I.ii.256, where the
Prince says: 'My father's spirit in arms! All is not well. / I doubt
some foul play.' Hence, also, the title of the film *Foul Play* (US
1978).

foundation garments Corsets. Since the 1920s. 'His wife ... would be plump, creating the greatest demand in the country for "roll-ons" and all-in-one foundation garments' – *Evergreen* (Spring 1985).

(a) four-letter word A monosyllabic obscenity (e.g. 'fuck', 'cunt', 'shit'). Since the 1920s when the term 'four-letter man' was applied to a person who spoke such words. The usage was much popularized at the time of the prosecution of Penguin Books Ltd in 1960 for the publication of an edition of D.H. Lawrence's *Lady Chatterley's Lover*. 'Having regard to the state of current writing, it seems that the prosecution against *Lady Chatterley* can only have been launched on the ground that the book contained so-called four-letter words' – *The Times* (7 November 1960); 'Nick Dear's boisterously idiomatic and theatrical version helps too, except for one thing: it bristles with expletives and some of those darling four-letter words that the British theatre fell in love with in the 1960s' – *The Sunday Times* (10 May 1992).

frank Obscene. By the mid-20th century. 'And we exchanged many frank words in our respective languages' – Peter Cook as Harold Macmillan, *Beyond the Fringe* (1961).

(to) fraternize To have relations (of whatever kind) with civilians, if you are an invading army, say. And vice versa. In which case the practice is known as 'fraternizing with the enemy' and usually there is nothing at all 'brotherly' about it. By the 1890s. In the Second World War, it came to mean '(albeit willing) sexual relations between conquering troops and civilians'. 'By his orders forbidding fraternisation, General Eisenhower is going to present his subordinate commanders and staffs with some knotty problems' – *New Statesman* (7 October 1944).

free Included in the cost, so no extra charge is made. 20th century.

free love Sexual relations free from legality and convention. Since the early 19th century.

(to be) free with one's favours Unchaste (usually of a woman). Since the 17th century when the phrase 'last favour' was also used to describe the ultimate concession to a man. 'One who had bestowed her favours on many' – Thomas Medwin, *Conversations with Byron* (1832), ch. 1.

(a) freedom fighter A terrorist, a GUERRILLA. When I was asked who first pointed out that 'One man's terrorist is another man's freedom fighter', I replied that I had been conscious of this view 'for, say, ten or twenty years' and wondered if it had started around the time of the Nicaraguan Contras whom President Reagan famously saluted as 'our brothers, these freedom fighters' (1985). I played for time by offering Hugh Gaitskell's remark – quoted by his widow, Dora, in a letter to *The Guardian* (23 August 1977) – 'All terrorists, at the invitation of the Government, end up with drinks at the Dorchester.' And there is also the observation from Joseph Conrad, *The Secret Agent* (1907), ch. 4: 'The terrorist and the policeman both come from the same basket. Revolution, legality – counter-moves in the same game; forms of idleness at bottom identical.'

Then I landed on this from the 1964 New York version of the revue *Beyond the Fringe*. Paxton Whitehead (taking over from Jonathan Miller) played the Duke of Edinburgh (something not then allowed on the London stage) and had him talk about his attending the independence celebrations in Kenya that had taken place in December 1963. Of Jomo Kenyatta, the first president, he says: 'That was when we thought he was a Mau-Mau terrorist. Now of course we realize that he was a freedom-fighter.'

Note also what Harold Nicolson wrote in his published diaries (entry for 29 October 1956): 'When people rise against foreign oppression, they are hailed as patriots and heroes; but the Greeks whom we are shooting and hanging in Cyprus are dismissed as terrorists. What cant!'

A similar delicacy invaded coverage by Reuters and ABC News of the 9/11 attacks in the United States. The word 'terrorist' was forbidden and 'attacker' substituted in various forms. In the London bombings of July 2005, 'terrorists' were not referred to on BBC News, only 'bombers', though that is hardly much of a euphemism, of course.

French lessons Services of a prostitute. As advertised on cards in doorways, shop windows, telephone booths, etc. By the 1960s. Presumably, 'French' rather than 'German', 'Italian' or any other nationality because of the time-honoured association of the French with sexual matters.

(to) freshen a drink To serve more alcohol. In fact, this may not be euphemism but just light-hearted periphrasis. Since the mid-to-late 20th century.

(a) friend A lover. Since the 15th century. 'The boy's mother ... was joined ... by a man described as her "friend". The mother is apparently divorced'– *The Guardian* (11 December 1967).

(a) friend of Dorothy A (male) homosexual. Probably the inquiry, 'Is she a friend of Dorothy?' originated among American homosexuals. It was current by 1984. Dorothy was the put-upon heroine of *The Wizard of Oz* and was played in the film by Judy Garland, a woman much revered in male homosexual circles.

friendly fire Killing or destruction by forces who are supposed to be on your side or in alliance with you. 'Friendly', in this case, seems to have been used first in the trenches of the First World War when it referred to 'one of our own shells' as it whizzed overhead. In 1976, presumably as a result of experiences in the Vietnam War, the term was taken up by the American military. C.D.B. Bryan's book *Friendly Fire* was published in 1976. 'Since the war began, more American troops are thought to have been killed by "friendly fire" than by the Iraqis, most by air-launched missiles' – *The Independent* (22 February 1991).

frigging Fucking – as in expletives. A milder and more humorous way of using the f-word without causing offence. The word has been known since the 16th century. 'The sooner we fix this girl up with a new life the better ... Bearing in mind that she's not serious, just friggin' around' – Joan Wyndham, *Love Lessons* (1985), diary entry for 2 February 1940.

(the) front door The VAGINA. *Partridge/Slang* offers these variations: 'front attic / garden / parlour / room / window / gut'. 'Front bum' and 'front passage' have also been recorded. 'Front door mat' rather sweetly has been used to describe the pubic hair. A very recent version (say, 2000) is **front bottom**. 'No front bottoms! That's a sight reserved for just one man in my life' – film *Calendar Girls* (UK 2003).

fuddled / befuddled Drunk. Since the 17th and 19th centuries, respectively. 'Freedom from the befuddlement of drink' – *Public Opinion* (11 August 1922).

fugly Fucking ugly / fuck ugly. Since the 1980s, especially in fashion circles.

full in the face Fat. 20th century. 'She was full in the face, full in the breasts, full in the hips because she'd been fed and pampered and spoiled until she was soft everywhere except in her attitude toward other people, women who crossed her and men who didn't snap to heel' – pulporiginals.com (2005).

(a) full relationship A marriage/partnership that involves SEXUAL INTERCOURSE. So, a divorce judge might ask: 'And did you have a full relationship with your husband?' 'It is probable, due to his character in every other aspect, that [Shaka Zulu] never managed to consummate a full relationship with any of these women' – campus.northpark.edu (1996–9).

full-figured Fat (of a woman). 'The Archduchess, a fair, blue-eyed, full-figured, round-lipped maiden' – Thomas Hardy, *The Dynasts* (1906), pt 2, act 4.

full-frontal (nudity) Bollock nakedness or, rather, nudity
that allows a man or woman's sexual parts to be seen. Before
the 1960s, naked people when being photographed had a way
of holding large beach balls in front of themselves, but with the
advent of naked actors in such shows as *Hair* (1967) and *Oh!
Calcutta!* (1969), a term obviously had to be invented for this great
leap forward in civilized behaviour. *OED2* does not find the term
until 1971. But the episode of TV's *Monty Python's Flying Circus*
broadcast on 7 December 1969 was entitled 'Full Frontal
Nudity' and my diary for 25 March 1970 notes a viewing of Ken
Russell's film *Women in Love*: 'Full frontal nudity, too, as they
call it, though I don't feel a better man for having seen Oliver
Reed's genitals.'

fun-loving Hedonistic. Although the term has been in use since
the 18th century, its coded suggestion of reckless and dissolute
excess probably dates only from the late 20th century.

funeral See DEATH

(a) funeral director / furnisher An undertaker. Originally
an American term, by the 1880s. ('Undertaker' was originally
itself a euphemism for the burial man, one who 'undertakes'
funerals. Through long association with death, the word has
become grim.)

(a) funeral home / parlour A mortuary. Originally an
American term, by the 1930s. 'From "undertaker" tout court
to "funeral parlor" to "funeral home" to "chapel" has been the
linguistic progression' – Jessica Mitford, *The American Way of Death*
(1963); 'Rev. James Earl Richardson. Interment will follow in
the Paradise North Cemetery in Houston. McClain-Clebourn
Funeral Home is in charge of arrangements' – kivy.com (2005).

funeral service operatives Undertakers' assistants. In
Britain, the National Union of Funeral and Cemetery Workers
and the British Funeral Workers' Association amalgamated
from 1927–50 to form the National Union of Funeral Service

Operatives. This then became part of the Furniture, Timber and Allied Trades Union.

funny money (1) Money acquired in an unscrupulous or illegal way; counterfeit money. (2) Ludicrously inflated sums paid in excess of what something is worth. The first meaning established by, say, 1960, the second by the 1970s.

Gg

gainful employment A paid job. 'Gainful' is a modern
elegance, sounding better than 'wage-earning' and invented
perhaps by the British Civil Service or at least the Inland
Revenue. The coinage has, however, antecedents as far back as
the 16th century, when a description of London referred to
carriers taking produce from the country into the city, 'whereby
they live very gainfully'. 'Many people … find themselves obliged
to take up gainful employment out of sheer embarrassment at the
inability to answer the question "what do you do?" in less than
eighty words' – N. Shulman, *Social Security* (1985), ch. 1.

(the) game Prostitution. Hence, 'She is on the game' means
'she is working as a prostitute'. In the 18th-century slang, the
'game' was that of 'thieving'. Applied to prostitution by the
1890s. Earlier, the term had been applied to not-necessarily
mercenary amorous activities: 'Sluttish spoils of opportunity /
And daughters of the game' – William Shakespeare, *Troilus and
Cressida* (1591), IV.v.62.

(a) garden of remembrance / rest A graveyard without
bodies. The term was originally applied to gardens where the
dead from the two World Wars were commemorated although
they were not buried there. Now applied to the area close to
a crematorium where ashes are scattered and where small
memorial plaques and such are positioned. Since the 1950s
or earlier.

gardening leave Suspension from office on full pay, usually pending job loss. The leave is taken at home by a civil servant or similar whose position has become untenable for some reason. 'Dave Jones had been suspended for 12 months as club manager while facing child abuse allegations ... He said he had received no indication that the club's board was withdrawing its full support until Mr Lowe arrived at his house and told him he was on "gardening leave" with Mr Hoddle stepping in for 12 months' – *The Times* (27 October 2005); 'Gardening leave of £1m for Barclays UK chief ... [Mr Davis] stands to pocket up to £1m in pay and bonus, provided he does no work for a competitor for at least a year ... [He] steps down from Barclays' board today and will leave the bank in April. He is available as a consultant until October.'

gastric flu Diarrhoea. Anything rather than use the d-word (which is very difficult to spell, anyway).

gathered to one's fathers Dead. The biblical phrase is 'gathered to one's people' (Genesis 25:8), though 'gathered to his fathers' does occur in the Apocryphal 1 Maccabees 2:69. The idea is of the dead person joining his ancestors. 'No change was to be made till MacFinnan Dhu had been gathered to his fathers' – James A. Froude, *The Two Chiefs of Dunboy* (1889), ch. 8. Compare the term **gathered to God**, meaning the same.

gave their lives / laid down their lives Died (of soldiers or others in action). 'They gave their lives that others might live' is probably the most common sentiment on war memorials, since the First World War at least. It is presumably intended to echo faintly Jesus Christ dying 'to save us all' and his commandment, 'greater love hath no man than this, that a man lay down his life for his friends' (John 15:13). On the tomb of the Unknown Warrior in Westminster Abbey (1920), the inscription reads in part: 'THUS ARE COMMEMORATED THE MANY / MULTITUDES WHO DURING THE GREAT / WAR OF 1914–1918 GAVE THE MOST THAT / MAN CAN GIVE LIFE ITSELF / FOR GOD / FOR

KING AND COUNTRY.' 'The Tomb Of The Unknown Soldier honors one who gave his life for his country and will never be known but to God' – thefossinstitute.org (2005).

gay Homosexual. In mainstream usage since the mid-1960s, this part euphemism/part alternative name became popular at a time when the US Gay Liberation Front came 'out of the closet' and used such slogans as 'Say it loud, we're gay and we're proud' and '2–4–6–8, gay is just as good as straight'. The word 'gay' had, however, been used in this sense since at least the 1930s and on both sides of the Atlantic. In the 19th century, 'gay' was used to describe female prostitutes and there is an even earlier use of the word applied to female licentiousness. Although one regrets the loss of the word to mean 'joyful, light-hearted', perhaps this use goes some way towards making up for the pejorative use of BENT , QUEER and POOF to describe homosexuals.

The French still manage to distinguish between the old and new meanings of the word (at least when writing): 'gay or joyful' is still *gai*; 'gay as homosexual' is *gay*. In English, however, mild confusion still exists. '"Great thing about gay people ..." "Gay?" Tessa said. "Bent, queer, you know. Homosexual"' – Frederic Raphael, *The Limits of Love* (1960); '"I had been aware for many years that my sexuality was different from that envisaged by traditional Judaism and tried to ignore it ..." said Rabbi Solomon. "But since I've begun to accept that I am gay, I've become a happier person"' – *The Daily Telegraph* (29 August 1992).

(a) gazunder A chamber pot. Because it 'goes under' the bed.

gee-whiz(z)! Jesus! A milder form of the oath, of American origin, since the 1880s. '"Gee whiz!" breathed William in ecstasy' – Richmal Crompton, *William and the Evacuees* (1940).

(the) gender The sex of a human being. Since the early 1960s. Intended (especially by feminists) to emphasize the social and cultural differences between men and women and not just the biological ones. 'Sex differences may be "natural", but gender differences have their source in culture' – A. Oakley, *Sex, Gender* *and Society* (1972), ch. 8; 'US Ambassador to Iraq turned scapegoat for all that was wrong with America's handling of the Gulf war, April Glaspie is under attack from all sides. And the first weapon used against her, declares Naomi Wolf, is her gender' – *The Guardian* (28 March 1991); 'Nobody can complain that The Men's Room exploits women, because the director, Antonia Bird, and the scriptwriter, Laura Lamson, are both of the female gender' – *The Sunday Times* (27 October 1991).

(a) gender reassignment operation A sex change operation. Not much of a euphemism and hardly a necessary one. This pre-PC coinage was used by a London hospital in the early 1980s. 'Myka Scott (née Michael Scott) is a pre-op transsexual...[and] doesn't like the term "sex change", preferring "gender reassignment operation"' – *The Independent* (22 August 1992).

(a) gender-bender A sexually ambiguous or confused person. The term arose in about 1980 to describe pop stars, like the bisexual David Bowie, who wore sexually ambiguous clothing and make-up or who affected a deliberately androgynous appearance. 'Gender benders are anything but gay. They make up and dress up out of a sense of fashion' – *Sunday Mirror* (22 January 1984).

generously cut Suitable for the extra-large (of clothing). 'Generously cut in quality wool gabardine – Mid-Fawn, Slate Grey or Lovat' – advertisement in the *National Observer* (US) (6 November 1976).

generously proportioned Fat. 20th century. 'Cassie, 25, is a generously proportioned girl with a masters in creative writing' – *The Observer* (23 November 2003).

gentility enforcement See COCKEREL; ROOSTER; SEE YOU NEXT THURSDAY; STICK (SOMETHING) WHERE THE SUN DOESN'T SHINE; SWEET F.A.

(a) gentleman A smuggler. In use since the 19th century. 'Watch the wall, my darling, while the Gentlemen go by!' – Rudyard Kipling, *Puck of Pook's Hill* (1906).

(a) gentleman caller / friend A man who calls on a woman and becomes a potential suitor. Also a euphemism for a male lover. The phrase occurs in the script of *Citizen Kane* (US 1941) – 'When I have a gentleman caller …' – but the concept is best known from Tennessee Williams's play *The Glass Menagerie* (1944).

(a) gentleman of fortune An adventurer (in the near criminal sense). 'By a "gentleman of fortune" they plainly meant neither more nor less than a common pirate' – Robert Louis Stevenson, *Treasure Island* (1883), ch. 11.

(a) gentleman of leisure An upper class person (presumably 'of independent means') but also now, loosely, anyone with nothing to do, no work to go to and so on. By 1899. P.G. Wodehouse's novel *A Gentleman of Leisure* was published in 1910.

(a) gentleman of the road A tramp, vagrant or down-and-out. Originally, a euphemistic name for a highwayman. In the 18th century, the nickname was used sarcastically as the roads became busy with stagecoaches as well as horse-riders and family carriages, but stories were told of certain courtesies during a robbery – a doffed hat to a lady, a wedding ring spared, a helping hand to the infirm. 'Even a highwayman, in the way of trade, may blow out your brains,' writes William Hazlitt in *The Fight* (1822), 'but if he uses foul language at the same time, I should say he was no gentleman.' 'Tramps may be costing the National Health Service millions of pounds by flitting from hospital to hospital … Gentlemen of the road get first-class accommodation plus medical care, costing up to £100 a week or more' – *The Guardian* (21 April 1975).

gentlemen / (the) gentlemen's / gents A men's LAVATORY – from the sign at the door. By 1929, but none of these forms seems to be recorded before this.

(the) gentlemen of the press Newspaper reporters en masse. Or 'reptiles', as Sir Denis Thatcher used to refer to them. Perhaps since the late 19th century. 'Sir, there are some journalists outside, and a gentleman from *The Times*' is a story that may date from then (though it has also been applied to *The New York Times*).

(a) geriatric An old and past-it person. By the 1960s. Is this a euphemism? Despite being an obscure medical-sounding word, it has become more insulting than the original. 'Nurses and patients barricaded themselves inside a ward in protest at the proposed mixing of geriatrics with surgical patients' – *The Guardian* (1 October 1980).

(to) get into bed with To act collusively. Late 20th century. Not the slightly earlier (1950s), **hop / jump into bed with**, meaning, to have a casual sexual relationship. 'I'm just glad I have what some would refer to as "questionable morals", the ones that allow me to jump into bed earlier rather than later' – *The Independent* (23 August 2005).

(to) get into trouble (Of a man) to seduce and impregnate a woman; (of a woman) to become pregnant illegitimately. By the 19th century.

(to) get off / out at Edge Hill To practise sexual withdrawal as a means of contraception, i.e. *coitus interruptus*, withdrawal in advance of ejaculation. Mid-20th century. One phrase in a whole group that evoke places that are *immediately before* you get to a major one. Edge Hill would be the last railway station you could get off at before arriving at Liverpool Lime Street. Others of this type include: Broadgreen (which is the station before Edge Hill – so this is even more prudent), Fratton (Bristol dockyard), Gateshead (Newcastle upon Tyne), Haymarket (Edinburgh), Paisley (Glasgow) and Redfern (Sydney, New South Wales). There is also the version **to leave before the Gospel.**

(to) get (something) off the ground To start (an enterprise). Allusively to a plane getting airborne. An example of a perfectly good word being replaced by a circumlocution when applied to an undertaking (from 1960 at least), but perhaps to indicate more than a simple beginning which the direct and stark 'start' might suggest. 'He needed a substantial loan to get the operation off the ground.' A correspondent in *The Daily Telegraph* (7 August 1976) satirically advocated a new Olympiad of self-righteous nations, but suggested that 'the organisers would be so busy arguing about the rules of entry that the games would never get off the ground'.

(to be) getting on in years To be old. By 1885. 'The Old Age Pensions Act (1908) supplied the language with at least one phrase: *to qualify for the pension* – to be getting on in years' – W.E. Collinson, *Contemporary English* (1927). Sometimes just **getting on.**

(a) gift from God A baby. Probably a Victorian conceit to avoid mentioning the b-word in mixed company.

gippy tummy Diarrhoea suffered by visitors to hot countries, typically Egypt (hence, the 'gippy'). By 1943.

girlie Sexually titillating, as in 'girlie magazine / show / pictures', in which scantily-clad or nude girls appear. By 1942 and probably of American origin.

(to) give head To perform fellatio or cunnilingus. Presumably because it is performed with the mouth (which is in one's head) rather than with one's genitals. Has also been said to derive from the head of the penis. Probably American in origin and since the 1960s.

(to) give oneself to To agree to have sex with. Since the 19th century. 'Under the hedge which divided the field from a distant plantation girls had given themselves to lovers' – Thomas Hardy, *Jude the Obscure* (1895), pt 1, ch. 2.

(to) give / teach someone a lesson   To punish. By 1855.
Sometimes **to learn someone a lesson**.

(to) give time to one's other commitments   To be
dismissed from employment. Compare SPEND MORE TIME
WITH MY (WIFE AND) FAMILY. Of course, it may not carry this
implication but, in that case, it is unwise to use this tainted
phraseology. 'K — A — will stand down as senior non-executive
director (SNED) at Cookson with effect from 15 April in order
to devote more time to his other commitments' – manifest.co.uk
(April 2005).

(a) glamour mag   A sexually titillating magazine. By the 1930s.
Hence, such uses as 'Linsey Dawn McKenzie, glamour model.
Have your picture taken with Dawn' – exhibitor at Erotica 2005,
London.

(to) go   (1) To die. Since the 14th century. 'Very, very ill. It is
only a matter of days now, I'm afraid. She may even go today' –
Flora Thompson, *Lark Rise to Candleford* (1945), ch. 36. (2) To
go to the LAVATORY. Recorded by 1926. 'Excuse me ... I've got
to go somewhere' – Frederic Mullally, *The Prizewinner* (1967), ch. 1.
Hence, in 20th-century seaside postcards, the proverbial saying,
'"Every little helps", as the old woman said when she piddled into
the sea' became '"Every little helps", as the old woman said as
she *went* in the sea.'

(to) go all the way   See ALL THE WAY

(to) go and check the blackout   To go to the LAVATORY.
'I'm just going to check the blackout' – Frank Deakin, Cheshire
(1996).

(to) go and check the plumbing   To go to the LAVATORY.
A loophemism volunteered by S. Davison, Nottinghamshire
(1996). Also: '(to) go and inspect the plumbing' – Adrian D.
Bull, North Yorkshire (1998).

(to) go and check the price of wheat in Chicago To go to the LAVATORY. 'My husband Peter, who is Canadian, goes "to check the price of wheat in Chicago"' – Edith Pink, Fife (1995). Dr Pink added: 'The origin dates back to the 1920s when my husband Peter's grandfather had a seat on the Toronto Stock Exchange and had at one time almost cornered the market in wheat futures! Of course, all was lost in the crash of '29, but the saying persisted in the family.'

(to) go and drain one's radiator To go to the LAVATORY. 'I'm going to drain my radiator' – S. Davison, Nottinghamshire (1996).

(to) go and empty the ashtrays To go to the LAVATORY. 'We lived in a terraced house, with no inside toilet or hot water, and when my mother was going to make the beds, she armed herself with a bucket and said, "I'll just go and empty the ashtrays"' – I. Moore, Greater Manchester (1994).

(to) go and empty the teapot to make room for the next cup of tea To go to the LAVATORY. 'Another [loophemism] is that I "am going to make room for a cup of tea"' – Hazel Stretton-Ballard, Buckinghamshire (1996).

(to) go and look at Africa To go to the LAVATORY. 'My father used to say "I'm going to look at Africa", despite the fact that we were living in India!' – Mrs R. Collins, Norfolk (1998).

(to) go and lower the level To go to the LAVATORY. Reported by Adrian D. Bull, North Yorkshire (1998).

(to) go and partake of a minor [or major] comfort To go to the LAVATORY. 'My one time chief, Fleming-Williams, used to offer visitors a minor comfort or a major comfort' – Clement R. Woodward, Hertfordshire (1995).

(to) go and pick a daisy To go to the LAVATORY. *Partridge/Slang* has this as 'mostly women's' use by 1860 and notes that a 'daisy'

was also the name for a chamber-pot, possibly because of the
floral design on it.

(to) go and pump ship To go to the LAVATORY. 'My late
father always used to say he was going to "pump ship"' – Molly
Anderson, Herefordshire (1996).

(to) go and see a friend off to the coast To go to the
LAVATORY. Revealed by the actor Jon Glover on BBC Radio
Quote...Unquote (30 May 1995).

(to) go and see a man about a dog (1) To undertake any
illicit or unmentionable job or task while providing this excuse
for leaving the scene. (2) To go and have a drink, while
withholding the fact that this is the purpose of your exit. (3)
To go to the LAVATORY. Since the mid-19th century. A caption
to a Ghilchik cartoon in *Punch* (22 January 1930) is: The Age
Old Excuse. Cave-dweller. 'I won't be long, dear. I've just got to
see a man about a brontosaurus.' But to which of the meanings
does this refer?

    Partridge/Catch Phrases seems to suggest that the phrase originally
indicated that the man was about to 'visit a woman – sexually',
then that he was 'going out for a drink', and then that he gave it
'in answer to an inconvenient question'. Only fourthly, does it
list 'go to the water-closet, usually to "the gents", merely to
URINATE'. At one time, *Brewer* also preferred the 'concealing
one's destination' purpose of this phrase, suggesting that it was a
late 19th-century American expression, and gave an example of
its use during Prohibition as disguising the fact that the speaker
was going to buy illegal alcohol from a bootlegger. A later edition
suggested that the phrase meant that the speaker was pretending
that he would see a man about placing a bet on a dog race (but
this strikes me as too literal).

    Sticking to what I take to be the now primary meaning: it has
been suggested that 'dog' is some sort of rhyming slang for 'bog',
a well-known term for a lavatory, but this is not true rhyming
slang and does not convince.

    To unravel all this a little: the earliest citation for the phrase, in any meaning, is Dion Boucicault's play, *The Flying Scud, or a Four-legged Fortune* (1866), act I, where a character says: 'Excuse me Mr Quail, I can't stop; I've got to see a man about a dog.' Here the meaning would appear to be that he is providing a limp excuse for absenting himself. This does not support an American origin for the phrase, for Boucicault was Irish and working mostly in London. However, there does seem to have been a US origin for the drinking/Prohibition meaning. In Barrère and Leland's *Dictionary of Slang* (1890) is this definition: '*To see a man (American), to go and have a drink at the bar.*' Later, *American Speech*, vol. 3 (1927) has: '*See a man about a dog, to go out and buy liquor.*' Early citations are lacking for the 'go and take a leak' application, in any country.

(to) go and see if one's hat is on straight To go to the LAVATORY. 'Asking if one wanted the loo when leaving, Jim remarked that Lady Lloyd, wife of George (Lord) Lloyd, proconsular figure to whom Jim was formerly secretary, used to enquire: "Do you want to put your hat straight?"' – Anthony Powell, *Journals 1982–1986* (1995); 'I always say, "I am just going to see if my hat's on straight", not that I ever wear one' – Mrs Jean Koba, Berkshire (1996).

(to) go and see the man I joined up with To go to the LAVATORY (i.e. joined up in the army with) – J. Skinner, Kent (1996).

(to) go and see the Turk – Mustapha Pee To go to the LAVATORY. Mrs Mac, Inverness-shire (1996).

(to) go and see the vicar and book a seat for evensong To go to the LAVATORY. 'An uncle of mine many years ago, when wanting to visit the loo, would say, "Shan't be long, just going to see the vicar and book a seat for evensong"' – Miss Nonnie P. Jaram, Isle of Wight (1998).

(to) go and see what time it is on the market clock To go to the LAVATORY. 'My mother always said: "I'm just going to see what time it is with the market clock"' – Frank J. Thomas, Bedfordshire (1995).

(to) go and shake hands with an old friend / the bishop / the unemployed / the wife's best friend To go to the LAVATORY. Date of origin unknown, although the 'friend' version was associated with the Australian cartoon character Barry McKenzie in *Private Eye* by 1971. *Partridge/Catch Phrases* also lists the variations: '... with my best friend', '... with an old friend', '... with the unemployed'. Also: 'I am just going to shake hands with the father of my son.'

(to) go and shake the dew from one's orchid To go to the LAVATORY. Told to me at a W.I. Federation meeting in Cumbria-Westmorland (1997). Compare: '"Must shake the dew off my violet" – said by my father' – Dave Hopkins, Kent (1998).

(to) go and shed a tear (for Nelson) To go to the LAVATORY. Date of origin unknown. Variations include, 'I'm just **going to shed a tear for the widows and orphans**' – adduced by Molly Anderson, Herefordshire (1996). 'My friend Floss always says "I'm just going to shed a tear"' – Ruby A. Richardson, Cleveland (1996).

(to) go and sit on the throne and rain over my subjects To go to the LAVATORY. 'My favourite expression is "I am going to sit on the throne and rain over my subjects"' – Hazel Stretton-Ballard, Buckinghamshire (1996).

(to) go and splash one's clogs as one's back teeth are all awash To go to the LAVATORY. Reported by John Hill, Dorset (1996).

(to) go and squeeze a peach To go to the LAVATORY. 'My late and very dear friend James McLean was for eleven years Private Secretary to HM Sultan Qaboos Bin Saeed Sultan of Oman. James always leaned forward and down to my ear especially at cocktail parties and whispered "Where can I go to squeeze a peach?"' – Allan Wilson, Merseyside (1996). 'A friend of mine, who is eight months pregnant, said as she headed for the loo: "I must go and squeeze a kidney!"' – Sonja Bailey, Kent (1995). Hardly a euphemism at all ...

(to) go and stand up To go to the LAVATORY. The poet John Betjeman's term for urinating was 'standing up' (as opposed to 'sitting down', naturally). He would say: 'I must go and stand up' – *Letters*, ed. Candida Lycett Green, vol. 1 (1994). 'As a very small boy I knew no other expressions than that I wanted "to stand up" (or "to sit down"), which seemed logically obvious and simple to me, but I can't remember what my sisters used to say' – Peter Newbolt, Norfolk (1997).

(to) go and telephone Hitler To go to the LAVATORY. 'In France in the war, members of the Resistance used to say "I'm going to telephone Hitler"' – Mrs Nan Bourne, West Midlands (1997). I recall that my uncle, Group Captain Tom Gleave, a Battle of Britain pilot, used to say 'I'm going to make a telephone call to Hitler.' Were he to be called away again, he would say 'Here comes the reply ...' Compare (TO) MAKE A CALL.

(to) go and turn one's bike round To go to the LAVATORY. Widely used, as in 'I'm just going to turn my bike round'. 'I have heard that one being used here in Suffolk and was given this explanation. Back in the days when policemen used cycles on the beat, the Suffolk and Norfolk bobbies would meet on the county boundary. They had a chat, attended to the wants of nature, then "turned their bikes round", hence the old saying!' – Marie Laflin, Suffolk (1995). 'At a recent tennis tournament at our small village club one of our ladies (middle-aged like myself) left the court saying "I'm just going to turn the *vicar's* bike round"' – Mrs H. Ball, Buckinghamshire (1996).

(to) go and wash one's hands To go to the LAVATORY. 'Friends of ours had a Swiss student staying with them to improve his English and he had been told that the British always say

"Would you like to wash your hands?" if inquiring whether a visitor wished to use the lavatory. So one day our friends brought him to afternoon tea with us and we first of all wandered around our large garden. On entering the house afterwards, I really thought Willy needed to wash his hands, but upon asking him, he replied, "Oh, no thank you. I have washed my hands behind a bush in your garden!"' – Anon., Cambridgeshire (1996). And then there is: '(to) wash one's hands before the train gets into the station' – Mr O. Barry, West Sussex (1996).

(to) go and wash the car To go to the LAVATORY. Reported by Margaret Walsh, Auckland, New Zealand (1987).

(to) go and water the horse(s) To go to the LAVATORY. '"I'm just going to water the horse" (spoken with a strong Black Country accent)' – Frank Deakin, Cheshire (1996).

(to) go and water the lilies To go to the LAVATORY. Reported by Margaret Walsh, Auckland, New Zealand (1987).

(to) go and wring out one's socks To go to the LAVATORY. 'My usual saying, "I've got to go and wring out my socks"' – Ted Farley, Kent (1996).

(to) go before To die. See GONE BEFORE

(to) go down the tubes To be lost, finished, in trouble. An Americanism meaning 'to go down the drain', where 'toob' = 'drain'. First recorded in the early 1960s.

(to) go for a quick burst on the banjo To go to the LAVATORY. 'A former colleague and friend used to say: "I'm going for a quick burst on the banjo." He picked it up when doing his National Service in the RAF. Apparently, the colloquial Japanese word for latrine is "benjo"' – Douglas J. Bolger, Dorset (1995).

(to) go for a sweet one To go to the LAVATORY. 'I knew a refined lady who used to go for "a sweet one" (= a sweet pea)' – Mrs D.M. Broom, Berkshire (1996).

(to) go for a wee walk To go to the LAVATORY. 'A friend with whom I used to ramble said, on wishing to disappear into the bushes, "I'm just going for a wee walk"' – Winifred Marks, West Midlands (1996).

go forth and multiply Fuck off. You might think it was in the Bible but the King James version of the Old Testament does not contain these words. The nearest is Genesis 1:28: 'Be fruitful and multiply.' Presumably, 'Go forth' is a phrase made up to sound biblical.

(to) go forth / be promoted to Higher Service To die. 'In happy memory ... of Allen Mawer ... who went forth to Higher Service on July 22, 1942' – In Memoriam notice in *The Times* (8 May 1945).

(to) go into a decline To have CONSUMPTION or any disease in which the body gradually fails. In the 18th/19th centuries. Fanny Burney wrote in her 1790 diary of the 'general opinion that I was falling into a decline'.

(to) go North To go to the LAVATORY. 'When I was a Girl Guide many years ago we used to call it "going north". Can you imagine our amazement when one day the main headline in one of the national papers read: King Goes North – Crowds Flock To See Him. It's absolutely true – I swear it!' – Norah Mayland, West Midlands (1996). It has been suggested that this usage may have been inspired by Noël Coward's song 'The Stately Homes of England' (1938): 'And the lavatory makes you fear the worst. / It was used by Charles the First, / Quite informally, / And later by George the Fourth / On the journey North.' *Punch* (28 August 1886) had the headline 'Going North!', but over a piece on trains.

(to) go out with To stay at home and have SEXUAL INTERCOURSE with (a partner). 'Going out with' or 'walking out with' or 'stepping out with' or simply 'seeing' someone are time-honoured ways of referring to courtship or 'being in one another's company'. The terms sit rather oddly on the possible true nature of the relationship. '[A "sex inspector" says] One photo is of my hip, the other is of my shoulder. They could be anything and were taken when I went out with a photographer' – *The Independent* (7 September 2005).

(to) go out without one's hat on To ignore another person. Perhaps originally from going to an outdoor privy. 'In our family, "He's gone out without his hat on" means that whoever you're speaking to, isn't listening (usually because they are reading the newspaper!)' – Betty Walker, Merseyside (1998). Partridge/*Slang* has 'hat on = formally dressed', which may not be much help.

(to) go slow To disrupt work as part of INDUSTRIAL ACTION. Originally, the action would take the form of performing normal work in as slow a manner as possible but then came to include non-cooperation and non-performance. By 1930. A 'go slow' on the railways would, of course, be literal. 'Drivers on the Morden–Edgware tube and the Bakerloo line had been adopting a "go-slow" policy because, it is alleged, they resented being reprimanded by inspectors for speeding on bends' – *Daily Herald* (11 February 1937).

(to) go through To go to the LAVATORY. 'I trained as a nurse at Barts in the 1940s and the expression used by us was "going through". The saying originated because in years gone by the sisters lived on the wards and had their bedrooms at the far end, but no toilet facilities. When they wanted to go to the loo at night a bell was rung and the patients put the bed clothes over their faces as sister "went through"' – Mrs E.M. Richard (1996).

(to) go to a better place To die. By the 18th century. Hence, presumably: 'It is a far, far better thing that I do than I have ever done; it is a far, far better rest that I go to, than I have ever known' – Charles Dickens, *A Tale of Two Cities* (1859), bk 3, ch. 15.

(to) go to do a job no one else can do for one To go to the LAVATORY. *Partridge/Catch Phrases* suggests this dates from about 1950.

(to) go to it To have SEXUAL INTERCOURSE. Since the 16th century. 'Die for adultery! No: / The wren goes to't, and the small gilded fly / Does lecher in my sight' – *King Lear* (1605), IV.vi.112. Literally, 'to act vigorously, set to with a will'. Hence, the slogan 'Go to it!', chosen somewhat daringly for a voluntary labour force in the Second World War. In the summer of 1940, the British Minister of Supply, Herbert Morrison, called for such a force in words that echoed the public mood after Dunkirk. The slogan was used in a campaign run by the S.H. Benson agency (which later indulged in self-parody on behalf of Bovril, with 'Glow to it' in 1951–2).

(to) go to La Pomme To go to the LAVATORY. 'Many years ago when I was nursing, the term used was "La Pomme". I never discovered why' – Mrs B. Jenkins, Cardiff (1996). 'The toilet at the Royal Victoria Infirmary [Newcastle] was "the La-Pom"' – A.O. Harbron, Tyne and Wear (1996). Now how did this come about? I can only observe that, in French, *la pomme d'arrosoir* = the rose of a watering can, and that *c'est une pomme à l'eau* = he's / she's a real twerp, nurd. Also there is the fact that 'la' = lavatory / latrine in certain Australian usage.

(to) go to meet one's maker To die. By the 1930s. Winston Churchill said in a speech on his 75th birthday (30 November 1949): 'I am ready to meet my Maker. Whether my Maker is ready for the ordeal of meeting me is another matter.' This euphemism is one of the roll-call in the *Monty Python's Flying Circus* 'Dead Parrot' sketch, first shown on BBC TV (7 December 1969). A man (named Praline in the script) who has just bought a parrot that turns out to be dead, registers a complaint with the pet shop owner in these words: 'This parrot is no more. It's ceased to be. It's expired. It's gone to meet its maker. This is a late parrot ...'

(to) go to one's death To be killed (in war, battle). 'Sometimes the band played "Destiny", the waltz so popular just before the war which had been the last tune, played on a squeaky gramophone, heard by thousands of young men before they went to their deaths' – Barbara Cartland, *We Danced All Night* (1970).

(to) go to page 54 To go to the LAVATORY. Joan Hassall (1906–88) was an artist and wood engraver. Betty Roe told me (1995) that this was Joan's polite way of referring to the matter. 'I'm going to page 54,' she would say.

(to) go to Paris To go to the LAVATORY. 'In my House at school it was traditional to say "I'm going to Paris" for the lavatory – which, not surprisingly, distressed the French under-matron' – Philippa Lawrence, Wiltshire (1996). Presumably, this derives from 'to go to P'?

(to) go to the gents / ladies To go to the LAVATORY. See GENTLEMEN'S / GENTS; LADIES.

(to) go to / pay a visit to the House of Commons To go to the LAVATORY. 'Our juniors have an interest in the Old English word for faeces. They use it a lot – the ones from polite homes do, I mean homes that talk of No. 2 and "going to the House of Commons"' – A.S. Neill, *That Dreadful School* (1937), ch. 7.

go to the lavatory See hereabouts and also grouped as a theme at LAVATORY, GOING TO THE.

(to) go to the off-stump To go to the LAVATORY. 'Among a group of my friends – all ex-Army National Service – we use the expression "going to the off-stump". This derives from a cricket commentary we once heard where the commentator said

something like – "He's just had a slash over the off-stump"' –
Rex Lanham, Hampshire (1996).

(to) go up the dubs To go to the LAVATORY. 'In the 'thirties
I went to a small village school in Wales, and when we wished to
visit the lavatories, we would say, "I'm going up the dubs." I've
never heard that expression since I left that school but only
recently did I realise that it must have been a shortened version
of WCs' – Mrs Thelma Collyer, Kent (1996).

(to) go up the river To go to jail. Because Sing Sing gaol
lies up the Hudson River from New York City. Known by 1891.
'I done it. Send me up the river. Give me the hot seat' –
Chicago Daily News (5 March 1946).

(to) go upstairs (1) To go to the LAVATORY. Even in flats or
bungalows. Since early in the 20th century? Not to be confused
with: (2) To have SEXUAL INTERCOURSE, as in 'They went
upstairs together.' 'As is the case with brothels throughout
Germany, the Leierkasten make much of their profit on the
drinks alone. A 100ml glass of weak beer will cost you something
like €15. A gin and tonic around €25. And if you'd like "to go
upstairs", that'll be another €100 for the basics' –
toytownmunich.com (18 January 2005).

(to) go west To die. Dates back to the 16th century and alludes
to the setting of the sun and may have entered American Indian
usage by 1801. However, another theory is that the term alludes
to the practice of taking condemned criminals westward out of
London to be executed at Tyburn. Additionally, the west gate of
Roman and Greek towns led to both the place of execution and
the cemetery. The pharaohs were buried on the west bank of the
Nile, and it seems that Egyptians referred to death as 'going
unto the western land'.

(to) go where kings go alone To go to the LAVATORY. 'I was
working in an office and a female Latvian sat next to me. When
a male member of staff had left the office and was wanted on the

phone etc., our Latvian friend would say: "He has gone where Kings go alone." Similarly when a female was missing, she had always gone "where the Queen goes alone"' – Miss Rosemary C. Black, West Midlands (1995). The Revd John Hagreen, Kent (1996), added: 'I heard the euphemism "*Où le roi va seul*" in southern France in the late 1920s.' Prof. Robin Jacoby, Oxfordshire (1999), mentioned the Russian euphemisms: 'I'm going where even the Tsar goes on foot' and 'I'm going where even the Tsar removes his gloves.' Compare: 'A place where even the King goes on foot – *enfin*, the toilet chamber' – Aldous Huxley, *Time Must Have a Stop* (1946).

God's acre A graveyard. More of a poetic alternative name than a full euphemism, but still. From a modern German phrase, according to the *OED2*. 'I like that ancient Saxon phrase, which calls / The burial ground God's Acre! / ... This is the field and acre of our God, / This is the place where human harvests grow' – H.W. Longfellow, 'God's Acre' (1844).

Godfrey Daniel! God damn you! Euphemistic expletive used by W.C. Fields in 1930s films to circumvent the strict Hollywood Hay's Code. Apparently, 'Godfrey' was a standard oath substitute from the early 1900s, in American use only. So, this is another 'minced oath' – like GORDON BENNETT! But who was Godfrey Daniel ... ?

(a) golden handshake A large compensatory payment made on dismissal or compulsory retirement. By 1960. Similarly, **golden handcuffs** are a payment made to deter a valued employee from leaving.

(a) golden-ager An old age pensioner. Another valiant attempt to come up with a gentler term – this was current in the US by 1961 – but it seems not to have weathered the trip across the Atlantic. Compare: 'The Japanese have a more elegant turn of phrase. Old age used to be known as the "silver age". Now jitsunen, meaning the "age of fruition", is replacing it' – *The Times* (22 January 1992). Similarly **the golden years** are those of retirement and old age. One suspects an American origin here.

(not dead / lost but) gone before Dead. A euphemism of condolence and bereavement. According to Benham's *Book of Quotations* (1907) 'Not lost but gone before' was the title of a song published in Smith's *Edinburgh Harmony* (1829), and it is one of the standard epitaphs now imprinted on countless graves. It may have been popularized by its use as the title of a poem by Caroline Norton (1808–77), which goes: 'For death and life in ceaseless strife, / Beat wild on this world's shore, / And all our calm is in that balm – / Not lost but gone before.'

The variant form occurs in *Human Life* (1819) by Samuel Rogers: 'Those whom he loved so long and sees no more, / Loved, and still loves – not dead – but gone before.' However, according to *Mencken's Dictionary of Quotations* (1942), the phrase occurs in one of Alexander Pope's epitaphs for 'Elijah Fenton, Easthampstead, England' (*circa* 1731) – though this one is not included in *Pope's Poetical Works*: 'Weep not, ye mourners, for the dead, / But in this hope your spirits soar, / That ye can say of those ye mourn, / They are not lost but gone before.'

And to Philip Henry (1631–96) is ascribed the couplet: 'They are not *amissi*, but *praemissi*; / Not lost but gone before.' Seneca wrote: *Non amittuntur sed praemittuntur* ['They are not lost but sent before'].

So the concept is, indeed, a very old one. The simple phrase 'gone before' meaning 'dead' was well established in English by the early 16th century. In *Heaven's Command* (1973), James Morris quotes the epitaph on Lt Christopher Hyland of the 62nd Regiment, who died in Bermuda in 1837: 'Alas, he is not lost, / But is gone before.' In 1982, a woman's gravestone was reported from Canada 'some years ago' that had: 'Dry up your tears, and weep no more, / I am not dead, but gone before, / Remember me, and bear in mind / You have not long to stay behind.'

A modern version of this would be 'he/she has **gone on ahead**' – which I first heard in 1998.

gone for a Burton Dead. Early in the Second World War, an RAF expression arose to describe what had happened to a missing person, presumed dead. He had 'gone for a Burton', meaning that he had gone for a drink (*in the drink* = the sea) or, as another phrase put it, 'he'd bought it'. Folk memory has it that during the 1930s 'Gone for a Burton' had been used in advertisements to promote a Bass beer known in the trade as 'a Burton' (though, in fact, several ales are produced at Burton-on-Trent). More positive proof is lacking. An advert for Carlsberg in the 1987 Egon Ronay *Good Food in Pubs and Bars* described Burton thus: 'A strong ale, dark in colour, made with a proportion of highly-dried or roasted malts. It is not necessarily brewed in Burton and a variety of strong or old ales were given the term.' Other fanciful theories are that RAF casualty records were kept in an office above or near a branch of Burton Menswear in Blackpool, and that Morse Code instruction for wireless operators/air gunners took place in a converted billiards hall above Burton's in the same town (and failure in tests meant posting off the course – a fairly minor kind of 'death'). Probably no more than a coincidental use of the name Burton and there are numerous other explanations for this involving other Burtons.

gone to one's eternal rest Dead. Hence, presumably, 'It is a far, far better thing that I do than I have ever done; it is a far, far better rest that I go to, than I have ever known' – Charles Dickens, *A Tale of Two Cities* (1859), bk 3, ch. 15.

(a) good career move Death – if you are a pop star or someone concerned about your reputation. Any number of pop stars have had their record sales enhanced by an untimely death. On hearing of Truman Capote's death in 1984, Gore Vidal pronounced it a 'Good career move' and this was confirmed by him in BBC TV *Gore Vidal's Gore Vidal* (1995). According to *Time* Magazine (8 April 1985), the graffito 'Good career move' had earlier appeared following Elvis Presley's death in 1977.

(a) good fellow A rake. A term used in Victorian club land. 'Oh, the immeasurable distance between a good man and a good fellow! A dissipated, self-indulgent man, like all the others in his set' – Rhoda Broughton, *Not Wisely but Too Well* (1867).

(we are just) good friends We are indeed having a sexual relationship but we are not going to admit to you, matey. This clichéd way for persons in the public eye, when being quizzed by the journalists, to express that their relationship with another is not sexual or romantic is just a fobbing-off phrase. Often the truth of the situation is otherwise. In James Joyce, *Ulysses* (1922), there occurs the original and straightforward form: 'They would be just good friends like a big brother and sister without all that other.'

The phrase probably established itself in the US during the 1930s, though in the film of Cole Porter's musical *Silk Stockings* (US 1957), the phrase is used several times as if not clichéd yet. 'The old fathead had got entirely the wrong angle on the relations between his ewe lamb and myself, we being just good friends, as the expression is' – P.G. Wodehouse, *Stiff Upper Lip, Jeeves* (1963), ch. 2.

From *Vivien: The Life of Vivien Leigh* by Alexander Walker (1987): 'At Cherbourg, Jack [Merivale – Vivien's lover when her marriage to Laurence Olivier was ending in 1960] experienced for the first time the bruising intrusiveness of the British Press who boarded the ship *en masse* to interrogate Vivien's handsome travelling companion. In self-defence, he fell back on the old "just good friends" cliché.' Now used as a consciously humorous evasion, especially when not true. A BBC sitcom current in 1984 was called *Just Good Friends* and several songs about that time also had the title.

(a) good-time girl A prostitute or a promiscuous amateur. Originally, by 1928, merely a pleasure-seeking girl.

(found under a) gooseberry bush How babies are born. Known by 1903. 'Many children said they were glad to *know* what

happened, and not be fobbed off with a lot of gooseberry bushes'
– *The Guardian* (28 October 1969).

Gordon Bennett! A euphemism for, presumably,
'Gorblimey', itself a euphemism for 'God blind me!' or similar
oaths including the word 'God'. It had a resurgence of popularity
in the Britain of the early 1980s. Understandably, people shrink
from blaspheming and 'Oh Gawd!' is felt to be less offensive than
'Oh God!' Around 1900, it was natural for people facetiously
to water down the exclamation 'God!' by saying 'Gordon!' The
name Gordon Bennett was to hand. The initial letters of the
name also had the explosive quality found in 'Gorblimey! [God
blind me!]'. But who was this man?
   James Gordon Bennett II (1841–1918) was the editor-in-chief
of the *New York Herald*, the man who sent Henry Morton Stanley to
find Dr Livingstone in Africa, and altogether quite a character.
He was exiled to Paris after a scandal but somehow managed to
run his New York newspaper from there. He disposed of some
$40 million in his lifetime. He offered numerous trophies to
stimulate French sport and, when the motor car was in its
infancy, presented the Gordon Bennett cup to be competed for.
He became, as the *Dictionary of American Biography* puts it, 'one of the
most picturesque figures of two continents'. This, if anything
does, probably explains why it was *his* name that ended up on
people's lips and why they did not go around exclaiming,
'Gordon of Khartoum!' or 'Gordon Selfridge!' or anything
else. Gordon Bennett was a man with an amazing reputation.
   'The plats de jour were ready, the sauces simmering; [but] not a
stove, not a hotplate was free. "Gordon Bennett," said the chef.
But the restaurant was in all the guides' – *The Guardian*
(24 June 1995).

grain-consuming units Livestock. As reported by the Plain
English Campaign and quoted in the *Northern Echo* (13 May 1997).

(a) grand horizontal / *grande horizontale* A prostitute.
From the French term. In English by 1888.

(a) grass widow A divorced woman or one apart from her
husband (because his job or some other preoccupation has taken
him elsewhere) and who does not, er, let the grass grow under
her feet. It originally meant an unmarried woman who had sexual
relations with one or more men – perhaps *on the grass* rather than
in the lawful marriage bed – and had had a child out of wedlock.
This sense was known by the 16th century. Later it seems to have
been applied to women in British India who were sent up to the
cool hill country (where grass grows) during the hottest season of
the year. An alternative derivation is from 'grace widow' or even
'Grace Widow', the name of an actual person.

(a) gratuity A tip. Since the 16th century. Hence, such modern-
day notices as: 'The attendants at this restaurant are forbidden to
accept gratuities.'

(to climb aboard the) gravy train To gain access to a
money-spinning scheme. Since the 1920s. This was an American
expression originally, possibly in sporting circles. An alternative
version is 'to climb aboard the gravy *boat*', which is a bit easier to
understand. Gravy boats exist for holding gravy in and take their
name from their shape. So, if money is perceived as being like
gravy, it is not hard to see how the expression arose. According to
Webster's Dictionary, the 'train' and 'boat' forms have been equally
popular in the US since the 1920s. 'Boat' is probably less popular
in the UK.

(the) great and the good / good and the great
Establishment figures – those who are on a British Government
list from which are selected members of Royal Commissions
and committees of inquiry. In 1983 the list stood at some 4,500
names. For the previous eight years, custodians of the list had
sought more women, more people under 40 and more from
outside the golden triangle of London and the South-East in an
attempt to break the stereotype enshrined in Lord Rothschild's
parody of it as containing only 53-year-old men 'who live in the
South-East, have the right accent and belong to the Reform
Club'.

In the 1950s, the Treasury division that kept the list was actually known as the 'G and G'. On one occasion, it really did nominate two dead people for service on a public body. 'At one level, the famous "List of the Good and Great", to which governments resort ... has added to the gaiety of the nation' – *The Times* (22 January 1983). 'A secret tome of *The Great and the Good* is kept, listing everyone who has the right, safe qualifications of worthiness, soundness and discretion; and from this tome came the stage army of committee people' – Anthony Sampson, *Anatomy of Britain Today* (1965).

(the) great game Power politics – specifically the struggle for power between Britain and Russia in the debatable lands of Central Asia, notably Afghanistan, in the late 19th century. Indeed, if we are talking about British imperialism, the term takes on the additional aspect of defence of the (British) realm as performed by heroic individuals. This is what Peter Hopkirk's book *The Great Game: on Secret Service in High Asia* (1990) is all about. The phrase was apparently coined in the 1830s and widely used from the 1870s onwards. 'When he comes to the Great Game he must go alone – alone, and at peril of his head' – Rudyard Kipling, *Kim* (1901), ch. 7; 'Some John Buchan hero, busily playing the Great Game for Queen and Country' – *The Guardian* (17 March 1961); 'Originally the Secret Service was entrusted to amateurs who played "the great game", as they romantically called it' – John Welcome, *Hard to Handle* (1964), ch. 2; 'The extensive action of *The Mulberry Empire* swirls between two great cities – London and Kabul – in the years that saw Afghanistan first become embroiled in the Great Game' – *The Observer* (2 March 2003).

(to join the) great majority To die – since the 18th century. Edward Yonge's *The Revenge* (1719) has: 'Death joins us to the great majority.' In the Epistle Dedicatory of *Urn-Burial* (1658), Sir Thomas Browne writes of: 'When the living might exceed, and to depart this world could not be properly said to go unto the greatest number.' There is also the Latin phrase *abiit ad plures*. The dying words of Lord Houghton in 1884 were: 'Yes, I am going to join the Majority and you know I have always preferred Minorities.' *Punch* (19 June 1907) carries an exchange between a parson and a parishioner after a funeral: 'Joined the great majority, eh?' 'Oh, I wouldn't like to say that, Sir. He was a good enough man as far as I know.' Sometimes just **the majority**.

Great Scott! Great God! A euphemistic expletive that sounds the same but is not blasphemous. The *Morris Dictionary of Word and Phrase Origins* (1977 edn) states that the expression became popular when the American Winfield Scott was the hero of the Mexican War (1847) and 'probably our most admired general between Washington and Lee'. No rival candidate seems to have been proposed and the origination is almost certainly American. The diary of Private Robert Knox Sneden, published as *Eye of the Storm: A Civil War Odyssey*, entry for 3 May 1864, has: '"Great Scott," who would have thought that this would be the destiny of the Union Volunteer in 1861–2 while marching down Broadway to the tune of "John Brown's Body".' *OED2*'s earliest British English example dates from 1885.

(one's) grey hairs / white hairs One's old age. Both forms have been used since the 16th century. Cardinal Wolsey's deathbed words (in 1530) are reported to have been: 'I see the matter against me how it is framed. But if I had served God as diligently as I have done the King, he would not have given me over in my grey hairs.'

(a) greybeard An old man. A term of respect of some antiquity – certainly dating from the time when old men were characterized by their beards. As indicated by Byron in *The Prisoner of Chillon* (1816): 'My hair is grey, but not with years.' Similarly, the title of a popular book of 1671, *A Cap of Gray Hairs for a Green Head*, with its explanatory subtitle, *Or the Fathers Counsel to his Son*.

(the) Grim Reaper Death. The terms 'The Reaper', 'The Great Reaper', 'The Old Reaper' come from the portrayal of Death carrying a scythe, though none seems to be recorded before the 1830s. 'The Grim Reaper' would appear to be a

20th-century coinage but currently perhaps the most used.
However, there are reports that 'old Mr Grim' was used in the
18th century. 'The Grim Reaper has been rather too vigorously
at work among us ... At least ten of the best have gone' –
New Statesman (2 September 1977).

gross indecency Sodomy or bestiality. A legal euphemism since
the 19th century.

(a) guerrilla A terrorist. By 1801. Originally (from the Spanish
guerrilla, a diminutive for *guerra*, 'war') used to describe those
taking part in irregular warfare. The euphemistic use became
more pointed in the second half of the 20th century.

(a) guest house A boarding house. Since the 1920s at least, in
this elevated sense.

(a) guest of Her / His Majesty A prisoner. In the US, a
guest of Uncle Sam.

Hh

haemorrhaging / hemorrhaging Bleeding. Possibly of American origin. By the 1920s?

haemorrhoids Piles. The medical term for this condition has been around since the 14th century and nicely distances ones thoughts from the matter in hand.

hair loss Balding. Also **hair-receding** and **hair-thinning**. All terms encountered by the 1970s.

(the) hair of the dog The drink of a drunk on the morning after; another drink of the same to attempt to cure a hangover. Perhaps originally, 'the hair of the dog *that bit me*', alluding to the old belief that a bite from a mad dog could be cured if you put hair from the same dog's tail on the wound. Known by 1760 but this unconfirmed couplet is said to date from 1546: 'I pray thee let me and my fellow have / A haire of the dog that bit us last night.'

(a) hair stylist A ladies' hairdresser (in the UK) or barber (in the US). In the UK since the 1930s. In the US, quoted in Willard R. Espy, *An Almanac of Words at Play* (1975).

hair-disadvantaged Bald/balding. A PC euphemism, known by 1992.

(a men's) hairdresser A barber. This term was substituted for the original from the 1960s/70s onwards. Perhaps it was thought to be a bit more elevated or perhaps it was because 'barber' had lost its meaning when shaving in a shop became unfashionable (that word comes from Latin *barba*, a beard). 'Hairdresser' had been used for 'barber' by the 18th century, however.

(a) hair-piece A wig. Strictly speaking, a hair-piece is a clump of hair used to supplement natural growth on part of the head but the term has been used in the US since the 1930s as one of several alternatives for the unmentionable w-word.

half-seas-over Half-drunk, almost-drunk. 'Half-seas-over' originally, by the 16th century, meant 'half way across the sea', then came to signify a half-way position between one thing and another. Finally, by 1700, it had acquired this meaning. 'Our friend the Alderman was half seas over before the bonfire was out' – *The Spectator*, No. 616 (1714).

halitosis Bad breath. Derived from Latin *halitus*, breath, this is one of the several examples of a medical term being popularly adopted because it sounds better or kinder, obscuring reality. Writing about 19th-century patent medicines in *The Pleasure of Your Company* (1972), Jean Latham says: 'Earlier doctors had been content to call a spade a spade and talked about bad breath, if ever they could be bothered to discuss such a minor ailment. A new word was coined later to euphemise this social handicap and "halitosis" became a money-spinner for the enterprising.'

And who did the coining? As a medical term, it was known by 1874 but Listerine mouthwash popularized it hugely, in the US, from 1921. At first, Listerine was promoted as a 'safe antiseptic' with countless hygienic uses. Then, in 1921, the Lambert Company decided to use a clinical term for the ordinary unpleasantness known as 'bad breath'. An anxiety was not only stimulated, it was labelled. Listerine sales climbed from 115,000 a year in 1921 to 4 million a year in 1927. The advertising slogans for it included 'Stops Halitosis!' and also 'For Halitosis, Use Listerine'.

From Rosser Reeves, *Reality in Advertising* (1960): 'Who can steal

"Stops Halitosis" from Listerine? Dozens of other mouth-washes stop halitosis. Many tried to move in on this great classic UNIQUE SELLING PROPOSITION, until it became almost a source of embarrassment to them, seeking ways to phrase their imitation, so that they did not advertise the leader. This U.S.P., in the public's mind, belongs to Listerine.'

'[Of Professor Tancred Borenius] Oh! that halitosis. It's so thick – a greyhound couldn't jump it' – Cecil Beaton, quoted in Hugo Vickers, *Cecil Beaton* (1985); 'Breathtaking New Doritos; The Modified Chip That's Halitosis-free' – *The Washington Post* (23 April 1992).

hallowed ground / soil A graveyard. 'Ground' since the 17th century, 'soil' since the 18th. 'Yet still, beneath the hallow'd soil / The peasant rests him from his toil' – Sir Walter Scott, *Marmion* (1808), Introduction to canto 2.

(a) hampton A penis. From rhyming slang: Hampton Wick (a place on the River Thames) / prick. By the early 20th century. The source of several sly allusions in *The Goon Show* (BBC radio 1951–60) in which mention was made of a character called Hugh Jampton.

(to) hand / pass / turn in one's dinner-pail To die. A dinner-pail is the name for what an American worker would carry his lunch in (from the mid-19th century). These expressions have been current since about 1900. 'A sliced ball, whizzing in at the open window, had come within an ace of incapacitating Raymond Parsloe Devine ... Two inches, indeed, to the right and Raymond must inevitably have handed in his dinner-pail' – P.G. Wodehouse, *The Clicking of Cuthbert* (1922), ch. 1.

(wandering) hand trouble / W.H.T. Inappropriate sexual fondling or groping of a woman by a man. Probably only British middle-class use. Known by the 1950s?

(a) hand-job Masturbation of a male, by another (usually paid) operative. By the 1930s.

(a) handful Difficult to manage, a menace (usually of children). By the second half of the 19th century. 'The troublesome boy ... that is generally described by his attendants as a "handful"' – *The Spectator* (17 January 1891).

(a) handicap A mental or physical disability. Disapproval of the word 'handicap' on the grounds that it alludes to being 'cap in hand' is questionable etymology. While it is true that 'handicap' in this sense derives from 'handicap' in the sporting sense of a 'disadvantage imposed on a competitor to make the chances more equal', the origin of this word has something obscurely to do with a 'hand i' cap' or 'hand in the cap'. Referring to physical and mental disabilities, especially in children, the word has been used since at least the 1910s. Disapproval has given rise to attempts to find a PC euphemism for this euphemism.

The words **inconvenienced** and **handi-capable** are sometimes employed to put a more positive slant on the problem, though whether 'inconvenienced' can be considered more positive is hard to say. 'If anything "the handicapped" is worse than "the disabled" as a blanket term because handicap can only be assessed in individual cases. It should not be used' BBC 'Guide to the Representation of People With Disabilities in Programmes', compiled by Geoffrey Prout (1990). 'The word "handicapped" carries powerful associations of disabled people as passive objects of charity, rather than individuals' – Briefing Note, The Royal Association for Disability and Rehabilitation (May 1992).

(a) handy little gadget A penis. This derives from the age-old remark from a little girl to a little boy when he dropped his trousers – 'My, that's a handy little gadget!' I date it 'by 1941' but in 2003, Alison Parker told me that her husband John heard it from his father in about 1922. 'John remembers his father telling him that two small children were taken on a picnic, and the rugs etc. were laid out in a corner of a field. After a while the little boy and girl wanted to spend pennies, so they walked over to some long grass at the edge of the field. The little girl squatted in it and discovered, too late, that it was full of nettles. The little boy had no such problems, and the little girl remarked, "My, that's a handy gadget to have on a picnic."'

I first included my version in a little collection I made of children's remarks entitled *Babes and Sucklings* (1983) and I specifically mentioned 'handy little gadget' as coming from the common stock of 'traditional' sayings that – as I found when compiling my earlier *Eavesdroppings* – does not prevent people from claiming it as their own. It had, I said, reached me from several sources. One said that it involved 'the daughter of a friend', another that 'it was told me by a friend who was a teacher about the local primary school at which he taught', and a third specifically said it concerned 'our 2-year-old son'.

(to) hang someone out to dry To punish by isolating a person from their group. Date of origin unknown. Probably American. 'Nasser has been hung out to dry; he could do nothing about it' – Mike Gatting, quoted in *The Observer* (16 February 2003); 'Even Mr Blair, America's most trusty ally but in dire political straits at home if he fails to get UN blessing, was hung out to dry' – *The Independent* (8 March 2003).

(to) hang up one's hat To die. By the 1940s, probably American in origin.

(a) happening An improvised theatrical event or deeply meaningful, possibly provocative act, supposedly of some significance but often disorganized and embarrassing to watch. An early example occurred at the Edinburgh Festival Drama Conference in 1963 when a nude woman was wheeled across a gallery above the speakers. A piper played, uproar ensued, and few delegates were any the wiser.

happy Slightly drunk. By the 18th century. 'To express the Condition of an Honest Fellow ... under the effects of good fellowship, it is said that he is ... Happy' – *The Gentlemen's Magazine*, No. 40 (1770).

(a) happy event The birth of a baby. Since the late 19th century.

(the) happy hunting grounds Death / the afterlife. A translation of the North American Indian name for 'heaven, paradise', the phrase is now also used of any field that appears fruitful. H.L. Mencken's *The American Language*, 4th edn (1947) has: 'There was also some translation of terms supposed to be in use among the Indians, e.g., squaw-man, heap big chief, Great White Father, Father of Waters, and happy hunting-grounds, but most of these, I suspect, owed more to the imagination of the pioneers than to the actual usage of the Indians.' In Supplement I (1945), Mencken says that 'happy hunting-grounds' was apparently first introduced by James Fenimore Cooper in his novel *Pathfinder* (1840). In fact, he also has it in *The Pioneers, or the Sources of the Susquehanna* (1823), ch. 38: 'Hawk-eye! my fathers call me to the happy hunting-grounds.' There is some doubt as to whether Cooper's Indianisms are genuine, however. 'My faithful Jasper [a spaniel] has gone to the happy hunting grounds' – Daphne du Maurier, *Rebecca* (1938), ch. 2.

hard of hearing Deaf. By the mid-19th century. Dickens has 'I am hard of hearing' in *Great Expectations* (1861), ch. 37. Also, **heavy of hearing** has been known as a variant. Now not considered a very PC euphemism – **with hearing difficulties** or **hearing impaired** preferred. As 'impaired hearing' this second term has been in use for some time: 'Ear phones ... are the most serviceable present means of aiding impaired hearing' – J.F. Barnhill, *Nose, Throat and Ear*, No. 583 (1928).

hard up Impecunious. Since the early 19th century. 'You don't feel nearly so hard up with elevenpence in your pocket as you do with a shilling' – J.K. Jerome, *Idle Thoughts of an Idle Fellow* (1886), ch. 2.

hardware Armaments. Of American origin. A history of the 5th New York Cavalry (1865) records: 'Capt. Hammond ... charged upon the rebels ... crying as he flew forward, "Give them your hardware, boys!"' 'Microelectronics, developed for American space and military hardware, is a way of miniaturising large circuits' – *The Daily Telegraph* (8 May 1970).

(to) have a motion To DEFECATE. 'Motion(s)' for the evacuation of the bowels has been a term since the 16th century (Shakespeare mentions it). Compare MOVE ONE'S BOWELS.

(to) have a screw loose To be eccentric, insane or mentally retarded. By the early 19th century.

(to) have a whistle To go to the LAVATORY. 'One of the many euphemisms for male urination – particularly among the boating fraternity' – John Phillips, Looe [*sic*], Cornwall (1996).

(to) have it off / away To have sexual intercourse. The notion of a man 'having' a woman in this way goes back to the 16th century (it is in Shakespeare) but these two developments seem to date only from the 20th century. There is also, of course, **to have one's way with** where the implication is that the sex is forced upon the woman. This was known by 1915. Note, however, this unusual reversal: 'Thus could Anne Bonny defend herself when she did not fancy a Man, but when she fancied one, she also had her Way with him' – Erica Jong, *Fanny* (1980), pt 3, ch. 13.

(to) have none of one's chairs at home To be mentally retarded. Elizabeth Monkhouse recalled (1997) that in her bit of Cheshire, 'He's got all his chairs at home' was an expression used to mean, 'He's all there, alert.' Hence, a home without furniture is empty, so 'no chairs at home' = empty headed, no longer at home, no longer 'there'. This was also reported from Lancashire. Meanwhile, Joyce Hanley wrote: 'In Yorkshire, if someone is a bit lacking in the head, we say that they haven't got all their furniture at home.' This information came to me when I was looking at the origin of the phrase 'to lose one's marbles', meaning 'to lose one's faculties', and was wondering whether it could have anything to do with the French word *meubles* (furniture). *Apperson* finds the Lancashire use by 1865, but also has a curious anticipation of the phrase by a man who writes, 'How slender furniture I have at home', referring to his accoutrements of 'eloquence, grace and good success'. See under (TO) LOSE ONE'S MARBLES.

(to) have sex To have SEXUAL INTERCOURSE. The abbreviation may be thought to dull the impact of the words or give the subject a clinical overlay. By 1929 (D.H. Lawrence). 'Why wasn't Bond "more tender" in his love-making? Why did he just "have sex" and disappear?' – *The Listener* (7 June 1962); 'Recently, book store displays were joined by a weighty tome about little grey aliens with blank eyes abducting large numbers of Americans and forcing them to have sex inside spaceships, followed by lectures on ecology' – *Financial Times* (23 July 1994).

(to) have words To have a row or altercation. 'Words' has been used in this way since the 15th century. 'I have lost my best friend & the best of fathers. I never had a word with him in his life' – King George V, quoted in Harold Nicolson, *George V* (1910), ch. 7.

(a) hawk See DOVE

(a/the) head of verbal communications A receptionist. Alleged by Susie Dent in *Fanboys and Overdogs: The Language Report* (2005).

(a) headache Menstruation. Since the 18th century. Hence, the woman's traditional way of declining to have sex: 'I've got a headache.'

health/illness/medical conditions See AS WELL AS CAN BE EXPECTED; BABY BLUES; BIG C; BLACK-COATED WORKERS; CEREBRAL PALSY; CERTAIN DISEASE; CHANGE OF LIFE; CHUNDER; COMFORTABLE; COMPANY; COMPLAINT; CONDITION; CONKED OUT; CONSUMPTION; FALSE TEETH; DOWN'S SYNDROME; EATING DISORDER; EMASCULATE; FARMER GILES; FEMININE COMPLAINT; GASTRIC FLU;

GENDER REASSIGNMENT OPERATION; GIPPY TUMMY; GO
INTO A DECLINE; HAEMORRHAGING; HAEMORRHOIDS;
HALITOSIS; HARD OF HEARING; HERNIA; ILL; IMPAIRED
HEARING; IMPOTENCE; INDISPOSED; INNER CLEANLINESS;
LITTLE VASCULAR ACCIDENT; MONTEZUMA'S REVENGE;
MOTION DISCOMFORT; NOSE SPASM; OFF-COLOUR;
OPENING MEDICINE; PARTIALLY SIGHTED; PERSONAL
HYGIENE; SOCIAL DISEASE; SPANISH TUMMY; SPEECH
DEFECT; SUBSTANCE ABUSE; SURGERY; T.B.; TERMINAL
ILLNESS; UNDER THE WEATHER; UNWELL; VENEREAL
DISEASE; WOMAN'S OPERATION; WORRIER ABOUT HEALTH

(to) hear something to one's advantage To receive good
news of a financial nature – for example, that money has been
left to one in somebody's will. Traditionally, when executors
are not able to contact a beneficiary, a small advertisement has
been placed in newspapers asking that so-and-so should contact
such-and-such solicitors 'where he will hear something to his
advantage'. In *Punch* by 1847. But as this citation shows, the
newspaper notices were not solely concerned with wills: 'If the
Gentleman who travelled from Yeovil Junction ... with a violin
case, will send his address he will hear of something to his
advantage' – *Daily News* (3 November 1882).

(in) heaven Dead or in the afterlife. 'The archbishop's few
public pronouncements have been notably acid. In October
2003, amid speculation that the pope was mortally ill, he said:
"Some journalists who in recent years have spoken and written a
lot about the pope's health are already in heaven"' – *The Independent*
(6 June 2005).

heavily built Large and fat. By about 1900. 'The prize-fighter,
a heavily built young man with a stupid, obstinate, slab-sided
face' – Conan Doyle, *The Case-Book of Sherlock Holmes* (1927), ch. 3.

heavy-going Boring, difficult. Seemingly a 20th century
development of the original meaning about the condition of
ground over which it is difficult to make progress. 'He found

such books heavy going and preferred a detective story' –
J.B. Priestley, *Angel Pavement* (1930), ch. 3.

heavy petting Sexual stimulation without penetration, possibly
to the point of orgasm. By 1960. '[A defending lawyer said that
his client's relationship] never progressed beyond heavy petting
... No intercourse took place, but every other sort of familiarity
did occur' – *Daily Mail* (19 January 1977).

(a) Hebrew A Jew. The word 'Hebrew' was used in the 19th
century to make clear that the word 'Jew' was not being used in
its derogatory sense of usurer, moneylender or extortionate
tradesman. When Laurence Olivier undertook to play Shylock
in a National Theatre production of *The Merchant of Venice* in 1970,
the director was Jonathan Miller, who was disconcerted to find
that Olivier intended to give the part with all the subtlety of
Fagin as he might have been played by Donald Wolfit. 'I do so
love the Hebrew!' Olivier declared (as Miller recalled in a TV
obituary in 1989). Miller responded by suggesting that his love
might be a little more appreciated if he did not wear false teeth
and a larger-than-life false nose. In Anthony Holden, *Olivier*
(1988), ch. 23, Olivier is quoted as replying, 'Certainly, dear
boy, certainly; we must do nothing to offend our beloved
Hebrew brethren ... many of them are, of course, my best
friends.'

(a) help A servant. Although the term has been used since the
17th century, the particular sense of a hired home help seems to
have originated in the US in the early 19th.

(to) help oneself to something To steal. Since the second
half of the 19th century.

(to) help the police (with their inquiries) To be
questioned by the British police about an offence for which one
has not been formally charged. Journalistic stock phrase, now a
cliché, this rather quaint euphemism is trotted out and eagerly
passed on by the media. It is quite possible, of course, that the

suspect in question is, in fact, being quite *unhelpful* to the police in their inquiries and that they are being impolite to him in equal measure. Current by 1957. 'A 17-year-old girl ... was found battered to death ... Later, a man was helping police with their inquiries' – *The Sunday Times* (14 October 1973); 'Woman knifed to death in garden. A man was arrested close to the scene and was later helping police with their inquiries' – *Evening Standard* (London) (23 November 1994); 'Several hurt in North beatings ... After a brief chase, three men were arrested and are now helping police with their inquiries' – *The Irish Times* (13 February 1995).

(the) hereafter Death / the afterlife. Since the 18th century. 'For he sang of ... life undying ... In the land of the Hereafter' – H.W. Longfellow, *Hiawatha* (1855), Pt 6.

(a) hernia A rupture. People seem to have been avoiding the r-word since the 14th century (Chaucer).

herstory History. A word coined by US feminists in the early 1970s as a way of removing the imagined male element from the term history. The 'his' in 'history' has nothing to do with masculinity, but the new term was adopted as a way of pointing out masculinist tendencies in the writing and teaching of history and its usual preoccupation with male historical figures. David Frost in his memoirs (1993) recalls feminists using this word as early as June/July 1969 on *The David Frost Show* on US TV. 'The fluidity and wit of the witches is evident in the ever-changing acronym: the basic, original title was Women's International Terrorist Conspiracy from Hell ... and the latest heard at this writing is Women Inspired to Commit Herstory' – Robin Morgan, *Sisterhood Is Powerful* (1970); 'I have tried to write a herstory of the inner psychic meaning of the ancient religion' – *Peace News* (2 October 1981). Sources include: *The Oxford Dictionary of New Words* (1991).

hesitancy of speech See DIFFICULTY/HESITANCY OF SPEECH

hidden in the earth Dead. An ancient Greek euphemism, now obsolete.

high Drunk. Since 1627 ('He's high with wine'). 'High as a kite' seems to be an Americanism (since the 1930s). Similarly, 'high' means 'under the influence of drugs' (since the 1930s).

(of a) high colour Flushed, red-faced, ruddy, blushing. Since the 17th century.

high-profile Evident. Since the 1960s – the reverse of the more common LOW-PROFILE. 'He [Jimmy Carter] delivered us from the courage of Wallace, and he consented to a high-profile relationship with blacks' – *The Guardian* (3 May 1976).

highly strung Excitable, neurotic. By the 1890s. A development of 'strung-up / strung-out'.

(a) home (1) A mental home, mental institution, lunatic asylum, loony bin, madhouse. Presumably 'loony bin' could also be considered as a euphemism of sorts. These expressions do still have a certain self-conscious currency even among those who administer such places. 'Asylum' was for a time a euphemism for 'lunatic asylum' but that, too, was considered politically correct in the early 19th century when it took over from the previous century's 'lunatic hospital/house' and, especially, was preferred to the 17th century term 'madhouse'. The earliest citation to hand for 'loony bin ... the facetious term for a mental hospital' is from *My Man Jeeves* (1919) by P.G. Wodehouse. Elsewhere, euphemisms rule. Now 'mental home' and 'mental institution' are still reasonably PC usage, though both frequently undergo a further euphemistic layer when used in such statements as 'Oh, he's in a home', 'he's in an institution', or even, 'he's had to be sent away'. 'There is still a strong streak of melancholia in the Lyttelton family ... His youngest son suffers, and from time to time has to go to a home' – James Lees-Milne, *Through Wood and Dale* (1998), diary entry for 18 April 1975.
 (2) An old folks' home. The original by 1915, the euphemism

soon afterwards. 'I deduced that he was the great-grandson of H.E. His mother is alive in a "home"' – James Lees-Milne, *Through Wood and Dale* (1998), diary entry for 28 April 1975.

(a) home entertainment center A combined radio and record-player (in the US). Quoted in Willard R. Espy, *An Almanac of Words at Play* (1975). The equally vague **music centre** also became known in Britain from the early 1970s.

(a) home plaque removal instrument A toothbrush. Cited in Ricks and Michaels, eds, *The State of the Language* (1991). Though surely it could never have caught on?

(a) home-protection officer A dog. This is a joke. 'Before the [1939–45] war a spade used to be called a spade – often brutally so ... But today a dustman has become a refuse collector ... and a dog a home-protection officer' – George Mikes, *How To Be Decadent* (1977).

homely (1) Lacking in refinement. (2) Plain. (3) Ugly. 'It was the homeliest members of your class who became teachers' – Mary McCarthy, *The Group* (1963).

(a) homemaker A housewife. An old word (around since the 1870s at least) which since the late 1970s has been the politically correct term for a housewife – than which there is no worse label in feminist eyes, particularly when self-applied ('What do you do?' – 'Oh, I'm just a housewife, you know ...') Alternatively, **householder** is another acceptable term but it is not clear whether it has caught on to any extent. The male term **househusband** has, against all the odds, gained a good deal of currency (though often uttered a touch self-consciously) to describe the relatively novel situation of a man running a household and looking after the children while his partner goes out to work.

'The Good Negotiator? What's this? A politically correct update of depressing old usage, which no more enhances domesticity than putting "home-maker" in your passport? Not at all. The housewife's near-demise is official. A sharp-eyed couple of advertising executives, Daryl Fielding and Cathy Clift of Lowe Howard-Spink, claim to have identified a new domestic breed and named it appropriately' – *The Guardian* (18 September 1991); 'As working novelist, professor and house-husband (his wife, Maureen Quilligan, is a professor of Renaissance studies at the University of Pennsylvania), he could lead a life of his own design. He could work all night when he wanted to. He could pick up his daughter after school. If he had any complaint, it was that he was a little lonely working at home' – *The Washington Post* (7 February 1992); '"Would you say that to Arthur Miller, who wrote two plays? Would you say: 'You chose to be a home-maker' to him? I've written two books," [Barbara Bush] snapped' – *The Independent* (21 August 1992); 'In 1981, an official from the Royal Borough of Windsor and Maidenhead wrote to a householder asking him to trim his hedge' – *Evening Standard* (London; 3 April 1995).

homosexuality See BENT; BUNNY; CAMP; CONFIRMED BACHELOR; CONSENTING ADULT; DEVIANT; EARNEST; EFFEMINATE; FRIEND OF DOROTHY; GAY; INVERT; LIGHT ON ONE'S TOES; LIKE THAT; LIMP-WRISTED; LOVE THAT DURST NOT SPEAK ITS NAME; MUSICAL; NEVER MARRIED; NOT THE MARRYING KIND; ONE OF THEM/THOSE; OPEN AND AFFIRMING; OTHER WAY; OUT OF THE CLOSET; PINK POUND; PLAY THE PINK OBOE; POOF; QUEER; RENT BOY; SAME-GENDER-ORIENTED; SAPPHIC; SEXUAL ORIENTATION; SHIRTLIFTER; SPECIAL MAN; TAKING LITTLE INTEREST IN THE OPPOSITE SEX; THAT WAY; UNMARRIED; UPHILL GARDENING

(a) honorarium A payment, fee. When applied to voluntary service or to a professional man, the word sounds smarter. Since the 17th century – perhaps much more recently as a euphemism.

(having) honourable intentions With a proposal of marriage in view. When the word 'proposal' connoted such considerations as dowry, division of property and other legalities, a girl's parents might ask the suitor if his intentions were honourable. 19th century.

(a) hooker A prostitute, in American usage. The term probably derives from Corlear's Hook (or 'The Hook'), a part of Manhattan where tarts used to ply their trade in the early 19th century. General Joseph Hooker may have helped popularize the name during the Civil War when an area of Washington DC became known as 'Hooker's Division' on account of the general's camp-followers. The term was well established by 1845, however, before the Civil War and the general came along.

(a) hope / promise of rain A threat of rain, drought. American TV weather-forecasters had to adopt PC terminology, according to *The Daily Telegraph* (14 January 1991).

horizontal aerobics / jogging SEXUAL INTERCOURSE. Late 20th century. 'This is truly, truly awful, but as others here have admitted to dreadful opinions, here's mine: I would really like to go horizontal jogging with Vanessa Feltz. I'd hate to have to chat her up first, though, as I can't stand her opinions' – forum.digitalspy.co.uk (10 November 2005).

(a) Horlick's A mess. By the 1980s. Posh-ish British slang, euphemizing 'bollocks' and employing the name of a well-known malted milk-powder drink. 'Jack Straw yesterday accused the government strategy director, Alastair Campbell, of presiding over "a complete horlicks" when he commissioned, received and published the "dodgy dossier" on Iraq's weapons threat in February' – *The Guardian* (25 June 2003).

(a) horticultural surgeon A tree trimmer (in the US). Quoted in Willard R. Espy, *An Almanac of Words at Play* (1975).

(a) hospice A hospital for the dying or incurable. The first one of these appears to have been in Dublin in the 1890s. Originally the name given to a place offering shelter to pilgrims. As such it was a long-needed euphemism for a 'hospital for incurable diseases', a term known since earlier in the 19th century. At Southsea in 1905 there was a '"Home of Comfort" for the last stage of incurable diseases'. I am not sure whether this euphemism was widely used. 'Before the [1939–45] war a spade used to be called a spade – often brutally so. I remember an institution named Hospital for Incurable Diseases. How gentle, how tactful, I thought, and tried to imagine the feelings of the patient driven through the gates' – George Mikes, *How To Be Decadent* (1977).

(a) hostess A prostitute. Perhaps by the 1930s. 'Many a prostitute, whether she calls herself a ... hostess, or a common whore, imagines that she is exploiting the male sex' – Germaine Greer, *The Female Eunuch* (1970).

hostilities Warfare. Since the 17th century.

hot Obscene (of publications etc). Since the mid-20th century. From the BBC radio show *Hancock's Half-Hour* (29 September 1959): 'Was it your intention to walk through customs with a string vest full of red-hot literature?'

(a) house A brothel. An abbreviation, possibly only in the 20th century, for all the other euphemistic 'house' phrases, e.g. **house of ill fame / ill repute / resort**. These since the 18th century. Hence, *A House Is Not a Home*, the title of the memoirs (1954) of Polly Adler. She was a notable New York madam in the 1920s/30s who finally closed her bordello in 1945 and spent part of her twilight years writing memoirs. Then: 'One day I happened to be spraying a rose-bush in my back yard, and Dora [Maugham] ... was profoundly impressed by this spectacle of suburban domesticity.

"I wonder what the cops would say," she mused, "if they could see you now."

"Oh," said I, "probably they'd be disappointed that my home is not a house." Dora's reaction to this remark was so unusual ...

"Eyeow!" she squealed. "Hold everything! ... Turn that around and you've got it!"

"What on earth are you talking about?"

"'The perfect title for your book ...'"

So far as I was concerned, I told her, it was the most inspired piece of thinking anyone had done in a garden since the day Isaac Newton got conked by an apple.'

When the book was filmed (US 1964), there had, of course, to be a theme song incorporating the title. It managed coyly to avoid any suggestion as to what sort of 'house' was being talked about. Hence, also, 'The House of the Rising Sun' ('There is a house in New Orleans ...'), the title of a song (1964).

'All houses in the suburbs of Vienna must be plucked down' – Shakespeare, *Measure for Measure* (1604), I.ii.88; 'We drove from the station to a remote and squalid door which was opened by a sinister gentleman in dirty pyjamas. We instantly decided the address we had been given was a house of ill fame' – James Lees-Milne, *Caves of Ice* (1983), diary entry for 11 October 1947.

(a) house of correction / detention   A prison or other form of penal institution. Since the 16th century but little used after the 19th century.

(a) housekeeper   A chambermaid. At least, according to Val Dumond in *The Elements of Nonsexist Usage* (New York, 1990). 'While young Kate Hardcastle is dressing as a housekeeper to overcome Marlow's reserve ("stooping to conquer" [in Goldsmith's play]) ...' – *The Washington Post* (22 March 1991).

(a spot of) how's your father   SEXUAL INTERCOURSE. Originally, an innocent catchphrase associated with the British music-hall comedian Harry Tate (1872–1940). Apparently, he would exclaim it as a way of changing the subject and in order to get out of a difficult situation. One account tells of a sketch in which he is on a sofa with a young woman. He was just saying something like, 'Let's get together for a bit of ...' when he saw her father enter the room and hastily said to the girl, 'And how's your dear father?' Possibly this gave rise to the phrase's use as a euphemism for sexual activity (as, 'indulging in a spot of how's-your-father').

It has been suggested that another source for the phrase might be George Robey's song 'In Other Words', written by N. Ayer and C. Grey (1916), of which some versions may contain these lines: 'A student of nature, I walked down the Strand / And there a fair maiden did see. / I didn't know her, but she seemed to know me, / For she said, "How's your father?" to me.'

A comic song performed from the early 1940s onwards by Flanagan and Allen in the character of a World War I veteran and his newly enlisted son contains the lines 'If a grey-haired lady asks "How's your father?", that'll be Madame Moselle' – obviously on the basis that she had been up to some 'how's your father' with the father long ago. This refers to the First World War song 'Mademoiselle from Armentieres' which, in its many versions, does not appear to contain the actual expression 'How's your father?' Whatever the case, the phrase also took on a third use, meaning the same as a 'thingummy' or anything the speaker does not wish to name.

human/personal characteristics/qualities See ADULT MALE; AGENT; ANORAK; BALLS; BASKET CASE; BIG GIRL; BIG GIRL'S BLOUSE; BIT OF A ROGUE; BOHEMIAN; BOTTLE; BROKEN ACCENT; CELEBRITY; CHARM-FREE; CHOSEN PEOPLE; CLIENT; COMPANY DIRECTOR; COUCH POTATO; DEMONSTRATORS; DICK'S HATBAND; DIFFERENTLY INTERESTING; EASY; EARTHY; DISADVANTAGED CHILDREN; ETHICALLY DIFFERENT; ETHICALLY DISORIENTATED; EUMENIDES; FACILITATOR; FISHING FLEET; FORWARD; FUN-LOVING; GENTLEMAN OF LEISURE; GENTLEMEN OF THE PRESS; GOOD FELLOW; GREAT AND THE GOOD; HANDFUL; HEAVY-GOING; HIGH-PROFILE; HIGHLY STRUNG; HOMELY; HUMOROUSLY CHALLENGED; HYGIENICALLY CHALLENGED; LACK OF MORAL FIBRE; LADIES; LAME DUCK; LEFT-FOOTER; LOOSE; LOOSE CANNON; LOW PROFILE; LOW-SPIRITED; LOWER ORDERS; MALADJUSTED CHILD; MAN IN A DARK/GREY SUIT; MATRON; METICULOSITY; MODEL; MUTTON DRESSED AS LAMB; MY NIECE; MYSTERY GIRL; NEW AGE TRAVELLERS; NEW AUSTRALIAN; NO BETTER THAN SHE OUGHT TO BE; NON-VEGETARIAN; OPERATIVE; OUR

BETTERS; OUTSPOKEN; OVER THE TOP; OVER-ACTIVE;
OVER-EMOTIONAL; OVER-FAMILIAR; OVER-INDULGE;
PEEPING TOM; PERSONALITY; PERSONNEL; PETITE; POINTY
HEAD; POODLE; PRESIDENTIAL PARTNER; PROBLEM
FAMILIES; PROLETARIAT; PROTESTERS; PUPPY; RAKE;
RELENTLESS RACONTEUR; SLOW; SOMETHING OF THE
NIGHT; SPARE WHEEL; STAR; TAKING HEAD; TARDATION
IN READING; THOSE IN THE LOWER INCOME BRACKET;
TOUCH OF THE TAR BRUSH; TURNCOAT; UNCLE;
UNCOURAGEOUS; UNDERACHIEVER; UNINHIBITED;
UNINTELLECTUAL; UNSOCIAL ELEMENTS; VICAR OF BRAY;
VIVACIOUS; WORKERS/WORKMEN; WORKFORCE; YOUNG
LADY; YOUTHFUL INDISCRETIONS

humankind Mankind. A PC de-'man'ing. 'To include women
in a word like *man* or *mankind* suggests that they don't merit their
own word, that they must be content to be included in the
generic *man*. Women become conditioned to borrowing men's
descriptions ... work ... and even men's ideas. The result of this
emphasis on men's contributions to civilization is the repetitious
message that women are also-rans, second-class citizens, tag-
alongs, things' – Val Dumond, *The Elements of Nonsexist Usage* (New
York, 1990); 'Columnists hoot at news of students boycotting
the classics, insisting on "humankind" rather than "mankind"' –
The Washington Post (3 February 1991).

humorously challenged Unfunny. Another suggested PC
euphemism from 1991/2. 'Be politically correct around
comedians. Never accuse them of not being funny. Call them
"humorously challenged"' – *The Washington Post* (4 August 1991).

hung See WELL-HUNG

hush money A bribe to ensure hush or silence. Since 1709
(*The Tatler*).

hygienically challenged Dirty, smelly. A nonce phrase waiting
to be coined. Compare the less-than-PC coinage **hygienically**

wanting – (the -*wanting* suffix is not acceptable, as this condition may result from poverty or some other cause for which whatever is so described is not responsible). 'Politically correct washing up liquid gave us plates that were found hygienically wanting compared with your grandmother's kitchen floor' – *The Independent* (10 March 1992).

I i

I hear you I hear what you say but am not going to do anything about it. Scots expression meaning that a remark is not worth considering or is untrue and is certainly not going to be responded to. Notably used by Lord Reith to fob off suggestions by Malcolm Muggeridge in the BBC TV programme *Lord Reith Looks Back* (1967) – 'Presented with an argument that he intended to ignore, Lord Reith would say in a matter-of-fact way: "I hear you." It was an admirably plonking rhetorical device' – *The Listener* (5 May 1977).

ill (1) Drunk. As used by Charlotte Bronte of her brother in a letter to a friend: 'Reaching Haworth from Hathersage at ten o'clock on Saturday night Charlotte found Branwell unexpectedly at home, ill' – this is probably a euphemism for drunk, for Charlotte wrote later: 'He is so, very often, owing to his own fault' – Phyllis Bentley, *The Brontes and Their World* (1947); 'Tommy's ill health was driving everything else from her mind. This time "ill health" was not a euphemism for alcohol-related problems or psychological ones' – Margaret Forster, *Daphne du Maurier* (1993), ch. 20.

(2) Menstruating. (3) Suffering from an unmentionable disease. (4) Mentally unwell.

illegitimate Bastard. Perhaps the main mid-20th century usage for this state. Since the 16th century.

illness See HEALTH

immoral Sexually misbehaved. The specific application of 'morals' to a person's sexual conduct seems to be mostly a 20th century usage. 'Perhaps he smarmed his hair with scented oil, / Perhaps he was "immoral" or a thief. / We did not mind the cause: for Angus now / The game was up' – John Betjeman, *Summoned By Bells* (1960), ch. 7; 'Turk shot sister dead "because of her morals"' – headline in *The Independent* (15 September 2005). Hence, **immoral earnings**, meaning money derived from prostitution, as in 'he lived off her immoral earnings'.

(with) impaired hearing Deaf. By the 1920s.

(to) importune To solicit for the purposes of prostitution. By the 1840s.

impotence Inability to achieve a sexual erection. The specific application to sexual powerlessness dates back to the 17th century. 'My impotence has altered my character [he had had his two testicles removed] ... The total absence of lust enables one to love without ulterior motives' – James Lees-Milne, *Holy Dread* (2001), diary entry for 1 December 1984.

improper Sexual. Probably by the late 19th century. As in 'he made improper advances / an improper suggestion to her'.

improved Lower, reduced, worse. As in 'the train company is now offering an improved service'. Late 20th century.

in drink Drunk. Somehow it seems a more amiable condition this way. 'I am, dear Prue, a little in drink, but at all times yr faithful husband' – letter to his wife from Sir Richard Steele (27 September 1708). 'The British are hypocritical, racist, secretive, arrogant, violent and boorish in drink' – *The Guardian* (3 April 1989). Also from the 18th century on: **in liquor**. Since the 16th century at least, there has also been **in one's cups**.

in flagrante (delicto) (Caught) having illicit SEXUAL INTERCOURSE. Literally, 'in the flames of the crime'. Originally, by the 18th century, a legal term for someone 'caught in the act' of committing any offence. The application specifically to a sexual 'crime', by the early 20th century. Perhaps now less disapprovingly used to convey simply that a couple is in the very act of 'doing it'.

(married) in name only Without sex being a part of it. Since the 17th century. 'She had hated her husband and been his wife only in name' – Robert Player, *Let's Talk of Graves, of Worms and Epitaphs* (1975), ch. 2.

in need of relief Poor, impecunious. Since the 18th century.

in the club Pregnant. Known since the 1930s. Hence, 'She's joined the club!', especially when the woman in question is unmarried. The club referred to – with a far from exclusive membership – was known in the 19th century as the 'Pudding' or 'Pudden Club' (where 'pudden' was seminal fluid). This latter expression has also been used to describe a girl's first menstrual period.

in-depth coverage Superficial coverage but a bit longer than usual. Media use. By the 1960s. 'What I do is history plus reportage, an in-depth extension of my former journalism' – *The Guardian* (20 February 1971); 'Maria Sharapova looks good *and* can win major tournaments. This profile includes an in-depth interview with the 18-year-old' – *The Independent* (26 August 2005).

in-store wastage Shoplifting. Late 20th century.

(one's) inamorata One's lover or sexual mistress. Curious periphrasis, fudging the language once more. Since the 17th century but now only used in a consciously archaic fashion.

(an) incentive (bonus) (A) payment for working harder. Second half of the 20th century.

(an) incident   An event that the police are investigating but are declining to go into any detail about. It might be a murder or a robbery or a motoring offence but, for whatever reason, they are being coy in the face of your understandable curiosity. Since the 1960s when 'incident rooms', 'incident posts' started being so called at crime scenes.

inclement weather   Bad weather. By 1868. Typical British understatement when describing rain, snow, storms. 'The inclement weather ... has enabled me to put off ... the first mow of the lawn' – *The Times* (10 April 1975).

inclinations   Sexual preferences. Since the second half of the 20th century. 'Bertie Hope-Davies died, as obituarists say, "unmarried" and never disguised, or obtruded, his inclinations but bubbled rather than seethed with indignation at the expression "gay"' – *The Independent* (2 September 2005).

inclusive language   Use of words that does not assume that the male includes the female. A PC term referring to language that does not exclude, by direct reference or implication, one gender, minority, group, or another. It is a word most usually employed to denote non-sexist language and has been used in the US since the late 1970s. Behaviour and thought may also, of course, be inclusive or exclusive. With particular reference to non-sexist language in religion, an *Inclusive Language Lectionary* has been available in the US since 1983. In Britain, the Liturgical Commission of the Church of England is inquiring whether women wish to go on being addressed by such non-inclusive terms as 'Brethren'.

(activities) incompatible with their diplomatic status   Spying. A phrase trotted out to explain what foreign diplomats had been up to in the UK and why they were being kicked out. Particularly in the 1970s. Of course, they may just have been failing to pay their parking fines.

incomplete success Failure. President Carter used the term in 1980 to describe an attempt to free American hostages held in Iran.

incontinent (1) Promiscuous, unchaste. By the 16th century. 'Manifold are the reasons for this my present wonderful continence. I am upon a plan of economy, and therefore cannot be at the expense of first-rate dames' – James Boswell, diary entry for 14 December 1762; 'Harwich for the Continent (Paris for the incontinent)' – travel poster with graffiti addition (recorded by 1977).

(2) Unable to control one's urinary functions. By the 19th century. 'Harwich for the Continent (Frinton for the incontinent)' – notice at Colchester station with graffiti addition (recorded by 1979); '[Two old sisters] first applied for rooms in a convent, and were presented with a questionnaire. The first question was, "Are you incontinent?" They had no idea what this meant, but imagined it must be a good thing and answered, "Yes, very." Both were refused admission' – James Lees-Milne, *Ceaseless Turmoil* (2004), diary entry for 23 December 1990.

indecent assault Rape – at least as popularly understood. However, the law applying to male and female victims, as in a British act of parliament dating from 1861, does not define what is meant by 'indecent'. It has been stated that in the majority of cases it simply means a man has put his hand up the clothing of an unwilling female but has not attempted rape. Compare SEXUAL ASSAULT.

indecent exposure Exhibiting one's genitals in public. Apparently this phrase was first used in a British act of parliament dating from 1851. 'The ultimate in indecent exposure: Patrick Collins witnesses Mike Tyson's release from jail with distaste' – headline in *Mail on Sunday* (26 March 1995). Consequently, **to expose oneself** (in the UK) or **to exhibit oneself** (in the US) are the verbs for this activity.

(of) independent means Upper class, i.e. having inherited wealth or income. Since the 1860s.

indigenous people(s) Natives. Only noticeable since the early days of PC in the 1980s/90s but no doubt earlier.

indigent Poor. A Victorian and early-20th-century euphemism, mainly applied to 'respectable' people fallen on hard times. Now rarely used. The word means simply 'lacking the necessary'.

(an) indiscretion A transgression of social morality – e.g. adultery. 'The Princess of Wales [later Queen Alexandra], who normally overlooked her husband's indiscretions' – Robert Massie, *Dreadnought* (1992).

indisposed (1) Ill. One of the commonest of euphemisms. Is this because 'ill' is simply too short and too blunt? (2) Menstruating. 'We have only the choice of three kinds of expression: the vulgar resentful, the genteel ("I've got my period", "I am indisposed"), and the scientific jargon of the *menses*' – Germaine Greer, *The Female Eunuch* (1970).

indoor games / sports Sexual activity. 20th century. 'We once again indulged in the oldest of indoor sports' – Ritchie Perry, *Fall Guy* (1972), ch. 4. The same thought lies behind the expressions **indoor sledging** and **interior decorating**.

industrial action A strike, work-to-rule, go-slow, or other form of union/worker protest. In the UK, since the late 1960s. 'The Times regrets that, in common with other national newspapers, it will probably be unable to publish tomorrow because of industrial action' – *The Times* (17 March 1971); 'Seventy-five journalists, working on three East Midland newspapers, start industrial action tomorrow ... They intend to refuse to handle copy from outside non-union journalists and will ban night work' – *The Observer* (15 August 1976).

industrial relations Resolving disagreements between employers and employees. By about 1900.

inebriated Drunk. Somehow the verbosity lightens the offence ... Since the 17th century.

infertile Barren, unable to bear children. The other PC term for such a woman is **sterile**, not least because both terms can refer to both men and women. 'Avoid "barren" which carries a certain unwarranted stigma and is used only of women,' says Rosalie Maggio in *The Nonsexist Word Finder: A Dictionary of Gender-Free Usage* (Boston, Mass., 1988): 'Saying that someone is "childless" or "has no children" is not recommended as these phrases tend to support a child-as-norm stereotype.' The condition was referred to by a correspondent in *The Times* (5 May 1976) as a **sub-fertility problem**.

(an) infestation officer A rat catcher. An alleged job-enhancer. Mid-to-late-20th century.

(an) inmate A prisoner. Because he is an inmate of a prison, but it does sound more matey, doesn't it? Perhaps not such an ancient usage as one might think. 'Set in 1963, it stars Charlie Sheen as Pvt. Bean, a defiant white loner who learns teamwork from fellow inmates in the Army brig' – *The Washington Post* (3 October 1991).

(an) inner-city (area) A slum, a run-down area where poverty and overcrowding are rife. Originally an American term from the 1960s, it rapidly became the only way of describing such things in the UK. 'The problems of the inner city – a work area where almost everyone has gone home' – *The Times* (19 January 1974); 'Edward Banfield, Harvard anthropologist professor, who had written a book called *The Unheavenly City*, which identified the growing phenomenon of the underclass in American inner cities' – *The Sunday Times* (16 June 1991).

inner cleanliness Keeping the bowels empty. From a slogan for Andrews Liver Salts (a laxative) in the UK, current from the 1950s: 'Andrews for inner cleanliness'. 'To complete your inner cleanliness, Andrews cleans the bowels. It sweeps away troublemaking poisons, relieves constipation, and purifies the blood ...'

Innuit / Inuit Eskimo. A PC term with the force of euphemism because the replaced term is, for some reason, thought to be reprehensible. The word means simply 'people' or 'men' and is variously pronounced, though an 1860 citation gives 'enn-oo-eet'. It has, apparently, always been the way in which Eskimos have referred to themselves. The Innuit are a people spread over an area from Greenland to eastern Siberia. Beard and Cerf in *The Official Politically Correct Dictionary and Handbook* (1992) prefer the spelling 'Inuit', say the word refers specifically to Canadian Eskimos, and attribute Inuit dislike of the word to the fact that they once believed it meant 'eater of raw meat'. For the appropriate sub-division, they recommend the use of 'Native Alaskan'.

'Prime Minister Brian Mulroney said ... the native deal created no new land rights, a big concern in Quebec, where Cree Indian and Inuit Eskimo groups claim large tracts' – *The Independent* (22 August 1982). 'Eskimo Pie' was the name given (in the US, from 1921) to an ice-cream bar covered with chocolate. Could this fact account in any way for the insistence (by others) on the change to Innuit?

inoperative To be ignored because it is a lie. Ron Ziegler, the White House press spokesman at the time of Watergate, famously said at a Washington DC press conference (17 April 1973): 'This is the operative statement. The others are inoperative.' Hence, **to render inoperative** means 'to disable'.

inside In prison. By 1888.

insolvent Bankrupt, unable to pay one's debts. Since the 16th century.

instruments of aggression Nuclear weapons (in the US). Quoted in Willard R. Espy, *An Almanac of Words at Play* (1975).

intelligence, lack of See under BRICK / FEW BRICKS SHORT OF A LOAD

interesting connexions Mistresses, prostitutes. The dating of this phrase's introduction can be found in a memorandum written by Lady Susan O'Brien (1745–1823) on 'changes between 1760-1818': 'Language has always been changing, & it has been said, as morals grow worse language grows more refined ... "fair Cyprians," & "tender" or "interesting connexions," have succeeded to "women on the town," & "kept mistresses".'

(to) interfere with To assault indecently. Since the 1940s. 'The girl was beheaded, chopped into pieces and placed in a trunk but was not interfered with' – from 'a Fleet Street report', quoted in John G. Murray, *Delightful Oddities* (1996).

interment Burial. Since the 14th century and, curiously, still much used. 'Rev. James Earl Richardson. Service will be Tuesday, November 29, 2005, at 11:00 a.m. at East Park Baptist Church, 8620 Tidwell, Houston, Texas. Interment will follow in the Paradise North Cemetery in Houston' – kivy.com (2005).

(an) internment camp A prison, though specifically for prisoners of war and detainees. Since the First World War.

intimacy took place SEXUAL INTERCOURSE took place – a standard form of words when a witness presented evidence of adultery in British courts, in the bad old days before divorce-law reform in the second half of the 20th century.

(an) invert A male homosexual. A short-lived usage, popularized (if at all) by the film *Victim* (US 1961). Dirk Bogarde played an English homosexual married lawyer who was being blackmailed in what was a rather sensational film for the time (homosexuality was still not a legal activity). Evidently, the director Basil Dearden insisted on this word being used and the h-word (or any other) was not. Quite how homosexuals are more inverted (i.e. whose sexual instincts are turned inwards) than anyone else is not clear. But at least it was an improvement on 'pervert'.

(an) investor A gambler (on football pools, horse racing). Since the 1950s.

involuntarily leisured Unemployed. A somewhat facetious attempt at softening the blow. A coinage from the early days of PC in the 1990s.

irregularities Law-breaking. 'Certain irregularities occurred.' By the 17th century.

islanders Natives. Anything but the n-word. A PC substitution by the early 1990s.

it (1) SEXUAL INTERCOURSE. Since the 16th century. As used in such expressions as 'to have it off' and 'to GO TO IT'. (2) Sex appeal. Hence, 'The It Girl' was the nickname or sobriquet of Clara Bow (1905–65), popular actress of the silent film era. She appeared in the film *It* (1928), based on an Elinor Glyn story and 'It' was the word used in billings to describe her vivacious sex appeal. A little earlier, 'It' was the title of a song in *The Desert Song* (1926). In 1904, Rudyard Kipling wrote in *Traffics and Discoveries*: ''Tisn't beauty, so to speak, nor good talk necessarily. It's just It. Some women'll stay in a man's memory if they once walk down a street.' *Punch* commented on another 'It' craze (18 March 1908), which may be relevant. In the 1990s, the phrase was resurrected and applied, in the UK, to certain young women of minor celebrity status.

J j

(a) J. Arthur A wank (male masturbation), from rhyming slang on J. Arthur Rank (the UK film distributor). Known by the 1980s.

jail bait A sexually attractive girl (and provocatively so) under the age of consent. Originally US, by the 1930s. 'I'm not interested in little girls. Particularly not in jail-bait like that one' – John Braine, *Room at the Top* (1957), ch. 24.

(a/the) jakes / jake's place A LAVATORY. Now archaic, if used at all and notable for supposedly commemorating Sir John Harrington (1561–1612) who invented a form of flush lavatory. He was Queen Elizabeth's godson and installed a prototype device at Hampton Court and published instructions as to how it could be manufactured. Either because of the difficulty of installation or frequent breakdowns, more than a century and a half elapsed before a household version was generally adopted. Unfortunately for this theory, the word 'jakes' was in use by the 1530s, before Harrington was born, and the etymology of the word is not clear.

(a/the) jelly roll A/the VAGINA. This was Southern Afro-American slang not only for the vagina but for a virile man and also for sundry sexual activities. It was derived from an item of food that you would get from a baker's shop (like a Swiss Roll or a doughnut with a hole at its centre). Here the word 'jelly' could refer to the meat of the coconut when it is still white (and

resembling semen). Hence, 'Jelly Roll' as the stage name of
Ferdinand Le Menthe Morton (who died in 1941), a pianist, and
one of the creators of New Orleans jazz.

jig-a-jig / jig-jig / jiggy-jiggy SEXUAL INTERCOURSE.
Since the 1930s at least – the sort of coy term that might be used
by a prostitute of, say, Oriental origin to a potential English-
speaking client: 'You want jig-jig?' Presumably, because the
offered activity requires a certain amount of jigging about.
'The boys' refrain ... "Captain want jig jig, my sister pretty girl
school-teacher, captain want jig jig"' – Graham Greene, *The Heart
of the Matter* (1948), pt 1, ch. 1; 'Health workers, trained to be
scrupulously non-judgemental in matters of jiggy-jiggy, bend
over backwards to accommodate the contraceptive needs of
children' – *The Independent* (24 September 2005).

(to) jilt To forsake/abandon a lover after initially raising hopes.
Originally said only of a woman. By the second half of the 17th
century.

(the) job axe The sack. Limited late 20th century use. 'The job
axe has finally fallen on Darlington wool workers' – *The Northern
Echo* (16 May 1976); 'Cabinet Axes Top Boffin Job' – headline in
The Guardian (1 June 1976). On the other hand, this is more brutal
than the original, so probably does not really count as a true
euphemism.

(a) job centre A labour exchange. In the UK from the 1970s.
'Britain's first Job Centre will be opened this afternoon. Job
Centres are the modern version of what have ... been called
employment exchanges or labour exchanges' – *The Guardian*
(23 May 1973).

job leaving See SACKING

job-title enhancement See AMBIENT REPLENISHMENT
ASSISTANT; APPEARANCE ENGINEER; APPOINTMENT; BAR
ASSISTANT; BOYS IN BLUE; BUSINESS EXECUTIVE; CANINE

CONTROL OFFICER; CAPTAIN; CHARLADY; CLEANSING
PERSONNEL; COMMERCIAL TRAVELLER; COMMISSION
AGENT; COMMUNITY NURSING OFFICER; COMPANY
REPRESENTATIVE; CONSULTANT; CUSTOMER OPERATIONS
LEADER; DAILY; DESPATCH ROOM FACILITATOR;
DESTINATION MANAGER; DISMAL TRADE; DOG WARDEN;
DOMESTIC; DOMESTIC ASSISTANT/HELP; DOMESTIC
ENGINEER; DOMESTICIAN; ECDYSIAST; EDUCATION
WELFARE MANAGER; EDUCATOR; EXECUTIVE; EXOTIC
DANCER; EXTERMINATING ENGINEER; FAMILY BUTCHER;
FIREFIGHTER; FLUEOLOGIST; FUNERAL DIRECTOR; FUNERAL
SERVICE OPERATIVES; HAIR STYLIST; HAIRDRESSER; HEAD
OF VERBAL COMMUNICATIONS; HELP; HOME PROTECTION
OFFICER; HORTICULTURAL SURGEON; HOUSEKEEPER;
INFESTATION OFFICER; LADY; LANDSCAPE TECHNICIAN;
LAVENDER JANE; MEAT DEALER; MULTIMEDIA SYSTEMS
TECHNICIAN; MY DAILY (HELP); OFFICE CLEANING
OPERATIVE; PERSONAL ASSISTANT; PEST CONTROL OFFICER;
PROFESSOR; PUBLIC HEALTH OFFICER; PURVEYOR; REFUSE
COLLECTOR; REUSED METAL PRODUCTS INDUSTRY; REVENUE
AGENT; RODENT OFFICER/OPERATIVE/OPERATOR; SALES
LADY; SALES REPRESENTATIVE; SANITARY ENGINEER;
SANITATION MAINTENANCE SUPERINTENDENT; SKILLED
FARM TECHNICIAN; SPECIAL (CONSTABLE); STOCKIST;
STREET ORDERLY; STRIP-TEASE ARTISTE; SUBTERRANEAN
SANITATION TECHNICIAN; TAX INSPECTOR; TONSORIAL
ARTIST; TURF ACCOUNTANT; UTENSIL MAINTENANCE MAN;
VENDOR; VERMIN EXTERMINATOR; VICTUALLER'S
ASSISTANT; WATER SYSTEMS SPECIALIST

(to) join the choir invisible To die. The phrase appears to
have originated in the hymn 'Oh May I Join the Choir Invisible'
written by the novelist George Eliot (1819–80). This is one of
the roll-call of euphemisms in the *Monty Python's Flying Circus* 'Dead
Parrot' sketch, first shown on BBC TV (7 December 1969).
A man (named Praline in the script) who has just bought a parrot
that turns out to be dead, registers a complaint with the pet shop
owner in these words: 'This is a late parrot. It's a stiff. Bereft of

life it rests in peace. It would be pushing up the daisies if you hadn't nailed it to the perch. It's rung down the curtain and joined the choir invisible. It's an ex-parrot.' See also CALLED TO JOIN.

joyriding Stealing a car (mostly for fun). Possibly of American origin, known by the 1910s. Popular in the UK in the early 1990s to describe the practice of young people stealing motor cars and then driving them at high speed. Believing that the euphemism was clearly inappropriate for such an anti-social activity, *The Daily Telegraph* (13 January 1993) attempted to engineer the language and impose 'mad-riding', 'bad-tripping', 'auto-abuse', instead, but inevitably failed. 'Recent incidents, including the spread of "hotting" or "joyriding" by youngsters in stolen cars, have taken juvenile crime to the top of the political agenda' – *The Scotsman* (22 February 1993).

Judas Priest! Jesus Christ!, as an oath. Mostly American usage, by 1922. Hence, Judas Priest, the name of a UK vocal/ instrumental group from about 1979.

Junoesque Large-breasted. References to the goddess Juno's voluptuous and stately beauty have been fairly common since the 17th century. The euphemistic allusion is probably no earlier than the 20th century. 'In *The Hollywood History of the World*, George MacDonald Fraser describes Miss O'Hara as being "Indispensable to 17th-century movies because she was Junoesque and looked like Nell Gwynne modelling for Vogue under the supervision of Sir Peter Lely"' – cooksley.org (28 July 2005).

justice See CRIMINAL

(a) juvenile delinquent A young thug. The coinage appears to date back to the 1816 *Report of the London Committee Investigating the Causes of the Increase in Juvenile Delinquency* which concluded: 'It was found that Juvenile delinquency existed in the metropolis to a very alarming extent.' The term had a revival in the 1950s but has now largely been superseded by (YOUNG) OFFENDER.

Kk

(a) kangaroo court An informal method of dispensing rough justice. The name is applied to a self-appointed court that has no proper legal authority – as in the disciplinary proceedings sometimes to be found among prisoners in gaol. Ironically, *Macquarie* (1981), the Australian dictionary, calls this an American and British colloquialism, but surely it must have something to do with the land of the kangaroo? Perhaps it alludes to the vicious streak that such animals sometimes display? *OED2*'s earliest citation is, however, from the US (dated 1853) and this may provide an explanation. In W.S. Ransom's *Australian English: An Historical Study of the Vocabulary 1788–1898* (1966), it is stated that over 800 Australians entered California for the 1849 gold rush. They presumably brought with them knowledge of the kangaroo's nature. On the other hand, between 1852 and 1856, when gold was found in Victoria, 16,000 miners arrived in Australia from California. They, likewise, would have taken home knowledge of the beast. In any case, American sealers and whalers had been putting into Sydney from about 1800.

(to) keep up with the Joneses To strive not to be outdone by one's neighbours. The expression came originally from a comic strip by Arthur R. 'Pop' Momand entitled *Keeping up with the Joneses* that appeared in the New York *Globe* from 1913 to 1931. It is said that Momand had at first intended to call his strip 'Keeping up with the Smiths' but refrained because his own neighbours

were actually of that name and some of the exploits he wished to
report had been acted out by them in real life.

(a) kept woman   A prostitute. Originally 'kept mistress' (by
1678) but the term changed in the 19th century, to describe a
woman who was maintained as a lover by (usually) just one man.
The term survives loosely to describe (sometimes jokingly) any
woman who is dependent on a man. 'There used to be a fine
family of words which described without reprobation or disgust
women who lived outside the accepted sexual laws, but they have
faded from current usage. Flatly contemptuous words like
kept-woman and *call-girl* have taken over from *adventuress ... courtesan,
mondaine*' – Germaine Greer, *The Female Eunuch* (1970).

(to) kick the bucket   To die. Recorded in Grose's *Dictionary of
the Vulgar Tongue* in 1785. Derived from either the suicide's kicking
away the bucket on which he/she is standing, in order to hang
him/herself, or from the 'bucket beam' on which pigs were hung
after being slaughtered. The odd *post mortem* spasm would lead to
the 'bucket' being kicked.

kinell!   Fucking hell! An oath substitute reported by Susie Dent
in *Fanboys and Overdogs: The Language Report* (2005).

(the) king over the water   King James II – also used to refer
to his son and grandson, the Old Pretender and the Young
Pretender. Hence, the toast incorporating the nickname given
to the exiled James II after his departure from the English throne
in 1688. Jacobites would propose the toast while passing the
glass over a water decanter.

(to) know / have (Biblical) knowledge of   To have SEXUAL
INTERCOURSE with. Genesis 4:1 started this off with: 'And
Adam knew Eve his wife; and she conceived, and bare Cain.'
Then presumably people must have started using 'to know ...
in the biblical sense'. And then, relatively recently, people have
played with the notion of 'having Biblical knowledge of'. 'And
though I can legitimately say that I do have Biblical knowledge

of Sharon – it's all right, Rodney, it was a long time ago and
I didn't like it very much' – *The Naff Sex Guide* (1984), 'Naff Best
Man's Speech'.

(well-) known to the police Having a criminal record or at
least having been investigated with a view to prosecution. 'It was
impossible for him to have won the Scripture-knowledge prize
without systematic cheating on an impressive scale. He went
so far as to suggest that Master Simmons was well known to the
police' – P.G. Wodehouse, *Right Ho, Jeeves* (1934), ch. 17;
'Regularly commuting at all hours ... [Jock Milne] was "well
known to the police" for his frantic driving' – obituary in
The Independent (19 May 2005).

Ll

(a) labour camp   A prison. Specifically, a penal institution where the prisoners are required to work. Since about 1900.

(a) lack of moral fibre / L.M.F.   A lack of courage. Since the late 19th century. 'Fanshawe was a boy in whom bad instincts had been nourished by his training, and who, from constant lack of moral fibre, had gradually deteriorated' – *Boy's Own Paper* (11 October 1884); 'When the Second World War began ... the term LMF ("lack of moral fibre") was coined as a pejorative for those pilots who would today be diagnosed and treated as having psychiatric illness' – *New Society* (22 July 1971).

ladies   Women. Used when the subject calls for a softer, more appealing or respectful synonym and euphemistically trans-ferring the original name for 'females of breeding' or high social standing to those of a lower. Yet there have been strange anomalies: in 1923, the British Broadcasting Company, as it then was, had a 'Ladies Advisory Committee' that was formed in Manchester to suggest a radio programme of special interest to female listeners. John Reith, manager of the company, who would not have addressed the distinguished amateur panel – including the wife of the Bishop of Manchester – other than as 'ladies', nevertheless accepted the title *Woman's Hour* which has persisted ever since. It is also the case that 'better class' females have been known as 'gentlewomen' rather than 'gentleladies'.

Quite how one distinguishes between a 'woman' and a 'lady'

has been the subject of amused discussion for decades. In *Collections and Recollections* (1904), G.W.E. Russell wrote: 'A good woman who let furnished apartments in a country town describing a lodger who had apparently known "better days", said, "I am positive she was a real born lady, for she hadn't the least idea how to do anything for herself; it took her hours to peel her potatoes".'

Until the suffragette movement and two world wars (in which women played so important a part), the word 'woman' was generally applied to the working class, 'lady' to females of leisure, and the distinction was acknowledged and unquestioned. ('Womanhood' honourably combined the two.) The mingling of classes in war usually made euphemism unnecessary. Then, with political changes, came a new emphasis on class consciousness. An illustration of use is the story of the housewife who answered a knock on the door and was asked, 'Are you the woman who's advertised for a lady to work for her?' See also LADY below.

(the) ladies' The ladies' LAVATORY. Curiously this designation, as on the sign over the door, does not appear to have been recorded before 1918. In *Clean and Decent* (1960), Lawrence Wright suggests that the first use of the equivalent of 'ladies' and 'gentlemen' in this context might have been at a ball in Paris in 1739 where *cabinets* were installed 'with inscriptions over the doors, *Garderobes pour les femmes* and *Garderobes pour les hommes*, with chambermaids on duty in the former and valets in the latter'. Such provisions were hailed as innovations.

(a) ladies' man A flirt. Or simply a man who pays a lot of attention to women. By the 1780s and latterly used in obituaries and such.

(a) lady (1) A cleaning lady, domestic help, a woman in a subservient role. Early 20th century. 'Twice a week a lady came to "oblige" in the house' – Adelaide Lubbock, *Australian Roundabout* (1963); 'The bracelet ... struck me as rather gloomy. Lady in shop said she might exchange if she wished' – James Lees-Milne, *Ceaseless Turmoil* (2004), diary entry for 12 November 1991.

(2) A prostitute. A shortened version of LADY OF THE NIGHT below.

(a) lady dog A bitch. By the 1880s. Probably redundant now.

(a) lady friend A woman who (it is assumed) has extramarital sex with another person. In use by the early 19th century. Plenty of scope for misapplication here. 'Hallo! Hallo! Who's Your Lady Friend?' – title of song (1913) by Bert Lee and Harry Frogson.

(a) lady of the night A prostitute (and nothing to do with the shrub of the same name). Sometimes **lady of the evening / of pleasure / of the town**. Since the mid-17th century. 'At night, Erskine and I strolled through the streets and St James's Park. We were accosted there by several ladies of the town' – James Boswell, diary entry for 4 December 1762; 'Janoo and Azizun are ... Ladies of the City and theirs is an ancient ... profession' – Rudyard Kipling, *Plain Tales from the Hills* (1888), 'In the House of Suddhoo'. Compare WOMAN OF EASY VIRTUE / PLEASURE.

laid in earth Buried. By the 17th century. 'When I am laid in earth, / May my wrongs create / No trouble in thy breast; / Remember me, but ah! forget my fate' – 'Dido's Lament' from Nahum Tate's libretto for Henry Purcell's opera *Dido and Aeneas* (1689), act 3. Dido sings the words about Aeneas just after he has told her he is leaving her. The corresponding scenes in Virgil, *Aeneid*, bk 4, do not use this metaphor, so presumably it is Tate's own.

laid to rest Buried. By the 14th century. 'Earth, receive an honoured guest: / William Yeats is laid to rest. / Let the Irish vessel lie / Emptied of its poetry' – W.H. Auden, 'In Memory of W.B. Yeats' (1939); 'The remains of Eva Peron, second wife of the late President Peron, have been laid to rest in the fashionable Recoleta cemetery in Buenos Aires' – *The Sunday Telegraph* (24 October 1976).

(a) lame duck A holder of an office who has failed to gain re-election and is thus unable to carry out his job effectively. Or referring to anyone or anything handicapped by misfortune or by incapacity. This was the name originally given to a defaulter on the London Stock Exchange in the 19th century. In William Thackeray's *Vanity Fair* (1847–8), ch. 13, the money-conscious Mr Osborne is suspicious of the financial position of Amelia's father: 'I'll have no lame duck's daughter in my family.' It is said that people who could not pay their debts would 'waddle' out of Exchange Alley in the City of London – hence perhaps, the 'duck'. In the US, the term has come to be applied to a president or other office-holder whose power is diminished because he is about to leave office or because he is handicapped by some scandal. In about 1970, the term came also to be applied by British politicians to industries unable to survive without government financial support.

(for the) land's sake (For the) Lord's sake. A blasphemy diffuser in American use by 1846. Also in phrases like 'the land knows' and 'Good land!' '"For the land's sake!" gasped Marilla ... "I believe the child is crazy"' – L.M. Montgomery, *Anne of Green Gables* (1908), ch. 14.

(to go into the) land of Nod To fall/be asleep (compare 'to nod off'). Jonathan Swift has the expression in *Polite Conversation* (1738). As such, this is a pun on the land of Nod ('on the East of Eden'), to which Cain was exiled after he had slain Abel (Genesis 4:16).

(in the) land of the living Alive. By 1700, but an Old Testament phrase before that. 'Heavens, is he still in the land of the living?'

(a) landscape technician A gardener (in the US). Quoted in Willard R. Espy, *An Almanac of Words at Play* (1975).

language Bad language, swear words. By 1860 (Dickens). As in the exclamation 'language!' when someone has just resorted to it.

larger (than average) Fat. Perhaps mostly an American 20th-century usage. 'Elongated vee neckline, especially becoming to the larger woman!' – advertisement in the Baltimore *Sun* (24 March 1949).

(a/the) last resting place A grave. In this sense, 'resting place' has been current since the late 18th century. 'His body's resting-place, of old' – Walter Scott, *Marmion* (1808), canto 2, st 14. 'Last resting place' is often used figuratively of a cause or idea rather than a person.

late Failing to menstruate. As in 'I am late this month'. By 1900?

(the) late lamented The (recently) dead. By 1859. 'One programme, *Subterranea Britannica* (BBC2), was the stuff of the late-lamented *40 Minutes* and at 50 minutes outstayed its welcome' – *The Herald* (Glasgow) (7 May 1994); 'Like the time when, as a callow 17-year-old during an Edinburgh Festival-time jam session, Travis suggested to the late, lamented alto saxophonist Joe Harriott that they play something up-tempo' – *The Herald* (Glasgow) (19 January 1995).

(the) late unpleasantness Recent war or HOSTILITIES. It was introduced by the US humorist David Ross Locke in *Ekkoes from Kentucky* (1868). Writing as 'Petroleum V. Nasby', he referred to the recently ended Civil War as 'the late onpleasantniss' and the coinage spread. It still survives: 'Here, for instance, is Dan Rather, America's father-figure, on the hot-line to Panama during the late unpleasantness [an invasion] ...' – *The Independent* (20 January 1990).

(the) later years Old age. By the 19th century. 'Polyalgia rheumatica ... affects subjects in the later years of life, the average age of onset being the late sixties' – Boyle and Buchanan, *Clinical Rheumatology* (1971), ch. 6. Compare **riper years**, since the 17th century, as in 'The Ministration of Baptism to Such as are of Riper Years, and Able to Answer for Themselves' – heading in the Book of Common Prayer (1662 version).

(a) latrine A LAVATORY. Though French, from Latin *latrina*, derived from *lavare*, to wash. Especially in camp, barracks, hospital use, since the 17th century. 'A "latrine", we learned, was not only a building, but also the name for any particularly exciting but quite unfounded rumour emanating therefrom' – F.A. Pottle, *Stretchers* (1930), ch. I.

(to) launder To process illegally acquired money so that it becomes 'clean'. A term that came to general notice during the Watergate inquiry in the US (1973–4).

(a) lavatory A place for urination and defecation. From the Latin *lavatorium*, for a place where you wash. The extension of this meaning to include the other activity may have occurred by the end of the 17th century (though it is not always possible to tell what people were writing or talking about ...) I suppose the modern abbreviation **lav.**, also a euphemism, should be mentioned here.

lavatory, going to the See ACCIDENT; ALONG THE PASSAGE; ANSWER THE CALL OF NATURE; ARRANGEMENTS; AUNT; AVAIL ONESELF OF THE FACILITIES; BATHROOM; BEEN; BOG; BUM-FODDER; CHAPEL OF EASE; CLOAKROOM; CLOSET; COMMODE; CONVENIENCE; COVER ONE'S FEET; DO (A) NUMBER ONE/TWO; DO ONE'S BUSINESS; DUTY; EARTH CLOSET; FACILITY; GENTLEMEN; GO; GO AND CHECK THE BLACKOUT; GO AND CHECK THE PLUMBING; GO AND CHECK THE PRICE OF WHEAT IN CHICAGO; GO AND DRAIN ONE'S RADIATOR; GO AND EMPTY THE ASHTRAYS; GO AND EMPTY THE TEAPOT; GO AND LOOK AT AFRICA; GO AND LOWER THE LEVEL; GO AND PARTAKE OF A MINOR/MAJOR COMFORT; GO AND PICK A DAISY; GO AND PUMP SHIP; GO AND SEE A FRIEND OFF TO THE COAST; GO AND SEE A MAN ABOUT A DOG; GO AND SEE IF ONE'S HAT IS STRAIGHT; GO AND SEE THE MAN I JOINED UP WITH; GO AND SEE THE TURK; GO AND SEE THE VICAR; GO AND SEE WHAT TIME IT IS; GO AND SHAKE HANDS WITH AN OLD FRIEND; GO AND SHAKE THE DEW; GO AND SHED A TEAR;

GO AND SIT ON THE THRONE; GO AND SPLASH ONE'S
CLOGS; GO AND SQUEEZE A PEACH; GO AND STAND UP;
GO AND TELEPHONE HITLER; GO AND TURN ONE'S BIKE
ROUND; GO AND WASH ONE'S HANDS; GO AND WASH THE
CAR; GO AND WATER THE HORSE; GO AND WATER THE
LILIES; GO AND WRING OUT ONE'S SOCKS; GO FOR A QUICK
BURST ON THE BANJO; GO FOR A SWEET ONE; GO FOR A
WEE WALK; GO NORTH; GO THROUGH; GO TO A JOB NO ONE
ELSE CAN DO FOR ONE; GO TO LA POMME; GO TO PAGE 54;
GO TO PARIS; GO TO/PAY A VISIT TO THE HOUSE OF
COMMONS; GO TO THE OFF-STUMP; GO UP THE DUBS; GO
UPSTAIRS; GO WHERE KINGS GO ALONE; HAVE A WHISTLE;
JAKES; LADIES; LATRINE; LEAVE THE ROOM; LITTLE
BOYS'/GIRLS' ROOM; LITTLE HOUSE; LOO; LOOK AT THE
GARDEN; MEN'S ROOM; NECESSARY; OUTSIDE PLUMBING;
PAY A CALL; PLUMBING; POWDER ONE'S NOSE; POWDER
ROOM; PRIVY; REST ROOM; RETIRE; SHOWN THE GEOGRAPHY
OF THE HOUSE; SMALLEST ROOM; SPEND A PENNY; TOILET;
TOILET TISSUE; USE THE EUPHEMISM; USUAL OFFICES;
W.C.; WASH ONE'S HANDS; WASHROOM; WATER CLOSET

(a) Lavender Jane A cesspit emptier. English rural use, by the 1950s, at least in Buckinghamshire, according to my wife.

(the) law The police. By the 1920/30s. 'I inquired of the Law where I might cash a cheque, and was directed to the nearest travel agency' – *The Times* (6 June 1972).

(a) law enforcement officer / official A policeman. A curious periphrasis, used perhaps when the actual status or rank of the person is not known. By the 1950s. 'Before the [1939–45] war a spade used to be called a spade – often brutally so ... But today a policeman has become a law enforcement officer' – George Mikes, *How To Be Decadent* (1977).

lawk-a-mussy / lawks ...! Lord have mercy! Since the late 19th century.

(to) lay down one's life To be killed (in war). See GAVE
THEIR LIVES / LAID DOWN THEIR LIVES.

(to) lead a normal married life To have SEXUAL
INTERCOURSE within marriage. Mid-20th century. '[*Doctor to
middle-aged woman patient "picking the words carefully for her"*:] How long
is it since you led a normal married life with him?' – Penelope
Gilliatt, screenplay for *Sunday Bloody Sunday* (UK 1971). The scene
continues with these other allusions: 'You mean he hasn't been
near you for a long time' / 'He never interfered with me without
a call ... It was never that sort of thing between us ... Not what
you're saying ... nothing physical.'

(to put) lead in one's pencil To make a man sexually
potent. Usually accompanying the offer of a strong and/or
alcoholic drink. As in 'Here y'are. That'll put lead in your
pencil.' From the similarity between the lead in a pencil and
a stiff prick. Possibly of Australian origin and recorded by the
1940s.

(to) leak To release information/secrets informally and
unofficially. Since the 1850s, at least. 'It was not sufficient for
the tribunal merely to establish by whose hand information ...
was improperly leaked' – *The Daily Telegraph* (14 July 1971);
'According to leaks, the 11-minute production is a combination
of Schwarzenegger-style action effects with a politically correct
plot' – *The Times* (15 November 1991).

(with) learning difficulties Of low intelligence, mentally
handicapped, cretinous, defective, imbecilic, paralytic, vegetable,
having a mental age of ——. Apparently first used at the time of
the Committee of Enquiry into the Education of Handicapped
Children and Young People 1976, whose chairman was Mary
Warnock (report published 1978). In this case, 'Children with
Moderate and Severe Learning Difficulties' was the term that
replaced 'EDUCATIONAL SUB-NORMAL (Moderate and Severe)'.
See citation below, however, for a slightly earlier Canadian use.
   As a substitute phrase for 'mentally handicapped', in deference

to political correctness, the new term was rejected by the charity,
Mencap, which after all has an interest in retaining the well-
established phrase alluded to in its name. In July 1992, the
charity said the new phrase was 'inaccurate' and that using it in
answer to demands from charity and social workers would cost
Mencap support because the public 'would not understand it'.
Steven Billington, Mencap's director of marketing and appeals,
said, 'It is only a matter of time before even the most right-on
expression becomes a term of abuse. It has been the same since
people talked about village idiots, and "learning difficulties" is
no exception. Children are already calling each other LDs as
an insult.'

'In cautioning against putting too much emphasis on early
French immersion for the majority of children, the report says
such programs may harm children with learning difficulties' – *The
Globe and Mail* (Toronto) (25 August 1976); 'When I heard that
someone had "learning difficulties", I had no idea what it meant
... If someone has learning difficulties, it could be because their
school was burnt down, because they are deaf, because they are in
the Tory Cabinet, because all their teachers are talking a foreign
language or many other reasons, one of which might be a physical
or psychological inability to learn' – *The Independent* (20 January
1992); '[Lord Rix, Mencap's chairman, said:] "learning
difficulties" is a misnomer. It implies that mental handicap is all
a matter of education ... My child [born mentally handicapped]
is 40 and to describe her as having a learning difficulty is a
travesty of the truth' – *The Independent* (20 July 1992). Alternatives
include: **to have learning disabilities / disorders** and **to be
learning disabled**.

(into) leather   Indulging in sado-masochism (or at least the
outward show of it). By the 1960s? 'I take it to be indisputably
a euphemism ... when it is said of a homosexual man who takes
part in sado-masochistic activity that he is "into leather"' –
J. Epstein in *Fair of Speech*, ed D.J. Enright (1985).

(to) leave   To forsake/abandon. 'He has left his wife in the
lurch.' Since the 17th century, if not much earlier. ''Tis better

to be left, than never to have been loved' – William Congreve, *The Way of the World* (1700), act 2, scene 1.

(to) leave (this world) To die. '"She left at 1.30 in her sleep quite peacefully and looks happy and beautiful." People always say these words, and I wonder if they are ever true' – James Lees-Milne, *Ancestral Voices* (1975), diary entry for 31 may 1942.

leave of absence Suspension from work. The 18th century term 'leave (of absence)', meaning official permission to go off duty was turned into a euphemism to cover another sort of absence, in the late 20th century. Usually this was used when an investigation was being held into an employee's alleged wrongdoing.

(to) leave one's chair vacant To die. A 1954 example – 'she left her chair vacant' – was found on a gravestone at Pinner and recorded in Hugh Meller, *London Cemeteries* (1981), ch. 5.

(to) leave one's shoes under the bed To have sex casually. As in, 'he can leave his boots (or shoes) under my bed anytime', in other words, 'I find him sexually attractive'. I recall it being said to me by a small lady of Iranian extraction regarding Robert Redford in April 1970. As far as I know, she still hasn't had a chance to make him the offer.

(to) leave the building To die. I first encountered this euphemism in 1998. Someone trying to establish whether a certain actress was alive or dead, asked me, 'Has she left the building?' It subsequently occurred to me that this euphemism may have derived from the phrase 'Elvis has left the building.' This was said by various tour managers and MCs in the 1950s when Elvis Presley was beginning to get swamped by fans. Spoken at the end of a stage show, it meant that Elvis would not be doing an encore and was designed to prevent fans from mobbing him at the stage door. Al Dvorin, one of those who uttered it, died in 2004. The phrase has also been given as the

title of a film about the murder of Elvis impersonators. After
Elvis's own untimely death in 1977, I think it may have been
transferred to this other form of departure.

(to) leave the room To go to the LAVATORY. 'Please, miss,
may I leave the room?' is a schoolroom euphemism and
continued facetiously into adult life. 'How to leave the room
during lessons – I solved ... by peeing in my trousers' –
C. Day Lewis, *The Buried Day* (1960).

(a) left-footer A Roman Catholic. 20th-century origin,
possibly a coinage of Northern Ireland Protestants. It is assumed
that in the Irish Republic, a spade is pushed into the ground
using the left foot by agricultural labourers. Hence, as anyone
from southern Ireland is likely to be a Roman Catholic, then
he is likely to be a left-footer. Recorded by 1944. Has also been
applied to homosexuals.

(a) left-handed compliment A dubious, ambiguous
compliment; one that can be taken either way. By the 1880s.
'What a splendidly loud singing voice you have, dear!'

legal See CRIMINAL

legless See WIDE-EYED AND LEGLESS

(a) leisure centre A sports centre also housing other
recreational activities that might not accurately be described as
'sporting'. By the 1970s.

(the) leisure years Retirement. This was reported in 1982 but
I am not sure it has lasted.

less-developed Poor. Usually when describing countries.
By 1940. Hence, also, **L.D.C.s** (Less-Developed Countries) –
according to *Brewer's Politics* (1995 edn).

(to) let go (1) To give a person the sack. A manager sacking an employee might say, 'I'm afraid we shall have to let you go.' By the 1970s?

(2) To kill (of animals). 'Took my poor old dog, Fop, to the vet ... Late in the afternoon while I was out he rang. A. said to me, "The vet had to let him go"' – James Lees-Milne, *Ancient As the Hills* (1997), diary entry for 20 December 1973.

(to) let off To fart (i.e. to let off a fart). Since the 1970s? Perhaps linked to the explosion that occurs when a firework is 'let off'.

(a) liaison An illicit sexual relationship. Since about 1800.

(to) liberate (1) To steal, loot, misappropriate. Since the 1940s. 'Or that was the story, until John Lennon "liberated" the [Victorian music-hall] poster [of "Being for the Benefit of Mr Kite"] from a café during the filming of promotional clips for the "Penny Lane/Strawberry Fields Forever" record' – Derek Taylor, *It Was Twenty Years Ago Today* (1987); '"I know what you're thinking: Rape, loot and pillage. No rape." Most took this as tacit permission to liberate anything of value' – *The Independent* (17 August 2005). (2) To subject to further oppression under the guise of liberation. Also since the 1940s. 'All your Italian friends must be starving now that we have "liberated" them' – Bernard Shaw, letter to a young actress (4 December 1944).

(to) lie with To have sexual intercourse with. Ancient usage, not least in the Bible. 'Thou shalt not lie with mankind, as with womankind: it is abomination. Neither shalt thou lie with any beast to defile thyself therewith' – Leviticus 18:21–2.

life drawing to a close Dying. To state that the 'king/queen/pope is dying' might seem too stark and disrespectful. On 20 January 1936, King George V lay dying at Sandringham. At 9.25 pm, Lord Dawson, the King's doctor, issued a bulletin that he had drafted on a menu-card: 'The King's life is moving peacefully towards its close.' It was taken up by the BBC.

All wireless programmes were cancelled and every quarter of
an hour the announcer, Stuart Hibberd, repeated the medical
bulletin until the King died at 11.55 pm and the announcement
of his death was made at 12.15. In 1980, at one stage in the long
final illness of President Tito of Yugoslavia, doctors announced
that 'his life is slipping away'.

(a) life preserver A cosh – so obviously the life preserved was
that of the wielder rather than the victim. Mostly 19th-century
use. The weapon of choice carried by burglars rather than
responsible citizens in that era.

lifestyle Sexual orientation. Originally, the term meant one's
complete life, physical and spiritual, and what one does with
it. The word was coined by the philosopher Alfred Adler
(1870–1937) in *Problems of Neurosis* (1929). He originally meant a
person's character as formed in early childhood, but the word
has come to mean a way of living. Latterly taken by those who
always prefer a longer word to a shorter. Where 'life' would be
the short direct way of saying what is meant, 'lifestyle' is wheeled
out instead. The euphemistic use for sexual orientation may
have been by the 1990s.

(to be) light on one's toes To be homosexual (male).
Possibly deriving from the old expression 'to be light on one's
feet/legs', meaning 'to be fortunate/successful', but given a
'camp', effeminate twist. Since the mid-20th century? The
American equivalent is reportedly 'light in the loafers' or 'light
on her feet'. 'This infamous loo was, for many years, a meeting
place for those who were a bit light on their feet – all right,
then – "ginger"' – Roy Hudd, *Book of Music-Hall, Variety and Showbiz
Anecdotes* (1993).

light-fingered Prone to petty theft, pilfering. By the 16th
century.

**like a cruel untimely frost death touched this lovely
flower** She died. From a 1942 epitaph 'at Lee' and recorded in

Hugh Meller, *London Cemeteries* (1981), ch. 5. From the same source, 'a lily bud has dropped and died'.

(to) like a drink To be a heavy drinker. 20th century. 'All Cloughie had were the simple, old-fashioned pleasures of hard work, team spirit and strong whisky. We all knew Cloughie liked a drink, but who didn't? I like a drink. I'm drinking now and have been all day. It never affected him and it doesn't affect me' – sportsoffensive.com (November 2005).

like that Homosexual. 20th century.

(to) like the ladies To be sexually promiscuous (or, at least, always in the pursuit). 20th century.

(the) limbs The legs. The usage is ancient but in this euphemistic sense it was established even before the 19th century. It came into its own at the height of Victorian prudery, though also in the US at that time. However, the legendary coverings said to have been put over too-shocking piano legs never really existed. 'One of my maids who slipped on the avenue yesterday and fractured one of her – er – limbs' – H.L. Wilson, *Spenders* (1902), ch. 31.

limp-wristed Homosexual (of a man). Since the mid-20th century?

(to) line one's pockets To steal money. Since the 19th century?

(the) lips The mouth. If one thinks of a dictionary definition like this from Cassell, 'The opening at which food is taken into the body, with the cavity behind containing the organs of mastication, insalivation and speech', the need for an elegant substitute is appreciated. As far as one can tell, the use of 'lips' in poetry has long been in this euphemistic mode. 'Take, O take those lips away' – William Shakespeare, *Measure for Measure* (1604), IV. i.1.

(a) liquid lunch An alcoholic drink taken with little or no food in place of a proper lunch. By the 1970s.

(to) liquidate To kill, assassinate. Probably started during the Soviet purges of opponents (like the Trotskyites) in the 1920s/30s. 'Once we killed bad men: now we liquidate unsocial elements' – C.S. Lewis, *The Abolition of Man* (1943), ch. 3; 'When the army units fanned out in Dacca on the evening of March 25 ... many of them carried lists of people to be liquidated' – *The Sunday Times* (13 June 1971).

(to have a) liquidity crisis To be unable to pay one's bills when they fall due or simply to be short of cash; insolvency. By the 1970s. Also **to have a temporary liquidity problem**.

(one's) little arrangements One's genitals. Perhaps a one-off, but Diana Athill, *Instead of a Letter* (1976) mentions that her aunt encouraged her to draw humans, even a naked man or woman, instead of horses, remarking: 'Go on, you needn't put in his – er – his little arrangements if you don't want to.'

(the) little boys' / girls' room A LAVATORY , echoic of nursery usage. Boys' more usual than girls'. Rather twee, a genteelism, but not uncommon. By the 1950s at least. 'Rodway pulled up in a lay-by. "All out for the little boys' room," he said' – Martin C. Woodhouse, *Blue Bone* (1973), ch. 2.

(a/the) little gentleman in black velvet A mole, after the one whose hillock caused William III's horse to stumble in 1702 and the subsequent death of the king, partly from the injuries sustained. Hence, the Jacobite toast: 'The little gentleman in black velvet!' Compare KING OVER THE WATER!

(a) little house An outside LAVATORY. Probably by the late 19th century. 'On the wall of the "little house" at Laura's home pictures cut from the newspapers were pasted' – Flora Thompson, *Lark Rise* (1939), ch. 1.

little jobs Urination. Nursery talk. Compare under BIGGIE.

(these) little local difficulties A major political crisis. Phrase used dismissively to show a lack of concern. In 1958, as British prime minister, Harold Macmillan made this characteristically airy reference to the fact that his entire Treasury team, including the Chancellor of the Exchequer, had resigned over disagreement about budget estimates. In a statement at London airport before leaving for a tour of the Commonwealth on 7 January, he said: 'I thought the best thing to do was to settle up these little local difficulties, and then turn to the wider vision of the Commonwealth.'

little Mary The abdomen, belly, stomach. Cited in Allen Walker Read, *Classic American Graffiti* (1935), but probably introduced by J.M. Barrie's play, *Little Mary*. 'And what is the subject of the piece? Who is Little Mary? It is nobody: it is simply a nursery name that the child-doctor invents as a kind of polite equivalent to what children ordinarily allude to as their "tum-tum"' – *Punch* (14 October 1903).

(a) little something A snack between meals. Since the 19th century. 'It was … as if somebody inside him were saying, "Now then, Pooh, time for a little something" … So he sat down and took the top off his jar of honey' – A.A. Milne, *Winnie-the-Pooh* (1926), ch. 6.

(a) little stranger A newborn child. *OED2* states that 'Welcome, little stranger!' was a common saying in the early part of the 19th century 'and sometimes printed or embroidered on articles for nursery use'. The expression 'little stranger' had been known, however, since the 17th century. 'Mrs. Custance was brought to bed of a Boy about 11 o'clock this Morn'. She with the little stranger as well as can be expected' – James Woodforde, diary entry for 6 May 1787.

(a) little vascular accident A mini-stroke. Given the medical profession's extreme reluctance to use the s-word, even when the

layman is convinced one has occurred, it was not surprising
that spokespersons played down what had happened to Jacques
Chirac, President of France, in September 2005. 'It appeared –
but was never clearly stated – that M. Chirac had suffered a
"mini-stroke", or minor failure of a cerebral vein ... He was
taken [to hospital] last Friday with what was described as *un petit
accident vasculaire"* which had impaired his vision' – *The Independent*
(10 September 2005).

(a) little visitor A flea. Since when? 'Next week they're
expecting a little visitor. Wee Georgie Wood is coming to tea' –
BBC Radio *Goon Show* (early 1950s); 'Get rid of their little
visitors' – advertisement for 'Anti-Flea and Tick Collar' (1981).

(a) little weakness A drink problem (usually). Date of origin
unknown. 'Esau ... undogcollared because of his little weakness,
was scythed to the bone one harvest by mistake' – Dylan Thomas,
Under Milk Wood (1954).

(to) live in sin See LIVING AS MAN AND WIFE

(to) live together To cohabit, to have a sexual relationship
outside marriage. By 1800. 'I am only concerned that their
living together before marriage took place, should be so generally
known' – Jane Austen, *Pride and Prejudice* (1813), pt 3, ch. 15;
'From that time on, they started living together "on a close basis".
They were married in October 2001, just over a year before he
died' – *The Times* (27 October 2005).

living as man and wife Cohabiting though not married. Also
living in (mortal) sin. Known by 1838. The phrase had earlier
been used with slightly different meanings. Margaret Cavendish,
Duchess of Newcastle, *Bell in Campo* (1662), pt 1, act 5, scene
25 has the phrase in a rather involved conceit. A twice-married
woman is said to 'live in sin herself by Cuckolding both her
Husbands, having had two'. 'Think women seek to match with
men, / To live in sin and not to saint' occurs in one version of
poem 18 in Shakespeare's 'The Passionate Pilgrim', though it is

difficult to understand what is meant by this. 'I said how strange it was that when Lloyd-George was premier he could be living in sin with Miss Stevenson and nobody knew ... in those days living in sin was no impediment to a politician's career' – James Lees-Milne, *Through Wood and Dale* (1998), diary entry for 21 February 1977.

(a) living curiosity A freak. 19th-century euphemism for dwarfs, giants, bearded ladies and the like.

(a) localized capacity deficiency A traffic bottle-neck – as reported by the Plain English Campaign and quoted in the *Northern Echo* (13 May 1997).

(the) loins The male genitalia in their reproductive capacity. A biblical term. 'Be fruitful and multiply ... and kings shall come out of thy loins' – Genesis 35:11.

(a) lone parent A single parent living alone. Describing a person who is bringing up a child without the assistance of a marital partner, SINGLE PARENT had been current since 1969. But then, Gingerbread, the UK organization catering for people in that position, substituted the term 'lone parent'. This was because 'single' may suggest 'unmarried' when it is hardly relevant whether the parents are married or not. The point is that the lone parent is on his or her own because of divorce, desertion, separation or death, or because the partner is in hospital or prison.

(a) long illness See AFTER A LONG ILLNESS

long in the tooth Old. Older people suffer from receding of the gums and so their teeth appear to have grown longer. Known by 1852 (Thackeray, *Esmond*). The same applies to horses, hence the reason one is advised 'not to look a gift horse in the mouth'.

(the) longer living Old age pensioners. An American term since the late 20th century.

(the) longest holiday Retirement. Possibly an American term, since the late 20th century.

(to go to the) loo To go to the LAVATORY. Established in well-to-do British society by the early 20th century and in general middle-class use after the Second World War. Of the several theories for its origin, perhaps the most well known is that the word comes from the French *gardez l'eau* [mind the water], dating from the days when chamber pots or dirty water were emptied out of the window into the street and recorded by Laurence Sterne as *garde d'eau* in *A Sentimental Journey* (1768). This cry was also rendered 'gardyloo' in old Edinburgh and recorded by Tobias Smollett in *Humphrey Clinker* (1771). However, Professor A.S.C. Ross who examined the various options in a 1974 issue of *Blackwood's Magazine* favoured a derivation, 'in some way which could not be determined', from 'Waterloo'. I would add that at one time people probably said: 'I must go to the water-closet' and, wishing not to be explicit, substituted 'Water–loo' as a weak little joke. The name 'Waterloo' was there, waiting to be used, from 1815 onwards.

(to) look after number one To be selfish. By 1700.

(to) look at the garden To go to the LAVATORY out of doors. Compare 'I will but look upon the hedge' – which is what Autolycus says in Shakespeare, *The Winter's Tale* (1611), IV.iv.827.

(a) looney bin A mad house. 'Sir Roderick Glossop ... is always called a nerve specialist, because it sounds better, but everybody knows that he's really a sort of janitor to the looney-bin' – P.G. Wodehouse, *The Inimitable Jeeves* (1924), ch. 7.

looney tunes Madmen. The reference is to the cinema cartoon comedies called *Looney Tunes*, produced by Warner Brothers since the 1940s. President Reagan commented on the hijacking of a US plane by Shi-ite Muslims: 'We are not going to tolerate these attacks from outlaw states run by the strangest collection of misfits, looney tunes, and squalid criminals since the advent of the Third Reich' (8 July 1985). The phrase had earlier been used in the Mel Brooks film *High Anxiety* (US 1977).

loose Immoral (of a woman). A favourite word in Bible translations, as 'You will be saved from the loose woman, from the adventuress with her smooth words' and 'For the lips of a loose woman drip honey, and her speech is smoother than oil' – Proverbs 2:16; 5:3 (in the Authorized Version, the phrase 'strange woman' is used here).

(a) loose cannon A person who is not attached to a particular faction and acts independently and, possibly, unreliably. Of American origin, popular since the 1980s. The reference is either to a cannon that is not properly secured to the deck of a ship or to an artilleryman who is working independently during a land battle. 'A subcategory of journalese involves the language used to indicate a powerful or celebrated person who is about to self-destruct or walk the plank ... Soon Mr Brilliant will be labeled a "loose cannon" and transmute himself into an adviser, the Washington version of self-imposed exile' – *Time* Magazine (1 September 1986); 'Gung-ho, loose cannon, cowboy, Jesus freak – there is already a cottage industry manufacturing Ollie epithets. Lynching [Oliver] North is quickly becoming a national sport' – *The Observer* (26 July 1987); 'The problem is that Mr Agha, like almost every other governor in Afghanistan, is a bit of a rogue. Taxes do not all go to central government. His own militia are better paid than government soldiers ... but it's no secret in Kabul that the governor is a loose cannon' – Robert Fisk in *The Independent* (9 August 2002).

(to) lose To have someone taken from you by death. As in the expressions, 'He has lost his wife' or a doctor advising, 'You're going to lose her' or a wife saying, 'I've just lost my husband.' Since the 16th century. In a letter of condolence to Robert Cecil in 1597, Walter Raleigh wrote: 'It is true that you have lost a good and virtuous wife.' Hence, someone's death is referred to as **a great loss**.

(to) lose one's cherry To have sex for the first time (usually of a female) and thus to lose one's virginity. By approximately 1900. 'Associated with the growing heterosexual awareness of high-school students are such words as *cherry*, which in appropriate contexts takes on the familiar slang meaning "hymen", while a *cherry-buster*, logically, is "a professional deflowerer"' – *American Speech*, vol. 39 (1964). Compare the venerable alternatives: **to lose one's honour / innocence / reputation / virtue**.

(to) lose one's life To die, be killed (especially in battle). 'Before the hymn the Skipper would announce / The latest names of those who'd lost their lives / For King and Country and the Dragon School' – John Betjeman, *Summoned By Bells* (1960), ch. 5.

(to) lose one's marbles To lose one's mental faculties. Almost everyone agrees that this euphemism is of American in origin, *OED2* finding it first recorded in the journal *American Speech* in 1927. *Partridge/Slang* also has it that 'marbles' = testicles, though *DOAS* rates this usage as 'not common'. Partridge also defines the word 'marbles' on its own as meaning 'furniture, movables', derived from the French *meubles*, and dating from 1864. Could one imagine 'to lose one's marbles' coming from the idea of losing one's 'mind furniture' or possessions? *Apperson* lends support to this account by showing that the English Dialect Society had included in a publication called *West Cornwall Words* (1880): 'Those that have marbles may play, but those that have none must look on.' Surely this admirably conveys the misfortune of those who are without the necessary wherewithal to participate in the game of life?

Again, Elizabeth Monkhouse recalled (1997) that in her part of Cheshire 'He's got all his chairs at home' was an expression used to mean 'He's all there, alert.' Hence, a home without furniture is empty, so 'lost one's marbles' = empty headed, no longer at home, no longer 'there'. This was also reported from Lancashire.

Meanwhile, Joyce Hanley wrote: 'In Yorkshire, if someone is a bit lacking in the head, we say that they haven't got all their furniture at home.' At the popular level, most people believe the phrase derives from a joke. When Lord Elgin brought back his famous marbles from the Parthenon and they ended up in the British Museum in 1816, the Greeks were hopping mad (and, indeed, remain so). But, with all due respect and however entertaining, this is not an origin to be taken seriously.

Dictionary explanations include this from Robert L. Chapman's *New Dictionary of American Slang* (1987): 'From an earlier phrase *let his marbles go with the monkey* from a story about a boy whose marbles were carried off by a monkey.' Chapman, basing himself on *DOAS*, also draws a parallel with the American expression 'to have all one's buttons', meaning 'to be of normal mentality or behavior' (by 1949). What is it about possessing small round things? *Chambers Dictionary* (1993) has: 'From Old French *marbre*, from Latin *marmor*; cf Greek *marmaros*, from *marmairein* to sparkle.' Is the suggestion that when we lose our marbles the sparkle goes out of our lives? These don't seem very winning explanations, to me, though the last does take us back to Greek ...

Other offers: Helen Rogers wrote (1997): 'I'm sure it comes from "cracked" meaning crazy. You kept your marbles in a glass jar to show the bright colours. If the jar cracked, it lost its marbles.' Mij Clarke: 'Brain cells do not renew themselves as other cells in the body do. Consequently when brain cells die, they are lost for ever.' Stephen Bristow noted that *Chambers* also gives the word 'bonce' as meaning both 'a large marble' and 'the head', 'so, if you have lost your head, you have also lost your bonce, or your marble'; Elizabeth Payne suggested that when playing the game of marbles, 'a person with a quick intellect might win all the marbles from a rather slower person'. And S.C. Upton recalled that when playing marbles as a boy, the balls would often fall through the grating of a drain at the side of the road, and be lost. 'This resulted in "losing your marbles" which made you quite angry and mad, hence the saying and meaning.'

(to) lose — posts To give people the sack. Announcing an economy drive in February 1980, the BBC stated that the proposals included 'losing about 1,500 permanent and temporary posts'.

(a) Lothario A man who pursues women for sex, a libertine, a RAKE. For a well-known term this has a relatively obscure origin. The character 'gay Lothario' appeared in Nicholas Rowe's play *The Fair Penitent* (1703), although the name had earlier been used for a man with the same disposition in Sir William D'Avenant's play *The Cruel Brother* (1630). 'A devil of a fellow – a regular Lothario' – W.S. Gilbert, *Ruddigore* (1887), act I.

(a) love child A bastard. By 1805.

love handles Rolls of fat at the waist, seen not as a sign of putting on weight but something useful to hold on to during SEXUAL INTERCOURSE. Late 20th century. 'Side steaks' is a similar term – and compare 'bugger's grips' for a man's cheek whiskers.

(a) love nest Where a man and his mistress may be found, according to the popular newspapers. By 1919, probably of American origin.

(the) love that durst not speak its name Male homosexuality. This expression is so much bound up with the Oscar Wilde case that it is sometimes assumed that he coined it. Not so. It was the person who had helped land him in his predicament, Lord Alfred Douglas (1870–1945), who wrote the poem 'Two Loves' (1892–3), that concludes with the line 'I am the love that dare not speak its name'. In both his trials, Wilde was asked about the poem. In the second (April–May 1895) he was asked to explain the line and gave a spontaneous explanation: 'In this century [it] is such a great affection of an elder for a younger man as there was between David and Jonathan, such as Plato made the very basis of his philosophy, and such as you find in the sonnets of Michelangelo and Shakespeare. It is that deep, spiritual affection that is as pure as it is perfect ... It is in this century misunderstood, so much misunderstood that it may be described as the "Love that dare not speak its name", and on account of it I am placed where I am now.'

love-making See MAKE LOVE

(a/the) loved one A dead relative (usually); a corpse. Since the 1920s. Hence, *The Loved One* – the title of Evelyn Waugh's novel (1948) satirizing American funerary procedures.

(a) lover A sexual partner, mistress or KEPT WOMAN. Since the 19th century? 'Under the hedge which divided the field from a distant plantation girls had given themselves to lovers' – Thomas Hardy, *Jude the Obscure* (1895), pt I, ch. 2.

low-budget See BUDGET

low-profile Inconspicuous, without publicity. Since the 1960s. It seems to have begun in American military contexts and became much used in reporting events in Northern Ireland. 'The army kept a low profile during the protest march', meaning the soldiers kept out of sight or were not prominent in the streets. It had a certain neatness and descriptiveness, suggesting a kind of tactical discretion. Its imagery was suspect – that of a man's outline merging into the background, or of a soldier crawling on his stomach (how else could he have a *low* profile?) – but it had the virtue of being understood in the context of the report. Then it was transferred to civilian use, over-use, and its glibness bordered on the tedious. It took the place of 'unobtrusive' and 'cautiously quiet' in general conversation. 'I adopted a low profile' was a new way of saying 'I kept out of the picture', or 'I didn't interfere', both of which were apparently thought to be too explicit. Probably more used than HIGH-PROFILE and, like it, a borderline euphemism, being above all just another way of saying something, albeit irritatingly.
    'I admire the brisk creativeness of American English. "Low profile" is a perfectly vivid phrase for "conciliatory demeanour"' – *The Listener* (4 January 1973); 'Low Profile Vigilantes a Success, Loyalists Claim' – *The Guardian* (1 June 1976); 'There have been times, however, when the council's politics have dictated that Atwell take a low profile on a controversial issue' – *The Washington Post* (3 November 1991).

low-spirited Depressed. Since the 18th century. This term seeks to play down what may be a serious medical condition. The same words meaning 'mean-spirited' go back further.

(the) lower orders The common people. James Boswell, snob though he was, probably had no derogatory intention when he wrote 'I have great pleasure in conversing with the lower part of mankind, who have very curious ideas.' Later he changed the synonym when he commented, 'The rudeness of the English vulgar is terrible' (in his *London Journal*). When 'common' began to imply rudeness and vulgarity (as in the vernacular 'She's common!') a politer word was called for, but 'lower orders' was never a completely satisfactory alternative and was later replaced by (THE) WORKERS. 'Really, if the lower orders don't set us a good example, what on earth is the use of them?' – Oscar Wilde, *The Importance of Being Earnest* (1895), act I.

(the) lower part of the body / lower regions The STOMACH, belly or other parts of the body in that general area. By the 17th century. '[The women] worked ... with coarse aprons of sacking enveloping the lower part of their bodies' – Flora Thompson, *Lark Rise* (1939), ch. 3. Since the 19th century, the phrase 'lower regions' has also been used to refer to the downstairs area of a house. Further, **lower stomach** can refer to the genitalia.

(to) lubricate (1) To grease the palm, to bribe. By the 1920s. (2) To drink alcohol or ply with alcohol. By 1900.
(3) To have SEXUAL INTERCOURSE. Probably obsolete. 'I met with a monstrous big whore in the Strand, with whom I had a great curiosity to lubricate, as the saying is' – James Boswell, diary entry for 13 April 1763.

(we must have) lunch (some time) We'll not meet up again, if I can avoid it. The suggested occasion for a future meeting has become widely interpreted as a coded expression of a wish that it should never, in fact, take place. This may date back to the 1960s when Jilly Cooper, then a journalist, reported

that 'We must have lunch some time' was 'London(-speak)' for
'goodbye'.

'[*Businessman talking into telephone*] 'No, Thursday's out. How about
never – is never good for you?' – caption to Robert Mankoff
cartoon in *The New Yorker* (3 May 1993); 'Paul Grice once observed
to me that in Oxford, when someone says, "We must have lunch
some time," it means, "I don't care if I never see you again in my
life"' – Thomas Nagel, *Concealment and Exposure and other Essays*
(2002).

(the) lunchbox The male genitalia. Since the late 20th century.
Much hilarity was caused in 1998 when a judge of the British
High Court was dealing with a case featuring the Olympic gold
medallist, Linford Christie. The athlete described his grievance
against the press for continually referring to the size of his
MANHOOD and vented his feelings of 'disgust' at newspaper
references to 'Linford Christie's lunchbox'. This led to a
bemused inquiry from the judge, Mr Justice Popplewell, who
asked, as such people do: 'What is Linford Christie's lunchbox?'
The athlete replied: 'They are making a reference to my genitals,
your honour.'

(the) lungs The female breasts. Second half of the 20th
century. '[*Boy, looking at her chest, to girl*] What lungs!' – film *Where the
Boys Are* (US 1960); 'A mother who had knitted her 5-year-old boy
a "V"-neck sweater was puzzled by his refusal to consider wearing
it. Finally the reason became clear: "I don't want one like that.
My teacher has one and when she bends down – you can see her
lungs"' – quoted in my *Babes and Sucklings* (1983).

lying See DISHONESTY

Mm

(a) madam / madame A brothel keeper. By the 1870s, probably at first in the US. 'There was a discipline in the old-time brothels. The madame ... played a role similar to that of the headmistress of Roedean' – Graham Greene, *Travels with My Aunt* (1969), pt 1, ch. 8.

(a) maiden A virgin. Except in medical circles and its special religious significance (the Virgin Mary), the word 'virgin' was almost taboo in literature and conversation for about a hundred years from the mid-19th century until the 1960s. The word was avoided by the use of euphemistic synonyms such as **pure, chaste** and **undefiled**. Nowadays, in contrast, not only do we have a Virgin record label, airline, rail company and so on, but one would be most unlikely to inquire if a girl or woman were chaste, unsullied or undefiled. Rather one would come right out with it and ask, 'Is she a virgin?' The direct approach is losing its indelicacy and therefore the need for euphemism is disappearing. We are returning to the forthrightness of the Bible when it could be said of Rebekah: 'The maiden was fair to look upon, a virgin, whom no man had known' – Genesis 24:16.

(a) maiden lady An unmarried (elderly) woman. Her virginity is, of course, not in question. By the 18th century and probably before. 'Maiden ladies of a certain age should have visiting cards of their own' – from a book of etiquette (1888).

(to) make a call To go to the LAVATORY. Probably just to URINATE. Compare GO AND TELEPHONE HITLER.

(to) make a decent woman of To marry a woman you have impregnated or at least seduced. Perhaps more commonly **to make an honest woman of** – known since 1629. 'There are several issues in Popeye and Olive Oyl's relationship that need reconciling. Despite Olive's obvious attraction to Popeye, she continues to lead Bluto along, and Popeye refuses to "make a decent woman" of Olive, whose biological clock must sound like Big Ben' – otal.umd.edu (2005).

(to) make a slip To become pregnant illegitimately. Since the 19th century?

(to) make eyes at To flirt, make amorous advances (usually said of a woman aiming at a man). By 1852. The song 'Ma, He's Making Eyes At Me' was written by Don Conrad in 1921.

(to) make love To have SEXUAL INTERCOURSE. Originally, 'to make love' simply meant 'to pay amorous attention to' and this, according to *OED2*, was established usage by 1580. It is often difficult to be sure which meaning is being applied but when Hamlet rails against Gertrude for 'honeying and making love' – *Hamlet* (1600–1), III.iv.94 – the context clearly shows that sex is being talked about. When the transition was finally made to the modern meaning is not easy to establish but probably by the 1950s. Mervyn Peake, *Gormenghast* (1950), ch. 29 clearly has it in this sense: 'One of the Carvers made love to her and she had a baby.' Since then its use in conversation, plays, newspapers and police courts has been well understood. The novelist Georges Simenon was reported in English newspapers as saying, 'I have made love to ten thousand women.' What he actually said during an interview in *L'Express* (21 February 1977) was: '*J'ai eu 10,000 femmes*... [I have had 10,000 women]'

Similarly, **lovemaking** can now refer to sexual intercourse whereas formerly it meant just courtship.

(to) make off with To steal. By 1829.

(to) make old bones To live a long time. Since the early 19th century. Usually employed when the opposite is expected: 'I don't think he'll make old bones' – i.e. 'I don't think he'll live very long.' 'Edward the Seventh and George the Fifth – they neither of them made old bones' – Nevil Shute, *In the Wet* (1953), ch. 8.

(to) make room for (my) tea To URINATE

(to) make up to To flirt, make amorous advances. By 1781.

(to) make water To URINATE. By the 14th century. In the transcript of the trial of John Lilburne in 1649, it was reported that he interrupted the proceedings to ask for a chamber pot. 'Whilst it was fetching, Mr Lilburne followed his papers and books close; and when the pot came he made water, and gave it to the foreman.'

(a) maladjusted child A backward, naughty, troublesome child. Early 20th century?

(to see a) man about a dog See GO AND SEE A MAN ABOUT A DOG

(a) man in a dark / grey suit / man in a suit A colourless administrator or technocrat who is probably as grey in his personality as in the colour of his suit. When the Beatles set up the Apple organization in the 1960s, John Lennon said this was an attempt 'to wrest control from the men in suits'. Sometimes such people are simply called **suits**. The plural 'men in grey suits' are, however, something a little different. In the November 1990 politicking that saw the British Prime Minister Margaret Thatcher eased out of office by her own party, there was much talk of the 'men in (grey) suits', those senior members of the Tory party who would advise Mrs Thatcher when it was time for her to go. Here, although still referring to faceless administrative types, the term is not quite so pejorative. In *The Observer* (1 December 1990), Alan Watkins adjusted the phrase slightly: 'I claim the paternity of "the men in suits" from an *Observer* column of the mid-1980s. Not you may notice, the men in dark suits, still less those in grey ones, which give quite the wrong idea.'

'With this latest career move can we expect to see the wunderkind [John Birt] transformed into the proverbial Man In A Grey Suit?' – *Broadcast* Magazine (1987); '[John] Major's spectacular ordinariness – the Treasury is now led by a "man in a suit" whose most distinguishing feature is his spectacles' – *The Observer* (29 October 1989); 'That was more than just a re-assertion of the company's mission statement. It was almost a threat to the new regime of financial "bean counters" from the ousted advertising "suit"' – *The Sunday Times* (8 January 1995).

(the) manhood The male genitals. By 1640. 'Topless kissogram girl Linzi Berry went on sick leave suffering from shock – after a naked miner coshed her with his manhood' – *Sun* (28 February 1991).

manure Dung. Since the 16th century. 'I knew a girl who was so pure / She couldn't say the word Manure' – Reginald Arkell, 'A Perfect Lady' in *Green Fingers* (1934).

marriage/relationships/singleness See ABUSE THE BED; AGREED TO PART; BACHELOR GIRL; CASUAL RELATIONSHIP; COHABITATION; COMMON LAW WIFE; COMPANION; CONJUGAL RELATIONS/RIGHTS; CONSENSUAL NON-MONOGAMY; CONSUMMATE A RELATIONSHIP; DALLIANCE; DAMAGED GOODS; EXTRAMARITAL RELATIONS; FRATERNIZE; FRIEND; FULL RELATIONSHIP; GENTLEMAN CALLER; GOOD FRIENDS; HONOURABLE INTENTIONS; JILT; LADIES' MAN; LADY FRIEND; LEAD A NORMAL MARRIED LIFE; LIVING TOGETHER; LIVING AS MAN AND WIFE; LONE PARENT; MARITAL RELATIONS; MENAGE A TROIS; MISCONDUCT; MISTRESS; NO LONGER LIVING TOGETHER; ONE-PARENT FAMILY; OPEN MARRIAGE; OTHER WOMAN; OVER THE

BROOMSTICK; PARTNER; POP THE QUESTION;
RELATIONSHIP; SEVEN YEAR ITCH; SIGNIFICANT OTHER;
SINGLE BY CHOICE; SINGLE PARENT; SLICE OFF A CUT
LOAF; SPLIT UP; THROW OVER; UNDERSTANDING;
UNFAITHFUL

(a) marital aid   An instrument used in sexual pleasuring, for
those married or not. By 1970?

marital relations   Sex within marriage – not your in-laws.
By 1893. Before the sexual revolution, 'marriage' and 'marital'
supposedly conferred dignity on discussions of sexual matters.
The Marriage Art was the title of a book on sex techniques by John
Eichenlaub, M.D. (1962). It contained, for example, this
suggestion for 'increasing feminine fervor': 'You are an A.1
tumble-bun.' Compare **marital rights** meaning sex by man with
his wife. By 1858. Mostly a legal term.

(a) massage establishment / parlour   A brothel. Probably
in the US originally. *Collier's* Magazine was referring to 'massage
parlors' in 1913. In the UK by the 1960s.

masturbation   See AUTO-EROTIC HABITS; BARCLAYS;
BASH/FLOG THE BISHOP; BEASTLINESS; BEAT ONE'S MEAT;
HAND-JOB; J. ARTHUR; MILK ONESELF; ONANISM; RELIEF;
SELF-ABUSE

(a) matron / mature woman   A middle-aged or elderly
woman. An equivalent of the French expression '*une femme d'une
certaine âge*' ('a woman of a certain age') has never caught on in
English. 'Matron' has meant a married woman since time
immemorial. The euphemistic use implies that simply by being
married, she is not in the first flush. As for 'mature woman', as
in the phrase 'fashions for the mature woman' – this is certainly
not PC. It might suggest that the woman was once immature.
'Do you want the whole countryside to be laughing at us? –
women of our years? – mature women, *dancing*?' – Brian Friel,
Dancing at Lughnasa (1990).

(of) mature years Old, not young. By 1832.

meaningful dialogue Discussion. 'Meaningful' would seem to suggest 'relevant, to the point', but it is still not clear why the Americans had to come up with this. By the 1960s/70s? 'We hope that international pressure will be increased and that meaningful dialogue will begin soon in Burma' – letter to the editor, *The Guardian* (22 July 1994).

(a) meat dealer / man / purveyor / technologist
A butcher. Anything to disguise the knacker/slaughter side of the trade. 'Meat man' is used particularly in the horse-meat trade and was current by 1910.

(to have a) medal showing (Of a man) to have a visibly undone trouser button. Say by 1900. From the days not only when trousers actually had fly buttons but also they were sometimes made of metal.

medical See HEALTH

(to) meet one's maker See GO TO MEET ONE'S MAKER

(to) meet with an accident To be murdered – or, at least, to die but not in your bed. 20th century. 'This is not the first time that an accident of this nature has occurred here. There have been several such cases earlier. The most recent being the case of Suresh Pavaskar, who met with an accident on Sept 29. The circumstances were the same; the only difference was that Pavaskar was on a bike' – mid-day.com (12 November 2005).

(at / in a) meeting Unwilling to speak to someone on the phone. A standard excuse given by secretaries – 'He's in a meeting.' By the mid-20th century? Sometimes it is actually true, of course. But then, sometimes people say 'We must have LUNCH' when they really mean it, too.

melanin-impoverished White-skinned. Alleged in the late 20th century. Melanin is the black pigment in the skin of Afro-Americans and other races.

mellow Quietly drunk. By the 17th century.

melons Large breasts. By the 1970s. 'She released the catch on her bra and slipped it off … Her full and shapely melons swung and swayed and drooped as she moved' – *Pussycat*, vol. 33, No. 59 (1972); '"Melons" [is the gossip column nickname] of Lady Helen Windsor, for two very good reasons' – Noble and Rees, eds, *A Who's Who of Nicknames* (1985).

(the male) member The penis. Also **carnal / privy / virile member** – the latter deriving from the medical Latin *membrum virile*. All mostly in use since the 13th century. In the plural, the genitals – as in the 16th/17th century death 'sentence': 'And your privy members cut off and thrown into the fire.' After intimacy with an actress, James Boswell 'began to feel an unaccountable alarm of unexpected evil: a little heat in the members of my body sacred to Cupid', diary entry for 18 January 1763. When the Family Planning Association inaugurated a sex-advice telephone service, one of the staff told the *Daily Mail* (13 October 1976) that most of the callers in the early stages were men: 'As for their principal worry, well – since you ask – it tends to concern the size of their "member", together with associated problems.'

(a) memorial garden A graveyard (in the US). Quoted in Willard R. Espy, *An Almanac of Words at Play* (1975).

men in white coats Doctors and orderlies (especially from mental hospitals) whose appearance on the scene suggests that someone is about to be taken away for treatment. The cry 'Send for the men in white coats' might have preceded their arrival. *OED2* finds the term 'whitecoat' for such a person in use by 1911.

(a) men's magazine A pornographic or semi-pornographic publication for male readers. Mid-20th century.

(to go to the) men's room To go to the [men's] LAVATORY. Curiously, there is no 'women's room' as the female equivalent. American in origin and still mostly confined to that place. By the 1920s. 'When one of the men asked to be excused to go to the men's room, Mrs [Dorothy] Parker softly explained, as if pleading for pity for a flustered young man. "He really needs to telephone, but he's too embarrassed to say so"' – John Keats, *You Might As Well Live* (1970), ch. 5.

(a) *ménage à trois* A sexual living arrangement involving three people, usually a husband, a wife and one of their lovers. From the French meaning 'household of three' and known in English by the 1890s.

menstruation See AUNT FLO IS VISITING; CAPTAIN IS AT HOME; COVERING THE WATERFRONT; CURSE; FEMALE / FEMININE HYGIENE / PHYSIOLOGY; FLOWERS; FLYING THE RED FLAG; HEADACHE; MY COUNTRY COUSIN HAS COME; RIDING THE RAG; REGULAR; TIME (OF THE MONTH); USUAL REASON; and also under PERIOD

mental matters See ACADEMICALLY SUBNORMAL; BACKWARD CHILDREN; BRICKS/FEW BRICKS SHORT OF A LOAD; BATS IN THE BELFRY; BROADMOOR PATIENT; CARE IN THE COMMUNITY; COMMIT; DEMENTIA CARE HOME; EDUCATIONALLY SUBNORMAL; HANDICAP; HAVE A SCREW LOOSE; HAVE NONE OF ONE'S CHAIRS AT HOME; HOME; ILL; LOONEY BIN; LOONEY TUNES; LOSE ONE'S MARBLES; MALADJUSTED CHILD; MEN IN WHITE COATS; MENTAL; MENTAL HOME; NERVE SPECIALIST; NERVOUS BREAKDOWN; NOT ALL THERE; NOT TO GO FURTHER THAN THURSDAY; OUT OF ONE'S MIND; OUT TO LUNCH; POSTAL; RETARDED; SEVERELY SUBNORMAL; SLOW LEARNER; SLOW ON THE UPTAKE

mental / mentally deranged / disordered / disturbed / unbalanced / suffering from a mental condition or **mental alienation** Mad, lunatic, insane. Most of these are no older than the 1920s and most are not acceptable to the PC for various reasons and the PC oracle has not come up with anything better, so it is quite in order to call mad people 'mad'. If they do not like this, they will probably point this out to you, forcibly.

(a) mental home / hospital A lunatic asylum. The former may be of American origin and has been in place since the 1920s, the latter by the 1890s. 'William Lutz, editor of the Quarterly Review of Doublespeak, says that the trend to make language politically correct is part of the larger, permanent trend of euphemization. Sometimes it's done out of embarrassment (ie, in sexual and bodily contexts), sometimes sensitivity (when we stopped calling the state mental hospital "the nuthouse")' – *The Washington Post* (2 July 1991); 'He was committed as a schizophrenic suffering from somatic delusions ... In 1976, he escaped and showed up at his mother's house. He was returned to the hospital, ending up at Beverly Manor, a facility for mental patients, where he earned the nickname "Dracula"' – crimelibrary.com (29 November 2005).

(a) mercy killing The deliberately induced death of, say, a terminally ill patient. By 1935.

merry Tipsy, inoffensively drunk. Since the 16th century.

(a) message An advertisement (in US TV usage). As in, 'We'll be right back after this message.' Since the 1940s?

meticulosity Great care. In *Chosen Words* (1961), Ivor Brown called it 'a recent pomposity' (though it had been around since the 17th century).

middle-aged spread Paunchiness or obesity around the waist. By the 1930s.

military enhancements See ADVISER; AIR STRIKE; AIR SUPPORT; ANTI-PERSONNEL BOMB; BATTLE FATIGUE; BLOW

AWAY; CASUALTY; COLLATERAL DAMAGE; COMBAT FATIGUE;
CONVENTIONAL WEAPONS; DEALING WITH POCKETS OF
RESISTANCE; DEFENCE EQUIPMENT; DETERRENT
CAPABILITY; DEVICE; FACTORS OF PEACE; FRIENDLY FIRE;
HARDWARE; MILITARY INTELLIGENCE; PRE-DAWN VERTICAL
INSERTION; PRECISION BOMBING; RETURNED TO UNIT;
SHOCK AND AWE; SURGICAL STRIKE; TAKE OUT; TARGET OF
OPPORTUNITY; WASTE; WITHDRAWAL TO PREPARED
POSITIONS

military intelligence Spying. By the early 20th century.
'Military Intelligence is a contradiction in terms' – quoted in
my book *Graffiti Lives, OK* (1979). Said to come from a Ministry of
Defence building in London (where it remained briefly). The
saying had earlier been attributed to Groucho Marx in Art
Spiegelman and Bob Schneider, *Whole Grains* (1973).

(to) milk oneself / another To masturbate (for obvious
reasons). Possibly by the late 19th century.

(a) minor function Urination. A 'major function' does not
seem to have been used for defecation. By 1900? Compare GO
AND PARTAKE OF A MINOR [OR MAJOR] COMFORT.

(to) misappropriate To steal. By the mid-19th century.

misconduct Adultery. A favourite euphemism in divorce cases.
Also latterly applied to sexual harassment. 'Women across the
country have the entire US Senate, only two of whose hundred
members are female, in their sights, accusing senators in
thousands of letters and telegrams of rank insensitivity to sexual
misconduct' – *The Times* (12 October 1991).

(the) missionary position SEXUAL INTERCOURSE in the
position which has the man lying on top of the woman, face-
to-face. Possibly also known as the 'Mamma-Papa' position,
indicating that it is considered a functional approach to love-
making. McConville and Shearlaw in *The Slanguage of Sex* (1984)

suggest that since the 1980s there was been a slang term 'missionary man' for an uninspired lover. The idea that Christian missionaries taught this method may have first been promoted by Alfred C. Kinsey, author of *Sexual Behavior in the Human Male* (1948). This could have been a misreading of the anthropologist Bronislaw Malinowski who, reportedly, wrote that Trobriand Islanders of the western Pacific mocked the sexual technique taught to them by European traders and planters. There is no evidence that any missionary ever promoted the 'missionary position'.

'In six States [in the US] a woman may still be awarded a divorce if her husband makes love to her in any other than the missionary position' – *The Daily Telegraph* Colour Supplement (10 January 1969); 'The face-to-face "missionary position" (so called because it is virtually unknown in primitive races) is actually said to have been invented by Roman courtesans to hinder conception' – *Vogue* (November 1971).

(to be engaged on) missionary work in Africa To be in prison. Probably a one-off coinage but it is how the character Percy Brand explains to his son his frequent long absences from home in the film *Law and Disorder* (UK 1958).

(a) mistake An unwanted pregnancy. By the 1950s. 'Owing to a "mistake", Bernadette was probably "caught". She was beginning to "show"' – *The New Yorker* (12 January 1957).

(a) mistress An established extramarital sexual partner. Since the 15th century, gradually replacing the other meaning of the term – a female head of household.

(of) mixed race Half-caste, half-breed, mongrel. By the 1970s? A correspondent in *The Journalist* (February 1981) describes this as 'accurate and neutral', whereas 'half-caste' 'has only ever been used in the derogatory sense'.

mixed reviews Uniformly bad (critical) reviews. By the 1950s. Sometimes, **a mixed critical reception**. 'Not only were the reviews unenthusiastic – or "mixed", as Daphne described them – but there was an air of embarrassment about them on both sides of the Atlantic' – Margaret Forster, *Daphne du Maurier* (1993), ch. 23.

(a) mobile home A caravan – possibly an attempt to rid the word 'caravan' of downmarket connotations. It has hardly succeeded. By the early 1960s, there was something called the *Mobile Home Journal* in the US.

mobility-impaired Crippled. By the 1990s – a PC coinage.

(a) model A mistress, a kept woman, a prostitute. A prostitute might well advertise herself as a 'model' but the word has also been much used as cautious journalistic shorthand when describing women who are not, strictly speaking, prostitutes. Since the 1960s in the UK. '"Company director" and "model" are useful euphemisms for those who appear in dubious court cases' – *The Observer* (3 November 1963); 'Working as hostesses in high-class clubs, as "models" or simply walking the streets' – Germaine Greer, *The Female Eunuch* (1970). 'Mandy Rice-Davies, British "model and show girl" (1944–)' – *Brewer's Quotations* (1994). (In the book *Mandy* (1980), Rice-Davies writes of herself and Christine Keeler: 'Whatever we were, we weren't prostitutes or whores, but this was the company we were now linked with.') The terms **actress** and **showgirl** are similarly used.

(all) modern conveniences An indoor lavatory; plumbing. By the mid-19th century. Now, standard estate agents' parlance and extended to include lots of power points.

(a) mole A spy, an infiltrator. Since the 1970s, though there are one or two instances of use before this. The name 'mole' is applied to one who 'tunnels' into a large organization, but particularly a spy who is placed in another country's intelligence network, often years before being needed. The CIA term for the process is 'penetration' and former CIA chief Richard Helms told *Safire* that he had never encountered use of the word 'mole' in this regard. Although flirted with by other writers (as early as Francis Bacon), the term was introduced by John Le Carré in his novel *Tinker, Tailor, Soldier, Spy* (1974). In a BBC TV interview in 1976, he said he *thought* it was a genuine KGB term that he had picked up.

(to) molest To assault indecently. 'She was molested in the park' – a legal as well as popular euphemism. By 1895 (Thomas Hardy, *Jude the Obscure*).

(a) Molotov cocktail A simple petrol bomb. This incendiary device acquired its name in Finland during the early days of the Second World War and was known as such by 1940. V.M. Molotov had become Soviet Minister for Foreign Affairs in 1939. The Russians invaded Finland and these home-made grenades proved an effective way for the Finns to oppose their tanks.

money/selling/trade See ACCOUNT; BUDGET; CAREFUL WITH ONE'S MONEY; CASH-FLOW PROBLEM; CLOSE/CLOSE-FISTED; COMFORTABLY OFF; COMPASSION FATIGUE; COMPLIMENTARY; CONSUMER; CONTRIBUTION; COURTESY; CREATIVE ACCOUNTANCY; CUSTOMER; CUSTOMER RESISTANCE; DESIGNER; DIRECT MAIL; DISPOSABLE INCOME; DONOR FATIGUE; ECONOMY; EXCLUSIVE; FAIRLY WELL-TO-DO; FAT CATS; FREE; FUNNY MONEY; GAINFUL EMPLOYMENT; GRATUITY; GRAVY TRAIN; HEAR SOMETHING TO ONE'S ADVANTAGE; HONORARIUM; HUSH MONEY; INDEPENDENT MEANS; INSOLVENT; INVESTOR; LAUNDER; LIQUIDITY CRISIS; LUBRICATE; MONEY-CONSCIOUS; MOTH IN YOUR WALLET; NECESSARY; NEVER-NEVER; NOT SHORT OF A FEW BOB; ON THE TAKE; PALM; PLENTY TUCKED AWAY; REFER TO DRAWER; REMUNERATION; SHOOT THE MOON; SIPHONING OFF; SLUSH FUND; SOMETHING FOR YOUR TROUBLE; SPECULATOR; STIPEND; SURPLUS; SWEETENER; VIABLE; WIPE OUT; and also under POVERTY

money-conscious / -minded Miserly. By the 1930s.

monkey business Deceitful, mischievous and foolish conduct, presumably on the basis of what the behaviour of actual monkeys appears to be like. Also casual sex. Of American origin. 'There must be no monkey business going on' – G.W. Peck, *Peck's Bad Boy* (1883). 'Monkey Business' is the title of a Mr Mulliner short story (1932) by P.G. Wodehouse. At least two films have been given the title, notably one featuring the Marx Brothers (US 1931) and another with Cary Grant and a chimpanzee (US 1952).

Montezuma's revenge Diarrhoea – as suffered by visitors to Mexico. Montezuma was the Aztec ruler at the time of the Spanish conquest of Mexico. By the 1960s. Also used: 'Mexican two-step', 'Mexican fox-trot', 'Mexican toothache', 'the Curse of Montezuma', 'the Aztec hop' and 'the Aztec two-step'. Elsewhere similar coinages include: 'GYPPY TUMMY', 'Delhi belly', 'Rangoon runs', 'Tokyo trots', 'Napoleon's revenge'.

monthly period / monthlies / months Menstruation. It was 'monthly terms' or 'monthly courses' by the early 16th century. For the reason that the procedure does occur every month. See also 'monthly FLOWERS'.

moo Cow (as a term of abuse for a woman). Since the 1940s, American in origin. As in 'Silly old moo!', the catchphrase popularized by Alf Garnett (Warren Mitchell) in the BBC TV comedy series *Till Death Us Do Part* (1964–74). He would say either form of the phrase to his wife, played by Dandy Nichols. Nichols said that people used to call it out to her in the street – affectionately, nonetheless – which rather suggests that the euphemism really did make it a gentler expression.

(a) mood enhancer A recreational drug (usually cocaine). 'Cocaine, or a "mood enhancer" as it was known in the advertising industry, was not difficult to obtain' – *The Observer* (16 February 1997). Hence, also, a **mood freshener** for an illicit narcotic.

(to do a) moonlight flit To remove one's goods at night in order to cheat the bailiff. By the early 18th century.

(a) mortician An undertaker. By 1895 – US origin. 'Read in the *Times* about some proposal to abolish the phrase "domestic servant," and substitute "domestician." What nonsense! An undertaker has the same ghastly function whether you call him that or a "mortician"' – James Agate, *Ego 3* (1938), diary entry for 1 February 1937. 'The world is a beautiful place / to be born into ... / Yes / but then right in the middle of it / comes the smiling / mortician' – Laurence Ferlinghetti, 'Pictures of the Gone World' (1955).

(the) most precious part The male genitals. By the 1930s? Compare *Trousers and the Most Precious Ornament*, the title of a book (1937) by the sculptor Eric Gill. According to Fiona McCarthy's *Eric Gill* (1989), this booklet is 'A grand defence of male supremacy, a plea for the reconsideration of the penis, tucked away into men's trousers, "all sideways, dishonoured, neglected, ridiculed and ridiculous – no longer the virile member". The dishonoured penis was a terrible indictment of the world's lost potency, the onset of commercialization and destructiveness. In their craziness and funniness Gill's penis-power writings remind one of the cunt-power movement of the 1970s. This is Eric Gill in pursuit of Germaine Greer.'

(the) *mot de Cambronne* The French expletive '*Merde!* [shit!]'. At the Battle of Waterloo in 1815 the commander of Napoleon's Old or Imperial Guard is *supposed* to have declined a British request for him to surrender with the words '*La garde meurt mais ne se rend jamais/pas* [The Guards die but never/do not surrender].' However, it is quite likely that what he said, in fact, was, '*Merde! La garde meurt...* [shit! The Guards die ...].' The commander in question was Pierre Jacques Etienne, Count Cambronne (1770–1842). At a banquet in 1835 Cambronne specifically denied saying the more polite version. That may have been invented for him by Rougemont in a newspaper, *L'Indépendent*. In consequence of all this, *merde* is sometimes known in France as *le mot de Cambronne*, a useful euphemism when needed. Unfortunately for Cambronne, the words he denied saying were put on his statue in Nantes, his home town.

(a) moth in your wallet A sign of stinginess. By the 1930s? Compare 'He [the taciturn Calvin Coolidge] opened his mouth and a moth flew out' – an anonymous remark quoted in Claude Fuess, *Calvin Coolidge* (1940), also in Auden and Kronenburger, *The Viking Book of Aphorisms* (1962).

(a) mother's little helper An 'upper' (drug) that enables a tired housewife to get through her daily tasks. Phrase that might once have been applied to a small child literally being of assistance to its mother around the house. Celebrated in a song poking fun at such pill-addiction – 'Mother's Little Helper', written and performed by the Rolling Stones on the *Aftermath* album (1966).

mother's ruin Gin. Known as such by the late 19th century, according to *Partridge/Slang*. Partridge wondered if it could be (rather poor) rhyming slang (ruin / gin) but Paul Beale thought it was just a literal epithet. There was, of course, the earlier 'mother's milk' to describe the same thing. Quite how and when the coinage arose is not known but it has a sort of Victorian music-hall feel to it.

(a) motion / motions Defecation, a BOWEL MOVEMENT. By the 16th century (Shakespeare, *The Merry Wives of Windsor*).

motion discomfort Air/travel sickness. One assumes an American origin. By the 1970s?

(to) mount (For a man) to get upon a woman to have SEXUAL INTERCOURSE. Since the 16th century (Shakespeare, *Venus and Adonis*). 'Men no longer want to mount women simply because, like Everest, they are there' – Jan Elsom, *Erotic Theatre* (1973), ch. 9; 'She mounted him and rode him ... until they climaxed together' – Stella Allan, *Inside Job* (1978), ch. 3.

multicultural Mixed-race. Used to describe a society in which different races are thrown together and left to get on with it. By the 1940s. 'Barrie's Never Never Land is a fantasy island that exists between waking and dreams ... Spielberg and his team transform this into the ponderously familiar: the Lost Boys are politically correct multicultural denizens of an urban adventure playground and the obstinately anchored pirate-ship is an ornate miniature city straight out of a theme park' – *The Guardian* (16 April 1992).

(a) multimedia systems technician A film projectionist (in the US). Quoted in Willard R. Espy, *An Almanac of Words at Play* (1975).

musical Homosexual. Since the early 20th century. Hence, possibly this anecdote: when Winston Churchill was asked by Somerset Maugham if he had ever had any homosexual affairs, he supposedly replied: 'I once went to bed with a man to see what it was like.' Maugham asked him who the man was. Churchill replied, 'Ivor Novello.' 'And what was it like?' 'Musical.' The source for this story as told to Ted Morgan for his biography *Somerset Maugham* (1980) was Alan Searle, one of Maugham's acolytes. Churchill's daughter, Mary Soames, questioned it when it was included in my *Dictionary of 20th Century Quotations* (1987), and it is surely of dubious veracity.

mutton dressed as lamb A woman's wearing clothes that are ridiculously and noticeably far too young for her. Used to describe something old got up to look like something younger. Since the late 19th century. In James Joyce, *Ulysses* (1922).

my country cousin has come Menstruation. Could this have anything to do with 'country matters', as in *Hamlet*: 'Do you think I meant country matters?' *Ophelia*: 'I think nothing, my lord.' *Hamlet*: 'That's a fair thought to lie between maids' legs.' Shakespeare's bawdy is sometimes obscure, but few can miss that 'country matters' means physical love-making or fail to note the pun in the first syllable – which also occurs in John Donne's

poem 'The Good-Morrow' (1635) and William Wycherley's
The Country Wife (1675).

my daily (help) / woman what does A cleaner. By the
mid-20th century.

my niece My (young) mistress. As in the introducing phrase
'Have you met my niece?', used by an older man when
introducing a female companion who is patently *not* his niece.
A well-known British political figure arriving at some function
with a nubile young girl on his arm tended to introduce her by
asking 'Have you met my niece?' He was not alone. According
to *The Independent*'s obituary of film producer Nat Cohen
(11 February 1988), 'He was much loved – not least by the young
ladies usually introduced as "Have you met my niece?"'
   According to *Soho* by Judith Summers (1989), the first Lord
Beaverbrook habitually dined upstairs at the French [restaurant]
with sundry 'nieces' – 'He had more nieces than any man I've
known,' one Gaston confided to the author. The film *Pretty Woman*
(1990) contains an entertaining disquisition between a hooker
and a hotel manager on 'niece' being used in this sense.
   Clearly, this is a well-established piece of usage. Working
backwards: from BBC radio *Round the Horne* (26 March 1967):
[A butler announces] 'Lord Grisley Makeshift and his niece (he
says) – Mrs Costello Funf.' In the film *Road to Utopia* (US 1945)
an elderly Bing Crosby introduces his two 'nieces' to an equally
aged Bob Hope. In James Thurber's story 'Something to Say'
(1927) there is this: 'Elliot Vereker ... arrived about noon on
4th July ... accompanied by a lady in black velvet whom he
introduced as "my niece, Olga Nethersole". She was, it turned
out, neither his niece nor Olga Nethersole.'
   The lines 'Moreover, if you please, a niece of mine / Shall there
attend you' – Shakespeare, *Pericles* (1609), III.iv.14 – are
unfortunately not connected.

(a) mystery girl / man A girl/man of whom a journalist has
not been able to establish the true identity. By 1984.

Nn

naff off! Go away/fuck off. Expletive (echoic of 'eff off!') which was once notably used by Princess Anne to press photographers at the Badminton horse trials (April 1982). It was used earlier in Keith Waterhouse's novel *Billy Liar* (1959), where there also appears the participle 'naffing', remembered from his service in the RAF (*circa* 1950). 'Naffing' and 'naff off' also featured in the BBC TV sitcom *Porridge* which began in 1974.

As such, the phrase seems to be derived from the adjective 'naff', meaning 'in poor taste; unfashionable; bad' and largely restricted to British use. This word had a sudden vogue in 1982. Attempts have been made to derive the word 'naff' from 'fanny' in back-slang, from the acronym NAAFI, and from the French '*rien à faire*', none very convincingly. In the BBC radio series *Round the Horne*, the word 'naph' (as it was spelt in the scripts) enjoyed an earlier resurgence as part of camp slang. From the edition of 30 April 1967: 'Don't talk to us about Malaga!' – 'Naph, is it?' – 'He's got the palare off, hasn't he?' – 'I should say it is naph, treashette. Jule had a nasty experience in Malaga ...'

(a) narrow bed A grave. By 1854.

National Assistance Poor relief – a form of welfare payment begun in 1948. Replaced in 1966 by Supplementary Benefits.

(the) national indoor game Sex. Late 20th century. The term is more usually applied to basket-ball in the US. Compare: INDOOR GAMES.

National Service Compulsory conscription into the British armed forces. By 1939, though the phrase had been mooted by 1916.

Native American Red Indian. As a name for the original inhabitants of North America, the term 'Red Indian' has never been acceptable (not least because the colour description seems curiously inaccurate). Since the 1730s at least, the *correct* term has been 'Native American' though this has often been used in a very general sense about old inhabitants of the North American continent. Since the 1970s, however, it has become the specifically correct term for 'Red Indians'. 'Appearing at the [Academy] awards in Brando's behalf was the beautiful, gracious, and now famous Native American woman, Sacheen Littlefeather, who, dressed in the traditional garments of her people, read a prepared statement' – *Black Panther* (7 April 1973); 'Political correctness seems to have infiltrated the BBC. This week's issue of BBC Playdays, the corporation's magazine for kids, contains detailed instructions on how to make a headdress using only thin card, glue and feathers. "Now you can pretend to be native Americans," it enthuses' – *The Times* (5 February 1992).

Never mind the pejorative sense often found in the term 'natives', 'Native American' is still very much the PC term. Equally acceptable, though requiring more precise usage, are the terms **plains Indian** or **Plains Indian**. These refer to the former Indian inhabitants of the North American plains (and have been so used since the 17th century).

Alternative forms are **(North) American Indian** or **Amerindian**, though, for whatever reason, these are less popular. 'Up with the Asians and Amerindians, down with the Europeans. Up the natives, down with the colonists if they are white, that is' – *The Times* (2 November 1991); 'Bruce Beresford's *Black Robe* ... has won critical plaudits but was attacked by American Indian leaders for showing "savage hostility – not (their) culture"' – *The Independent*

(24 January 1992); 'Will the dictates of political correctness force the Washington Redskins, victors of the Super Bowl, to change their name? After their triumph over the Buffalo Bills on Sunday night, the American Indian Movement was demanding that the team make the change' – *The Times* (28 January 1992).

There is a rights organization called the American Indian Movement. It should be noted, however, that all groups including the term 'American' fall foul of the fact that the word was introduced from Europe (after the Italian Amerigo Vespucci), which simply won't do if Eurocentrism and DWEMs [Dead White European Males] are to be avoided. It is much safer to refer to the members of a specific Indian 'nation' – Cherokee, Navajo, or whatever.

A joke nonce-coinage in 'The Way of the World' column in *The Daily Telegraph* (2 December 1991) was 'quasi-autochthonous American Indigenes'.

(a) natural break An unnatural and irritating interruption of a TV programme by advertisements. The concept was arrived at in Britain before the introduction of commercial television in 1955. There were fears that programmes (hitherto free of interruptions on the BBC) would be broken up willy-nilly by advertisements when ITV started. An assurance was demanded that commercials would only be placed at 'natural breaks' in the programmes. The consequence of this was, of course, that artificial cliff-hangers were introduced in plays and such so that the breaks would indeed occur 'naturally'. 'What was meant by the term was a break which would have occurred even had there been no advertisement: for example, in the interval between the acts of a play, or at half-time in football matches' – *Report of the Committee on Broadcasting* (1962).

(a) natural child A bastard. By the 16th century. Byron, in letters to friends from Venice in 1818, did not hesitate to refer to his daughter Allegra by Clair Clairmont as 'my bastard', but later he wrote, 'I have here my natural daughter ... a pretty little girl enough, and reckoned like her papa' – included in *The Flesh Is Frail: Byron's Letters and Journals* (1976).

(the) natural functions Defecation and urination. By the 1940s.

natural wastage People leaving employment without being sacked, whether through ill health, child rearing and other commitments or death. By the 1940s. 'The savings which the bank is seeking will involve natural wastage, retraining, redeployment and some measure of redundancy' –*Financial Times* (23 April 1983).

(a) naturist A nudist. By the 1920s. 'The description "a nudist camp", according to the naturist terminology, is defunct ... Instead club members are asked to use the expression "sun club" or "naturist club"' – *The Daily Telegraph* (20 March 1963).

(the) naughty bits Male or female genitals. Probably since the 1970s, though, of course, the word 'naughty', implying sexual titillation, was already long established. BBC TV, *Monty Python's Flying Circus* (24 November 1970) begins with a spoof lecture on 'How to recognise parts of the body'. The voice-over gets to 'Number five. The naughty bits' and eventually to 'Number eleven. More naughty bits. *Cut to full length shot of lady in Bermuda shorts and Bermuda bra. Superimposed arrow on each side of her body. One points to the bra, one to the Bermuda shorts.*' By 1978–81, the disc jockey Kenny Everett had managed to elevate this to a catchphrase, usually referring to the way in which the sexy dancing group Hot Gossip flaunted their bodies on *The Kenny Everett Video Show* on TV. Then the term came to refer to the actual dance routines, as in the title of the DVD *Kenny Everett: The Complete Naughty Bits!* (2004).

near her hour About to give birth. As in Shakespeare, *Measure for Measure* (1604), II.ii, referring to 'groaning Juliet'.

(the) necessary (1) Money in cash. By the early 18th century. (2) A lavatory. By the early 17th century – a 'necessary house'.

(a) necktie party A lynching. Of American origin, by 1871.

(the) needy The poor. 'When I first came to live in America I was struck by how "the poor" had vanished – vanished from the American lexicon. I discovered they were constantly being rescued by euphemism. First they became needy, then deprived, then underprivileged or disadvantaged' – Harold Evans, BBC Radio 4, *A Point of View* (18 September 2005).

negative care outcome Death. Of American origin, 1980s. In medical jargon.

(to have a) nerve To have a cheek, audacity, impudence. By 1900. 'The very word "nerve" was used in a different sense to the modern one. "My word! An' 'aven't she got a nerve!" they would say of any one who expected more than was reasonable' – Flora Thompson, *Lark Rise* (1939), ch. 1.

(a) nerve specialist A specialist in the treatment of lunatics. Also **nerve doctor**. 'Sir Roderick Glossop ... is always called a nerve specialist, because it sounds better, but everybody knows that he's really a sort of janitor to the looney-bin' – P.G. Wodehouse, *The Inimitable Jeeves*, ch. 7 (1924).

(a) nervous breakdown A mental or emotional illness. By the mid-19th century.

nether garment(s) Trousers. By the early 19th century.

never married / unmarried Homosexual, in obituary-speak. Second half of the 20th century. Sometimes it does not have this imputation, of course. 'But it was still a shock to find at the end of [a bishop's] obituary, in place of the traditional "He never married", the single, defiant sentence, "He remained celibate"' – *The Church Times* (3 October 1998); 'Bertie Hope-Davies died, as obituarists say, "unmarried" and never disguised, or obtruded, his inclinations but bubbled rather than seethed with indignation at the expression "gay"' – *The Independent* (2 September 2005).

(the) never-never (1) A mythical place to which things
disappear. Winston Churchill said in the House of Commons
(5 April 1906): 'That constitution now passes away into the never
never land, into a sort of chilly limbo ...' It is also the name
given to the land where the Lost Boys live in J.M. Barrie's *Peter Pan*
(1904) – 'Never Never Never Land' in early versions, but simply
'Never Land' in the published text. Not an original coinage:
a play by Wilson Barrett was called *The Never Never Land* (1902).
'Never Never Land' was the English title of a song, *Naar de Specituin*
(1954), by Beryenberg and Froboess. (2) The Australian outback,
known as such by 1882, and as in *We of the Never Never* (1908) by
Mrs Aeneas Gunn. (3) An alternative name for hire purchase,
as 'the never-never' (by 1926).

New Age travellers Vagrants. 'New Age' has been used since
the 1970s as an alternative phrase for the 'ALTERNATIVE culture'
of that time.

(a) New Australian A recently arrived immigrant. By the
1920s.

(a) nice time Sex with a prostitute. As in the traditional
invitation 'Like a nice time, dearie?' 20th century.

niece See MY NIECE

night and fog [*Nacht und Nebel*] What people disappear
into when they are 'disposed of'. This was the name of a 1941
decree issued under Adolf Hitler's signature. It described a
simple process: anyone suspected of a crime against occupying
German forces was to disappear into 'night and fog'. Such
people were thrown into the concentration camp system, in
most cases never to be heard of again. Alain Resnais, the French
film director, made a cinema short about a concentration camp
called *Nuit et Brouillard* (1955). The phrase comes from Wagner's
opera *Das Rheingold* (1869): '*Nacht und Nebel niemand gleich*' is the spell
that Alberich puts on the magic Tarnhelm which renders him

invisible and omnipresent. It means, approximately, 'In night and fog no one is seen'.

(a) night hostel A doss house. 20th century.

(the) night of broken glass [*Kristallnacht*] A Nazi pogrom against Jewish people. Attributed to Walther Funk to describe the moves made against Jews in Germany on the night of 9/10 November 1938.

night soil Human shit. So called because domestic excrement from cesspools, cellars and outside lavatories was collected at night. By the 1770s. Hence, the honourable and often lucrative trade of the night-soil man who by the early 17th century was known simply as the 'nightman', either in private business or employed by a local authority.

(a) nightstick A policeman's truncheon. By the 1880s. Used instead of 'baton' in the US. Quoted in Willard R. Espy, *An Almanac of Words at Play* (1975).

no better than she ought to be / should be Of loose morals (invariably of a woman). A phrase of understated criticism, established by 1815 and probably much older. Beaumont and Fletcher, *The Coxcomb* (1612), act 4, scene 3, has: 'You are no better than you should be.' Motteux's translation (1712) of Cervantes's *Don Quixote*, bk 3, ch. 20, has: 'The shepherd fell out with his sweetheart ... thought her no better than she should be, a little loose in the hilts, and free of her behaviour.' A cartoon caption from James Thurber, *Men, Women and Dogs* (1943) is: 'She used to be no better than she ought to be, but she is now.' Also: **not all she should be**.

no chicken No longer young. As in 'he/she's no chicken'. By the early 18th century (Swift).

no comment I am not going to be drawn into incriminating statements. Useful phrase, when people in the news are being hounded by journalists. Not quite condemnable as a cliché. After all, why should people in such a position be required to find something original to say? Nevertheless, it has come to be used as a consciously inadequate form of evasion, often in an obviously jokey way. The phrase probably arose by way of reaction to the ferretings of Hollywood gossip columnists in the 1920s and 30s, though perhaps it was simply a general reaction to the rise of the popular press in the first half of the 20th century. Winston Churchill appears not to have known it until 1946, so perhaps it was not generally known until then, at least not outside the US. After a meeting with President Truman, Churchill said, 'I think "No Comment" is a splendid expression. I got it from Sumner Welles.' Also in 1946, critic C.A. Lejeune's entire review of the US film *No Leave, No Love* was 'No comment'.

A good example of the phrase in something like straight-forward use can be found in a terse broadcast interview conducted with Kim Philby on 10 November 1955 after the diplomat had been cleared of being the 'Third Man' in the Burgess/Maclean spy case. He later defected to Moscow in 1963 and was shown to have been a liar and a spy all along. *Interviewer*: 'Mr Philby, Mr Macmillan, the Foreign Secretary, said there was no evidence that you were the so-called "third man" who allegedly tipped off Burgess and Maclean. Are you satisfied with that clearance that he gave you?' *Philby*: 'Yes, I am.' *Interviewer*: 'Well, if there was a "third man", were you in fact the "third man"?' *Philby*: 'No, I was not.' *Interviewer*: 'Do you think there was one?' *Philby*: 'No comment.'

Martha 'The Mouth' Mitchell, the blabber who helped get the Watergate investigations under way and who was the wife of President Nixon's disgraced Attorney-General, once declared: 'I don't believe in that "no comment" business. I always have a comment' (quoted 1979). Desmond Wilcox, a TV executive, came up with a variant for the TV age in 1980. When ducking a question, he said, 'Sorry, your camera's run out of film.' The *Financial Times* for many years has used the slogan 'No *FT* ... no comment' (current 1982). 'Mr [Norman] Willis [TUC General Secretary at book award ceremony] is not going to rock the boat by descending to literary chat. "No comment," he says vigorously when asked if he has read any of the short-listed books' – *The Guardian* (25 January 1989).

no longer living / no longer with us Dead. 19th/20th century?

no longer living together (Of a couple) separated or divorced. 20th century?

no oil painting Unattractive, not good-looking, unprepossessing – of a woman (though sometimes of a man). Since the 1920s. 'The poor girl's certainly no oil painting' – Nancy Mitford, *Christmas Pudding* (1932), ch. 3.

(a) nocturnal emission An involuntary ejaculation of semen at night. By the 1820s.

(a) noggin A small serving of an intoxicating drink. Made to sound harmless. By about 1700.

(a) non-aboriginal A white Australian, an immigrant Australian. 'Though [Bob] Hawke, the son of a congregational minister and nephew of a former Australian premier, will talk about the programme he instituted to have "aboriginal Australians and non-aboriginal Australians" (political correctness has clearly crossed the last frontier) holding hands by the millennium' – *The Sunday Times* (22 March 1992).

non-aligned Shifting in allegiance (of countries). By 1960.

non-available Out of stock. 20th century.

(a) non-traditional shopper A looter. Surely a joke coinage of the peak PC years, 1991–3?

non-vegetarian Meat-eating. Actually, a joke-coinage: 'There was a box-office jackpot for *Robin Hood Prince of Thieves*, whose hero knocked off more Normans in his time than Hannibal Lecter had non-vegetarian dinners' – *Financial Times* (2 January 1992).

(a) North American Indian A Red Indian. See NATIVE AMERICAN.

North Britain / N.B. Scotland. Following the Act of Union in 1707, Acts of Parliament in both countries referred to England as 'South Britain' and to Scotland as 'North Britain'. The term for Scotland lingered a little longer than the one for England, say until the mid-19th century.

(a) nose job Cosmetic surgery upon the nose. By the 1960s. Hence the question, 'What sort of job did Peter O'Toole have before he starred in *Lawrence of Arabia*?' – 'A nose job.'

(a) nose spasm A sneeze. Cited in Allen Walker Read, *Classic American Graffiti* (1935).

not —— A euphemistic format, properly called 'litotes', where the negative of the opposite is presented as a way of expressing an opinion gently. Hence:

> **not a great reader** means that the person so described is 'illiterate'
> **not quite straight** means 'hypocritical'
> **not so slim as one would like to be** means 'fat'
> **not the most energetic of people** means 'lazy'
> **not too brave** means 'cowardly'
> **not very bright** means 'ignorant, stupid'
> **not very tall** means 'short'
> **not very well** means 'ill/very ill' (Compare NOT TOO WELL.)
> **not well-off** means 'poor'

Other expedient negatives follow ...

not a million miles from Close to. A venerable phrase of ironic exaggeration and much used in this form by *Private Eye* since the 1960s, though traditionally the number of miles has been a hundred. Nelson's *English Idioms* (about 1890) explains 'not a hundred miles off/from' thus: 'A phrase often used to avoid a direct reference to any place. The place itself or its immediate neighbourhood is always intended ... the phrase is also used of events not far distant in time.' The example given is from H. Rider Haggard: 'From all of which wise reflections the reader will gather that our friend Arthur was not a hundred miles off an awkward situation.'

'Mr C's address is not a hundred miles from here, sir' – Charles Dickens, *Bleak House* (1853), ch. 51; 'Girls are sometimes inclined to be vain. I know a little girl not a hundred miles from this room who was so proud of her new panties that she ran out in the street in them' – P.G. Wodehouse, 'Portrait of a Disciplinarian' (1927); Casson and Grenfell, *Nanny Says* (1972) has the nannyism: 'There's someone not a hundred miles from here who's being rather stupid.' Peter Cook is credited in *The Life and Times of Private Eye* (1971) with introducing 'not a million miles from the truth' to the magazine. Another, almost facetious variant, appears in the *Private Eye* phrase, **a sum not unadjacent to ...** (meaning, 'a sum very close to ...')

not a pretty sight Ugly, horrible, a mess. Phrase of under-statement for something that the speaker wishes to criticize. Possibly from parodies of old British imperial-speak. Perhaps usually said about the appearance of a body that has been involved in an accident or death. In the BBC radio *Goon Show*, 'The Yehti' (8 March 1955) and, indeed, in most editions. Observed by Fritz Spiegl in an article on drama cliché lines in *The Listener* (7 February 1985). 'The swelling's gone down ... Not a pretty sight, is it, Fiona?' – BBC radio, *Round the Horne* (15 May 1966); 'Take a long, hard look at this picture. No, it's not a pretty sight but, sad to say, it's the brutal face of Britain, 1994' – *The People* (11 September 1994); 'In-yer-face investment banking, as practised by Swiss Bank Corporation, is not a pretty sight. Swiss Bank has specialised in upsetting the City's establishment, rather as S.G. Warburg did 30 years ago' – *The Daily Telegraph* (14 January 1995).

not all there Mentally subnormal, of low intelligence. By 1864.

not as / so young as he / she was / used to be No longer young. By 1852.

not at home At home but unavailable to callers. By 1700. In the heyday of calling and visiting in the 19th century, this would be the coded way for servants to turn away unwanted visitors.

not available for comment Unwilling to be interviewed. Journalist's get-out clause at the end of an article. From the mid-20th century. It really means to say: 'You may be wondering why we haven't got any reaction from the allegedly guilty party/person criticized/man of the moment, but we failed to get hold of him.' Sometimes, 'Mr So-and-So could not be contacted/reached last night.'

not dead but gone before See GONE BEFORE

not in one's first youth No longer young. 'First youth' has been a phrase since 1390, but this form of the euphemism really dates from the 18th century. 'She was not pretty ... Neither was she in her first youth' – Henry James, *The Europeans* (1878), pt I, ch. I. Also **past one's first youth** and **not in the first flush of youth**.

not long for this world About to die. By the early 19th century. 'I fear she is not long for this world.'

not much to look at Ugly, unattractive. Since the mid-19th century (Dickens, *Great Expectations* (1861)).

not rocket science Simple, not requiring any great intelligence to understand. Based on the (somewhat debatable) view that rocket scientists require formidable powers of mind to do what they do – a view that may have gained ground as a result of the achievements of the US space programme in the 1960s/70s. An exchange from the film *Roxanne* (US 1987) –

Chris (of Roxanne): 'Why am I afraid of her? She's not a rocket scientist.' *Charlie*: 'Actually, she is a rocket scientist.' 'The military is saying that during the day we need more [fire-fighting services], and during the night we need less. It is not rocket science' – Tony Blair, quoted in *The Independent* (30 November 2002); 'It's not rocket science: free access to museums works' – headline in *The Independent* (1 January 2003). Sometimes **not brain surgery** – where no great skill is required.

not short of a few bob Comparatively rich. First half of the 20th century. A 'bob' was the nickname for a shilling.

not the marrying kind / sort Homosexual. Formerly said of men who clung to their bachelor status but only more recently used to imply that they are homosexual (compare CONFIRMED BACHELOR). 'There were plenty of pretty girls, but none of them caught him, none of them could get hold of his heart; evidently he [Dr Barry] was not a marrying man' – Mark Twain, *Following the Equator* (1897); when Hugh Montefiore, an Anglican clergyman and later bishop, wondered at a conference in Oxford (26 July 1967), 'Why did He not marry? Could the answer be that Jesus was not by nature the marrying sort?' – people were outraged at the suggestion that Christ might have been a homosexual; in Anthony Powell's autobiographical volume *Infants of the Spring* (1976), he writes of an entertainer called Varda that she 'had been married for a short time to a Greek surrealist painter, Jean Varda, a lively figure ... but not the marrying sort'. It is not quite clear what is to be inferred from this.

Usually encountered in the negative sense, positive use of 'the marrying kind/sort' has nevertheless existed in its own right. In fact, the phrase may sometimes have originally implied that the man was a womanizer – that is to say, not 'homosexual' but '*too* heterosexual'. For example, from Thomas Moore, *M.P., or The Blue-Stocking, a Comic Opera* (1811), act 3, scene 2: 'So it *is* a hoax, if he told you he / Was going to marry any such thing – La! sir – he is / Not one of your marrying sort'; from Allan Cunningham, *The Maid of Elvar* (1832): 'He wed her? He's none of the marrying kind, – / Let her beware ...'

From Shaw's *Pygmalion* (1916): *Prof. Higgins to Liza*: 'All men are not confirmed old bachelors like me and the Colonel. Most men are the marrying sort (poor devils!).' *The Marrying Kind* is the title of a play (1957) by Garson Kanin and Ruth Gordon derived from their film script (US 1952). *Rugby Songs* (1967) contains a ribald piece of verse entitled 'If I Were the Marrying Kind' that continues ' ... Which thank the Lord I'm not, sir, / The kind of man that I would wed / Would be a rugby full-back ...', and so on. Compare: **not interested in the opposite sex**.

not to go further than Thursday Simple-minded. 'In Norfolk, of a person considered a bit simple, it was said: "He/she don't go no further than Thursday"' – Mrs Monica Nash, Nottinghamshire (1995).

not too well Seriously ill or with a serious medical condition. 'I have a child who's not too well, so I've seen a lot of the NHS from the inside' – David Cameron, in speech as leader of the Conservative Party, delivered at the King's Fund in London (4 January 2006). In fact, his son has an autism-related disorder.

notice Notice of dismissal. Since the 17th century.

Notre Dame de Paris *The Hunchback of Notre Dame*. Since there appears to be no agreed PC term for a hunchback, even the Disney cartoon version (US 1996) of Victor Hugo's novel was allowed to keep the standard English translation of its title. However, when a short-lived French musical version was presented (in translation) on the London stage in 2000, could it have been PC that dictated the title was given as in the 1831 French original, *Notre Dame de Paris*?

nuclear capability Having the means/power of mass destruction. Mid-20th century. 'As Soviet nuclear capability has grown, the Soviets have ... become less aggressive' – Herman Kahn, *On Escalation* (1965), ch. 6.

(your) number is up You are about to die. Originally, perhaps, 'number has gone up', meaning 'dead' and dating from the First World War. Hence, *The Night My Number Came Up*, the title of a film (UK 1955), about a passenger on a flight to Tokyo who fears it is doomed.

(a) nursing home A home for old people. In the original general sense, this was known by the late 19th century, but seems to have narrowed to the care of the old by the second half of the 20th century.

nutritional shortfall Hunger. Late 20th century. Why this euphemism was ever needed, I have no idea.

(a) nymph of darkness / the pavement A prostitute. Both known by 1900.

Oo

oath control See B.; BALLY; BLEEDING; BLINKING;
BLOODY; DARN; DASH(ED); EXPLETIVE (DELETED); F-WORD;
FLIPPING; FOR GOODNESS SAKE; FOUR-LETTER WORD;
FRANK; FRIGGING; GEE-WHIZ; GO FORTH AND MULTIPLY;
GODFREY DANIEL; GORDON BENNETT; GREAT SCOTT; JUDAS
PRIEST; KINELL; LAND'S SAKE; LANGUAGE; LAWKS-A-
MUSSY; MOO; MOT DE CAMBRONNE; NAFF OFF; PYGMALION;
RIPE LANGUAGE; ROUND OBJECTS; S.H.ONE.T; STRONG
LANGUAGE; UNPARLIAMENTARY LANGUAGE; WHAT IN THE
SAM HILL; WHAT THE DICKENS; YOU KNOW WHERE TO GO

(to get / have one's) oats To be having sex. Since the 1920s.
Compare SOW ONE'S WILD OATS.

obese Fat. As the 'opposite of slim' becomes a major problem
in Western societies, the word 'obese' is in danger of swallowing
up the shorter word. Originally, 'obese' was more precisely used
to describe the *very* fat and fleshy and the *excessively* corpulent.
'[Social] workers often hold common biases ... an unconscious
rejection of very obese clients' – Claudia L. Jewett, *Adopting the
Older Child* (1978); 'Two New York writers, meanwhile, have come
up with an essential reference work for those who fear that they
may unwittingly be demonstrating insensitivity to minorities or
damaging the self-esteem of "oppressed" groups, such as the
obese' – *The Times* (13 April 1992).

(to) oblige (1) To act as a charwoman, domestic help. Since the 1930s. 'They fared little better with the women brought in "to oblige". One excellent charwoman in her own line of washing and scrubbing ... was expected to cook for dinner ... and bolted' – Flora Thompson, *Lark Rise to Candleford* (1945), ch. 39. 'Twice a week a lady came to "oblige" in the house' – Adelaide Lubbock, *Australian Roundabout* (1963).

(2) To make oneself sexually available (usually of a woman to a man). By the first half of the 20th century. *Partridge/Slang* gives as an example 'She soon found that she would never get promoted unless she were willing to oblige her boss.' Hence, the amusement with which the drama critic James Agate recalled in his diary (5 November 1937) this splendid sign from a pub: 'Ladies Unaccompanied Are Respectfully Requested To Use Tables For Their Refreshments And Not To Stand At The Bar And Oblige' – *Ego 3* (1938).

obsequies Funeral arrangements, rituals. This consciously used archaism goes back to the 14th century. 'When the last Badminton agent, by name Rooke, died, he and Master attended the obsequies' – James Lees-Milne, *Through Wood and Dale* (1998), diary entry for 13 August 1976.

odiferous / odoriferant / odoriferousness Smelly. Grandiloquent avoidance words. Since the 14th century.

off-colour (1) Vulgar, offensive (usually of jokes). By the late 19th century. (2) Ill. By the late 19th century.

(an) offender A burglar, criminal, murderer. Since the 15th century. Specifically, a JUVENILE OFFENDER (known since the 1840s) and YOUNG OFFENDER – which may have been coined as the title of D.J. West's 1967 study, *Young Offender*. I am told that Reading Gaol, famous for the incarceration of Oscar Wilde and for his ballad named after it, now rejoices under the name of Reading Young Offenders Centre.

offering enormous potential for improvement Derelict. Estate agents' parlance. Second half of the 20th century.

(an) office cleaning operative A cleaning lady, charwoman. Second half of the 20th century.

(the) offspring of unmarried parents Bastard(s). 'That offspring of unmarried parents, P.P. Bassinger' – P.G. Wodehouse, 'George and Alfred' (1967).

old age See ADVANCED YEARS; AGEFUL; ANECDOTAGE; ANNO DOMINI; CERTAIN AGE; ELDERLY; EVENING OF ONE'S DAYS; EVENTIDE HOME; EXPERIENTIALLY ENHANCED; GERIATRIC; GETTING ON IN YEARS; GOLDEN AGER; GREY HAIRS; GREYBEARD; HOME; LATER YEARS; LEISURE YEARS; LONG IN THE TOOTH; LONGER LIVING; LONGEST HOLIDAY; MAKE OLD BONES; MATURE YEARS; NO CHICKEN; NOT AS YOUNG AS HE/SHE WAS; NOT IN ONE'S FIRST YOUTH; NURSING HOME; OLDER WOMAN; POSITIVE AGE CENTRE; RETIREMENT PENSION; SEASONED; SENIOR CITIZEN; SENIOR MOMENT; SUNSET DAYS/YEARS; THIRD AGE; TWILIGHT YEARS; VENERABLE; VETERAN; VINTAGE YEARS

(an) old friend A penis. Hence, expressions such as 'shake hands with an old friend / the wife's best friend', as euphemisms for going to the LAVATORY (by the 1950s).

Old Nick The Devil – sometimes just **Nick / Nicker / Nickie Ben**. Since the 17th century. A nickname of obscure origin and one of numerous ways of referring in a roundabout way to someone whose name it was bad luck to use directly – such an utterance might conjure 'him' into the speaker's presence. A euphemism in the sense that it makes the Devil sound more likeable and friendly. It has a long history, either derived in some way from 'Nicholas' or going back to *nicker*, the water goblin with hoofs in Scandinavian legend. The word is used in the oldest of English narrative poems, the Beowulf saga. In a trans-lation by Henry Morley a couplet reads: 'Naked high nesses, /

Nicker houses many.' Among the numerous other names for the
Devil are:

Auld Clootie
Auld Hangie
(the) Arch Enemy
(the old) black lad
(the) dark man
(the) dickens See also WHAT THE DICKENS.
(the) Father of Lies
His Satanic Majesty
Nickie-ben
Old Harry
Old Scratch
Horny
(the) Lord of the Flies Hence, *Lord of the Flies*, title of the novel
    (1954; films UK, 1963, US, 1990) by William Golding that derives
    from the literal meaning of the Hebrew word 'Beelzebub', the
    devil.
Nathaniel
(the) Tempter

See also DEUCE; PRINCE OF DARKNESS.

(the) older woman The elderly woman. Older than what?
Since the mid-20th century, especially in fashion advertising.
'Unfortunately everybody can't be sweet 16 and there are many
shops catering for the older woman' – *Grimsby Evening Telegraph*
(5 May 1977).

(the world's) oldest profession Prostitution. The first
reference found, in these terms, to prostitution, is 'Lalun is a
member of the most ancient profession in the world' – Rudyard
Kipling, *In Black and White* (1888), 'On the City Wall'. 'In the
House of Suddhoo' from Kipling's *Plain Tales from the Hills* (also
1888) has: 'Janoo and Azizun are ... Ladies of the City and theirs
is an ancient ... profession.' From Alexander Woollcott, *Shouts
and Murmurs* (1922): 'The Actor and the Streetwalker ... the two

oldest professions in the world – ruined by amateurs.' This last
has also been attributed to Sir Henry Irving who, on being
approached by a prostitute in London, is said to have remarked:
'You and I, madam, are members of the world's two oldest
professions, and both of them, if I may say so, are being ruined
by a bunch of damned amateurs.'

(resigning / retiring) on health grounds Unable to cling
on to a job in politics or elsewhere. The reason usually has
nothing whatever to do with health. Second half of the 20th
century.

(to be) on the carpet (Of a servant or employee) to be
reprimanded or hauled over the coals. The carpet here probably
refers to the covering on a table at which officials would sit
rather than to the floor covering on which the person to be
reprimanded might stand. Indeed, 'on the carpet' (*sur le tapis*, in
French) originally referred to what was up for discussion by, say,
members of a council who would be seated at a table. This sense
was established by the 18th century. The second (disciplinary)
meaning, possibly of American origin, was well known by the
early 19th century.

on the game See GAME

on the job Having sex. By the 1960s at least. Hence the
merriment caused when Margaret Thatcher informed a TV
chat-show host, 'I am always on the job' – ITV, *Aspel and Company*
(21 July 1984).

(a bit) on the side Something secret. So a person might make
extra money through unauthorized means or have casual sex
extramaritally. 20th century.

(to be) on the streets / to walk the streets To be engaged
in prostitution. By the 1890s. Also **a woman who walks the
streets**, meaning 'a prostitute' or **a streetwalker**, the latter term
known since the 16th century. Hence, the subtle humour of the

remark made by Mae West as Lady Lou in the film *She Done Him Wrong* (US 1933): 'One of the finest women who ever walked the streets.'

on the take   In receipt of bribes or underhand payments. Of American origin since the 1930s.

on the tiles   On a debauch / spree – in the way of a cat's nocturnal activities. By the 1880s.

on the wagon   Abstaining from drinking alcohol, teetotal. This term probably began in 19th-century America where people who had signed the pledge would say they were 'on the water cart', meaning they would rather drink water from the cart than take the demon drink. This somehow became 'on the wagon'. Perhaps temperance campaigners also invited would-be abstainers to climb aboard their campaign wagon? If they strayed, they would be said to have fallen off the wagon. A colourful theory, said to date back to the early 18th century and the days of public executions at Tyburn (now Marble Arch in west central London), is that when the condemned were being transported there from prison, they were allowed to stop at an inn for a last drink ('one for the road', so to speak). When the drink was over, they climbed back 'on the wagon' and would, indeed, never drink again.

onanism   Masturbation. By the early 17th century. This is mistakenly derived from the name of Onan in Genesis 38:9 because he 'spilled it [his seed] on the ground'. But he was not masturbating. He withdrew from intercourse with his brother's wife before he ejaculated. 'It is amusing that a virtue is made of the vice of chastity; and it is a pretty odd sort of chastity at that, which leads men straight into the sin of Onan, and girls to the waning of their colour' – Voltaire, in a letter to M. Mariott (28 March 1766).

(to have) one foot in the grave   To be near death. The earliest citation in *OED2* is from Burton's *Anatomy of Melancholy*

(1621): 'An old acherontic dizzard that hath one foot in his grave.' The idea is older, however, and occurs in Barclay's *Ship of Fools* (1509) and the precise phrase is in J. Case, *Praise of Music* (1586). Swift in *Gulliver's Travels* (1726) uses the phrase in connection with the immortal Struldbruggs of Laputa. There is also a punning inscription upon the grave of the actor and dramatist Samuel Foote (died 1777) in Westminster Abbey: 'Here lies one Foote, whose death may thousands save, / For death has now one foot within the grave.' David Renwick wrote a popular BBC TV comedy series *One Foot in the Grave* (1990–2000) about a man having to endure premature retirement.

one for the road A final drink before setting off on a journey (even if just a journey home after a night in the pub). By the 1940s. 'We're drinking my friend / To the end of a brief episode / So make it one for my baby / And one more for the road' – Johnny Mercer/Harold Arlen, song, 'One For My Baby', *The Sky's the Limit* (1943); 'If you are driving do not have one for the road' – *South Notts Echo* (16 December 1976).

one of them / those Homosexual. 'One of them' is a derogatory phrase, known by the 1950s/60s; 'one of those' by 1977. Homosexuals were known to say of their own kind that 'He is one of us', by 1961.

one of us Sharing our beliefs and values. By 1900. 'Is he one of us?' was a remark ascribed to Margaret Thatcher when reviewing candidates for appointments (by 1985). From *The Independent* (28 January 1989): 'Mr [Kenneth] Clarke also failed the is-he-one-of-us? test applied by Mrs Thatcher to favoured colleagues.' Hence, *One of Us*, the title of Hugo Young's political study of Mrs Thatcher (1989).

one over the eight Drunk, intoxicated. Services' slang, but not, apparently, before the 20th century. For some reason, eight beers was considered to be a reasonable and safe amount for an average man to drink. One more and you were incapable.

(having taken) one too many Drunk, intoxicated. By the 1940s. It may be an abbreviation of 'one too many quick ones'.

(a) one-night stand A sexual relationship that lasts only one night. By the 1960s – derived from the theatrical sense of a single performance at each of several venues in different towns (American origin by the 1880s). 'I am always looking for meaningful one-night stands' – Dudley Moore, quoted in Bob Chieger, *Was It Good for You Too?* (1983).

(a) one-parent family A divorced/abandoned parent living on his/her own with dependent children. By 1969. Quite how this euphemism makes things any better is not clear, though as with LONE PARENT, the point may be that the parent is on his or her own because of divorce, desertion, separation or death, or because the partner is in hospital or prison.

open and affirming Not anti-gay but welcoming. American church use, noted in Hartford, Connecticut, in May 1998.

(an) open marriage / relationship A marriage or relationship that allows either or both partners to indulge in other sexual relationships. Since the 1970s.

(to) open one's bowels To DEFECATE. Though hardly much of an obscuring euphemism.

(to) open one's legs To engage in SEXUAL INTERCOURSE. Though as explicit, really, as the original.

(an) opening medicine A laxative, an aperient. Since the 18th-century. Before that, simply an **opener**.

(because of) operational difficulties Excuse universally given to explain transport delays. Meaning 'the reason why things aren't working is because they are not working.' Second half of the 20th century.

(an) operative A worker. Since the 1820s. Since about 1900 the word has had a separate career meaning a detective or secret service agent.

optical enhancement Obscuring an image for reasons of censorship. 'Despite causing a headache for the censors, Oshima's bizarre sexual parable [*Ai No Corrida*] was admired and championed by chief censor James Ferman. A subtle "optical enhancement" of one scene finally facilitated its UK certification' – *The Observer* (11 September 2005). The 'enhancement' in question was the zooming in on an image in order to exclude hand/genital contact between an adult and a minor that fell foul of the British Child Protection Act.

oral sex Cunnilingus or fellatio, sexual practices involving the mouth. Since the 1940s (Kinsey uses the word 'oral').

(one's) organ One's penis. A contraction of 'organ of generation', which can also be applied to the female. In the plural, **organs** refers to the genitals of either sex. Hence, the humour of: 'It's organ organ all the time with him … Up every night until midnight playing the organ … I'm a martyr to music' – Dylan Thomas, *Under Milk Wood* (1954).

(contains many) original features Has never been done up (of houses) – in estate agent-speak. Second half of the 20th century.

orthodontically challenged Having bad teeth. A joke variation on the – CHALLENGED theme. 'The Singing Postman's orthodontically challenged grin and his bucolic lamentations might have seemed archaic even in a record chart crowded out by Pink Floyd and Jimi Hendrix, but at least he was being true to himself' – *The Independent* Magazine (3 December 2005).

(a bit of the) other Sex. 'Other' in this way has been in use since the 1920s. 'I usually managed to get Mary behind a haystack for a "bit of the other"' – Frank Norman, *Banana Boy* (1969).

(the) other place (1) Hell, i.e. not Heaven. Since the mid-19th century. (2) The House of Commons / House of Lords when referring to either in the other one. (3) Oxford / Cambridge – it depends on where you are standing.

(the) other side Death / the afterlife. Derived ultimately from the crossing of the river Styx in classical mythology. 'So he [Mr Valiant-for-Truth] passed over, and the trumpets sounded for him on the other side' – John Bunyan, *Pilgrim's Progress* (1684), pt 2.

(born on the) other side / wrong side of the tracks Born poor in the socially inferior part of town. By the 1940s/50s. Of American origin. The railroad would often segregate a town's population. 'I'm just a girl from Little Rock. / We lived on the wrong side of the tracks' – from the Robin/Styne lyric for 'A Little Girl from Little Rock' in *Gentlemen Prefer Blondes* (1949).

(the) other way Homosexual. 'Is he "the other way"?' From the mid-20th century.

(the) other woman The mistress or third party in an affair, in relation to the wife or original amatory partner. By the mid-19th century. '[Robert Stephens and Maggie Smith] married in 1967 after Miss Smith was named as the "other woman" by Mr Stephens' first wife' – *Daily Mirror* (29 April 1975).

otherly abled Disabled. Another attempt at removing the stigma from disability. A pre-PC coinage from the 1980s. As also **otherwise-abled**.

our betters Superior people, those of a higher class. A subservient expression put into the mouths of rural tenants by some Victorian writers, but one suspects that it was rarely used by the peasantry themselves (who would have more appropriate euphemisms). Since the 17th century. Somerset Maugham's play *Our Betters* was first performed in 1923.

(taken) out of context Accurately quoted to the embarrassment of the speaker. Second half of the 20th century. A politician who has been quoted when he does not wish to be, would bleat, 'My words have been taken out of context.'

(to be/go) out of one's mind / senses / skull Mad. Since the 15th century.

(to come) out of the closet To proclaim one's homosexuality openly. The starting point was the term 'closet homosexual' or 'closet queen' for one who hid his inclinations away in a closet ('cupboard' in American usage rather than 'lavatory' or 'small room' in British English). Hence, 'out of the closets and into the streets', a slogan for the US homosexual rights organization known as the Gay Liberation Front, in about 1969.

out to lunch Mad, crazy. Known by 1955 in the US. Presumably, because the person 'is not *there*' or 'not *all there*'. Originally, absence at lunch would have been a perfectly reasonable explanation of why a person was not physically 'there'.

(executive) outplacement Losing your job, being made redundant. By the late 1960s. 'Employers with unwanted executives ... resort to "the dehiring process" or "executive outplacement"' – *The Daily Telegraph* (10 July 1970).

outside plumbing A privy outside the house. Of American origin, by the late 1940s. See also PLUMBING.

outsize(d) Fat. Both forms since the 19th century.

outsourcing Farming out work to where it is cheaper, i.e. outside some business or organization. Since the 1970s.

outspoken Rude/contentious. When told that she was 'very outspoken', Dorothy Parker replied: 'Outspoken by whom?' – quoted in Ralph L. Marquard, *Jokes and Anecdotes for All Occasions* (1977).

(to jump) over the broomstick To live together as though married. Also **to live over the brush / get married over the brush**. Since the 17th century. These expressions possibly derive from some form of informal ceremony that involved the couple jumping over a stick.

over the limit Drunk, according to the legal limits set on the amount of alcohol in one's blood when driving a vehicle. Of American origin. In British use since the introduction of the breathalyser in the 1960s. 'Attempting to drive while over the 80 mg/100 ml. limit can be punished ... Being in charge of a vehicle while "over the limit" can lead to up to four months' imprisonment' – *The Daily Telegraph* (11 August 1966).

over the top / O.T.T. Exaggerated in manner of performance; 'too much'. The expression 'to go over the top' originated in the trenches of the First World War. It was used to describe the method of charging over the parapet and out of the trenches on the attack. In a curious transition, the phrase was later adopted for use by show business people when describing a performance that had gone beyond the bounds of restraint, possibly to the point of embarrassment: 'They are forced by a dagger, some over the top acting and Don Quixote forcing Lorenzo to bless the union of Kitri and an apparently dying Basilio' – screen title in film of ballet *Don Quixote* (Australia 1973). In 1982, a near-the-bone TV series reflected this by calling itself *OTT*. After which, you heard people saying that something was 'a bit OTT' instead of the full expression. On 15 February 1989, *The Independent* quoted from a play called *State of Play* at the Soho Poly theatre: 'Look at sport – I'm sure you'll agree: / It's much more fun when it's OTT.' Another euphemistic application of 'to go over the top' means 'to achieve orgasm'.

over there Waging war in a foreign country. Since the First World War when this was how Europe was viewed from the US. Irving Berlin's near-anthem 'Over There' was written in 1917: 'Over there, over there, / Send the word, send the word over there – / That the Yanks are coming ... / And we won't come back till it's over / Over there.'

over-active Naughty (of children). 20th century.

over-availability A glut (of goods). 20th century.

over-emotional Hysterical. 20th century.

over-familiar Sexually predatory. The basic phrase has been with us since the 15th century but acquired this overlay in the 20th.

(to) over-indulge To eat or drink to excess. Since the late 19th century.

over-shapely Fat. Michael Barratt used this word when talking about a slimming competition on the BBC TV programme *Nationwide* (3 May 1977). Being humorous and faintly patronizing, it will qualify for the PC Seal of Approval.

over-tired See under TIRED

(to score an) own goal To bring misfortune upon oneself. In the original footballing sense (by 1947), this meant a goal scored against one's own side. With grim humour, the phrase was adapted to describe bringing harm upon oneself – most usually, a terrorist being blown up by a bomb that he has made to kill someone else. As such, it originated with the security forces in Northern Ireland and was in use by 1976. '[Princess Anne added] "It could be said that the Aids pandemic is a classic own goal, scored by the human race on itself, a self-inflicted wound that only serves to remind *Homo sapiens* of his fallibility"' – *The Guardian* (27 January 1988); 'Ozal risks own goal in move to kick life into slack election [by attending a Turkish football team's foray into European soccer – when it might have lost the game]' – *The Guardian* (20 March 1989).

Compare **to be hoist with one's own petard**, meaning 'to be caught in one's own trap'. In origin, nothing to do with being stabbed by one's own knife (poniard = dagger), or hanged with one's own rope. The context in which Hamlet uses it in Shakespeare's play (1600–1), III.iv.209 makes the source clear: 'For 'tis the sport to have the engineer / Hoist with his own petard.' A petard was a newly invented device in Shakespeare's day, used for blowing up walls, etc. with gunpowder. Thus the image is of the operative being blown up into the air by his own device.

Pp

pacification Conquering. 'Political language has to consist largely of euphemism, question-begging and sheer cloudy vagueness. Defenceless villages are bombarded from the air, the inhabitants driven out into the countryside, the huts set on fire with incendiary bullets: this is called *pacification*'– George Orwell, 'Politics and the English Language' (1946).

(to) pack it in (1) To give up or retire from some activity. (2) To die. (3) To stop talking (when told to). The third of these meanings seems to have arisen first – in the 1940s. The third citation below might seem almost to combine meanings 1 and 2. 'Rob Millar didn't finish work until gone eleven, and then decided he'd have to pack it in' – J. Wilson, *Hide and Seek* (1972), ch. 7; 'He had long ago "packed it in", and spent his life sitting by the window dozing, with a volume of Pepys' Diary upside down on his knee' – Kenneth Clark, *Another Part of the Wood* (1974), ch. 2; 'I want to be part of the Royal Court's history before I pack it in ... I don't want to fall under a bus before having a play on its stage' – Tom Stoppard, quoted in *The Independent* (12 October 2005).

(to) paint the town red To carouse, go on a spree. American origin, well before the 1880s.

(a) painted lady / woman A prostitute. Coincidentally, 'painted lady' is also the name of a butterfly. 'Painted woman', by the 1960s.

(to grease the) palm To bribe. Since the 18th century.

(to) paper the house To give away free theatre tickets in order to fill up an under-subscribed performance. Since the mid-19th century.

(a) parent care facility Nappy-changing and breast-feeding room in a public place. Previously 'mother and baby unit'. On a sign in the Royal Borough of Kensington and Chelsea by the 1990s. I expect the PC police thought that fathers should not be left out it.

parentally disadvantaged Orphan. 'When the time comes for Pan to depart, which of the orphans does he pass his magic sword to? Obviously: the fat black kid (or perhaps I should say the parentally disadvantaged, differently sized Afro American)' – *The Times* (14 April 1992).

(a) park home A caravan that is stationary and therefore not a *mobile* home. Seen on an advertisement in Dorset (July 1991).

partially sighted Nearly blind. By 1949.

(a) partner A (sexual) lover, either one of a couple. Since the 1970s. This may refer to a mistress, girlfriend, wife, boyfriend, homosexual paramour, or husband. The term's political correctness presumably lies, thus, in its imprecision. 'It's on the train line to Woodmansterne, the little village in Surrey where I live with my partner' – *The Observer* (22 May 1988).

parts of the body See ABDOMEN; ANATOMY; ATTRIBUTES; BACK PASSAGE; BACKSIDE; BALLS; BEHIND; BOOBS; BOSOM(S); BOTTIE; BRISTOLS; BUM; BUST; CHARMS; CHEEKS; CHEST; CLEAVAGE; CROWN JEWELS; DECOLLETAGE;

DERRIERE; DOWN BELOW; EXTREMITIES; FLESHY PART
OF THE THIGH; JUNOESQUE; LIMBS; LIPS; LITTLE MARY;
LOINS; LOVE HANDLES; LOWER PART OF THE BODY; LUNGS;
MELONS; PLUMBING; POSTERIOR; REAR; RUMP; SEAT;
SIT-UPON; STOMACH; SWEETBREADS; TRUNK; TUMMY

(to make a) pass To make a sexual advance by word or gesture.
Originally, the sort of thing a man would do to a woman, but
nowadays ... By the 1920s.

(to) pass away / on / over To die. 'Pass away' since the 14th
century; 'pass on' by 1800; 'pass over' by 1900 (especially in
connection with spiritualism). 'So Men pass on; but States
remain permanent for ever' – William Blake, *Jerusalem* (1804–20);
'In treasured memory of Benchara Branford ... who passed away
May 8, 1944' – In Memoriam notice in *The Times* (8 May 1945);
'Some neighbour's father or mother or sister or aunt was
"sinking fast" or had "passed peacefully away this morning"' –
Flora Thompson, *Lark Rise to Candleford* (1945), ch. 27.
   Note this development on the grave of the author of *Wind in the
Willows*: 'To The Beautiful Memory Of Kenneth Grahame ...
Who Passed The River On The 6th Of July 1932 Leaving
Childhood & Literature Through Him The More Blest For All
Time.' The use of the phrase 'passing the river' for death is
absolutely appropriate for an author who wrote so enchantingly
of the river bank and 'messing about in boats'. It may also be
taken to allude to the classical use of **to cross the Styx**, Acheron,
Lethe, and so on, as a symbol of death, but chiefly to the
Christian use. In John Bunyan's *The Pilgrim's Progress*, Christian
passes through the River of Death (which has no Bridge) and
quotes Isaiah 43:2, 'When thou passest through the waters, I will
be with thee, and through the Rivers, they shall not overflow
thee.' See also OTHER SIDE.

**(to) pass into the keeping of the Great Architect of the
Universe** To die. A 1938 example was found at Plaistow and
recorded in Hugh Meller, *London Cemeteries* (1981), ch. 5: 'He
passed into the keeping of the Great Architect of the Universe.'

(to) pass water To URINATE. Barely a euphemism, because it is more explicit than the original, but still. By 1860 (Florence Nightingale). 'To pass water (terrible doctors' phrase) gives him much pain' – James Lees-Milne, *Midway on the Waves* (1985), diary entry for 24 September 1949.

(to have a) past To have a sexually disreputable history. By the 1870s (Ouida).

past its sell-by date Out of date, old-fashioned, past its best. Originally applied to foodstuffs – which were marked with the sell-by date in supermarkets and shops from the 1970s onwards – the expression soon became applied to other things and to people. 'Socialism: the package that's passed its sell-by date' – *The Daily Telegraph* (13 March 1987); 'Once described by an over-enthusiastic newspaper as "one of London's most eligible bachelors", Stacpoole is now grey, portly and, at 55, looking rather past his sell-by date' – *Today* (1 September 1994).

(the) patter of tiny feet The arrival of a baby in a household. Longfellow has 'patter of little feet' in 1863. 'Four months after her marriage [1932], she was reporting to Tod that there was "no sign of the pattering of tiny feet"' – Margaret Forster, *Daphne du Maurier* (1993), ch. 7; 'Going to have little feet pattering about the home?' – P.G. Wodehouse, *Ice in the Bedroom* (1961), ch. 6; 'Expectant motherhood these days is marked less by the patter of tiny feet than the tinkling of cash registers' – *The Times* (29 October 1977); 'Newlyweds Nicolas Cage and Patricia Arquette are expecting the patter of tiny feet' – *Hello!* Magazine (13 May 1995).

(to) pay a call / visit To go to the LAVATORY, principally to URINATE. Both forms by the 1950s.

(to) pay last respects to To attend a funeral. By the 1970s, but surely much earlier.

(to) pay lip service To promise a service that is not performed. Since the 17th century, but now indicating respect that is insincere.

(to) pay nature's debt / one's debt to nature To die. By the 16th century. 'Finally he paid the debt of nature' – Robert Fabyan, *The New Chronicles of England and France* (1516), vol. I, ch. 41. Compare **to pay one's debt to society** = to be hanged / put to death.

(a) paying guest / P.G. A lodger. Here the euphemism is more explicit than the original but is conceivably a notch up in status. By the 1890s. 'Her voice paused at the word *lodger* as if considering ... the euphemisms – paying guest ... and so on' – John Braine, *Room at the Top* (1957), ch. I.

(at) peace in heaven Dead. The phrase occurs in a slightly different way on the gravestone of Sarah Fletcher in Dorchester Abbey, Oxfordshire: '*Mrs SARAH FLETCHER* Wife of Captain *FLETCHER*, departed this Life at the Village of Clifton, on the 7 of June 1799. In the 29 Year of her Age. May her Soul meet that Peace in Heaven which this Earth denied her.'

(to go) pear-shaped To go out of control, become chaotic – because it is a collapse from the perfect sphere. Known by the mid-20th century. Suggested sources for the phrase include the making of lead shot (where molten lead was dropped through a sieve and by the time it reached the bottom of the shot tower it had solidified into a spherical lead shot – or not, in which case it was pear-shaped) or on the potter's wheel, where collapsed clay has this appearance. Compare (and make anything of it, if you can) what W.C. Fields says to Mae West when he is locked out of the bridal suite in the film *My Little Chickadee* (US 1940): 'Come, my phlox, my flower. I have some very definite pear-shaped ideas I'd like to discuss with thee.'

peccadilloes Social transgressions (e.g. adultery). From the 17th century the term was applied to little faults. Now used to gloss over the harsh nature of certain behaviour.

(to have a) pee To URINATE. By the 1870s. From the first letter of 'piss' and certainly an acceptable euphemism for it, acceptable usage in all but the staidest company.

(a) Peeping Tom A voyeur. The name derives from Tom the Tailor who was struck blind because he peeped when Lady Godiva rode by. In the legend, Lady Godiva's husband, the Lord of Coventry, only agreed to abolish some harsh taxes if she would ride naked through the town. The townspeople responded to her request that they should stay behind closed doors – all except Peeping Tom. This element of the story was probably grafted on to the record of an actual happening of the 11th century. *Peeping Tom* was the title of a film (UK 1959) about a man who films his victims while murdering them.

(a/the) people's – Something imposed on the people by an autocracy. There is, of course, a long history of usage of the formula in egalitarian and/or communistic contexts: we have had the People's Car – Volkswagen, known as such by 1938 – and then the People's War, not to mention Bureau, Court, Army, and much else. The People's Palace (a London educational institution for the working class) was being referred to as such by 1854 though not formally opened until 1887. Flora Thompson's *Lark Rise* (1939), recalling her Victorian country childhood, tells us that Prime Minister Gladstone was referred to as 'The People's William' – as in the song: 'God bless the people's William, / Long may he lead the van / Of Liberty and Freedom, / God bless the Grand Old Man.'

   The most noted use of this formula in recent years has been British Prime Minister Tony Blair's rapid-response TV statement on hearing of the death of Diana, Princess of Wales (31 August 1997): 'She was the People's Princess, and that is how she will stay ... in our hearts and in our memories forever.' The phrase was suggested to the PM by his press secretary, Alastair

Campbell, though it had already been used regarding the
Princess by journalists. Also, in 1984, *The People's Princess* had been
the title of a book by S.W. Jackman about Princess Mary, Duchess
of Teck, the 'crowd-pleasing' mother of Queen Mary.

people in poverty The poor. Hard to see how this alleviates
the situation for those concerned but, importantly for the PC, it
does call them people. By the 1990s.

people of colour See PERSON OF COLOUR

(the) people of the book Jews – but also Christians, Muslims
and anyone whose religion is based on a work of authority. By
the 19th century in English but the term originates in the Koran.

people with differing abilities Disabled people. This
alternative term emerged from 66,000 entries as the winner
of a competition organized by an American charitable group in
1991. Objections to the phrase were soon raised. Dianne Piastro,
a syndicated columnist, said the new construction suggested
that disability was somehow shameful and needed to be treated
in a vague generality. Mary Johnson, editor of the *Disability Rag*,
a disability rights magazine, said, '[It's a] nice sentiment but it
doesn't have any soul. It has no power to it.' And quite right, too.

Percy A/the penis. Since the mid-20th century. A
personification most notably to be found in the euphemism
POINT PERCY AT THE PORCELAIN.

(a) period Menstruation. Since the 19th century. 'We have
only the choice of three kinds of expression: the vulgar resentful,
the genteel ("I've got my period", "I am indisposed"), and the
scientific jargon of the *menses*' – Germaine Greer, *The Female
Eunuch* (1970). However, note this earlier roundabout expression:
'She informed me that Saturday could not be the hoped-for
time to bestow perfect felicity upon me ... I understood that
Nature's periodical effects on the human, or more properly
female, constitution forbade it' – James Boswell, diary entry for

7 January 1763. Among the numerous euphemisms for this
otherwise unmentionable are:

(a) bad week
(my) blood
(a) caller
(to) come around
(to) come on
courses
cramps
(the) danger signal is up
domestic afflictions
(to) fall off (the roof)
(the) flag is up
(my) (little) friend has come
(to have a little) friend to stay / have friends to stay
(to have) grandmother to stay
holy week
in purdah
Kit has come
leaky
menses
off-duty
off-games
old faithful
(my) others
out of circulation
(to have the) painters in
(the) Prince
(a) problem day
(the) red flag is up
(the) red rag
(the) Red Sea is in
(a) red-haired visitor
(the) reds
(my) relations have come
(the) road is up for repair
(your) roses

(to have a) run on
stomach cramps
Tampax time
terms
those days
tummy ache
unavailable
(a) visitor
(the) visitor with the red hair is come
(to) wear a pad
(a) wet weekend
(the) wretched calendar

See others listed under MENSTRUATION.

(the) permissive society Moral laxness, sexual promiscuity (among the general public). 'Permissive' was a term popularized in the 1960s, euphemizing the lowering or changing standards of morality. 'The permissive society has been allowed to become a dirty phrase. A better phrase is the civilised society' – Roy Jenkins, speech at Abingdon (19 July 1969). Jenkins had been Home Secretary in a Labour government (1965–7). He had a notably liberal record, presiding over or setting the tone for liberalization of divorce and anti-homosexual laws, the abolition of theatre censorship, and much else.

(the) person The genitals. 'Did he expose his person?' asked a magistrate in an indecency case. From an Act of Parliament of the reign of George IV in 1824: 'Every Person wilfully, openly, lewdly and obscenely exposing his Person in any Street, Road or public Highway, or in View thereof, or in any place of public resort, with intent to insult any Female ... shall be deemed a Rogue and Vagabond within the true Intent and Meaning of this Act.'

(a) person in a wheelchair See WHEELCHAIR USER

(a) person living with — / (a) person with — A person afflicted / crippled / deformed / stricken by —, suffering from —, victim of —. Especially, when replacing 'patient' used in conjunction with 'AIDS', which is non-PC usage. Here, the acceptable alternatives include, for example, 'person with AIDS' and 'person living with AIDS', often abbreviated to PWA, PLA or PLWA. The emphasis in these alternatives is designed to show that the people are 'living with' rather than 'dying from' AIDS. At the second AIDS forum in the US, held at Denver, Colorado, in December 1983, a statement was issued, saying: 'We condemn attempts to label us as "victims", which implies defeat, and we are only occasionally "patients", which implies passivity, helplessness, and dependence upon the care of others.'

For the same reasons, the word 'victim' should not be used of any other person with mental or physical illness or handicap. Hence, 'Jane Smith has polio / has contracted polio.' As the Briefing Note (May 1992) from the Royal Association for Disability and Rehabilitation, puts it: 'Instead use the phrases "someone who has" or "a person with" a disease or disability. These phrases are more neutral and less value-laden.'

(a) person of color / colour A black person, Negro, nigger, a coloured person, a non-white. At the time of the great PC boom in the early 1990s, this term – and **people of color / colour** – caught on to a considerable degree in the US, though less so elsewhere. They are, of course, purposely less specific than 'African-American' or 'Asian-American', though for this reason some people have objected to them on the grounds that they lump all colours together and 'obscure diversity'.

The terms are older than they may seem: 'A free person of colour is now entitled to give evidence against a white, in any Court of Justice, upon producing his privilege papers' – *The Gentleman's Magazine*, No. 95 (1825); '[Long John Silver] leaves his wife to manage the inn; and as she is a woman of colour ... I may be excused for guessing that it is the wife ... that sends him back to roving' – R.L. Stevenson, *Treasure Island* (1883), ch. 7; 'The east was represented among "the saints" by an excellent Irish peer who had, in his early youth, converted and married a lady of colour' – Edmund Gosse, *Father and Son* (1907), ch. I.

Even earlier, an epitaph in St Andrew's Church, Chesterton, Cambridgeshire, on a girl who died aged four in 1797 (the daughter of 'Gustavus Vassa, the African'), states: 'Know that there lies beside this humble stone / A child of colour haply not thine own.' 'The great ambition of students today is to be truly ethical ... They patiently say "people of color"' – *The Washington Post* (17 January 1991); 'Reporter Kristi King was castigated for using the phrase "colored women" instead of the politically correct "women of color"' – *The Washington Post* (27 September 1991); 'Black, Hispanic and Indian activists, meeting in Washington from October 24th to 27th for the first "National People of Colour Environmental Leadership Summit", will press this argument in exploring the relationship between environmentalism and racial justice' – *The Economist* (26 October 1991); 'For a while at the beginning of the [Oprah] Winfrey show, everyone ... talked about "people of colour", before the hostess herself opted for a blunt "black"' – *The Guardian* (19 March 1992); 'A public gallery that aims to place "artists of colour" in a wider contemporary art context is to be set up by the Arts Council and the London Arts Board ... The Institute of New International Visual Arts ... sets out to place artists from Africa, the Caribbean and Asia alongside their European and American peers' – *The Independent* (25 August 1992).

'Might I suggest an alternative for Emily Tasao and others uncomfortable with the "PC" term "people of color" for all minorities except women? What if we refer to the aforementioned peoples as "colorful people" and "whites" as "colorless people"' – letter to *The Washington Post* (9 October 1992).

(a) **person of non-colour** A white person. Probably only a joke coinage from the great PC boom of the early 1990s. 'A person of paleface' has also been jokingly suggested.

(a) **person of restricted growth** A dwarf, midget. The politically correct term, though how much currency it has is doubtful. The expression first came to general attention when

Lord Snowdon made a TV film on the subject, with the title
'Born To Be Small' (1971). 'An international dwarf-throwing
competition in West Germany next month has been cancelled ...
The Hamburg-based Organisation of People of Restricted
Growth protested about what it called a macabre spectacle' –
The Daily Telegraph (18 February 1986); 'Let us get this absolutely
clear: Mickey Rooney is not a dwarf, nor a midget, nor a person
of stunted nor restricted nor diminished growth, nor is he waist-
high to the average grasshopper. Such opening conversational
gambits as "Hi there, shortie", or "What's the weather like down
in the carpet?" would not be recommended unless you fancy a
sharp head-butt in the ankle' – *The Times* (15 March 1992).

(a) person of size   A fat person. A PC coinage from the US,
about 1990.

(a) person of substance   A fat person. Late 20th century.
Presumably, playing on the phrase 'man/woman of substance',
meaning 'wealthy, well-to-do', as in *A Woman of Substance*, title of
a novel (1979) by Barbara Taylor Bradford and the TV film of
the book.

(a) person with a drink / drinking problem   An alcoholic,
heavy drinker. Since the 1960s/70s. 'He has what our American
friends call a drinking problem. Not an alcoholic, but certainly a
heavy drinker' – Eric Ambler, *The Intercom Conspiracy* (1969), ch. 2;
'We don't speak of alcoholics: we call them problem drinkers' –
from a BBC interview (September 1977).

(a) person with an alternative body image   A fat person.
A PC coinage. '[In the US] it is unacceptable to describe even a
38-stone man as fat. All you can say is that he has "an alternative
body image"' – *The Times* (19 April 1992).

personal   See HUMAN

(a) personal assistant / P.A.   A secretary. Job enhancement
has been at work here since the 1960s/70s.

personal hygiene (1) To do with one's dirtiness and smelliness. Since the 1920s. 'The sloth ... pays such little attention to its personal hygiene that green algae grow on its coarse hair' – David Attenborough, *Life on Earth* (1979), ch. 9. (2) To do with menstruation – the paraphernalia and methods of coping with it. Late 20th century. Compare FEMININE HYGIENE.

(the provision of) personal services Prostitution. In the straightforward sense, since the 19th century; in the new sense, since the late 20th century. Hence, the title of the film *Personal Services* (UK 1987) about the 'Luncheon Voucher' madam, Cynthia Payne.

personal violence Beating someone up. Since the 19th century.

(a) personality A person who appears on radio or television. Since the 1920s/30s. 'I apply what may seem a whimsical test to broadcasting personalities. I ask myself if I would care to meet and talk with them in the flesh' – *Radio Times* (14 April 1933). I once read a suggestion that these people should be called instead 'appearers', which rather nicely gets to the bottom of what they do.

personkind Humankind. An early 1990s humorous invention, designed to poke fun at the feminist hostility to the m-word. Similarly, how about 'cowperson' (as in 'cowpersons and native americans')? Of these inventions, 'personkind' has almost taken on a life of its own – 'Sonja fights for her life and the lives of all personkind' – *Video Today* (April 1986), whereas Wagner's 'Flying Dutchperson' has not.

personnel People (in the US). Usually in an employment context and following military usage. Quoted in Willard R. Espy, *An Almanac of Words at Play* (1975). 'Responsibility was decentralised to the "front-line" personnel and the whole staff was sent on service courses – which quickly became known as charm schools' – *Financial Times* (15 September 1986); 'It is against the law of land warfare to employ WP [white phosphorous] against personnel targets' – *The Independent* (19 November 2005).

(to) perspire To sweat. Hence: 'Horses sweat, men perspire – and women merely glow', a saying used to reprove someone who talks of 'sweating'. Casson and Grenfell, *Nanny Says* (1972) lists it as a nanny's reprimand in the form: 'Horses sweat, gentlemen perspire, but ladies only gently glow.' J.M. Cohen includes it in *More Comic and Curious Verse* (1956) as merely by Anon., in the form: 'Here's a little proverb that you surely ought to know: / Horses sweat and men perspire, but ladies only glow.'

(a) pest control officer A rat catcher. Apparently, since the 1940s: 'A rat-catcher is a Pest Control Officer and a rook-scarer a Corvine Operator' – James Wentworth Day, *Harvest Adventure* (1946), ch. 16.

petite Small. Of a female, especially in the garment industry. 'Emily hated being "petite", which was a euphemism for getting stuck with all the short boys on blind dates' – Rona Jaffe, *Class Reunion* (1979); 'For a profession that is supposed to be hardboiled, journalism is remarkably chivalrous with its adjectives ... Small young women are *petite*. Small old women are *tiny*' – Keith Waterhouse, *Waterhouse on Newspaper Style* (1989).

(a) photo opportunity A publicity-seeking occasion. Its only *raison d'être* is to attract the media's cameras and thus publicity for the subject of the photo call. Given the contrivance involved – it is a form of pseudo-event – it is surprising how the media invariably fall for it. Of American origin in the 1970s. Said to have been raised to an art form by Ronald Reagan's advisers when he was US President. 'Heseltine visits ... tend to be one long photo-opportunity ... Whatever the occasion you could be sure it would produce pictures and copy' – *The Listener* (16 January 1986); 'They operate in the slick new tradition of political handlers, whose job is to reduce a campaign to photo ops and sound bites' – *Time* Magazine (21 November 1988); 'Political "photo opportunities" are not supposed to be life-or-death affairs. But the Socialist candidate in the French presidential election, Lionel Jospin, broke the rule on Sunday when he very nearly fell into a watery grave while attempting to board a fishing boat in the Breton port of Concarneau' – *Evening Standard* (London) (19 April 1995); 'Mr Bush's travels have not quelled the bitter complaints that the federal government was far too slow in its response to the crisis. "I'm not interested in hand shaking and photo-ops, this is going to take a lot of money," said Mildred Brown who has been in the shelter since Tuesday' – *The Independent* (6 September 2005).

physically challenged Disabled, physically handicapped. By 1985. Originating in the US, the first coinage in the '–challenged' mode would appear to have been 'physically challenged' in the 'disabled' sense. 'This bestselling author [Richard Simmons] of *The Never Say Diet Book* creates a comprehensive fitness program for the physically challenged' – *Publishers Weekly* (US) (10 January 1986). This is rare among the –challenged constructions in that it is not simply a joke. Indeed, it may be the example which inspired all the serious and not-so-serious suggestions. Nancy Mairs, an essayist and poet with multiple sclerosis, is one of those who has voiced her opposition to it: 'Physically challenged doesn't distinguish me from a woman climbing Mt. Everest. It blurs the distinction between our lives' – *The Washington Post* (25 August 1991).

physically different Physically handicapped. This is one of several attempts to get away from the labels of 'handicap' and 'disability'. It is also the most controversial of the coinages. 'The society we [people with thalidomide] were born into is not adapted to physically different people' – speaker on *David Frost on Sunday*, ITV (24 July 1988).

A modest proposal put forward in a letter to *The Independent* (25 July 1992) by a wheelchair-user who has multiple sclerosis was **physiologically disenfranchised**.

(to) pick a daisy To URINATE (usually), in the open air. Since the 19th century.

(to) pilfer To steal. A word used with hardness in the 18th century but softened to euphemism in the 20th. 'We have to set aside a sum each year for shrinkage due to staff pilfering in addition to petty theft by the public' said a chain store's representative in a radio interview (1982).

(the) pink pound The homosexual economy. By 1984. 'The economic strength of the "pink pound" was important in establishing the idea of a gay community' – *The Independent* (4 September 1990). A **pink dollar** has been reported from the US.

(a) pit-stop An opportunity to URINATE on a journey. After the motor-racing use. Possibly of American origin, by the 1960s.

pixilated Nicely drunk, tipsy, intoxicated. Originally American in the 19th century meaning 'fey, whimsical', if not mildly insane. 'Why, *everybody* in Mandrake Falls is pixilated – except us' – Jane Faulkner in the film *Mr Deeds Goes to Town* (US 1936); 'We were both ever so slightly inebriated, no not even that, pixilated, to use the lovely movie euphemism' – Cathleen Nesbitt, *Little Love and Good Company* (1975), ch. 17.

(a) plains / Plains Indian See under NATIVE AMERICAN

(to) play the harp To die/be dead. 20th century. After the harp-playing angels in heaven.

(to) play the pink oboe To engage in homosexual fellatio. The 'pink oboe' came to popular attention after June 1979 when Peter Cook used it in his satirical version of the summing up by the judge in the recently completed Jeremy Thorpe trial. An unreliable witness was termed 'A self-confessed player of the pink oboe'. It is said that Cook acquired this term from the comedian Billy Connolly when preparing to perform the piece in the Amnesty Gala, *The Secret Policeman's Ball*, but, long before, Spike Milligan had entitled an episode of *The Goon Show* 'Who is Pink Oboe?' on BBC radio (12 January 1959). The similar **to**

play the skin flute was defined as 'to engage in buggery', by 1984, whereas fellatio is the more obvious activity described here.

please adjust your dress before leaving See ADJUST

(to) pleasure To engage in sexual relations with. Since the 17th century. 'His Grace returned from the wars today and pleasured me twice in his top-boots' – attributed to Sarah, Duchess of Marlborough, wife of the 1st Duke (1660–1744). James Agate, *Ego 4* (1940), diary entry for 28 July 1938, talking of pageants, has this version: 'How can yonder stout party hope to be Sarah, Duchess of Marlborough – "His Grace returned from the wars this morning and pleasured me twice in his top-boots" – when we know her to be the vicar's sister and quite unpleasurable?'

(to sign the) pledge To promise that one will abstain from the demon drink. From the 1830s, the temperance movement in Britain encouraged people literally to sign a pledge to 'refrain forever from ingesting spirituous and malt liquors, wine, or cider'. On some pledges a letter was put after each signature indicating how far a pledger wanted to go. *M* stood for moderation; *A* stood for abstinence from ardent spirits only; *T* stood for total abstinence, hence the expression '*tee*total'.

(to have) plenty tucked away To be rich, well-off. 20th century.

(a) plod A policeman. Since approximately the 1960s when people who had encountered P.C. Plod, a character in the Noddy children's books by Enid Blyton that first appeared in 1949, were of an age to look for a critical nickname for the British police. These were perceived at the time as having lumbering ineptitude in the catching of criminals and a plodding walk while on the beat. 'The BBC is reviving Noddy this autumn, but would Enid Blyton recognise the lad? ... Grumpy old PC Plod will be "less aggressive", while the golliwogs will be replaced by monkeys and gremlins' – *The Independent* (10 April 1992).

(a) ploughman's lunch A basic meal made to sound redolent of olden days through a marketing ploy. The popularization of this term for a meal of bread, cheese and pickle came as the result of an intervention by the English Country Cheese Council in the 1960s. B.H. Axler's *The Cheese Handbook* (1970) has a preface by Sir Richard Trehane, Chairman of the English Country Cheese Council & Milk Marketing Board, who writes: 'English cheese and beer have for centuries formed a perfect combination enjoyed as the Ploughman's Lunch.' Another source credits Trehane himself with introducing the term as a marketing tool. It is clear, however, that the concept and the name had long existed. In Lockhart's *Memoirs of the Life of Sir Walter Scott* (1837), there is this: 'The surprised poet swung forth to join them, with an extemporised sandwich, that looked like a ploughman's luncheon, in his hand.' *The Ploughman's Lunch* was subsequently the title of a film (UK 1983), scripted by Ian McEwan, whose theme was the way that history (especially recent history) tends to get rewritten. The title, unexplained in the film, must have puzzled many, including those who were familiar with the ploughman's lunch in the other context.

(the) plumbing (1) A lavatory. Since the 1950s? (2) The parts of the body to do with urination. From about the same time. See also OUTSIDE PLUMBING.

plump Fat, fleshy. Since the 16th century. 'Banish plump Jack, and banish all the world' – Falstaff in Shakespeare, *Henry IV, Part 1* (1597), II.iv.473.

(to) pocket To steal. Since the 17th century.

(to) point Percy at the porcelain To URINATE. An Australian loophemism, by 1965. Though not of his own invention, it was introduced to Britain by Barry Humphries through the 'Barry Mackenzie' strip in *Private Eye* (before 1971). See also PERCY.

(a) pointy head An intellectual. Of American origin, by
the 1970s, possibly a coinage of George Wallace, the populist
American politician who would refer to 'pointy-headed
professors' and 'pointy-headed intellectuals who can't park their
bicycles straight'. 'George Wallace attacked Muskie, Humphrey,
and his other "pointy-headed" opponents' – *The Guardian*
(21 February 1972).

police See CRIMINAL

police action War – or rather military intervention without a
formal declaration of war. By the 1930s. 'He would have been
able to avoid the Vietnam War – or "police action", to properly
designate that valiant attempt to save Southeast Asia for the free
world' – Gore Vidal, *Kalki* (1978), ch. 3.

police officers Policemen – a locution avoided by the non-
sexist. After all, 'Policewomen are often involved. Police, police
officers, detectives, policemen and women can be used' –
'Guidelines for Factual Programmes', BBC (1989); 'He claimed
a police officer punched and kicked him, and he was also
assaulted in a police van' – *The Guardian* (17 May 1994).

political correctness See ACCESS HOLE; ADULT MALE;
AFRICAN-AMERICAN; AFRO-CARIBBEAN; AMERINDIAN;
ANIMAL COMPANION; APPROPRIATE; ASIAN-AMERICAN;
BIRTH NAME; BODY HARASSMENT; BRIDE'S ATTENDANT;
CAUCASIAN; CHAIR/CHAIRPERSON; COFFEE WITH MILK;
COLLABORATIVE PIANIST; COLOURED MAN; COUNCIL
MEMBER; CULTURALLY DIFFERENT; DARK; DEMOCRATIC;
DISEMPOWERED; ENGLISH PERSON; ENSLAVED PERSON;
ETHNIC; ETHNIC ORIGIN; FAMILY NAME; FEMHOLE;
FESTIVITIES OF A LUMINARY NATURE; FIRST NAME;
FLIER/FLYER; HEBREW; HERSTORY; HOMEMAKER;
HUMANKIND; INCLUSIVE LANGUAGE; INDIGENOUS PEOPLE;
INNUIT; INSTRUMENTS OF AGGRESSION; ISLANDERS;
LEARNING DIFFICULTIES; MELANIN IMPOVERISHED; MIXED
RACE; MOBILITY IMPAIRED; MULTICULTURAL; NATIVE

AMERICAN; NON-ABORIGINAL; NOTRE DAME DE PARIS;
PACIFICATION; PARENT CARE FACILITY; PARENTALLY
DISADVANTAGED; PEOPLE OF THE BOOK; PERSON OF
COLOUR; PERSON OF NON-COLOUR; PERSON OF RESTRICTED
GROWTH; PERSON LIVING WITH – ; PERSON OF SIZE; PERSON
OF SUBSTANCE; PERSON WITH A DRINK PROBLEM; PERSON
WITH AN ALTERNATIVE BODY IMAGE; PERSONKIND; POLICE
OFFICERS; POSITIVE DISCRIMINATION; PRE-WOMAN;
PSYCHOLOGICALLY DISADVANTAGED; RAPE SURVIVOR;
ROMANIES; SEWER HOLE; SHOPPER; SNOW CREATURE;
SPECIAL NEEDS; SPOKESPERSON; STAFFING; STREET
PERSON; TEMPORALLY ABLED; TRAVELLERS/TRAVELLING
PEOPLE; TROPICAL RAIN FOREST; VERBALLY DEFICIENT;
VERTICALLY CHALLENGED; VISIBLE MINORITY;
WAITPERSON; WHEELCHAIR USER; and also under
DISABILITIES

(to be) politically correct To avoid actions or words that
might exclude or reflect badly upon minorities or groups
perceived as being disadvantaged. These groups might be
identified on the grounds of their race, sex, sexual orientation,
class or politics. To conform with dogmatic assertions. People
in the US started talking about 'political correctness' in the
current, specific sense, in about 1984. From *The Washington Post*
(12 March 1984): 'Langer ... is saying that novelists have a duty
higher than the one they owe to their art and their private vision
of the world; they have a duty to be politically correct ... In
thus construing, Langer reveals herself to be a captive of the
assumption, widespread among the academic and literary left,
that art exists to serve politics.'

By the following year, the phrase in its modern sense is fully
formed and stands alone in the same paper (11 March 1985):
'It is the only caffeinated coffee served by the "wait-persons", as
they are called, at the politically correct Takoma Cafe in Takoma
Park.' Really, 'politically correct' and 'political correctness' are
the wrong terms for the idea, in that they may make people think
it has to do with Politics with a capital P, whereas it has much
more to do with social concerns. Why not 'socially correct',

then? – because that would make it sound as though it had something to do with manners and etiquette. 'Ideologically correct' would give the game away, of course, and leads us back to politics. As it is, 'political' hints at the coercion that is all too much part of the PC movement.

politics See ANNEXE; ANSCHLUSS; APPEASEMENT; ARMED CONFLICT; ARMED STRUGGLE; BEER AND SANDWICHES AT NO. 10; CONCENTRATION CAMP; CROSS THE FLOOR; DEVELOPING COUNTRIES; DOVE/HAWK; ELDER STATESMAN; EMERGENT; ETHNIC CLEANSING; FACT-FINDING MISSION; FELLOW TRAVELLER; FIFTH COLUMNIST; FINAL SOLUTION; FREEDOM FIGHTER; GREAT GAME; GUERRILLA; HOSTILITIES; INCOMPATIBLE WITH THEIR DIPLOMATIC STATUS; INTERNMENT CAMP; LATE UNPLEASANTNESS; LIBERATE; LITTLE LOCAL DIFFICULTIES; MOLE; NIGHT AND FOG; NIGHT OF BROKEN GLASS; NON-ALIGNED; NUCLEAR CAPABILITY; PEOPLE'S – ; POLICE ACTION; RE-EDUCATE; REGIME CHANGE; RESEARCH VESSEL; ROOTLESS COSMOPOLITANS; SEPARATE DEVELOPMENT; SOPHISTICATED WEAPONS; SOUNDBITE; SOURCES CLOSE TO THE PRIME MINISTER; SPIN DOCTOR; THIRD WORLD; TROUBLES; WEAPONS OF MASS DESTRUCTION

(a) poodle A sycophant, lackey or cat's-paw. Since 1907, in the form 'Mr Balfour's poodle', a reference to the House of Lords. David Lloyd George spoke in the House of Commons on 26 June 1907 in the controversy over the power of the upper house. He questioned the Lords' role as a 'watchdog' of the constitution and suggested that A.J. Balfour, the Conservative leader, was using the party's majority in the upper chamber to block legislation by the Liberal government (in which Lloyd George was President of the Board of Trade). He said: '[The House of Lords] is the leal and trusty mastiff which is to watch over our interests, but which runs away at the first snarl of the trade unions. A mastiff? It is the Right Honourable Gentleman's poodle. It fetches and carries for him. It bites anybody that he sets it on to.'

Hence, all the subsequent '——'s poodle' jibes, usually applied to one politician's (or government's) subservience to another. 'Ninety per cent of respondents feared military action against Baghdad would result in more September 11-style attacks on the West, while 54 per cent thought it fair to describe Mr Blair as "Bush's poodle"' – *The Age* (Australia) (13 August 2002).

(a) poof A homosexual male – also **pouff, poove, poofdah** and the Australian **poofter**. Dates back at least to the 1850s, and 'puff' (pointing to the likely origin) was apparently tramps' slang for homosexual by 1870. *Private Eye* certainly popularized 'poof' in the 1960s but clearly did not invent it, as has been claimed, though possibly it did coin the 'poove' version. 'I may be a poove but I'm a terrific engineer' – *Private Eye* (30 November 1962).

(to) pop off To die. Since the 18th century.

(to) pop one's clogs To die. Judging from its absence from *Partridge/Slang* and *OED2*, this must be a fairly recent blending of 'to pop off', 'to die with one's boots on' and possibly 'to pop' in the sense of 'to pawn'. An unconfirmed 18th-century use has been reported. *Street Talk: The Language of Coronation Street* (1986) definitely has it.

(to) pop the question To propose marriage. By the early 19th century.

popular justice Lynching. A euphemism used by a newspaper in Budapest during the uprising against the Hungarian Communist regime in 1956.

pork pies / porkies Lies. From rhyming slang, but a relatively recent coinage (by 1996). The traditional rhyming phrase was 'collar and tie' for 'lie'. 'Made up stories about what they were doing on the night in question, faked alibis, any sort of "pork pies", as Chippy used to call them' – John Mortimer, *Quite Honestly* (2005), ch. 24.

porridge Time spent in prison. This term has been current since the 1950s at least. It is said to be (a touch unconvincingly) from rhyming slang 'borage and thyme = time'. The porridge-stirring connection with the (more American) expressions 'stir' (meaning 'prison'), 'in stir' (in prison) and 'stir crazy' (insane as a result of long imprisonment) may just be coincidental. These terms are said to derive from the Anglo-Saxon word *styr*, meaning 'punishment', reinforced by the Romany *steripen*, meaning 'prison' (*DOAS*).

On the other hand, if porridge was once the prisoner's basic food – and it was known as 'stirabout' – it may be more than coincidence that we have here. *Porridge* was the title of a BBC TV comedy series (1974–7) about prison life. In *Something Nasty in the Woodshed* (1976), Kyril Bonfiglioli provides another angle: '"Porridge" ... means penal servitude. There is a legend ... that if ... on the last morning of your "stretch", you do not eat up all your nice porridge, you will be back in durance vile within the year.'

portly Fat, overweight. Since the 16th century. '[Falstaff on himself] A goodly portly man, i'faith, and a corpulent' – Shakespeare, *Henry IV, Part 1* (1597), II.iv.416. Falstaff uses the word to mean 'of stately bearing' as also 'corpulent' in the sense of 'full-bodied', rather than 'extremely stout', but his audience probably heard otherwise. 'My mother-in-law told of a phrase overheard on a bus in Huddersfield, spoken by a portly woman to her equally portly husband who in true Northern fashion had got on the bus first. As they sat together, she said: "Move over, Daddy, I've only got one cheek on' – from my collection *Eavesdroppings* (1981). 'Once described by an over-enthusiastic newspaper as "one of London's most eligible bachelors", Stacpoole is now grey, portly and, at 55, looking rather past his sell-by date' – *Today* (1 September 1994).

(a) positive age centre An old folks' club. One of these was discovered in London W10 in 2005: 'The Positive Age Centre, which is part of the Open Age Project, aims to provide a range of health and creative activities which keep people of 50+ active, fit and healthy.'

positive discrimination The favouring of minority groups considered to be underprivileged, in order to compensate for racism, male chauvinism etc. Or unfair discrimination in support of such an oppressed minority (depending on where you are standing). An expression familiar by 1967 in the UK. 'With this victory over the successors of the once mighty Lords Commissioners of the Admiralty, in forcing them into this blatant sex discrimination (or, in politically correct language, positive discrimination), I cannot understand why the feminists are getting so excited about a small skirmish like membership of the Garrick Club. All they should do – as would any commander on encountering a pocket of resistance – is leave it behind in their drive towards superiority, and return to starve it out or beat it into submission at a later date' – *The Daily Telegraph* (15 July 1992).

(to go) postal To go berserk or to have an outburst, after the reported behaviour of postal workers in the US when they came under pressure. Recorded in the February 1994 issue of *Wired*. Confirmed by *The Economist* (21 June 1997), saying such workers went on shooting rampages when stressed out.

(the) posterior The arse, buttocks. Since the 17th century.

poverty See BENEFIT; BOTHER; DEPRIVED PEOPLE; DIFFERENTIATED INCOME GROUP; DIFFERENTLY-ADVANTAGED; DISADVANTAGED PEOPLE; DOWN ON ONE'S LUCK; ECONOMICALLY-ABUSED; HARD UP; IN NEED OF RELIEF; INDIGENT; LESS-DEVELOPED; NATIONAL ASSISTANCE; NEEDY; PEOPLE IN POVERTY; SOCIAL SECURITY; UNDERPRIVILEGED (CLASS)

(to) powder one's nose To go to the LAVATORY – female use only. By the 1920s, in the UK and US, but in the latter less so because of possible confusion with the side-effects of cocaine-sniffing. *OED2* doesn't find it before 1921 when Somerset Maugham daringly put it in his play *The Circle*. Cole Porter put it in *The New Yorkers* (1930) – though there is some doubt whether the song was actually used in the show: 'The girls today / Have but one thing to say, / "Where can one powder one's nose?"' 'We are invited to wash our hands, or, if we wear dresses, to powder our noses' – Isaac Goldberg, *The Wonder of Words* (1938), ch. 6; *Honey*: 'I wonder if you could show me where the ... I want to ... put some powder on my nose.' *George*: 'Martha, won't you show her where we keep the ... euphemism?' – Edward Albee, *Who's Afraid of Virginia Woolf?* (1962), act I.

(a/the) powder room A/the LAVATORY for female use. Originally American, by the 1940s. Formerly, a powder room was (domestic) a closet where you had your wig powdered and (nautical) where gunpowder was stored on board.

(a) pre-dawn vertical insertion An early-morning parachute drop. US military talk after the invasion of Grenada (27 October 1983).

pre-owned Second-hand, used. American usage, almost exclusively, and established by the early 1960s. So, a 'pre-owned vehicle' is a 'used car'. Quoted in Willard R. Espy, *An Almanac of Words at Play* (1975).

(a) pre-woman A girl. This word for a pre-pubertal person was a joke coinage by the American cartoonist Jeff Sheshol in his strip 'Politically Correct Person' (by 1990). 'Imagine the shift a children's tale would have to undergo to rid itself of all offending elements. "It's raining nonhuman animal companions," said Wendy and Melissa's father. "Why don't you pre-women have an herbal tea party for your nonsexist dolls, and then we'll bake some gingerbread persons!"' – *The Washington Post* (8 June 1992), quoting Beard and Cerf, *The Official Politically Correct Dictionary and Handbook*, 1992.

precipitation Rain. Favoured by meteorological officers and TV weather-forecasters and sometimes used grandiloquently in other circles, perhaps because it does not make the rain sound so wet. By the mid-19th century in scientific circles.

'Some television news people here [the US] like to refer to
"precipitation situations" when they mean it is raining.
I sometimes wonder if they speak like this off-screen, whether
they actually go home and say they had just been caught in a
heavy precipitation situation' – Harold Evans, BBC Radio 4,
A Point of View (18 September 2005).

precision bombing Bombing where there is more chance
of hitting the target (in comparison with 'saturation bombing',
where little or no attempt is made to be precise). By 1939.
'Strategic bombing as carried out by the American 8th and 15th
Air Forces in Europe was "precision bombing" directed, so
far as operational accuracy permitted, against specific military
targets' – *The New York Times* Magazine (27 August 1950). But
whether it was precise or imprecise was presumably of no great
concern to those who were killed by the bombing.

(to) predecease To die before. By the 16th century
(Shakespeare).

preggers Pregnant. Possibly schoolgirl slang originally and used
to avoid the ominous word. By the 1940s. 'I would only offer my
seat to a woman if she were carrying a baby, if she were preggers,
or if she were obviously infirm' – *The Times* (4 February 1964).

pregnancy See BIRTH

(a) presentation session A class (for instruction) (in the
US). Quoted in Willard R. Espy, *An Almanac of Words at Play* (1975).

(a/the) Presidential Partner A/the first lady, i.e. the spouse
of the US president. The first 'first Lady of the Land' to be so
called may have been the wife of Abraham Lincoln, who was
mentioned thus by William Howard Russell in 1863. Clearly
not PC nowadays. The spouse of the President should simply be
referred to as 'Ms' or 'Mrs' (until such time as there is a male
one, that is). On the other hand, Hillary Clinton was making it
known that she would wish to be known as the 'Presidential

Partner' even before her husband was elected in November 1992. A euphemism that does not seem to have caught on.

(caused by) pressure of work A common excuse for inefficiency, discourtesy etc. By the early 20th century?

prestigious Expensive, over-priced. It is appropriate that this word has acquired a euphemistic overlay. Now meaning 'having prestige', originally 'prestigious' meant quite the opposite: 'cheating, deceptive, illusory'. Compare 'prestidigitation' ('juggling, trickery'). But that meaning slips easily into the idea of 'dazzling', and has done so. Original meaning by 1546, second by 1913, a euphemism by the 1980s.

prevarication Lying. By the 17th century – originally in legal use.

preventive / preventative detention Imprisonment preventing the imprisoned from getting up to what they would get up to if they were still free. By the 1930s. 'Paris reports that the French police have released from "preventive detention" P.G. Wodehouse, British novelist' – *Facts On File* (28 February 1945).

(a/the) price spiral Increasing costs. Originally 'wage–price spiral', by the 1950s.

(the) pride of the morning / morning pride An erect penis on waking. By the late 19th century. More caused by the need to URINATE than to use it for sex. Not to be confused with the term for a morning shower that betokens a fine day (in rural use since the 1850s).

(the) Prince of Darkness The Devil. By the 16th century. 'The prince of darkness is a gentleman' – Edgar in Shakespeare, *King Lear* (1605), III.iv.140.

(a) prison officer / warder A gaoler/jailer. Both known by about 1900 but 'prison warder' less apparent from about 1930.

(the) private part(s) The male/female genitals. Since the 17th century. Sometimes just **part(s)**. 'Private Parts on Public View' – headline on report of nude photographic trip on Thames boat in *The Guardian* (13 September 1976).

privileged Upper-class, or at least not working-class. By the 16th century? '[An official of the Independent Schools Information Service asserted] The image of "privileged classes" has gone for good' – *The Daily Telegraph* (5 August 1977).

(a) privy A LAVATORY (usually outside the house). Since the 14th century. Derived from 'private' because it is a 'private place of easement'. 'The "privies" [were] as good an index as any to the characters of their owners. Some were horrible holes, others were fairly decent' – Flora Thompson, *Lark Rise* (1939), ch. 1.

pro-choice In favour of a woman's right to choose whether or not to have an abortion. An American coinage, by 1975. On the other hand, **pro-life** is a euphemism for being opposed to abortion. 'Instead of presenting the pro-choice position as the politically correct, women's rights position, it suggested it was anti-big government, keep the government out of our bedroom. For Jeffersonian conservatives, that was the proper approach' – *The Washington Post* (23 March 1992).

(a) problem drinker See PERSON WITH A DRINK PROBLEM

problem families Noisy/quarrelsome families. By 1937. 'Troublesome council tenants in Birmingham ... are to be moved into special areas where they can "do their worst" among themselves. The present policy of dispersing problem families to estates in the city has caused growing anger among normal tenants whose lives have been disrupted' – *The Daily Telegraph* (24 November 1977). The euphemism was for families described by the chairman of the housing committee as 'making threats of personal injury to neighbours, pouring paint into car petrol tanks, and down house windows, ripping fittings in their own homes, trampling on cultivated gardens and tearing down fences ... Recently, one family threatened to blow up a neighbour's house.'

(a) professional foul A foul committed in football and designed to prevent the other team from scoring. By the mid-20th century. In American basketball, this is known as a 'profit foul'. Hence, the title of Tom Stoppard's play *Professional Foul* (1978).

(a) professor A school teacher. Perhaps mostly in the US. '*Professor*, a male teacher. This abuse of the word "professor" seems to have grown up in the country districts recently. It is now applied indiscriminately to any schoolmaster' – *Dialect Notes* (US) (1903), pt 2, ch. 5.

profoundly deaf Stone deaf, i.e. having no useful hearing. Perhaps late 20th century?

(the) proletariat The common people. Originally, the lowest ranks in ancient Rome but from the mid-19th century, specifically those who had only their hands to work with and no laid-up capital. Hence, the Marxist/Communist notion of the Dictatorship of the Proletariat. 'Ford glumly sees the bird-catcher Papageno as "an objectification of the proletariat as abstract labour to be dominated"' – *The Observer* (17 November 1991).

(a/the) promise of rain A/the threat of drought. During a drought, American TV weather-forecasters had to adopt PC terminology. They had to talk about the **hope of rain** or 'the promise of rain'. Source: *The Daily Telegraph* (14 January 1991).

prostitution See CAMP FOLLOWER; COURTESAN; DISORDERLY HOUSE; FALLEN WOMAN; FRENCH LESSONS;

GAME; GOOD-TIME GIRL; GRAND HORIZONTAL; HOOKER;
HOSTESS; HOT; HOUSE; IMPORTUNE; KEPT WOMAN; LADY;
LADY OF THE NIGHT; MASSAGE ESTABLISHMENT; NICE
TIME; NYMPH OF DARKNESS; WORLD'S OLDEST PROFESSION;
ON THE STREETS; PAINTED LADY; PERSONAL SERVICES;
QUICK TIME; RENT BOY; SCARLET WOMAN; SEX WORKER;
SOCIAL WORKER; UNFORTUNATE; WOMAN OF EASY VIRTUE;
WORKING GIRL

protected sex Sex with a condom (to protect the participant
from sexually transmitted diseases). Since the 1980s. See also
UNPROTECTED SEX.

protective custody Imprisonment, supposedly for the
prisoner's own safety. Borrowed from the German *Schutzhaft*
(protective detention), a term used in the 1930s to give cover to
Nazi arrests.

protesters A mob. Since about 1960.

psychologically disadvantaged Spaced out on drugs. A joke
would-be PC coinage by 1993.

(a) public health officer A SANITARY ENGINEER. 'Last year
the sanitary engineers suggested that they should be known as
Public Health Officers. We should be lucky they did not want
to call themselves Privy Counsellors' – Lord Mancroft, speech
to auctioneers and estate agents, Dorchester Hotel (31 October
1957). Whether this was based in fact or just an after-dinner
joke is not known.

(a) puffback An explosion on an oil burner (in the US).
Quoted in Willard R. Espy, *An Almanac of Words at Play* (1975).

(a) puppy An impudent, conceited or silly young man, a
coxcomb. Since about 1600. Mrs Elton remarked to Mr Weston
that she thought his son 'truly the gentleman, without the least
conceit or puppyism. You must know I have a vast dislike of

328

puppies – quite a horror of them' – Jane Austen, *Emma* (1816), pt 3, ch. 2.

(to) purloin To steal. Since the 16th century. 'I took an opportunity of purloining his key from his breeches-pocket' – Henry Fielding, *Tom Jones* (1749), pt 8, ch. 9; 'James and I ran around the bedrooms, gossiping and giggling, he purloining a black coal-scuttle glove and some india rubbers' – James Lees-Milne, *Ancestral Voices* (1975), diary entry for 18 April 1943; 'The Garden, an assemblage of sanctities purloined from the New Testament and grafted on to youthful gayness, was plainly Derek Jarman's own plot in Dungeness' – *The Guardian* (9 April 1992).

(a) purser A buffet-car steward on British railways. Noted in August 1993.

(a) purveyor A seller. In an effort to raise the word's dignity. Since the 16th century. Hence, 'a purveyor of meat' is a butcher.

(to) push the envelope To take a risk, to expand the possibilities. A phrase suddenly popular in the mid-1990s, though the allusion was not immediately clear. Probably the expression refers to 'envelope' in the sense of the structure containing the gas in an airship or balloon or, more probably, in the sense of the limitations of speed and other technical specifications which dictate an aircraft's performance. It has been suggested that if the aviation context is the original one (dating back to the 1940s), the phrase meant pushing a plane in test flights up to and even beyond its known endurance limits in order to find out its exact capabilities.

'Messrs E & V want you to know that if you thought *Basic Instinct* was pushing the envelope, this year's trendy phrase for taking a risk, *Showgirls* is, according to the publicity material, "pushing the edge of the envelope"' – *The Sunday Times* (10 September 1995); 'This film, set against the background of the Mexican Revolution, aroused enormous controversy over the extent of the violence, which pushed the already bulging envelope out still further' – Simon Rose, *Classic Film Guide* (1995).

pushing up the daisies Dead. 'To turn one's toes up to the daisies' has been an expression since the 1840s. 'Under the daisies' has been known since the 1860s. '"Pushing up the daisies" is their creed, you know' occurs in a poem by Wilfred Owen (about 1918). One of the roll-call of euphemisms in the *Monty Python's Flying Circus* 'Dead parrot' sketch, first shown on BBC TV (7 December 1969). A man (named Praline in the script) who has just bought a parrot that turns out to be dead, registers a complaint with the pet shop owner in these words: 'It's a stiff. Bereft of life it rests in peace. It would be pushing up the daisies if you hadn't nailed it to the perch.'

(to) put away (1) To arrest, imprison. (2) (also **put down / put to sleep**) To destroy (pets and animals). 'I had my dog put down.' 'Dog put down after biting baby.' 'A man has been fined £425 for wounding a woman in a passing car while trying to put down a friend's cow with a rifle' – *The Times* (28 October 2005). (3) To eat a lot of food.

(to) put it about To be sexually promiscuous. Date of origin unknown, but whereas *Partridge/Catch Phrases* guesses that it originated in the late 1940s, it does occur much earlier in a letter of Byron's dated 20th January 1817. Speaking of Mary Shelley's sister Claire Clairmont he says, 'I never loved nor pretended to love her – but a man is a man – & if a girl of eighteen comes prancing to you at all hours – there is but one way – the suite of all this is that she was with *child* – & returned to England to assist in peopling that desolate island ... The next question is is the brat *mine*? – I have reason to think so – for I know as much as one can know such a thing – that she had *not lived* with S[helley] during the time of our acquaintance – & that she had a good deal of that same with me. – This comes of "putting it about" (as Jackson calls it) & be damned to it – and thus people come into the world.' 'Gentleman' John Jackson was a pugilist Byron cultivated. 'The simplest explanation was that he had just got tired of Jacqui ... He was a man who had always put it about a bit' – Simon Brett, *Cast, In Order of Disappearance* (1975).

putting on weight / putting it on   Fat. By the 1890s. 'She had put on a lot of weight .. I could see her checking herself against Veronica – who has definitely been putting it on' – Adam Diment, *The Dolly Dolly Spy* (1967), ch. 7.

Pygmalion   Bloody – as in 'not Pygmalion likely!' for 'not bloody likely!' The latter phrase of emphatic refusal is a famous quotation from George Bernard Shaw's play *Pygmalion* (1914): '*Freddy*: "Are you walking across the Park, Miss Doolittle? If so –" *Liza*: "Walk! Not bloody likely." (*Sensation*).' The shock of the original was that it was uttered at a polite tea-party and the word 'bloody' had rarely, if ever before, been uttered on the British stage. The euphemistic 'Not Pygmalion likely!' had a certain currency in the 1920s. By the time *My Fair Lady*, the musical version, was filmed in 1964, the shock effect of 'bloody' was so mild that Liza was given the line 'Come on, Dover, move your bloomin' arse!' in the Ascot racing sequence.

Qq

queer Homosexual. 'Queer' has been a pejorative alternative name since the 1920s at least, but some queers take delight in applying the derogatory term to themselves. 'Young American homosexuals want to be called queer rather than gay because it has more "political potency". They chant at rallies: "We're here, we're queer – get used to it." The trend, led by Militants Queer Nation, is also set to sweep Britain. Lesbian, Liza Powers, 34, said: "Using a word that is offensive is a way of showing anger. Gay is white middle class"' – *Sun* (9 April 1991); 'Just when the message had finally got through to the shires, queer is back, this time appropriated by gay people themselves in a development known as the New Queer Politics. Suddenly, gay is bourgeois, it's boring, it's the politics of compromise and reaction. Queer is where it's at' – *The Guardian* (23 June 1992); in the summer of 1992, at a Promenade Concert in the Royal Albert Hall, London, I spotted a man wearing a T-shirt emblazoned with the slogan 'Queer to Eternity'.

Not everyone seems capable of going along with this, however: 'All 21 of [Enid Blyton's] Famous Five adventures are being published in an updated, bowdlerised edition ... Blyton's frequently-used adjective "queer" has given way to "strange/ peculiar/funny/odd"' – *The Observer* (6 September 1992).

(a) quick time A brief sexual act with a prostitute. 'Want a quick time, long time, companionship, black leather bondage?

Ring Maggie and Maureen. Edinburgh **** (mourning [*sic*] only)' – graffito in a phone booth, Princes St, Edinburgh, quoted in my book *Graffiti 2* (1980).

Rr

(to have the) rag / rags on To be menstruating. Before the mid-20th century. Also **riding the rag**. 'The attitude that regards menstruation as divinely ordained and yet unmentionable leads to the intensification of the female revolt against it, which can be traced in all the common words for it, like the *curse*, and male disgust expressed in terms like *having the rags on*' – Germaine Greer, *The Female Eunuch* (1970).

(a) rake An immoral, dissipated man. Since the 17th century.

(a) rape survivor A rape victim. 'On the frontiers of political correctness and social sensitivity, a rape victim is not a rape victim, but a "rape survivor"' – *The Washington Post* (22 November 1991).

(to blow a) raspberry To make a noise like a fart. From rhyming slang, 'raspberry tart/fart'. Since the 1890s. Hence, also 'to show disapproval'.

(to) re-educate To brainwash. Since the 1950s, when goings-on in Chinese prisoner-of-war camps in Korea were made known to the world audience. 'Enforcement of political correctness then extends to "sensitivity" sessions in which students are encouraged to confess publicly their racism. This middle-class take on the Chinese reeducation camp, like the other forms of psychological coercion on campus, serves a specific agenda: to identify nonconforming ideas as illegitimate and, by doing so, banish them' – *The Washington Post* (8 February 1991).

readjustment Reduction. 'It had been found necessary to make a readjustment of rations (Squealer always spoke of it as a "readjustment," never as a "reduction")' – George Orwell, *Animal Farm* (1945), ch. 9.

(the) rear The arse, buttocks. Since the late 18th century. Agnetha Faltskog, the singer with Abba, was awarded the title 'Rear of the Year' in 1975.

(to) receive punishment To be in pain (boxing). A report on Richard Dunn's unsuccessful fight with Muhammad Ali (May 1976) said the referee stopped the fight 'to save him from further punishment'.

(a) reception centre A doss house. Providing temporary accommodation for the destitute. Since the 1940s.

(a) recreational facility A playground (also used by some local authorities for a park, 1976–7). Probably American in origin. 'A new recreational facility featuring tennis, paddle tennis and a barbecue and picnic area with charming pavilion has been completed' – advertisement in *The New York Times* (3 November 1972). See also under FACILITY.

redundancy See under SACK

(to make) redundant / (to) reduce the headcount / staffing levels To give people the sack. By 1991. 'About 50 employees at Brown's store in Chester have received redundancy notices, despite previous assurances that the recent takeover would not affect staffing levels' – *Manchester Evening News* (13 August 1976). Also **redundancy elimination**, by 1991.

refer to drawer This cheque has bounced. Since the 1880s. From the notice instructing the payee to send back to the drawer a cheque that cannot be honoured or for which there are 'insufficient funds'.

(a) reformatory A prison for first offenders/women where the emphasis is supposedly on reformation rather than punishment. Since the 1830s.

refuse Rubbish. Since the mid-19th century. 'At the back or side of each cottage ... the house refuse was thrown on a nearby pile called "the muck'll"' – Flora Thompson, *Lark Rise* (1939), ch. 1; 'Areas previously wasted by chemical contamination, domestic refuse and coal-mining were given a new lease of life by redevelopment for recreational or industrial purposes' – *The Independent* (6 October 1994).

(a) refuse collector / refuse disposal operative / refuse operative A dustbin man, dustman. Since the 1940s? 'It happened to the rat-catcher (he's now a rodent operator), the dustman (refuse collector), and the sweeper (street orderly)' – *The Daily Mail* (25 October 1958); 'Before the [1939–45] war a spade used to be called a spade – often brutally so ... But today a dustman has become a refuse collector' – George Mikes, *How To Be Decadent* (1977).

regime change Overthrowing a government you dislike. The phrase came to prominence in the run-up to the US invasion of Iraq in 2003 but had been used by international-relations experts since the late 1970s, albeit in the simple sense of 'change of government'. Regimes tend only to be run by bad guys.

regular Regularly defecating, perhaps on a daily basis. Hence, 'Keep "Regular" With Ex-Lax', the slogan for Ex-Lax chocolate laxative in the US (current by 1934). Also, 'All-Bran Keeps You Regular' in the UK, in about the 1950s. Is also applied to menstruation.

(a) relationship An extramarital sexual relationship. Perhaps since the mid-20th century. 'The FA's director of public affairs tried to broker a deal with the *News of the World* to expose Ms Alam's relationship with Mr Eriksson if the paper would keep her six-month fling with Mr Palios out of the public eye' – *The Independent* (10 September 2005).

relationships See under MARRIAGE

(a) relentless raconteur A boring person – in obituary-speak. Second half of the 20th century. In fact, just 'raconteur' on its own is enough to signal this.

(hand) relief Masturbation, especially as provided by a prostitute. Compare HAND JOB.

(to) relieve oneself To DEFECATE / URINATE. Since the 16th century but really since the 19th. 'An army captain has sparked a security alert after accidentally leaving a gun in a supermarket lavatory ... She removed her holster and put the weapon on the cistern while relieving herself but forgot it when she left' – *The Independent* (17 October 2005).

(to) relieve someone of his / her virginity To have SEXUAL INTERCOURSE with a virgin (female, usually).

(mortal) remains A dead body, ashes. Since the 19th century; 'remains' on its own since 1700. 'Beneath this Stone lie the Remains of William Cobbett, Son of George and Anne Cobbett [who died in 1835]' – grave in St Andrew's Parish Church, Farnham, Surrey; 'Here At The Feet Of Walter Scott Lie The Mortal Remains Of John Gibson Lockhart His Son-In-Law [who died in 1854]' – grave in the ruins of the Abbey church at Dryburgh, Berwickshire; 'Marie Curie, who discovered radium, was yesterday chosen to be the first woman for burial in the Paris Pantheon, resting place of France's illustrious dead. President François Mitterrand ordered her remains to be transferred

there along with her husband Pierre' – *The Herald* (Glasgow)
(15 March 1995); '[A] six year battle with activists which
culminated in the unsolved theft of the remains of the owner's
late mother-in-law' – *The Independent* (24 August 2005).

(to) remove To assassinate, kill, murder. By 1653.

remuneration Payment. In the euphemistic way, from the 19th
century onwards.

rendition See EXTRAORDINARY RENDITION

(a) rent boy A male (homosexual) prostitute. By 1969.

(a) research vessel A spy ship. During the Cold War, mid-
20th century.

(a) rescheduled train A late train. Noted in British railway
use by 1992.

(to) rest in peace To be dead. 'Here rest in peace, till angels
bid thee rise, / To join thy Saviour's concert in the skies' – on
a 1732 grave in Wolverhampton. The abbreviation 'R.I.P.' for
the injunction *requiescat in pace* was known by 1816. Latterly, one
of the roll-call of euphemisms in the *Monty Python's Flying Circus*
'Dead parrot' sketch, first shown on BBC TV (7 December
1969). A man (named Praline in the script) who has just bought
a parrot that turns out to be dead, registers a complaint with
the pet shop owner in these words: 'It's a stiff. Bereft of life,
it rests in peace', etc.

(a) rest room A lavatory, in American parlance. In this sense,
I am not sure the term was much used before the 1950s.

resting Unemployed (of actors). By the 1920s. 'My theatrical
colleagues who are only too familiar with the long periods of
"resting" – which being out of work is so politely called' – *The Times*
(28 September 1960); '"Are you on holiday?" ... "Resting, to

use a theatrical term. Between jobs"' – Reginald Hill, *Another Death in Venice* (1976).

(to come to one's) resting place To die. 'This is the last long resting place / Of Aunt Jemima Jones / Her soul ascended into space / Amidst our tears and groans' – said to be on a Shropshire tombstone dating from 1803. 'Marie Curie, who discovered radium, was yesterday chosen to be the first woman for burial in the Paris Pantheon, resting place of France's illustrious dead. President François Mitterrand ordered her remains to be transferred there along with her husband Pierre' – *The Herald* (Glasgow) (15 March 1995).

retarded Dull-witted, mentally deficient. By 1895 and originally applied to children.

(to) retire To go to the LAVATORY. Since about the 17th century.

(a) retirement pension An old-age pension. Seemingly since the 1960s: 'Matthew's father-in-law had also been receiving the state old age pension, or national assurance retirement pension, as it is properly called' – Edith Rudinger (ed.), *Wills & Probate* (1967).

returned to unit / R.T.U. Failure to get promotion, in military parlance. Since the First World War.

(in the) reused metal products industry A junk dealer (in the US). Quoted in Willard R. Espy, *An Almanac of Words at Play* (1975).

(a) revenue agent A tax inspector (in the US). Quoted in Willard R. Espy, *An Almanac of Words at Play* (1975).

(a) revenue protection inspector / officer A ticket inspector – as in a recruitment advertisement in the *Notting Hill and Bayswater Times* (16 January 1998). If one likes, one can see this as a

prime example of status enhancement. Even a 'ticket inspector'
is really a 'cheat catcher'.

(to) ride (Usually of a man) to engage in SEXUAL
INTERCOURSE with a woman, but sometimes *vice versa*. Since the
16th century. 'She mounted him and rode him ... until they
climaxed together' – Stella Allan, *Inside Job* (1978), ch. 3.

ripe language Bad language, swearing. Since about the 19th
century.

robbed of her honour / virtue Seduced, forcibly relieved of
her virginity. By the 18th century? The Victorian 'parlour poem'
entitled 'Village-Born Beauty' (author unknown) has the lines:
'From a post-chaise and four / She's in London set down, /
Where robbed of her virtue, / She's launched on the town'
(as a prostitute).

(a) rodent officer / operative / operator A rat catcher.
An early form of political correctness was presumably at work
when this occupation was so renamed. 'Westminster City
Council's rat-catcher is in future to be called Rodent Officer' –
The Liverpool Echo (31 January 1944); 'When it comes to official
jargon, can you beat turning our old friend the rat-catcher into
a "Rodent Operative"?' – *The Sunday Times* (5 November 1944);
'Euphemisms ... *rodent operator* for *rat-catcher*' – *Word Study* (May
1946); 'It happened to the rat-catcher (he's now a rodent
operator), the dustman (refuse collector), and the sweeper
(street orderly)' – *Daily Mail* (25 October 1958).

(to) roger To have SEXUAL INTERCOURSE with a woman, as
in 'I rogered my wife'. By 1650. A 'roger' is one of the numerous
terms for the penis and may derive from the fact that 'Roger'
was once a common name for a farm bull or ram. 'Swear to have
no more rogering before you leave England except Mrs. —— in
chambers ...' – a memorandum to himself by James Boswell
(16 July 1763).

(a) Roman spring A sexual last hurrah for the elderly. After *The Roman Spring of Mrs Stone* – title of a novel (1950; filmed UK/US 1961) by Tennessee Williams. It tells of an ageing beauty who uses her wealth to bed a young lover.

Romanies Gypsies. A slang term by 1812 but then a useful euphemism, avoiding the g-word.

(a) rooster A cock. By the 1770s. More common in the US and presumably used in order to avoid confusion with the other sort of cock.

rootless cosmopolitans Jews. A Stalinist euphemism from 1948 onwards. The basic Russian is *'bezrodnye kosmopolity'* (*'bezrodnyi'* literally means 'homeless' or 'stateless') and was used with reference to Soviet Jews, and particularly those who supported the newly emerging Zionist movement in Israel, at a time when the Soviet Union was once more insulating itself from the West after the relatively relaxed relationship with its allies during the war. 'Kosmopolit' on its own had been in use by the 1930s and Hitler spoke of *'eine wurzellose internationale Clique* [a rootless international clique]' in a speech (also broadcast on radio) at Berlin-Siemensstadt on 11 November 1933.

The Russian phrase seems first to have been used by Anatoly Sofronov in an article ('For the Further Development of Soviet Dramaturgy') in *Pravda* (23 December 1948). At Stalin's behest, his henchman Andrey Zhdanov had, in 1948, launched an official attack on Jewish artistic figures, including the internationally famous Yiddish actor, Solomon Mikhoels, who was murdered that year, probably by Soviet secret police. But the term became a derogatory tag for anyone who did not toe the official party line and who was thus perceived as being unpatriotic.

(to have) round heels To be sexually promiscuous (of a woman) – in other words, she's anybody's, she's an easy lay. American origin, current by 1957. A sharp image, suggesting that a woman's heels are so curved that the slightest push from a man would put her on her back and in a position to have sexual intercourse. *A Round-Heeled Woman : My Late-Life Adventures in Sex and Romance* (2003), by Jane Juska.

round objects / spherical objects BALLS. An anecdote told by Kingsley Amis on BBC Radio *Quote ... Unquote* (1978) goes as follows: A civil servant made a marginal comment on an official document that was circulating in the Foreign Office but instead of putting what he thought – i.e. 'Balls!' – he chose the more diplomatic words, 'Round objects!' When the document passed before the eyes of the then Foreign Secretary – Lord Halifax (1881–1959) – he inquired who this Mr Round was and what precisely were the grounds for his objection? A version of this anecdote involving Winston Churchill and Pug Ismay is told in *Pass the Port Again* (1980). Another version is recounted in Gerald Kersh, *Clean, Bright and Slightly Oiled* (1946).

Hence, also, **the answer is in the plural and they bounce**. This was reputedly the response given by the architect Sir Edwin Lutyens to a Royal Commission. However, according to Robert Jackson, *The Chief* (1959), when Gordon (later Lord) Hewart was in the House of Commons, he was answering questions on behalf of David Lloyd George. For some time, one afternoon, he had given answers in the customary brief parliamentary manner – 'The answer is in the affirmative' or 'The answer is in the negative.' After one such non-committal reply, several members arose to bait Hewart with a series of rapid supplementary questions. He waited until they had all finished and then replied: 'The answer is in the plural!'

(having a) rounded stomach Obese. 'Mr Ivell, looking every inch the happy publican, with his open-neck shirt, hearty handshake, rounded stomach and amiable disposition' – *The Independent* (4 June 2005).

(a) rubber A contraceptive sheath or condom. From the material it is made of. By 1947. Hence, **rubber goods** is a general name for contraceptive devices when discretion is the watchword. In the US, were a man or woman to say 'I've got my rubbers', this commendable state of preparedness would only apply to their overshoes or galoshes.

(the) rubber-chicken circuit The celebrity speaking circuit in the US (but also elsewhere) where rubbery chicken is invariably on the menu. By the 1980s. The British Conservative politician Michael Heseltine was known as 'Rubber Chicken' by 1990 because when he resigned from Margaret Thatcher's Cabinet, he spent almost every night speaking to political meetings up and down the country.

Rubenesque / Rubensesque (Of a woman) PLUMP, well-rounded, large-breasted, as in portraits by Rubens. Since about 1900.

(a) rug A wig. Of American origin by 1940. Because of what it does and because of its appearance.

(to) ruin To seduce. By 1679. 'Tell me, hussy, are you ruin'd or no?' – John Gay, *The Beggar's Opera* (1727), act 1.

(a/the) rump The arse, buttocks. By the 14th century. An interesting euphemistic transference is quoted by Samuel Pepys in his diary entry for 7 February 1660: 'Boys do now cry "Kiss my Parliament" instead of "Kiss my arse," so great and general a contempt is the Rump come to among all men, good and bad'; 'Adorer of the adulterous rump!' – James Joyce, *Ulysses* (1922).

(to) rusticate To expel (from university), either for a specified period (as a punishment) or permanently. By 1714. Originally, to return to the *rus* or countryside. 'This son had been first rusticated from Oxford and then expelled' – Anthony Trollope, *Dr Thorne* (1858), ch. 2.

Ss

S.H.One.T. Shit. A way of avoiding it by misspelling it out loud. Noted in the 1990s.

(the) sack Dismissal from employment. Known in English since 1825, but in French since the 17th century as '*On luy a donné son sac.*' The suggestion is that this expression dates from the days when workers would carry the tools of their trade around with them, from job to job, in a bag which they would leave with their employer. When their services were no longer required, they would be given the bag back. Hence, the expression **(to) give someone** (or **get given**) **the sack**.

The second half of the 20th century saw a boom in euphemisms for this activity. The following had all been recorded by 1991:

> **career change opportunity**
> **chemistry change**
> **(the) chop**
> **coerced transition**
> **de-accession**
> **decruitment**
> **degrowing**
> **dehiring**
> **delayering**
> **destaffing**

dispensing with someone's services / assistance
downsizing
dropping
early release / retirement
executive culling
force reduction
giving time to one's other commitments
head-count reduction
indefinite idling
internal reorganization
involuntary separation
laying off
losing
negotiated departure
no longer with us
not renewing someone's contract
(given one's) notice
(putting) out to grass
personnel surplus reduction

rationalization (of the workforce) (since the 1970s)
redeployment (since the 1940s)
reducing someone's commitments
reduction in force / rif
releasing
relieving (as in 'to relieve of duties' or 'to relieve someone of his/
    her responsibilities')
restructuring
retrenching
rightsizing
schedule adjustment
selective separation
services no longer being required
shedding labour
shelving
skill-mix adjustment
standing down / stepping down
surplussing

transitioning

vocational relocation

voluntary redundancy / severance / termination

workforce adjustment

workforce imbalance correction

working on private projects (this is what it is said people are doing when they have been relieved of their formal jobs).

Sources include David Crystal, *The Cambridge Encyclopedia of the English Language* (1995).

sacking/dismissal/job leaving See above and also CARDS; CLEARING ONE'S DESK; CONSIDER ONE'S POSITION; CONSULTANT; DESELECT; EARLY BATH; EXCESS; EXCLUDE; GARDENING LEAVE; GIVE TIME TO ONE'S OTHER COMMITMENTS; GOLDEN HANDSHAKE; JOB AXE; LEAVE OF ABSENCE; LET GO; LOSE – POSTS; NATURAL WASTAGE; NOTICE; ON HEALTH GROUNDS; OUTPLACEMENT; REDUNDANT/REDUCE THE HEADCOUNT; SPEND MORE TIME WITH MY (WIFE AND) FAMILY; STEP DOWN; STOOD DOWN; TERMINATE

salami tactics / technique The gradual removal of an opponent (especially political) or anything else that you do not wish to exist, as though slicing a salami. By 1952. 'Alan Bullock and Oliver Stallybrass credit the coinage to Matyas Rakosi of the Hungarian Communist party, who in 1945 described how he came to power by getting his opposition to slice off its right wing, then its centrists, until only those collaborating with Communists remained in power' – *Safire*.

(a) sales lady A shop assistant. Of American origin, by 1856.

(a) sales representative A salesman. By 1949.

(a) saloon A bar. From the 1840s, in the US, 'saloon' was applied to anywhere, shop or bar, where intoxicating liquor was available. In the UK, 'saloon' is still used to describe a rather more exclusive bar within a pub, one that is not a 'public bar'.

same-gender-oriented Homosexual. Second half of the 20th century.

sanctions Disruption of work in the work-place. In the UK, since the 1960s/70s. 'Shop-floor workers at the two Triumph factories have been applying sanctions – designed to reduce output by 5 per cent – for nearly two weeks in protest at the management's failure to pay an increase' – *The Guardian* (22 April 1976).

(a) sanitary engineer A sewage worker. 'Last year the sanitary engineers suggested that they should be known as Public Health Officers. We should be lucky they did not want to call themselves Privy Counsellors' – Lord Mancroft, speech to auctioneers and estate agents, Dorchester Hotel (31 October 1957). Whether this was based in fact or just an after-dinner joke is not known. Originally, in the 1870s, the term had been applied to those who *built* such works rather than just operated them. The American TV comedian Art Carney played a character called Ed Norton, who was described as a **sanitation engineer**, in *The Honeymooners* in the early 1950s. Compare **a sanitary assistant / man** who is, rather, a dustbin man or dustman. A nice distinction.

(a) sanitary napkin / towel A tampon or pad used to absorb menstrual flow. Since the mid-19th century. 'She's not going to walk in here ... and turn it into a Golden Sanitary Towel Award Presentation' – John Osborne, *The Hotel in Amsterdam* (1968).

(a) sanitation maintenance superintendent A janitor (in the US). Quoted in Willard R. Espy, *An Almanac of Words at Play* (1975).

Sapphic Lesbian. Since the late 19th century. Originally used to describe the metres used by the famous poetess of Lesbos (about 600 BC). 'In England there are no laws against "Lesbianism" or intercourse of an erotic character between women, and yet there are several women in London whose friendship with other women does carry a taint and a suspicion, simply because these women are obviously "sapphic" in their loves' – an 1895 letter from Lord Alfred Douglas, quoted in H. Montgomery Hyde, *The Trials of Oscar Wilde* (1948).

sartorially challenged Badly dressed. A would-be PC coinage from the early 1990s.

sayings, euphemistic See CHEQUE IS IN THE POST; CONVERSATION ABOUT SEX AND TRAVEL; DUE TO A PRODUCTION ERROR; ELEGANT SUFFICIENCY; FITS WHERE IT TOUCHES; FOR YOUR CONVENIENCE; I HEAR YOU; ANOTHER CHANCE TO SEE; KING OVER THE WATER; LITTLE GENTLEMAN IN BLACK VELVET; (WE MUST HAVE) LUNCH; NO COMMENT; OPERATIONAL DIFFICULTIES; SCOTTISH PLAY; UP TO A POINT LORD COPPER; WAYS (AND MEANS) OF MAKING YOU TALK; WHEN ARE YOU GOING TO FINISH OFF THAT DRESS

(a) Scarborough warning No warning at all. This is sometimes wrongly said to derive from the occasion when Thomas Stafford entered and took possession of Scarborough Castle before the townsmen were aware of his approach. But that took place in 1557 and the phrase had been recorded by 1546.

(a) scarlet woman A harlot or what later would be called a prostitute. Occasionally, **scarlet lady / whore**. Also used as an abusive nickname by Protestants for the Roman Catholic church (known by the mid-19th century), selecting a phrase from Revelation 17:1–5, where a whore is described as 'arrayed in purple and scarlet colour'.

(the) Scottish play *Macbeth*. Theatrical superstition is understandable in a profession so dependent on luck. However, the euphemism 'Scottish play', invariably used for Shakespeare's play (1606), is based on a well-documented history of bad luck associated with productions of *Macbeth*. Merely to utter the name of the play would be enough to invoke misfortune. Date of origin unknown.

(the) seasoned   Old age pensioners. Does not seem likely to catch on – for culinary reasons.

(the) seat   The arse. Since about 1600. Hence, the somewhat unfortunate book titles like the Revd Francis Orpen Morris's *A Series of Picturesque Views of Seats of Noblemen and Gentlemen of Great Britain and Ireland* (1880).

(to) see (someone)   To have SEXUAL INTERCOURSE with that person. By about the mid-20th century. Hence, 'he's seeing her' could really mean 'he's screwing her' and 'he's not seeing anybody' mean 'he's not having sexual relations with anybody'.

(to) see a man about a dog   See GO AND SEE A MAN ABOUT A DOG

see you next Thursday   Cunt (say the first two words aloud and take the initial letters of the second two ...). Used as the title of a play, adapted by Ronald Harwood from Francis Verber's comedy, presented in London (October 2003) – 'Set in Paris, it is about the complicated life of a publisher, involving his wife, mistress, friends ...' Compared: 'If you see kay / Tell him he may / See you in tea / Tell him from me' – in James Joyce, *Ulysses* (1922).

(people with) seeing difficulties   The blind/part blind. By 1993.

self-abuse   Masturbation. *Chambers Cyclopedia* (1728) explained: 'Self-Abuse is a Phrase used by some late Writers for the Crime of Self-Pollution' (and there's another one). So also **self-pollution**, by the 17th century.

self-inflicted death Suicide. Only marginally more positive. The phrase had been around since the 1870s. 'Shaw was then 83, Mrs [Virginia] Woolf in her late 50s and within a year of her self-inflicted death' – *Radio Times* (May 1977).

semi-detached Attached – or, if you insist, joined to the neighbouring house but only on one side. Since 1859.

(to) send down To expel (from university, permanently or for a time). By 1853. '"I understand, too, that you left your University rather suddenly. Now – why was that?" "I was sent down, sir, for indecent behaviour"' – Evelyn Waugh, *Decline and Fall* (1928), ch. 1.

(a) senior citizen An elderly person, probably over retirement age; an old age pensioner. This term originated in the US in about 1938. It began to take hold in the UK by the 1970s. Sometimes just **a senior**. 'Sir, Are weather forecasters an unnecessary luxury? Now being a senior citizen, I survived the vagaries of the English climate long before weather forecasters came to such prominence' – letter to *The Times* (31 July 1993).

(a) senior conductor A guard (on British railway trains). Noted by 1992. Compare TRAIN MANAGER.

(a) senior moment An incident of memory loss in a middle-aged or older person. Known by 1997 and probably of American origin, this phrase is used by baby-boomers in middle age to describe failures of memory that can't be blamed on anything but age. It may derive ultimately from SENIOR CITIZEN. It has been suggested that referring to experiences as '— moments' may have been encouraged by the 'Kodak Moments' in Kodak film advertising, later used with or without irony to mean any heart-warming moment. 'The senior moments don't freak me out as much as the "Death in Venice" moments' – caption to cartoon (showing a group of elderly people) in *The New Yorker* (7 July 2003).

sensible shoes Ugly or unfashionable shoes for female wear. Since the 1880s (Kipling). Also sometimes taken to indicate lesbian tendencies in the wearer.

separate development Apartheid, separation and suppression of blacks by whites in South Africa, racial discrimination. *Apartheid* is the Afrikaans word meaning 'separateness'. The English version of this hated policy seems to have come into use in the mid-1950s.

(a) service A train. Noted on British railways by 1992. As in the loudspeaker announcement: 'This service will shortly be arriving at ...'

(a) service of thanksgiving A memorial service. By the 1980s. 'This morning to Archie Aberdeen's memorial service at St Margaret's, Westminster ... Service of Thanksgiving is a new term which I don't much like. It is a euphemism, a cowardly term, a not-facing-up to grief. We must all be cheery instead' – James Lees-Milne, *Holy Dread* (2001), diary entry for 16 October 1984.

(to) settle one's account / settle up See ACCOUNT

(the) seven year itch The urge to be unfaithful to a spouse after a certain period of matrimony. *OED2* provides various examples of this phrase going back from the mid-20th to the mid-19th century, but without the specific matrimonial context. For example, the 'seven year itch' describes a rash from poison ivy which was believed to recur every year for a seven-year period. Then one has to recall that since biblical days seven-year periods (of lean or fat) have had especial significance, and there has also been the Army saying, 'Cheer up – the first seven years are the worst!' But the specific matrimonial meaning was not popularized until the phrase was used as the title of George Axelrod's play (1952) and then film (US 1955).
  'Itch' had long been used for the sexual urge but, as Axelrod commented on BBC Radio *Quote ... Unquote* (15 June 1979):

'There was a phrase which referred to a somewhat unpleasant disease but nobody had used it in a sexual [he meant 'matrimonial'] context before. I do believe I invented it in that sense.' 'Itch', oddly, does not seem to have been used in connection with venereal diseases. Nonetheless, note the following remark in *W. C. Fields: His Follies and Fortunes* (1950) by Robert Lewis Taylor: 'Bill exchanged women every seven years, as some people get rid of the itch.'

severely subnormal / S.S.N. Dunce-like. By 1961. 'Down below the plimsoll line of an IQ of fifty are the erstwhile imbeciles and idiots, now classed as SSN – severely subnormal' – *Punch* Magazine (20 August 1972).

(a) sewer hole A manhole. Another attempt at avoiding the dreaded m-word. About 1988.

(a) (commercial) sex worker / C.S.W. A prostitute. Though presumably this could as easily be applied to a pimp or someone that merely serves in a sex shop. Another example – probably – of bureaucratic euphemism that has become PC. It may also be a way of heading off sexism into the bargain, as a 'prostitute' is invariably taken as female ('male prostitute' being employed, pointedly, for those of the other sex). By the 1980s. 'Now we are promised a campaign against prostitutes, or "sex workers", as our officialdom puts it' – *The Sunday Telegraph* (23 July 1989). By 2003, there was an International Union of Sex Workers who campaigned under the slogan 'Sex Workers of the World Unite'.

(a) sexual assault An attempted rape. A **serious sexual assault** is therefore a rape that succeeds? Compare INDECENT ASSAULT.

(to have) sexual intercourse To fuck. Is this really a euphemism? Probably. It is pretty explicit, though neutral, and has 'intercourse' which is suitably vague. By 1799 and initially in medical contexts. 'The young man and the young woman went and had sexual intercourse together' – D.H. Lawrence, *Pornography* *and Obscenity* (1929). There is any number of phrases like this that tend to fudge the issue. For example, **sexual relations** or simply **relations**. 'I am fifty-one years old and have recently experienced some pain and difficulty in relations with my husband' – Penelope Mortimer, *The Pumpkin Eater* (1962), ch. 9. Indeed, how vague can a euphemism be? Here is one that nevertheless leaves you in no doubt what is being talked about. It comes from Flora Thompson's *Lark Rise* (1939), ch. 2: 'Laura, at about twelve years old, stumbled into a rickyard where a bull was **in the act of justifying its existence**.'

(of a certain) sexual orientation / preference / proclivity Homosexual. Second half of the 20th century.

sexual parts See APPENDAGE; BEAVER; FAMILY JEWELS; FRONT DOOR; HAMPTON; HANDY LITTLE GADGET; JELLY ROLL; LITTLE ARRANGEMENTS; LUNCHBOX; MANHOOD; MEMBER; MOST PRECIOUS PART; NAUGHTY BITS; OLD FRIEND; ORGAN; PERCY; PERSON; PRIVATE PARTS; THING; TUNNEL OF LOVE; UNDERCARRIAGE; VAGINA; WEDDING KIT; WELL-ENDOWED; WELL-HUNG; WELL-UPHOLSTERED; WILLY

sexuality See AC/DC; ACCIDENT; ACT OF SHAME; ADMIRER; ADULT; ADVANCED SOCIAL LIFE; AFFAIR; ALL THE WAY; AMBIDEXTROUS; ANY; ARMOUR; AROUSE; ART/ARTISTIC; ASSIGNATION; AT IT; ATHLETE; AVAILABLE; BACKWARD; BEAST WITH TWO BACKS; BED WITH SOMEONE; BEDROOM; BETRAY; BETWEEN THE SHEETS; BIG; BIRDS AND THE BEES; BIRTH CONTROL; BLOW JOB; BLUE; BOTHER; BOYFRIEND; BROADMINDED; BUSINESS; CARNAL; CARRY A TORCH FOR SOMEONE; CARRYINGS-ON; CASTING COUCH; CERTAIN SUGGESTION; CLIMAX; COME; COPULATE; COVER; CREAM ONE'S JEANS; CRUMPET; CRUSH; DARING; DEFLOWER; DESIGNS ON; DIFFERENTLY PLEASURED; DISCUSS UGANDAN AFFAIRS; DON JUAN; DOWN (ON)/DOWN SOUTH; DROIT DE SEIGNEUR; EARTH MOVES FOR ONE; EMBRACE; ERECTION; EROTICA; EXERCISE THE FERRET; EXPERIENCED; EXPLICIT; EXTRA-CURRICULAR ACTIVITIES; FAST; FATE WORSE THAN

DEATH; FEEL (UP); FLING; FREE LOVE; FREE WITH ONE'S
FAVOURS; GENDER-BENDER; GET OFF/OUT AT EDGE HILL;
GIVE HEAD; GIVE ONESELF TO; GLAMOUR MAG; GO OUT
WITH; GO TO IT; GO UPSTAIRS; GRASS WIDOW; HAND
TROUBLE; HAVE IT OFF/AWAY; HAVE SEX; HEAVY PETTING;
HORIZONTAL JOGGING; HOW'S YOUR FATHER; IMMORAL;
IMPOTENCE; IMPROPER; IN FLAGRANTE (DELICTO); IN NAME
ONLY; INAMORATA; INCLINATIONS; INCONTINENT;
INDISCRETION; INDOOR GAMES; INTIMACY TOOK PLACE; IT;
JAIL BAIT; JIG-A-JIG; KNOW/HAVE (BIBLICAL) KNOWLEDGE
OF; LEATHER; LEAVE ONE'S SHOES UNDER THE BED;
LIAISON; LIE WITH; LIFESTYLE; LIKE THE LADIES; LOSE
ONE'S CHERRY; LOTHARIO; LOVE NEST; LUBRICATE; MAKE
EYES AT; MAKE LOVE; MAKE UP TO; MARITAL AID; MEN'S
MAGAZINE; MISSIONARY POSITION; MOUNT; NATIONAL
INDOOR GAME; NOCTURNAL EMISSION; OATS; OBLIGE; ON
THE JOB; ON THE SIDE; ONE-NIGHT STAND; OPEN ONE'S
LEGS; ORAL SEX; OTHER; PASS; PAST; PLEASURE; PRIDE OF
THE MORNING; PROTECTED SEX; PUT IT ABOUT; RELIEVE
SOMEONE OF HIS/HER VIRGINITY; RIDE; ROBBED OF HER
HONOUR/VIRTUE; ROGER; ROMAN SPRING; ROUND HEELS;
RUBBER; RUIN; SEE; SEXUAL INTERCOURSE; SEXUALLY
IRRESPONSIVE; SILLY; SIZE MATTERS; SLEEP AROUND; SLEEP
WITH; SLIPPERY HEELS; SOMETHING FOR THE WEEKEND;
SPEND; SPEND THE NIGHT WITH; STATE OF SEXUAL
EXCITEMENT; SUGGESTIVE; SWING BOTH WAYS; SWINGING;
TAKE ADVANTAGE OF; TROUBLE; UNDOING; UNNATURAL
PRACTICES; UNPROTECTED SEX; VICE ANGLAISE; VIOLATE;
WEAR IRON KNICKERS; WET DREAM; WOLF; WRONG; and
under HOMOSEXUALITY, MARRIAGE, MASTURBATION and
PROSTITUTION

sexually irresponsive Frigid. A psycho-medical invention, an
upgrading of the simple **cold**. Since 1660.

(to) shake hands with the bishop To URINATE. By the late
19th century, probably.

sham Fraudulent. Since the 17th century.

shapely Sexually attractive (of a woman). By the 16th century.

(three) sheets in the wind Drunk. Known by 1821. The 'sheets' in question are not, as you might expect, sails but the ropes or chains attached to sails to trim them with. If the sheet is free, the sail is unrestrained. As Robert L. Shook in *The Book of Why* (1983) puts it, 'If these sheets are loose, the ship will be as unstable on the water as a thoroughly drunk man is on his feet.' Sometimes 'three sheets *to* the wind' and sometimes '*four* sheets ...'.

(a) shirtlifter A bugger. Now what does this word mean? I first encountered it in the late 1970s when it was being used to describe a meal made up of lentils and beans and other currently fashionable fibre-full ingredients. The net result would be a good deal of farting on the part of the diners, lifting the shirts of those who happened to be wearing them.

However, 'shirtlifter' was then found being used to describe a male homosexual, i.e. one who lifts the shirt of another man in the course of obtaining his pleasure (though *Partridge/Slang*, curiously, hears it as rhyming slang for 'poofter'). *OED2* labels it as Australian slang, yet it is commonly used elsewhere. *OED2*'s earliest citation is from 1966. It has also been used to describe anything (a pornographic book or film) that would cause a man to have an erection. '"Gay" was a perfectly useful word which I dropped into my ordinary conversation at least three times a day until the shirtlifters got hold of it' – *The Times* (14 May 1992).

shock and awe The psychological destruction of an enemy's will to fight. The term was given to the instilling of fear and doubt in the minds of Iraqis while their country was being invaded by American forces for REGIME CHANGE purposes in 2003. The phrase had first appeared publicly in a book entitled *Shock and Awe: Achieving Rapid Dominance* (1996) by Harlan K. Ullman and James P. Wade, which came out of a report by the Rapid Dominance Study Group, an informal association of mainly ex-military men. 'It is all part of the administration's basic approach toward foreign policy, which is best described by the phrase used for its war plan – "shock and awe". The notion is that the United States needs to intimidate countries with its power and assertiveness, always threatening, always denouncing, never showing weakness' – *Newsweek* Magazine (March 2003).

(to) shoot a line To boast, to talk pretentiously. By the 1940s. '[He] was an awful line-shooter. He claimed to have been at Oxford, but he hadn't been at Oxford' – *The Listener* (15 March 1973).

(to) shoot the breeze (1) To chat. (2) To chat up. Of American origin, by the 1940s.

(to) shoot the moon To leave without paying your bills, rent, etc. or to remove your goods at night in order to cheat the bailiff. A chiefly American expression, the equivalent of the British 'to do a MOONLIGHT FLIT'. Current by 1869 when it was discussed in *Notes and Queries*. G.K. Chesterton alludes to it in *The Club of Queer Trades* (1904), ch. 4: 'His slangier acquaintances were of opinion that "the moon" had been not unfrequently amid the victims of his victorious rifle.' '"Mr Ukridge owes a considerable amount of money round about here to tradesmen ... Well, when they find out he has – er –" "Shot the moon, sir," suggested the Hired Retainer helpfully' – P.G. Wodehouse, *Love Among the Chickens* (1906). *Shoot the Moon* was the title of a film (US 1981). 'To shoot the moon' can also mean 'to go for broke' in card playing.

(a) shopper A housewife. So as to avoid use of this w-word. Or indeed the h-word in 'househusband'. In PC use by 1993 and recommended by the BBC's 'Guidelines for Factual Programmes' (1989).

(a) shorn crown Decapitation, the beheading of a monarch. 'A shorn crown ... a euphemism for decapitation' – J.A. Froude, *A History of England*, vol. 6 (1860), ch. 27.

(a) shortfall A shortage. By 1895. More grandiloquent – by one letter.

(to be) shown the geography of the house To be shown where the LAVATORY is. Hence, 'the geography' can also refer to a lavatory. Probably by the mid-19th century. 'For a man to show a woman the way to the lavatory ... an evasive phrase had to be used ... "Have you been shown the geography of the house?"' – Robert Graves, *Lars Porsena, or the Future of Swearing and Improper Language* (1920); 'It is all very baffling for the uninitiated foreigner, who when his host offers to "show him the geography of the house" finds that his tour begins and ends with the smallest room' – A. Lyall, *It Isn't Done* (1930).

shrinkage of stock Theft (in stores). 'We have to set aside a sum each year for shrinkage due to staff pilfering in addition to petty theft by the public' said a chain stores representative in a radio interview (1982).

(to) shuffle off (this mortal coil) To die. 19th/20th century? After William Shakespeare, *Hamlet* (1600–1), III.i.66: 'For in that sleep of death what dreams may come / When we have shuffled off this mortal coil, / Must give us pause.'

(a) significant other A LOVER or PARTNER. A euphemism for a euphemism – in other words, the person with whom one is having a relationship or to whom one is actually married – though whom, for some reason of political correctness, one does not wish to describe in terms of dependency or dominance. Of American origin, since the mid-1980s. 'We are envious when we feel that the significant other has all the power. We feel envy in a relationship of one to one, jealousy in a relationship of one to two. When one partner in an alliance has all the power the other, however apparently loved and cherished, feels envy' – *The Sunday Times* (19 January 1986); 'After all, the business is becoming much more dangerous with Aids. But it seemed a little tactless to take this up with Sharon as she was by now heavily entangled with my significant other person' – *The Sunday Times* (2 November 1986);

'If there's anything I can stand less than the term Significant Other it's hearing its defence mounted in unblushing terms of political correctness' – *The Times* (14 May 1992).

(a bit) silly Sexually misbehaved. 'Tommy, too, had been "a bit silly in 1957 or whenever it was", but she had not divorced him' – Margaret Forster, *Daphne du Maurier* (1993), ch. 23.

silver Grey (when applied to hair). By the 19th century. 'There were scarce three lines of silver in her soft brown hair' – William Thackeray, *Vanity Fair* (1848), ch. 58. 'Darling, I am growing old, / Silver threads among the gold / Shine upon my brow today; / Life is fading fast away' – Eben Rexford, song, 'Silver Threads Among the Gold' (about 1900).

simpleness See under BRICK / FEW BRICKS SHORT OF A LOAD

(a person) single by choice A spinster, an old maid. By the 1980s – a bit PC.

(a) single parent (family) A divorced/abandoned parent bringing up a child without the assistance of a marital partner. Since 1969. For some reason, **one-parent family** never caught on. 'Their daughter is a single parent (and journalist) with a halfway house accent and her two daughters talk wiv a proper London accent' – *The Times* (28 February 1992). Compare LONE PARENT; ONE-PARENT FAMILY.

singleness See MARRIAGE

(to) sink To be in the last stages of dying. By the early 18th century. 'Some neighbour's father or mother or sister or aunt was "sinking fast" or had "passed peacefully away this morning"' – Flora Thompson, *Lark Rise to Candleford* (1945), ch. 27.

siphoning off Embezzlement. By the 1960s.

(a) sit-upon An arse. Sometimes **sit-me-down**. British use, mainly. Either way, an abbreviation: 'He's left the impression of his sit-me-down-upon on the cushion' – Dorothy L. Sayers, *Clouds of Witness* (1926), ch. 2. In the US, 'sit-upons' were, rather, 'trousers'.

size matters Penis size is important. 'Penis size is unimportant' is described as a 'Naff sexual myth' in *The Complete Naff Guide* (1983). Alex Comfort, *The Joy of Sex* (1972) refers to: 'The irrational male preoccupation with penile size. Size has absolutely nothing to do with their physical serviceability in intercourse ... though many women are turned on by the idea of a large one ... Smaller ones work equally well in most positions ... Excessive preoccupation with size is an irrational anxiety.'

The idea is much played with, nudgingly. 'The programme's handling of sex ... [includes] one planned item [looking] at things people say to each afterwards ("You were fantastic; of course size doesn't matter")' – *The Times* (30 May 1990); 'Does this prove once and for all that size does matter?' – James Cameron, director of the film *Titanic* on winning an award, quoted in *The Observer* (25 January 1998); 'Where size doesn't have to matter' – headline over article on charities in *The Independent* (11 May 1998); 'Size does matter' – slogan for film *Godzilla* (US 1998); 'Size matters' – slogan for Renault Clio motor-car, in the UK (1998).

(a) skilled farm technician A farm worker. A resolution was put before a conference of the National Union of Agricultural Workers in May 1976 which advocated that a British farm worker should be thus described, giving him credit for the skill and training demanded of him. I don't think it was passed, nor did the term catch on.

(to) sleep around To be sexually promiscuous. By the 1920s; **to screw around** from the late 1930s. '"Sleeping around" – that was how he had heard a young American girl describe the amorous side of the ideal life, as lived in Hollywood' – Aldous Huxley, *Point Counter Point* (1928), ch. 27.

(to) sleep with To have SEXUAL INTERCOURSE with. Implying sexual intimacy, this euphemism would seem to date back to the 10th century. By the time of Shelley's *The Cenci* (1819), I.iii.63, it was clearly well established and understood: 'Whilst she he loved was sleeping with his rival'; '"Oh, let us sleep together," I burst out. "It's impossible." I coaxed and carnied. "Do, – look what a state you've put me in," and in rutting excitement, out I pulled my prick, in its randy rigidity' – 'Walter', *My Secret Life*, Vol. 5, Ch. 1 (1880-94); 'I've made it to the top without sleeping all the way, but I know girls, mentioning no names, who do, and they've made it, too' – *Sunday Mirror* (29 August 1976), quoting what it called 'a sex goddess'; 'The proposition that the painter automatically slept with his models has become an unquestioned tenet of Matisse scholarship' – Hilary Spurling, *Matisse the Master* (2005), Preface. The curious thing about this euphemism is that – as with GO OUT WITH – it means the opposite of what it says. 'To sleep with' really means 'to stay very much awake with' ...

slender Thin (usually of females only). Since the 14th century. 'That most elegant female charm, a slender waist' – *Figure Training* (1871).

(a) slice off a cut loaf An extramarital affair. Hence, the proverbial expression 'a slice off a cut loaf is never missed'. In other words, it doesn't matter having a bit on the side once you've taken the plunge and got married. In her autobiography *Billie Whitelaw: Who He?* (1995), the actress recounts how her mother drew her aside when she was about to get married for the first time and told her to remember this bit of advice. 'After forty years I'm still trying to work out what she meant.' Well, I took it upon myself to tell her. One has to say that it was an extraordinary thing for a mother to say on such an occasion, but it is a very old saying indeed. *Apperson* has it as 'It is safe taking a shive [= slice] of a cut loaf' and traces it back to Shakespeare, *Titus Andronicus* (1591), II.i.87: 'What, man! more water glideth by the mill / Than wots the miller of; and easy it is / Of a cut loaf to steal a shive, we know.' *Partridge/Slang* has it that 'to take a slice' means 'to intrigue, particularly with a married woman'.

(to) slip into something more comfortable To change
into more sexually alluring clothes. After the line spoken by
Helen (Jean Harlow) to Monte (Ben Lyon) in the film *Hell's Angels*
(US 1930): 'Would you be shocked if I put on something more
comfortable?' What Helen says is, of course, by way of a
proposition and she duly exchanges her fur wrap for a dressing
gown.

Invariably misquoted – e.g. 'Do you mind if I put on something
more comfortable?' or 'Excuse me while I slip into something
more comfortable.' 'Pardon me while I slip into something more
comfortable' was perpetrated by Denis Gifford in *The Independent*
(22 July 1995).

(to have) slippery heels To be promiscuous (of a woman).
'Of a girl of easy virtue – a hussy (said with a sniff)' – UK, 20th
century.

slow Lazy. By the mid-19th century (Mark Twain).

(a) slow learner A person of low intelligence. By the late
1930s. *'Slow learner.* A term often used rather loosely of any child
whose attainments have always fallen noticeably behind those of
other children of the same age, without any implication as to
what might be thought to be the cause ... or whether the child
might be enabled to speed up or catch up. Sometimes, however,
the term is used to indicate children who are not only expected
to remain slow learners but also to be unable ever to learn as
much as others. Some people would even restrict the term to
pupils who are educationally subnormal' – Derek Rowntree,
A Dictionary of Education (1981).

slow on the uptake Dull-witted, mentally deficient. Since
the early 19th century. 'An energetic, likeable, cockily pugnacious
figure, but slow, almost Neanderthally slow, on the uptake' –
Here and Now (NZ) (October 1949).

(a) slumber chamber A coffin. Of American origin. By the
1950s.

(a) slush fund Money reserved for financing bribes.
A (probably) illegal stash of money used (perhaps by a politician)
to pay off people. William Safire in *Safire's Political Dictionary* (1978)
says the word is probably 'derived from the Swedish *slask*,
meaning wet, or filth. Naval vessels would sell the slush and other
refuse on board; the proceeds went into a fund to purchase
luxuries for the crew. Later this practice was extended to war-
damaged equipment as well.' Known in this sense by 1839.

Robert L. Shook in *The Book of Why* (1983) specifically defines the
slush as grease from the cook's galley which was used to lubricate
the masts. 'Whatever was left over was sold, and the money
put into a fund for the enlisted men.' Both meanings were
established by the end of the 19th century – the political one via
the US. 'A dawn barrage was launched on the already heavily
bombarded reputation of Pavel Grachev, Russia's defence
minister, yesterday, with front-page accusations linking him to
a secret hard-currency slush fund in a German bank' –
The Guardian (4 February 1995).

(to go to the) smallest room To go to the LAVATORY.
OED2's earliest citation for this phrase also contains another
loophemism (see SHOWN THE GEOGRAPHY): 'It is all very
baffling for the uninitiated foreigner, who when his host offers
to "show him the geography of the house" finds that his tour
begins and ends with the smallest room' – A. Lyall, *It Isn't Done*
(1930).

smoke and mirrors Trickery and illusion (in politics).
From William Safire, *New Political Dictionary* (1993): 'Jimmy Breslin
coined the term in a 1975 book, *How the Good Guys Finally Won*, about
House Speaker Tip O'Neill's involvement in the removal of
Richard Nixon from the Presidency. Quoting Thomas Hobbes's
"The reputation of power is power," Breslin opined that political
power is primarily an illusion: "Mirrors and blue smoke,
beautiful blue smoke rolling over the surface of highly polished
mirrors, first a thin veil of blue smoke, then a thick cloud that
suddenly dissolves into wisps of blue smoke, the mirrors catching
it all, bouncing it back and forth. If somebody tells you how to

look, there can be seen in the smoke great, magnificent shapes, castles and kingdoms, and maybe they can be yours".'

'The "blue smoke and mirrors" of Reaganomics, said Mr Mondale, had caused industrial blight to descend on once prosperous states' – *The Economist* (12 May 1984).

(a) smoking gun / pistol Incriminating evidence. As though a person holding a smoking gun could be assumed to have committed an offence with it – as in Conan Doyle's Sherlock Holmes story 'The "Gloria Scott"' (1894): 'Then we rushed on into the captain's cabin ... and there he lay ... while the chaplain stood, with a smoking pistol in his hand.' The term was popularized during Watergate. For example, Representative Barber Conable said of a tape of President Nixon's conversation with H.R. Haldeman, his chief of staff, on 23 June 1972, containing discussion of how the FBI's investigation of the Watergate burglary could be limited, 'I guess we have found the smoking pistol, haven't we?'

'As President Bush so vividly says, "The smoking gun will be a mushroom cloud"' – *The Spectator* (14/21 December 2002).

(a) snifter / snort An alcoholic drink. By the 1840s/by the 1880s, both versions of American origin. 'And now, old horse, you may lead me across the street to the Coal Hole for a short snifter' – P.G. Wodehouse, *Ukridge* (1924), ch. 3; 'We were taking a quiet snort in a corner' – P.G. Wodehouse, *Carry On, Jeeves* (1925), ch. 4. Compare **a sharpener** for an alcoholic drink that livens you up.

(a) snow creature / figure / sculpture A snowman. The non-sexist euphemisms are these and not, apparently, 'snowperson', as you might expect. Except that you can use 'snowwoman *or* snowman *if it really is*' – Rosalie Maggio, *The Nonsexist Word Finder: A Dictionary of Gender-Free Usage* (1988).

(it's) snowing down South A girl's petticoat is showing below her skirt. Iona and Peter Opie include this in *The Lore and Language of Schoolchildren* (1959) as a 'juvenile corrective', along with **SOS**

(Slip On Show) and **is your name Seymour?** To which one might add another: **it's snowing in Paris**.

(a) social group A class. Euphemism is demanded by those who deplore the division of people into 'classes' or who are sensitive to accusations of class distinction, so that words such as BRACKET or 'group' have been adopted. By the mid-19th century.

(a) social disease Syphilis. Also **social infection**. Hence, 'Social Diseases and Worse Remedies' –title of a paper (1891) by T.H. Huxley. 'She was probably an ODESSA agent and you've come down with a social disease, as planned' – Robert Ludlum, *The Holcroft Covenant* (1978), ch. 27.

social security Poor relief/payment of money by the state to the poor or needy. By the early 1900s. Sometimes abbreviated to **the social** (by the 1980s).

(a) social worker A prostitute. A usage encountered when used by Stubby Kaye on BBC Radio 2's *Where Were You in '62?* (27 November 1984). Compare: 'They call themselves "working girls" ... Their work is a "business", or even a "social service"' – *The New York Times* (9 August 1971).

something (anything) for the weekend Male contraceptive supplies. From the traditional parting question from British barbers (in the days before they were called men's hairdressers) inviting customers to stock up with condoms (which, for no very obvious reason, they sold): 'Something for the weekend, sir?' 1930s to 1950s, at a guess.

something for your trouble A tip. 'Here's something for your trouble.' By the early 20th century?

something of the night Dark/evil/mysterious traits in a person's character. *Something of the Night* is the title of a crime novel (1980) by the American writer Mary McMullen. The British politician Ann Widdecombe MP famously used the phrase to describe her former Home Office colleague Michael Howard in May 1997, and thus helped scupper his chances as a contender for the leadership of the Conservative Party at that time (though he later got the job).

sophisticated weapons A nuclear bomb or missile. By the 1960s.

(a) soundbite A pre-arranged form of words that a politician expects to be quoted and thus become a very short extract from a speech or interview used in a television news programme. Originating in American broadcasters' jargon (compare 'clip'), the word is now used to suggest that meaning and context are often lost in the process and that it is a worthless activity for politicians and similar public figures to speak in soundbites in the hope that they will thereby acquire media coverage for themselves. Known in the US by 1980, in the UK somewhat later, especially after its wide use in the American presidential election campaign of 1988. '"Gaffe" ... [is] monosyllabic, which is a help of course, to the Editor; and, to them, it signifies "soundbite", or "unpalatable truth"' – Alan Clark, diary entry for 18 November 1986; 'They operate in the slick new tradition of political handlers, whose job is to reduce a campaign to photo ops and sound bites' – *Time* Magazine (21 November 1988).

sources close to the Prime Minister The Downing Street press secretary who, at one time, under the rules of the parliamentary lobby system, could not be named unless speaking 'on the record'. In journalistic sourcing, by the 1960s and possibly of American origin. 'Sources close to the chief executive report he is planning to request the Legislature to approve state purchase' – citation given in *Webster*, 3rd edn (1961). Hence, *Sources Close To the Prime Minister* – the title of a book (1984) by Michael Cockerell and others.

(to) sow one's wild oats. To behave wildly, irresponsibly, promiscuously. A wild oat is a common weed, so for anyone to sow it means that (usually) he is doing something useless or worthless. Hence, the expression is employed to describe behaviour prior to a man's 'settling down'. In use by 1576. Quite how much implication there is of him wasting his semen in unfruitful couplings is hard to judge, though the expression often has reference to sexual dissipation. Perhaps this connotation has increased with the popularity of such expressions as 'getting one's OATS' (for having sex).

Spanish practices / old Spanish customs Dishonest methods used by workers to hold employers to ransom. The phrases also refer to practices that are of long standing but unauthorized. Although the journal *Notes and Queries* was vainly seeking the origin of the phrase in 1932, the term came to prominence in the 1980s to describe the irregular behaviour of British newspaper production workers in Fleet Street (cheating over pay-packets, especially). The use seems mainly British, though this does not explain how Groucho Marx came to make the pun 'old Spinach customs' in *Animal Crackers* (US 1930). Why the Spanish are blamed is not clear, except that Spaniards tend to attract pejoratives – not least with regard to working practices (the *mañana* attitude).

In Elizabethan times, William Cecil is quoted as saying of Sir Thomas Tresham, architect of Rushton Triangular Lodge, that he was not given to Spanish practices (i.e. Roman Catholic ones). In 1584, also, Lord Walsingham referred to 'Spanish practices' in a way that meant they were 'deceitful, perfidious and treacherous'. This could provide us with an origin for the modern phrase. Indeed, in the late 1980s, the two were used interchangeably in the newspaper context. 'Receiving visits ... when you are from Home, is not consisting with our Spanish Customs' – William R. Chetwood, *The Voyages and Adventures of Captain Robert Boyle* (1724); 'The biggest internal cost is production wages ... embroidered round with "old Spanish customs", which was regarded as virtually outside management control' – Simon Jenkins, *Newspapers: The Power and the Money* (1979).

Spanish tummy Diarrhoea. Compare MONTEZUMA'S REVENGE.

(a) spare tyre Bulging round the waist. By 1961 – probably of American origin.

(a) spare wheel A child seen as one who would replace a lost child. By the 1950s, at a guess.

(to) speak with forked tongue To dissimulate. Hence, 'white man speak with forked tongue', supposedly the way a Native American chief would pronounce on the duplicitous ways of the white man, in Western movies. It is hard to believe a chief would have said this in real life. In the film *Yukon Vengeance* (US 1954), Carol Thurston as Princess Yellow Flower gets to say: 'White man's tongue is forked.' From the BBC radio show *Round the Horne* (28 April 1968): 'He speaks with forked tongue.'

special / (with) special needs With a mental handicap, of low intelligence. This has caught on quite widely – **exceptional needs** less so. *Adopting Children with Special Needs* was the title of a book edited by Joan McNamara (1975). 'Yes, there is a meeting *tonight* at one of the area high schools for people interested in being parents for special needs children' – Claudia L. Jewett, *Adopting the Older Child* (Boston, Mass., 1978); 'The Strangest Village in Britain was a thoughtful, touching documentary … about Botton in North Yorkshire, a community inhabited entirely by people with various sorts of mental handicap ("special needs" was the programme's preferred, but too vague, euphemism)' – *The Independent* (17 June 2005).

(a) special (constable) A part-time policeman. Since 1801.

(a) special man A homosexual. In Egypt in 1989, I encountered this term used about male homosexuals. Although spoken in a slightly mocking way, it now strikes me as an utterly PC phrase, should anyone care to take it up – though 'person' or 'adult male' would, of course, be more PC than 'man'.

(a) speculator A gambler (on football pools). 20th century. Compare INVESTOR.

(a) speech defect A stammer, stutter. By the mid-20th century. Also **(a) speech impediment**.

(to) spend To ejaculate semen. A very old euphemism (Shakespeare's 'The expense of spirit in a waste of shame / Is lust in action' in Sonnet 129 alludes to it) and one familiar in Victorian speech and pornographic writing, alluding to both male and female orgasm. 'I went up to her and played and talked with her and, God forgive me, did feel her; which I am much ashamed of, but I did no more, though I had so much a mind to it that I spent in my breeches' – Samuel Pepys, diary entry for 7 September 1662.

(to) spend a penny To go to the LAVATORY (mostly female use). *OED2* does not have a citation for the phrase before 1945 though it is believed that lavatory accommodation was provided at the Great Exhibition in Hyde Park, London, in 1851 at a cost of one penny. The first public convenience to charge one penny opened in London in 1855. A little before, one is curious about this passage from ch. 6 of Charles Dickens's *Dombey and Son* (1846–8): 'The young Toodles, victims of a pious fraud, were deluded into repairing in a body to a chandler's shop in the neighbourhood, for the ostensible purpose of spending a penny' – but this is probably using the phrase in the literal sense.

(I would like to) spend more time with my (wife and) family I have been sacked from my job in politics and am attempting to put a positive construction on it. A cliché of political resignations. '[The Duke of Omnium, after deciding to give up the prime ministership, is asked what he will do:] 'I am a private gentleman who will now be able to devote more of his time to his wife and children than has hitherto been possible with him' – Anthony Trollope, *The Prime Minister* (1876), 'The New Ministry'. *Woodward (to Deep Throat)*: 'John Mitchell resigns as the head of C.R.E.E.P. and says that he wants to spend more time with his family. Sounds like bullshit. We don't exactly believe that' – film *All the President's Men* (US 1976).

In March 1990, two of Prime Minister Thatcher's ministers –

Norman Fowler and Peter Walker – withdrew from the Cabinet, both giving as their reason for going that they wished to 'spend more time with their families'. Fowler, in his resignation letter, wrote: 'I have a young family and for the next few years I should like to devote more time to them while they are still so young.' Prime Minister Thatcher replied: 'I am naturally very sorry to see you go, but understand your reasons for doing this, particularly your wish to be able to spend more time with your family.' These were both withdrawals rather than sackings, but even so. Subsequently, Gordon Brown, the Labour MP, suggested in the House of Commons that Nicholas Ridley might care to follow suit. But the Secretary of State for Industry was having none of it. 'The last thing I want to do,' he said, 'is spend more time with my family' – quoted in *The Independent* (14 July 1990).

(to) spend the night with To have SEXUAL INTERCOURSE with. By the 1930s: 'She meant to come back and bed down with Garcia ... you know – to spend the night with him' – Ngaio Marsh, *Artists in Crime* (1938), ch. 9.

(a) spin doctor A public relations practitioner or political aide who puts a positive interpretation upon events, usually in the political sphere, by briefing journalists and correspondents. Out of the US in the mid-1980s, particularly during the 1988 presidential election, and taken from the game of baseball where spin has to be put on the ball by a pitcher to make it go where it is wanted. 'The spin doctors, the PR generals, argued after the Reykjavik talks that Reagan still stands by Star Wars' – *Newsweek* (27 October 1986); 'The theme of the two men having talked bluntly yet courteously ... is likely to be stressed further by Reagan Administration 'spin doctors' who will try to present the summit in a favourable light in the days to come' – *The Daily Telegraph* (11 December 1987).

(to) splash one's boots To URINATE (for obvious reasons). 20th century.

(to) split (up) To separate / divorce (of a couple). 'They've split/split up.' Of American origin, by the 1940s.

(a) spokesperson A spokesman. 'The spokesperson (non-sexist term) for UCWR complained that she had been "physically assaulted by a university administrator"' – *The Guardian* (18 February 1972); 'Mrs Sally Oppenheim MP ... [the Conservative] spokesperson on consumer affairs' – BBC radio news (15 January 1978).

staffing Manning. To be used in preference to the m-word, according to the 'Guidelines for Factual Programmes', BBC (1989). Also 'jobs', 'job levels' would apparently do the non-sexist trick.

standard class Second class. Noted on British railways by 1992. 'If you have a First Class ticket (or the equivalent) and no First Class accommodation (or the equivalent) is available, and you travel in Standard Class accommodation (where it is provided), you may claim a refund of the difference in fare' – National Rail Conditions of Carriage (2005).

(a) star An actor or actress who happens to have got a part. A tendency noted by the 1980s: 'Anybody who is appearing in stage, film, radio or TV productions should be described as a "star" and "starring in". Carrying a spear at Stratford? Got a walk-on part in *Crossroads*? Doing the boring old weather forecast? You are a star, dear' – in my book *The Joy of Clichés* (1984).

(a) star in the east An undone fly button. *Partridge/Slang* suggests a date of origin around the First World War.

(in a/the) state of nature Naked. By 1802.

(in a) state of sexual excitement With an erect penis. By the 1970s. Perhaps mostly a legal euphemism.

(a) state room A cabin on certain passenger liners, containing one or two berths. Seemingly of American origin, since 1774. 'Single stateroom? Always our pleasure on QE2. Your stateroom is always a restorative haven of calm – what a joy to come back to' – Cunard 2005 cruise brochure.

states of affairs See CONDITIONS

(a) station manager A (railway/train) station master. Since the 1980s? Compare TRAIN MANAGER.

(a) station stop A (railway) stop. By 1986. I am told that this usage came about in order to help passengers distinguish between the train coming to a halt (in which case it would be foolish to try to get out of it) and stopping in an actual station.

stealing See ACQUIRE; ANNEX; APPROPRIATE; BORROW; COMMANDEER; FALLEN OFF THE BACK OF A LORRY; HELP ONESELF TO SOMETHING; LIBERATE; LIGHT-FINGERED; LINE ONE'S POCKETS; MAKE OFF WITH; MISAPPROPRIATE; PILFER; POCKET; PURLOIN; SHRINKAGE OF STOCK; TAKING AND DRIVING AWAY; TEA LEAF

(to be asked to) step down To have to accept forced retirement. Of American origin, by the 1890s.

sterile Barren. Because the original word carries a certain unwarranted stigma – according to Rosalie Maggio, *The Nonsexist Word Finder: A Dictionary of Gender-Free Usage* (1988). To me, 'sterile' sounds equally to be avoided.

(to) stick (something) somewhere the sun doesn't shine To stick it up one's arse. Second half of the 20th century. 'She's living proof that you can stick all that pious crap about working mothers all being useless somewhere the sun doesn't shine' – *The Independent* (12 October 2005).

(a) stipend A clergyman's salary or wage. The original words being considered undignified or inappropriate for a vocation. By the 15th century.

(a) stockist A shopkeeper. 'Your local stockist will give you details', state some advertisements. By the 1920s.

stomach (1) anything internal and not necessarily to do with the digestive tract. The dating of its introduction can be found in a memorandum written by Lady Susan O'Brien (1745–1823) on 'changes between 1760–1818': 'Language has always been changing … "Cholic" and "bowels" are exploded words. "Stomach" signifies everything. This is delicate, but to very many unintelligible.' (2) Obesity. 'He has something of a stomach.' 'Repeating "Keep down, proud stomach", patting the said organ meanwhile' – Flora Thompson, *Lark Rise to Candleford* (1945), ch. 27.

(to be) stood down To be sacked. After the military expression 'stand down', meaning 'to come off duty or relax after a state of alert'. 19th century?

(a) stool A portion of excrement. By the 16th century and probably deriving from the 'close stool' or 'stool of ease' upon which one sat in an early form of LAVATORY. 'Having taken one of Mr Holliard's pills last night it brought a stool or two this morning' – Samuel Pepys, diary entry for 24 May 1663.

(to tell) stories To tell lies. Since the 17th century. 'You were always good Children, and never told stories' – John Wesley, *Journal*, entry for 21 March 1770.

(the) stork has come A child has been born. From German and Dutch nursery fiction. In English by the 19th century?

stout Fat. By 1800. '*The Official Politically Correct Dictionary and Handbook*, by Henry Beard and Christopher Cerf, sets out to help the unwary avoid such faux pas as "fat", or any of its old synonyms, like stout, instead of "differently sized"' – *The Times* (13 April 1992).

(a) street person A tramp, vagrant, bag lady. Suggested PC euphemism, by 1993.

(a) street orderly A street sweeper, road sweeper. However unlikely a name, the street orderly has a long and distinguished history. 'Street orderly bins' were known by the 1890s and were so called after an 'orderly plan' for keeping the streets continually swept had been instituted. Though known in the US, **street sweeper** is barely used in the UK. 'It happened to the rat-catcher (he's now a rodent operator), the dustman (refuse collector), and the sweeper (street orderly)' – *The Daily Mail* (25 October 1958).

(to) stretch one's legs To URINATE.

(a) strip-tease artiste A stripper. By the mid-20th century, of American origin.

(a) stroking session An informal meeting at which an attempt is made to persuade and win over somebody – a political opponent, say – to a cause. The term emerged from the White House occupancy of President Richard Nixon and was known by 1973. The choice of the word 'stroking' may have a sexual connotation. Sometimes envoys would be sent on a **stroking mission**. 'President Nixon, revolted by such direct methods, preferred what he called "stroking", a process of jawboning so sweet to the strokee's earbones that the victim fell into a hypnotic state in which he could be deboned without realizing it' – Russell Baker, *The New York Times* (4 April 1978); 'As if the "stroking missions" were not enough, Nixon began to write Lon Nol a series of warm optimistic letters' – William Shawcross, *Sideshow* (1986).

strong language Bad language / swearing. By 1910.

(with a) sub-fertility problem Barren (of a woman). The condition was thus described in *The Times* (5 May 1976) – but this is plainly not PC because of the non-positive word 'problem'.

sub-standard housing Slums. By the 1970s?

substance abuse Drug/alcohol addiction. Mostly US use, by 1975. 'The authors had noted the PC tendency to slide over from the well-accepted ("substance abuser" already has largely replaced drug addict and drunk) to the semi-reasonable' – *The Washington Post* (8 June 1992).

(a) subterranean sanitation technician A sewer worker (in the US). Quoted in Willard R. Espy, *An Almanac of Words at Play* (1975).

suggestive Lewd. By the 1880s.

(the) sun is over the yardarm It is time to start drinking. Since the late 19th century. Among naval people this might have some meaning, but for most it represents a rather far-fetched excuse. Depending on where the boat is, the sun would be over the yardarm (a spar on a mast) after noon. So, we are talking a lunchtime tipple here. In the evening, drinkers might wait until the sun was 'below the horizon'.

sunset days / years Old age. By the late 20th century, of American origin.

(a) supplier A shopkeeper. By the 17th century.

(to make / pay the) supreme penalty / sacrifice To die for a cause, a friend, etc., especially in the 1914–18 war. 'These young men ... have gone down not only to the horror of the battlefield but to the gates of death as they made the supreme sacrifice' – W.M. Clow, *The Evangelist of the Strait Gate* (1916). A (perhaps) forgivable cliché since then. Additional popularity arose from its use by Sir John Arkwright as the title of a poem in *The Supreme Sacrifice and Other Poems in Time of War* (1919). Sung to an already-existing tune, 'Ellers' by E.J. Hopkins, this became the hymn 'O valiant hearts'. In the 1950s this moving hymn suffered a backlash and was dropped from Remembrance Day services by those who believed it was insufficiently critical of militarism.

'Governor Nelson Rockefeller ... has emerged from the dark night of the soul that afflicts all politicians pondering the supreme sacrifice' – *The Guardian* (22 December 1970); 'Only when we dare to question the necessity for the "supreme" sacrifice, and examine truthfully the quality of life that all the survivors are destined to lead afterwards ...' – *The Independent* (1 May 1995).

surgery An operation. 'I am undergoing surgery at the hospital' (even if a knife is not involved). '[Groucho Marx] recently underwent surgery to replace a hip joint' – *The Sunday Times* (17 April 1977).

(a) surgical appliance See APPLIANCE

(a) surgical strike A bombing raid – held to be precise but more likely to require surgical assistance in the aftermath. By 1965 and out of American usage in the Vietnam War. 'Even the language of the bureaucracy – the diminutive "nukes" for instruments that kill and mutilate millions of human beings, the "surgical strike" for chasing and mowing down peasants from the air by spraying them with 8,000 bullets a minute – takes the mystery, awe, and pain out of violence' – *Harper's Magazine* (November 1971).

(a) surplus A profit. Profit became a dirty word in some quarters in the 1970s. James Callaghan, Labour prime minister, acknowledged this in a speech to the Labour Party Conference at Blackpool (28 September 1986), when he spoke of the need for industry to make a surplus: this, he said, was a euphemism for profit.

sweet F.A. / sweet Fanny Adams Sweet fuck-all, nothing. There actually was a person called Fanny Adams from Alton in Hampshire, who was murdered, aged eight, in 1867. At about the same time, tinned meat was introduced to the Royal Navy, and sailors – unimpressed – said it was probably made up from the remains of the murdered girl. 'Fanny Adams' became the naval nickname for mutton or stew, and then the meaning was extended to cover anything that was worthless. The euphemisms (known as phrases in their own right by the First World War) have been applied to the more recent coinage 'Sweet Fuck-All' (perhaps by the mid-20th century).

sweetbreads Animal glands (specifically the pancreas or testicles) used as food. Since the 16th century.

(a) sweetener A bribe. By the 1820s.

(to) swing both ways To be actively bisexual. By the 1970s.

swinging Fornication. By 1964. 'Swinging' had been a musician's commendation for many years (certainly by 1958) before it was adopted to describe the free-wheeling, uninhibited atmosphere associated with the 1960s. By extension, 'swinging' came to denote sexual promiscuity. 'A swinger' was one who indulged in such activity. One suggestion is that 'swinging' in the sense of changing partners derives from the caller's words in square dancing. How the phrase caught on is not totally clear. Frank Sinatra had an album entitled *Songs for Swinging Lovers* (1958), Peter Sellers, *Songs for Swinging Sellers* (1959), and Diana Dors *Swinging Dors*. Could the square-dancing use of 'swing your partners' have contributed?

sylph-like Thin (of females only). By 1801.

Tt

T.B. Tuberculosis (strictly-speaking 'tubercle-bacillus'), consumption. By 1912. 'Poor Laura has left the first-aid post – the conditions there have apparently brought back her TB and she may have to go into a sanatorium' – Joan Wyndham, *Love Lessons* (1985), diary entry for 23 January 1940.

(to have one's) tail between one's legs To act in a cowardly manner, to appear cowed, defeated, dejected. From the indication of retreat or submission in many animals. By 1400.

(to) take a break To interrupt the programme and make way for advertisements on TV. By the 1940s/50s. 'Let's take a break now ...'

(to) take advantage of To seduce. Lorenz Hart's lyric for the song 'You Took Advantage of Me' (1928) tip-toes allusively round this meaning. Also **to take the virtue of.**

(to) take into custody To arrest, imprison, lock up. By 1802. *PC Trubshawe* (Arthur Mullard): 'I was proceeding along Bond Street in an easterly direction ... whereupon we apprehended him and took him into custard ... y' – BBC TV *Hancock's Half-Hour* (2 December 1957).

(to) take no prisoners To be utterly ruthless and not take on any liabilities. From *The Times* (30 July 1900): '[Kaiser Wilhelm II

said at Bremerhaven] "No quarter will be given, no prisoners
will be taken. Let all who fall into your hands be at your mercy".'
'The history of her [Catherine Zeta Jones's] career resembles a
military campaign in which no prisoners are taken' – *The
Independent* (12 February 2003).

(to) take out To destroy (an enemy). Military use. By the
second half of the 20th century.

(to) take the Mickey To send up, tease. Possibly from rhyming
slang, 'Mickey Bliss' = 'piss', in the 1950s. But who was Mickey
Bliss to be so honoured? We may never know. The Revd Geoffrey
Knee wrote to *Radio Times* (in April 1994) thus: 'I have long
understood that the phrase is a less vulgar form of "Taking the
p***" [his asterisks] and that it's derived from the term "p***
proud", meaning an erection caused by pressure in the bladder
and not, therefore, a sign of sexual prowess; hence, someone who
is "p*** proud" has an exaggerated sense of his own importance.
Such a one might be to told to "p*** off", meaning, not "go
away", but "get rid of the p***" and stop boasting. Thus, to "take
the p*** out of someone" means to deride him into lowering his
self-esteem.'
   However, with respect to the reverend etymologist, an earlier
form – **to take the Mike** – is remembered by some from the
1920s and would seem to demolish his suggested origin. More
recently, the verbose and grandiose 'are you by any chance
extracting the Michael?', and '**extracting the urine**' have
become reasonably common. Another explanation is that the
'mickey' = 'piss' derives from the word 'micturition'.

(to) take things easy To be lazy. By 1905.

taking and driving away Stealing a car. Probably legal
euphemism, by the 1960s.

taking little interest in the opposite sex Homosexual.
Mid-20th century.

(a) talking head A pundit on TV. By the 1960s. Because a head is all that is most commonly shown on the screen. Originally, the term was used somewhat differently in British broadcasting for the type of TV programme that is composed mainly of people talking, shown in 'head and shoulder' shots and sometimes addressing the camera directly. Often used critically by those who would prefer a programme to show more physical action or to get out of the confines of the studio. Granada TV's booklet *Some Technical Terms and Slang* (1976) defined the term solely as 'a documentary programme which uses the technique of people talking directly to the camera'.

Earlier (*circa* 1968), the term 'talking head' seems to have been applied to anyone addressing the TV camera in a presenter's role. The US/UK pop group with the name Talking Heads performed from 1981. Alan Bennett wrote a series of dramatic monologues for TV called *Talking Heads* in 1988.

(a) tall story A lie. Thus **to tell a tall story** means 'to lie / exaggerate'.

tardation in reading Backward in reading and writing. Heard in a BBC Radio *World at One* interview (7 May 1976).

(a) target of opportunity Random bombing. Second half of the 20th century, of American origin.

(a) taskforce A working group, a committee. Since the 1980s. Originally in American military use (by 1941), a group of armed forces convened to carry out a special operation. A 1949 film called *Task Force* was a 'flag-waver' (according to *Halliwell's Film Guide*) portraying an admiral about to retire recalling his struggle to promote the cause of aircraft carriers. In the early 1970s (according to *Halliwell's Television Companion*) there was a BBC TV series 'rather clumsily' entitled *Softly, Softly: Task Force*. Then, finally, in 1982, the Falkland Islands were liberated from the Argentinians by what was widely referred to as the British Task Force. From thence it has been more generally and loosely applied.

(a) tax inspector A taxman. By 1959. To be used instead of the sexist m-word and because it is also accurate, according to the 'Guidelines for Factual Programmes', BBC (1989). Not that such an easy adjustment can be effected with 'policeman', except where appropriate, of course. 'Use also the Inland Revenue and Revenue staff', the Guide goes on. Additionally, the euphemism perhaps enhances the status of the job.

tea and sympathy Caring behaviour towards a troubled person, sometimes erring beyond the provision of literal tea and sympathy. In Robert Anderson's play *Tea and Sympathy* (1953; film US 1956), it is provided towards a teenage boy at a New England boarding school by the housemaster's wife. To sort out his possible homosexuality, she goes to bed with him, and is reprimanded with: 'All you're supposed to do is every once in a while give the boys a little tea and sympathy.' The phrase undoubtedly predates the Anderson use, however.

(a) tea leaf A thief. Rhyming slang. By 1899.

temporally / temporarily abled What hitherto we may have thought of as 'able(d)'. A menacing, Orwellian coinage designed to make those who are not disabled realize that they could become so at any moment. It seems to be saying that it is only a question of time – though there seems to be a certain amount of doubt as to which adverb is intended. In the form 'temporarily able', it was noted by Jerry Ardler *et al.*, 'Thought Police', *Newsweek* Magazine (14 January 1991); 'Did you realise you were "temporarily abled", meaning "non-physically challenged"' – *The Sunday Times* (9 February 1992).

temporarily immobile Broken down. Of British railway trains. Noted in the *Northern Echo* (10 August 1993).

(to have a) terminal illness To be dying, because you have an illness from which you won't recover. Certainly by 1961, but probably since the 1890s.

(to) terminate To SACK. Becoming euphemistic from the 1950s, its pomposity intending to dull the fact, as in 'terminate your employment', 'we must terminate this conversion' and even in 'this service terminates here'. 'Terminated' for 'fired' (in the US) is quoted in Willard R. Espy, *An Almanac of Words at Play* (1975). Hence, also, **termination of employment** meaning 'the sack, firing'.

(to) terminate with extreme prejudice To kill, execute, assassinate – in American CIA parlance. Also, in a weaker sense, simply to dispose of, get rid of. It became known to a wider audience in 1972 and was used in the film *Apocalypse Now* (US 1979). 'Taylor is the design supremo who stood at the right hand of Harold Evans for 15 years, accompanying him from the *Sunday Times* to refashion *The Times*. His relations with Times Newspapers terminated with extreme prejudice after he had collected a staff petition in support of the sacked Evans' – *The Guardian* (31 August 1985).

(induced) termination of pregnancy Abortion. By the 1920s, though more popularly used from the 1960s. 'Women are being turned away from all the main hospitals, and even gynaecologists in private practice are thinking twice before agreeing to operate on women who want to terminate their pregnancy' – *The Times* (10 June 1992).

(a) terminological inexactitude A lie. Now taken as a humorously long-winded way of saying this, but the context of the coinage shows that 'over-simplication' was really the original meaning implied. In 1906, the status of Chinese workers in South Africa was mentioned in the King's speech to Parliament as 'slavery'. An Opposition amendment of 22 February of the same year was tabled regretting 'That Your Majesty's ministers should have brought the reputation of this country into contempt by describing the employment of Chinese indentured labour as slavery'.

Winston Churchill, as Under-Secretary at the Colonial Office, replied by quoting what he had said in the previous election campaign. He went on: 'The conditions of the Transvaal ordinance under which Chinese Labour is now being carried on do not, in my opinion, constitute a state of slavery. A labour contract into which men enter voluntarily for a limited and for a brief period, under which they are paid wages which they consider adequate, under which they are not bought or sold and from which they can obtain relief on payment of seventeen pounds ten shillings may not be a desirable contract ... but it cannot in the opinion of His Majesty's Government be classified as slavery in the extreme acceptance of the word without some risk of terminological inexactitude.'

One of the first to misunderstand Churchill's phrase was Joseph Chamberlain. Of 'terminological inexactitude' he said: 'Eleven syllables, many of them of Latin or Greek derivation, when one good English word, a Saxon word of a single syllable, would do!' Following Churchill's coinage, *Punch* Magazine ran a series of 'terminological exactitudes' from 6 May 1908.

that way (1) Homosexual. By the 1960s. 'I divined that he was homosexual, or as we put it, "one of us," "that way", "so", or "queer"' – J.R. Ackerley, *My Father and Myself* (1967), ch. 16. (2) Pregnant. As 'in that way', by 1817 (Jane Austen).

thin on top Balding. By the 1930s.

(a/the) thing A/the penis. Since the 14th century (Chaucer). Shakespeare plays on the word 'thing' in this sense in *King Lear*, I.v. and *Henry IV, Part 1*, III.iii. 'One had opened his pants and was shaking what my circle called "his thing"' – Lillian Hellman, *An Unfinished Woman* (1969), ch. 2.

(the) third age Old age. Of French origin (*troisième âge*), the phrase can also be used specifically to refer to retirement. The University of the Third Age – set up for retired people in France by Pierre Vellus in 1973 has also been introduced to the UK. Learning is for pleasure: there are no qualifications, examinations or age limits. The phrase 'the third age of your life' had been used much earlier – in 1446, in English.

(the) third degree Violent treatment, torture, to bring about a confession. Of American origin, by 1900.

(the) Third World Underdeveloped and developing countries. An early example of PC-speak, coined in French in 1956, to describe the developing countries generally not aligned with the Communist and non-Communist blocs. Hence also, to describe the same phenomenon, the term 'non-aligned nations'. 'Euro-tunnel's debt is now like that owed by a third world republic. It has ceased to be real money' – *Lloyd's List* (5 June 1995).

those in the lower income bracket The poor. Originally an advertising classification but adopted by politicians. Probably of American origin, by 1940.

though his body is under hatches his soul has gone aloft He's dead. An 1874 example was found at Lambeth and recorded in Hugh Meller, *London Cemeteries* (1981), ch. 5.

thought showers Brainstorming (generating ideas in a group session). This curious PC euphemism was revealed in *The Observer* (26 June 2005). The Department of Enterprise, Trade and Investment in Belfast was apparently concerned 'that the term ["brainstorming"] would cause offence to people with epilepsy as well as those with brain tumours or brain injuries'. It remains to see whether the new term 'has legs'. A spokesperson for the Campaign for Plain English ridiculed the innovation: 'You do sometimes wonder if some people haven't got anything better to do with their time.'

(to) throw over To abandon/forsake/jilt. By 1910.

(a) ticket A legal summons. 'Parking ticket', of American origin, by the 1940s; 'speeding ticket', ditto, by the 1960s. 'I have yet to see one of your crazy drivers pulled over for a traffic violation. Your policemen are wonderful, but why don't they throw away that halo and get on to a little ticket-writing?' – letter to the editor, *Today* (20 January 1987).

tight Drunk. By the early 19th century. 'What was Mr Snellgrave up to when he fell down those stone steps? "Was he a bit tight, think you?"' – Flora Thompson, *Lark Rise to Candleford* (1945), ch. 25.

time Death – as in 'your time has come'. By AD 1000. 'And he [Jesus] said, Go into the city to such a man, and say unto him, The Master saith, My time is at hand; I will keep the passover at thy house with my disciples' – Matthew 26:18.

(doing) time In prison. By the 1860s: '"I was doing time" ... A cant term for serving a sentence in prison' – *The Daily Telegraph* (1 March 1865).

(the) time Childbirth. By the 15th century. 'Now Elizabeth's full time came that she should be delivered; and she brought forth a son' – Luke 1:57; 'There's that Mrs Wren, only a month from her time, and not a stitch put into a rag yet' – Flora Thompson, *Lark Rise* (1939), ch. 6.

(the) time (of the month) / that time The period of menstruation. 'Time' by the 16th century; 'time of the month' by the 1960s. Sometimes also **the wrong time of the month**.

(a) tincture An alcoholic (usually) drink. Since the early 20th century. 'Rough diamond, especially after a tincture or two' – Richard Ingrams and John Wells, *Dear Bill* (1980) – supposedly reproducing the conversational style of Sir Denis Thatcher Bt.

(a) tipple An alcoholic (usually) drink. Since the 16th century. Caption from a painting entitled 'Three Sober Preachers' (about 1860) at Compton Verney: 'Tippling, Do You Say, I call this Down, Right, Hard, Drinking.'

(to be) tired and emotional To be drunk. A pleasant euphemism, ideally suited to British newspapers which have to operate under libel laws effectively preventing any direct statement of a person's fondness for the bottle. The expression 't. and e.' (to which it is sometimes abbreviated) is said to have arisen when *Private Eye* printed a spoof Foreign Office memo suggesting it was a useful way of describing the antics of George Brown when he was Foreign Secretary (1966–8). On 29 September 1967, the *Eye* described him as 'tired and overwrought on many occasions' and a cover showed him gesticulating while Harold Wilson explained to General de Gaulle: '*George est un peu fatigué, votre Majesté.*'

There was never any question that Brown *did* get drunk. Peter Paterson entitled his biography of Brown, *Tired and Emotional* (1993). *Private Eye* may not actually have coined the phrase, though it undoubtedly popularized it. It has been suggested that a BBC spokesman said of Brown 'He was very tired and emotional' after the much-criticized appearance he made on TV on the night of President Kennedy's death in November 1963. In fact, it was ITV Brown appeared on and the remark, even if it was made, has not been traced. Also **over-tired**.

(a) toilet A LAVATORY (itself a euphemism). The word is originally a diminutive of the French *toile*, 'a cloth', so this points to the washing function of what was at first a dressing room with bathing facilities, a closet in fact. This was how 'toilet' was used in English by 1819 (Byron). The fact that a lavatory might also be found in such a place gradually meant that the word became descriptive of just that. By the time of the First World War.

toilet tissue LAVATORY paper (another euphemism for a euphemism). By the 1960s/70s and of American origin? 'Take lavatory paper, or, in the genteel euphemism of Adspeak, toilet tissue' – *Verbatim* (Summer 1982).

(a) tonsorial artist A barber, hairdresser. By 1910 – but 'tonsorial' had been used as a facetious adjective for two hundred years before this.

(a) touch / lick / dash of the tar brush Showing traces of non-white ancestry in one's skin. By 1796, as 'lick of the tar-brush'. Because the tar would be black.

(a) toupee A wig. Since the 18th century, but originally an additional piece of artificial hair rather than something covering all or most of the pate.

(a) trade union member A worker. British use since the 1960s.

(a) trademark Animal dung. As in, 'a cow had left its trademark on the path'.

(a) train manager A SENIOR CONDUCTOR, formerly guard. Reported in 2005. Job enhancement continues.

(a) train station A railroad/railway station. Seemingly of American origin, perhaps from the 1950s onwards. 'When was the last time you heard a young, rich-affluent-wealthy type use the phrase *railroad station*? Upper-class use is now *train station*' – *The New York Times Magazine* (21 June 1981).

transport/travel See AIR SICKNESS CONTAINER; DEFECTIVE TRAIN; DELAYED; DETRAIN; FLIGHT ATTENDANT; PURSER; RESCHEDULED TRAIN; SENIOR CONDUCTOR; SERVICE; STANDARD CLASS; STATION MANAGER; STATION STOP; TEMPORARILY-IMMOBILE; TRAIN MANAGER; TRAIN STATION; TRANSPORTATION FACILITY; TRAVEL CENTRE; TRAVEL DOCUMENTS; UPLIFTING PURPOSES

(penal) transportation Sending to an overseas prison. By 1669.

(a) transportation facility A bus or train service. 'A lady in the north-east of England complained to her local council that although living close to a main road she had to walk a mile to the shops in all weathers. "What you need, madam," said an official, "is a transportation facility." What she needed, she told him, was a bus' – Vernon Noble, *Speak Softly* (1982).

(a) travel centre A railway station with bus station, taxi-stand adjacent. Noted by 1992.

travel documents Tickets. Noted in use on British railways by 1992, as in the loudspeaker announcement: 'Before leaving the train, please make sure you have all your belongings and travel documents with you.' Originally, when used in connection with foreign travel, it might have had some point – visas and passports could indeed be considered as 'documents'. For all one knows, there may be plans to call train drivers 'pilots', as clearly the whole drift is to make travelling by train seem as superficially glamorous as air travel.

travellers / travelling people Gypsies. Such people have been known as this since the 18th century at least and it is their own name for themselves. But the term 'traveller' has also been applied, not least by themselves, to other types – tinkers, beggars, tramps and vagrants – who are not ethnically Romany. In recent years, wandering groups of hippies have also tended to be termed travellers by the media. 'The Government last night pledged new laws to control travellers, as the last hippies evicted from an illegal festival site at Otterbourne, Hampshire, packed up and left, leaving behind a £1m bill for damages' – *The Independent* (11 August 1992).

I wonder what view traditional travellers have of their word being applied to these newcomers? On the other hand, it appears that proper gypsies do not mind being called 'gypsies'. Indeed, they have good reason to hold on to the name. 'Of all those who live in caravans in Britain, gypsies are the only ones that have the distinction of being recognised as an ethnic group and thus protected from discrimination under the 1976 Race Relations Act. Their small victory was the result of a Court of Appeal ruling in 1989 which made this distinction after a pub in Hackney, east London, put a sign on the door banning travellers. Travellers were not held to be an ethnic group, but gypsies were, so the sign was deemed discriminatory' – *The Independent* (21 August 1992).

(a) tribute band A money-making rip-off under the guise of respectful recreation. The first such, in Britain, may have been the Bootleg Beatles, formed in 1980. By the early 21st century there were thought to be 20–30 Abba perform-a-likes around the world – including Abbacadabra, ABBALanche, Abbasolutely and Bjorn Again. Now the number of tribute bands performing on any one night seems likely to exceed the number of original bands.

(a) tropical rain forest A jungle. This word is unacceptable these days, because of derogatory associations with the 'law of the jungle', 'The Blackboard Jungle', 'The Asphalt Jungle', 'just down from the trees' etc. The PC Tarzan now has to hack his way through the 'tropical rain forest' which, alas, just isn't quite the same somehow. Since the early 1990s.

(in) trouble (1) Undergoing an unpleasant experience. (2) In gaol. (3) Unmarried and with child. All venerable usages, perhaps since the 19th century.

(to) trouble To approach sexually in or out of wedlock, especially when the bothered party is unwilling. Since the early 20th century? 'Shortly after Edward had been born [Mrs Green] had taken Barbara aside, and hinted that there were Things You Could Use, and that she had heard it rumoured that there were Clinics where they gave you the Things, not that she had any experience of them herself, she had never been troubled that way with poor Mr G., he was more for the fretwork' – David Lodge, *The British Museum Is Falling Down*, Chap. 2 (1965).

(The) Troubles Murderous mayhem in Ireland. Before the recent round of civil strife in Northern Ireland started in 1969, 'The Troubles' had been applied specifically to the outburst of Civil War in (1919–23), but it had also been applied generally to any nationalist unrest – even to events as far back as 1641.

(a/the) trunk A (man's) body. In the mid-19th century 'body' was considered indelicate in female conversation.

(a/the) tummy A/the STOMACH. A childish alteration of the original word but also reflecting the 19th century avoidance of mentioning this s-word – so a euphemism for a euphemism. 'Why should I hesitate to own / That pain was in his little tummy?' – W.S. Gilbert, *The Bab Ballads* (1869).

(the) tunnel of love The VAGINA. A euphemism perpetrated by a doctor answering readers' questions in the magazine *She* (May 1977). After the fairground attraction, of course, once much favoured by courting couples.

(a) turf accountant A bookmaker (in horse racing). By 1915.

(to) turn one's face to the wall To give up the will to live. Since the 16th century. 'He would turn his face to the wall, and die with that word unsaid' – Mark Twain, *The Adventures of Tom Sawyer* (1876), ch. 3.

(to) turn one's toes up (to the daisies) To die. Since the mid-19th century. 'It is a commonplace remark to hear young men boast of the time when the "old man turns up his toes", and they can "collar the chips"' – *Daily Chronicle* (11 September 1905).

(a) turncoat A traitor. By the 16th century.

twilight housing Slums. By the 1970s. These are said to be found in **twilight areas**, often in the INNER CITY.

(the) twilight years Old age. Late 20th century.

(a/the) twilight zone An indistinct boundary area. The phrase had existed in the early 1900s, for undoubtedly *The Twilight Zone*, a TV series about the supernatural (US 1959–65), reinforced it, e.g.: 'Several key officials charged with formulating foreign policy remain in a bureaucratic twilight zone one hundred days after Reagan's inauguration' – *The Washington Post* (26 April 1981);

'Musicians are not normal human beings. They are a species out of the Twilight Zone with something different in their brains' – Bob Monkhouse, *Crying with Laughter* (1993).

Uu

Ugandan affairs See DISCUSS UGANDAN AFFAIRS

(an) uncle A parent's unmarried lover as described for the benefit of a child. 'Mum often had guys she called my uncles around. Most of the time, of course, these uncles weren't uncles at all' – John Mortimer, *Quite Honestly* (2005), ch. 2.

uncourageous Cowardly. By the 19th century. 'Wordsworth's uncourageous elder years' – Edward Dowden, *Studies in Literature 1789–1877* (1878).

under review Put in a drawer and forgotten about. Accordingly, 'I am unable to tell you when this matter will be dealt with but it is under review' means get lost. Late 20th century.

under the counter Transacted in a dubious or illegal way. By 1926 (Aldous Huxley). '*De Sade Illustrated*, another version of the same under-the-counter classic, is also around' – *The New Yorker* (31 May 1969).

under the weather (1) Ill, not very well. Of American origin, by the 1820s. (2) Menstruating. (3) Drunk. (4) Depressed.

underachievement / (an) underachiever Failure / a failure. In educational psychology use, by about 1950. Bart Simpson's slogan 'underachiever and proud of it' became a curiously potent slogan from near the start of Twentieth-Century Fox's TV cartoon series *The Simpsons* (US 1989–).

(the) undercarriage   The genitals – especially the VAGINA. By the 1990s.

underfashions   Underwear (in the US). Quoted in Willard R. Espy, *An Almanac of Words at Play* (1975).

(the) underprivileged (class)   The poor. Especially in the US, by the 1890s. Quoted in Willard R. Espy, *An Almanac of Words at Play* (1975). 'Barbara Bush, the former first lady, courted controversy by pointing out that many of the people forced out of their homes by Hurricane Katrina "were underprivileged anyway" ... "they all want to stay in Texas. Everyone is so overwhelmed by the hospitality"' – *The Independent* (7 September 1995); 'When I first came to live in America I was struck by how "the poor" had vanished – vanished from the American lexicon. I discovered they were constantly being rescued by euphemism. First they became needy, then deprived, then underprivileged or disadvantaged' – Harold Evans, BBC Radio 4, *A Point of View* (18 September 2005).

understains   Stains of bodily functions on underwear. Used in advertising for Omo washing powder from 1968. 'Coined for Omo Biological to epitomize the ultimate in human residue on clothing, the word seemed to strike at the very heart of human frailty; it was universally objected to and finally crept away in silence' – Jo Gable, *The Tuppeny Punch and Judy Show* (1980), pt 6.

(to have an) understanding   To have a (possibly sexual) relationship. 'In *Cranford*, when Lady X after her *mésalliance* with the doctor, explained that the two of them had long had an "understanding", the ladies of Cranford found the word coarse. The Duke of Windsor had had an "understanding" with Mrs Simpson right enough' – James Lees-Milne, *Ancestral Voices* (1975), diary entry for 26 June 1942. As the term could also be applied to innocent courtship, there was plenty of scope for confusion.

(the) underworld Criminals, especially those involved in organized crime. Since 1900. 'True stories from the Underworld ... to understand as thoroughly as possible the motives and methods of that great part of the community which they describe as "The Under-World"' – *McClure's Magazine* (New York) (August 1900).

undeveloped areas Slums. By about the mid-1950s in the UK.

(the) undiscovered country Death. From Shakespeare, *Hamlet* (1600-1), III.i: 'Who would fardels bear, / To grunt and sweat under a weary life, / But that the dread of something after death, / The undiscovered country, from whose bourn / No traveller returns, puzzles the will, / And makes us rather bear those ills we have / Than fly to others that we know not of?'

undoing Loss of virginity by rape, seduction, whatever. By the 16th century. 'His proximity made me feel self-conscious. I must have been no more than fifteen ... when I met my "undoing" from his hands ... I rather enjoyed it, though of course pretending not to' – James Lees-Milne, *Caves of Ice* (1983) – diary entry for 13 November 1947.

undraped Naked, nude. Mostly of statuary and paintings and already well-established usage by the early 19th century. 'Eve ... is the only undraped figure which is allowable in sacred art' – Anna Jameson, *A Commonplace Book of Thoughts* (1854/1877). Curiously, when Mrs George Hammond Lucy (of Charlecote Park) was in Rome on the Grand Tour in June/July 1841, she used the word 'undraped' in her diaries for a passage that ended up in her actually published memoirs thus: 'I fear much of my modesty will wear away before I return to England, as naked Statues & *shocking* Pictures meet my eye in every Palace.'

unfaithful Adulterous or not restricting oneself to a single sexual partner. Since the early 19th century. 'Shall we condone the slaying of unfaithful wives by husbands avenging their honor if that was the custom in their native countries?' – *The Washington Post* (29 March 1992).

(an) unfortunate A prostitute. Before 1800. '*Frank*. Where is the reparation to the unfortunate he has deserted? *Shuffleton*. A great many unfortunates sport a stilish carriage' – George Colman, *John Bull* (1803), act 2, scene 2.

uninhibited Bawdy/immoral. Since the mid-20th century? 'Attractive, broad-minded, uninhibited, bi-minded couple' – advertisement in *Screw* Magazine (12 June 1972).

unintellectual Unintelligent. By the 17th century.

unlawful Illegal. Since the 14th century. 'Public authorities must beware of surrendering to the dictates of unlawful pressure groups. Indeed, they have an active responsibility not to' – *The Independent* (13 April 1995).

unlawful or arbitrary deprivation of life Killing. 'We found the term "killing" too broad and have substituted the more precise, if more verbose, "unlawful or arbitrary deprivation of life"' – Elliott Abrams, Assistant Secretary of State for Inter-American Affairs during the Reagan administration, quoted in *The New York Times* (11 February 1984). He was referring to State Department reports on human rights practices in 163 countries.

unmarried Homosexual. Coded use – since the mid-20th century? 'Bertie Hope-Davies died, as obituarists say, "unmarried" and never disguised, or obtruded, his inclinations but bubbled rather than seethed with indignation at the expression "gay"' – *The Independent* (2 September 2005).

unmentionables (1) Trousers. Now only used as a consciously archaic euphemism. Sometimes **indescribables** (by 1794). 'Mr Trotter ... gave four distinct slaps on the pocket of his mulberry indescribables' – Charles Dickens, *The Pickwick Papers* (1837), ch. 16. Also **indispensables, inexplicables, innominables,** and **ineffables, inexpressibles, unwhisperables**, the last three cited in Allen Walker Read, *Classic American Graffiti* (1935). (2) Underpants and, especially, female underwear. (3) What trousers and underwear contain: '[Coarse stories included] a lavish enumeration of those parts of the human body then known as "the unmentionables"' – Flora Thompson, *Lark Rise* (1939), ch. 3.

unnatural practices   Sodomy (usually). By about the late 19th century.

unofficial action   A strike in breach of an agreement. British trades union euphemism since the 1960s. 'Severe disruption of the production of the *Daily Mirror* took place last night as a result of unofficial action by some members of the Natsopa union' – *The Times* (11 February 1963).

unparliamentary language   Bad language/swearing. By 1887 (Kipling). Because the limits of language are policed in both houses of parliament by the Speaker and the Lord Chancellor. 'At Westminster words regarded as unparliamentary include blackguard, cad, corrupt, coward, criminal, hypocrite, jackass, murderer, rat and traitor ... In the US Congress ... Speaker Sam Rayburn once declared, "If they're from the Bible, they're not unparliamentary"' – Nicholas Comfort, *Brewer's Politics* (1995 edn).

unprepossessing   Ugly. By the early 19th century.

unprotected sex   SEXUAL INTERCOURSE without some form of prophylactic. Since the 1980s. 'We have a drug that can save people from possible death, but we hold back from telling them about it in case they might get the idea that unprotected sex is OK'; 'Gay writer whose advocacy of unprotected sex enraged other activists' – *The Times* (27 October 2005).

unseasonable weather   Bad weather. By the 17th century.

(an) unseeing person A blind or partly blind person. An American suggestion, from about 1990. 'Unseeing' for 'without sight' has been known since the 16th century (Shakespeare).

unsightly Unpleasing to the eye. Since the 16th century.

unsocial elements Poor citizens, bad men. 'Once we killed bad men: now we liquidate unsocial elements' – C.S. Lewis, *The Abolition of Man* (1943), ch. 3.

unwaged Out of work, unemployed. Sometimes a marginally more dignified way of saying 'out of work', at others, a means of recognizing the contribution to society made by people (like non-working mothers) who do not receive wages. By the 1980s. 'The cost will be £2 per line for waged persons or £1 per line for those who are unwaged' – *Library Association Record* (30 November 1982).

(to feel) unwell (1) To be menstruating. By the 1840s. 'When I was unwell for the first time it was she who explained to me, so that it seemed quite all right' – Jean Rhys, *Voyage in the Dark* (1934), pt 1, ch. 6. (2) To be drunk / have a hangover – a euphemism used by Queen Victoria in excuse for her Scottish servant John Brown's excess of whisky taking. (3) To be ill. 'Jeffrey Bernard is unwell' was the occasional editorial explanation for the non-appearance of his articles in *The Spectator* and was used as the title of a London play (1989) by Keith Waterhouse, based on Bernard's writings and life. Given his chief penchant, it could equally have been referring to meaning (2).

up the spout Pregnant. By the 1930s.

(to go) up the wooden hill to Bedfordshire To go up to bed. Originally a nursery euphemism, this has become part of grown-up 'golf-club slang', as someone once termed it – i.e. a conversational cliché. Sir Hugh Casson and Joyce Grenfell included it in their *Nanny Says* (1972), together with 'Come on, up wooden hill, down sheet lane'. 'Up the Wooden Hill to

Bedfordshire' was the title of the first song recorded by Vera Lynn, in 1936. The 'bed-fordshire' joke occurs in a synopsis of *Ali Baba and the Forty Thieves, or, Harlequin and the Magic Donkey* staged at the Alexandra Theatre, Liverpool, in 1868. Indeed, as so often, Jonathan Swift found it even earlier. In *Polite Conversation* (1738), the Colonel says, 'I'm going to the Land of Nod.' Neverout replies: 'Faith, I'm for *Bedfordshire*.' But then again, the poet Charles Cotton had used it in 1665.

up to a point, Lord Copper I disagree with you but I know on which side my bread is buttered. This phrase is employed when disagreeing with someone it is prudent not to differ with, or when simply disagreeing without being objectionable about it. It comes from Evelyn Waugh's novel about journalists, *Scoop* (1938), ch. 3, pt 3: 'Mr Salter's side of the conversation was limited to expressions of assent. When Lord Copper [a newspaper proprietor] was right he said, "Definitely, Lord Copper"; when he was wrong, "Up to a point".' 'We are told that [Norman Tebbit] was only trying to help ... he was out to "stop Heseltine". Well, up to a point, Lord Whitelaw' – *The Independent* (4 April 1990).

uphill gardening Sodomy. By the 1990s. Like 'pillow biting' and 'Vegemite drilling', this does not bear too detailed an explanation. A hapless individual (who was mortified when it was explained to him) put it among his hobbies in the 2000 edition of *Who's Who* – and all he meant to say was that his garden was on a slope ...

(for) uplifting purposes For picking up. 'The new British Rail summer timetable ... states that the 2025 Fort William to London Euston service will call at Roy Bridge, Corrour and Ardlui "for uplifting purposes only"' – letter to *The Independent* (25 April 1990).

upstate In prison. Of American origin, by the 1930s. 'She got married while I was upstate doing time' – Ed McBain, *Long Time No See* (1977), ch. 11. Compare **to send someone up the river**,

meaning 'to imprison', because Sing Sing gaol lies up the
Hudson River from New York City. Known by 1891. 'I done it.
Send me up the river. Give me the hot seat' – *Chicago Daily News*
(5 March 1946).

(to) urinate   To piss. Since the 16th century – a medical term.

urination   See COMFORT BREAK; COMMIT A NUISANCE;
DRAIN ONE'S LIZARD/SNAKE; INCONTINENT; MAKE ROOM
FOR MY TEA; MAKE WATER; MINOR FUNCTION; PASS WATER;
PEE; PICK A DAISY; PIT-STOP; POINT PERCY AT THE
PORCELAIN; SHAKE HANDS WITH THE BISHOP; SPLASH
ONE'S BOOTS; WATERWORKS; WEE-WEE; and see under
LAVATORY.

(to) use the euphemism   To go to the LAVATORY. *Honey*:
'I wonder if you could show me where the ... I want to ... put
some powder on my nose.' *George*: 'Martha, won't you show her
where we keep the ... euphemism?' – Edward Albee, *Who's
Afraid of Virginia Woolf?* (1962), act 1.

(the) usual offices   LAVATORY (and also washing facilities)
in a house. 'You will find the usual offices at the end of the
corridor.' By the 1930s, though the term 'office of ease' had
been used for 'privy' since the early 18th century. 'The
bathroom's to the right and the usual offices next to it' –
John Braine, *Room at the Top* (1957), ch. 1.

(the) usual reason   Menstruation, i.e. the usual reason for
not being able or wishing to take part in sex. The actress Liv
Ullman, writing about her girlhood in Norway in *Changing* (1977),
recalled: 'Gym classes, which most girls missed once a month by
saying "usual reason" in a matter-of-fact voice when their names
were called out.'

(a) utensil maintenance man   A dishwasher. Probably a
one-off, maybe joke-, coinage. 'Euphemism has upgraded other
jobs. In parts of the country, dishwashers have been called

utensil maintenance men, though back at the sink they may still be "pearl divers"' – *Daily Progress* (Charlottesville) (15 January 1970).

(a) utility (access) hole See ACCESS HOLE

Vv

(the) vagina The cunt. This medical term has been elevated to almost the sole way of euphemizing the 'c-word', which is still publicly unacceptable usage. 'The real reason ... why women are loath to describe their private parts must surely be that there is no acceptable word ... Feminist linguist Deborah Cameron suggests "ginny" pronounced with a "j" sound, a nicely inoffensive abbreviation of vagina which, unfortunately, is unlikely to pass into the lexicon except through a very concerted politically correct effort' – *The Guardian* (9 July 1992).

(a) vendor A seller. In legal use by the 16th century. Now would-be dignification by mortgage-lenders and estate agents. By the 1970s.

venerable Old. Originally because the old were worthy of respect because of their age. By the 16th century.

venereal disease / V.D. Syphilis. Hardly euphemistic now but, in the 17th century, an attempt by invoking the name of Venus, goddess of love, to provide a term more softly-sounding than 'pox' or 'clap'.

verbally deficient Illiterate. A joke PC invention from the early 1990s.

(a) vermin exterminator A rat-catcher. 'My father's father ... [ended up] as a rat-catcher on the Royal Sandringham estate. My mother, who had a distinct aura of piss-elegance, always insisted that he was a "vermin exterminator"' – Peter Hall, *Making an Exhibition of Myself* (1993).

vertically challenged Small, dwarf; smaller or taller than average. A joke PC invention from the early 1990s. 'Usually [PC] is noticed here through its more ridiculous contortions: the handicapped being "differently abled"', the short "vertically challenged"' – *The Observer* (15 December 1991). Also **vertically impaired**.

(a) veteran An old age pensioner or a retired soldier. By the 16th century.

viable Profitable. A strange use of the word to avoid the accusation of making money or producing a profit. 'At the present time it is not a viable proposition to process potatoes into frozen chips', commented a manufacturer in *The Observer* (2 May 1976). 'Viable' was one of the 'in' words of the 1970s, used on a multitude of occasions, sometimes meaning 'workable' and sometimes without any discernible meaning.

(a) Vicar of Bray A vacillating opportunist, a person who changes allegiance according to the way the wind blows, a turncoat. So named after a vicar of Bray, Berkshire, in the 16th century who is supposed to have changed his religious affiliation from Roman Catholic to Protestant more than once during the reigns of Henry VIII to Elizabeth I. However, there was more than one vicar of Bray in this period. Whatever the case, by the time of Thomas Fuller's *Worthies* (1662) there was a proverb: 'The Vicar of Bray will be Vicar of Bray still.' As for the song beginning 'In Good King Charles's Golden Days ...', it was probably written at the beginning of the 18th century and describes a different (perhaps completely fictional) vicar of Bray who changed his religion to suit the different faiths of monarchs from Charles II to George I. Can there have been two such turncoat vicars – or was the song merely an updating of the circumstances of the actual first vicar?

vice Prostitution, drug abuse, illegal gambling. A catch-all name for crime on the recreational side. Of American origin, by 1900, as was also the term (police) Vice Squad. The concept of 'vice' seems to have been transferred to Britain in the 1930s, though it is doubtful whether Scotland Yard's Vice Squad was ever officially known as such – it may just have been journalistic labelling. The word 'Vice' now appears to be obsolete in this context but was certainly well alive in the UK at the time of the Profumo Affair in the summer of 1963. Having just left school, I remember my mother inquiring whether I knew what it meant. 'Of course!', I replied confidently.

(la/the) vice anglaise [the English vice] Flagellation. From the curious French view that this is the chief sexual predilection of the English (derived in turn from his supposed enjoyment of corporal punishment during his schooldays). Often thought to be the French term for the Englishman's predilection for homosexual over heterosexual behaviour. *OED2* does not find the 'flagellation' use until 1942. On the other hand, Sir Richard Burton's 'Terminal Essay' in his translation of the *Arabian Nights* (1885), includes this observation on homosexuality: 'In our modern capitals, London, Berlin and Paris for instance, the Vice seems subject to periodical outbreaks. For many years, also, England sent her pederasts to Italy, and especially to Naples whence originated the term *"Il vizio Inglese"*.'

(a) victualler's assistant A barmaid. The search for a less pejorative term is ongoing: in John Osborne, *A Better Class of Person* (1981), he recalls his mother saying: *'I'm* not a barmaid. I'm a victualler's assistant.'

(the) vintage years Old age. Late 20th century. Of American origin.

(to) violate To rape (a woman). Since the 15th century. '"Tell me, Mr Strachey, what would you do if you saw a German soldier trying to violate your sister?" [He] replied with an air of noble virtue: "I would try to get between them"' – Robert Graves, *Goodbye To All That* (1929), ch. 23.

visible minority Black, African-American. By the early 1990s.

(a) visually impaired individual A blind/partly blind person. By the early 1990s. Note also **loss of vision** = blindness.

vital statistics Body measurements (usually of a female). A jocular twisting of the original 19th-century meaning which related to births, marriages and deaths, being a euphemism for bust, waist and hip measurements. Probably coined by Hollywood film publicists in the 1930s as a way of avoiding restraints against too much emphasis on sexual attraction. 'Regina wrote haphazardly to men, giving her age and vital statistics' – C.R. Cooper, *Teen-Age Vice* (1952), ch. 8.

vivacious (Of a woman) not backward in coming forward, possibly drunk and generally rather an embarrassment. Newspaper gossip-column shorthand. Late 20th century. 'Adjectives should not be allowed in a newspaper unless they have something to say. *Red-haired* tells us that a person has red hair. *Vivacious* – a word belonging to the lost world of Marcel waves and cocktail cherries – tells us nothing except that someone has sat down at a VDU and keyed in the word "vivacious"' – Keith Waterhouse, *Waterhouse on Newspaper Style* (1989).

voluntary death Suicide. Since the second half of the 19th century. 'I would like to represent this voluntary death as an exemplary case' – Peter Handke (on the death by suicide of his mother), *A Sorrow Beyond Dreams* (1976). 'Suicide' has long disappeared as an inquest verdict – hence such formulations as 'He took his life while the balance of his mind was disturbed'.

(with a) voluptuous figure Fat, on the large side (of a woman). 'You might think that adopting a royal title is a little cheeky, but Queen Latifah can pull it off. With her no-nonsense attitude and voluptuous figure, the brazen first lady of hip-hop is perhaps an unlikely movie star' – *The Independent* (26 April 2005).

(a/the) W.C. / w. A/the LAVATORY (itself a euphemism). By 1815. An abbreviation of WATER CLOSET that has quite definitely taken on a life of its own.

(the) wages of sin Death; punishment or retribution for one's actions – now often jocularly used. After Romans 6:23, St Paul speaking: 'For the wages of sin is death; but the gift of God is eternal life through Jesus Christ our Lord.' 'For sin pays a wage, and the wage is death' is the New English Bible's version. The strength of the expression derives from the perfectly correct singular verb 'is', where the hearer might be more comfortable with 'are'. There may possibly be an allusion in *The Wages of Fear*, English title of the film *Le Salaire de la Peur* (France/Italy 1953).

(a) waitperson A waiter/waitress. An American non-sexist coinage. There is nothing wrong with using 'waiter' to apply to a male or female, but 'waitperson' did have a certain amount of use. 'It is the only caffeinated coffee served by the "wait-persons", as they are called, at the politically correct Takoma Cafe in Takoma Park' – *The Washington Post* (11 March 1985); 'Waitperson wanted ... Olive Tree Cafe' – *Village Voice* (14 June 1988). Another attempt was waitron]ax[but this one never seemed to get off the launching pad.

(a) wardrobe malfunction Accidental exposure of a body part usually kept hidden and caused by the clothes giving way.

The phrase was coined by the singer Justin Timberlake to explain how Janet Jackson's breast popped out of her costume for a few seconds while she was singing before a TV audience of millions during the halftime show at Super Bowl XXXVIII (1 February 2004). She never heard the end of it.

(to) wash one's hands To go to the LAVATORY. By the 1930s. 'We are invited to wash our hands, or, if we wear dresses, to powder our noses' – Isaac Goldberg, *The Wonder of Words* (1938), ch. 6.

(a) washroom A LAVATORY. From the mid-19th century. Merely an English translation of the original Latin. 'Washroom sex can mean a hand reaching for a groin under toilet cubicles or it can involve two men in a cubicle' – *The Ottawa Citizen* (16 June 1980).

(to) waste (1) To destroy (an enemy), particularly in military usage. Since the 1960s. 'The intention to "waste" My Lai' – *The Guardian* (2 April 1971). (2) To DEFECATE / URINATE.

(a) water closet A flush LAVATORY. Since the mid-18th century. Hence, the abbreviation W.C.

(a) water systems specialist A plumber (in the US). Quoted in Willard R. Espy, *An Almanac of Words at Play* (1975).

(the) waterworks The male urinating equipment. By 1900. 'Little scotch, lot of soda. Got to keep the old waterworks going in this climate' – Eric Ambler, *Passage of Arms* (1959), ch. 5. A one-off but delightful euphemism is to be found in Flora Thompson's *Lark Rise* (1939), ch. 2: 'In summer they would make mud pies in the dust, moistening them from **their own most intimate water supply**.'

(to go the) way of all flesh To die. After 'I enter into the way of all flesh' – 1 Kings 2:2 – in the 1609 Douai Bible translation, repeating an old mistranslation of 'the way of all the earth' (which is what the Authorized Version has). The phrase can also mean the opposite, 'to experience life'. Hence, *The Way of All Flesh*, title of a novel (1903) by Samuel Butler.

(we have) ways (and means) of making you talk We have weapons of torture. This threat by evil inquisitor to victim appears to have come originally from 1930s Hollywood villains and was then handed on to Nazi characters from the 1940s onwards. Douglass Dumbrille, as the evil Mohammed Khan, says, 'We have ways to make men talk' in the film *The Lives of a Bengal Lancer* (US 1934). He means by forcing slivers of wood under the fingernails and setting fire to them ... A typical 'film Nazi' use can be found in the film *Odette* (UK 1950) in which the French Resistance worker (Anna Neagle) is threatened with unmentioned nastiness by one of her captors. Says he: 'We have ways and means of making you talk.' Then, after a little stoking of the fire with a poker, he urges her on with: 'We have ways and means of making a woman talk.'

Later, used in caricature, the phrase saw further action in programmes like the BBC radio show *Round the Horne* (e.g. 18 April 1965) and *Laugh-In* (*circa* 1968) – invariably pronounced with a German accent. Frank Muir presented a comedy series for London Weekend Television with the title *We Have Ways of Making You Laugh* (1968).

we must have lunch See LUNCH

weapons of mass destruction / W.M.D.s Weapons that could kill a great number of people. Since the 1950s. 'I've got the United Nations delegate staying at my hotel ... he's trying to get them [dumplings] put on the list ... of banned weapons of mass destruction' – BBC Radio *Hancock's Half-Hour*, 'The Chef That Died of Shame' (24 May 1955); 'Various means of mass destruction such as atomic, thermonuclear, chemical and bacteriological weapons' – G.K. Zhukov, Soviet Minister of Defence to 20th Party Congress (1956); 'Nuclear weapons or any other kinds of weapons of mass destruction' – the Outer Space [arms control] Treaty (January 1967); 'States like these

[Iraq, Iran, North Korea], and their terrorist allies, constitute an axis of evil, arming to threaten the peace of the world. By seeking weapons of mass destruction, these regimes pose a grave and growing danger' – George W. Bush, State of the Union address to Congress (29 January 2002).

(to) wear iron knickers To cling to one's virginity (or, at least, to refrain from sexual intercourse). This 20th-century version of the chastity belt seems to have been coined in the 1970/80s. The novelist Jilly Cooper was once described as being like the romantic novelist Barbara Cartland – 'but without the iron knickers' – quoted in my book *A Year of Stings and Squelches* (1985).

(the) wedding kit / tackle The male genitals. Since the First World War.

(the) weed Tobacco (and later marijuana). Originally sometimes 'fragrant weed'. By the 17th century. 'Smoking Cars ... we mean cars expressly provided for the lovers of the "weed"' – *The American Railroad Journal* (1846).

(to do a) wee-wee To URINATE. In imitation of children's talk. By the 1930s. Also the noun 'wee-wee' for 'urine' (but also occasionally for 'penis'). Could it derive from the 'w' at the front of 'water closet' and 'W.C.'? 'I suddenly rushed into the sea ... and wee-weed in the water for a joke' – Dannie Absie, *Ash on a Young Man's Sleeve* (1967).

(a) welfare home A doss house. American use only, since the 1960s? 'Did some purely personal demons hound her to the point where she went to work as a domestic (she claimed she was doing research for a book) and ended up in a welfare home?' – *The Washington Post* (31 January 1992).

well-built Fat, PLUMP. Since the 17th century, but it is often not clear precisely what is being hinted at by this word. 'This Gentleman was of a middle size, and what is called well built' –

Henry Fielding, *Tom Jones* (1749), pt I, ch. 10. From the BBC radio show *Hancock's Half-Hour* (23 December 1956) – *Kid* [of Hattie Jacques]: 'Who is the, er, well-built lady?' *Hancock*: 'Do you know, that is the kindest thing anyone ever said about her.' Also **well-covered**. 'A mild, well-covered person, with crinkly hair and rather piggy eyes' – Denton Welch, *Maiden Voyage* (1943), ch. 17.

well-endowed (I) Having large genitals/breasts. By the 1950s. '"I'm not rich." "You are doubtless well-endowed ... It's better, really ... A lot of women think so"' – Nicholas Monsarrat, *The Cruel Sea* (1951), ch. 5. (2) Fat.

well-hung (Of a man) having large genitals. Since the mid-20th century. 'Hung like a horse, my dear!' 'As the vagina is an elastic organ that can stretch – or shrink – to accommodate, unless a man is literally hung like a horse, this is probably not an issue any man need worry about' – *The Independent* (15 November 2005).

(a) well-informed source (I) Someone the journalist met in a pub. (2) The person quoted himself/herself. Journalistic code when half-heartedly trying to obscure a source. Both by the mid-20th century.

well-upholstered (I) Having large genitals/breasts. 'Could that be a sigh I hear, emanating from Anouska Hempel's well-upholstered chest?' – *The Independent* (16 June 2005). (2) Fat. By the 1930s.

(a) wet dream An erotic dream that produces an orgasm and/or ejaculation in a male sleeper. Known as a medical term since the mid-19th century. '(*He gazes ahead reading on the wall a scrawled chalk legend* Wet Dream *and a phallic design*)' – James Joyce, *Ulysses* (1922).

what in the Sam Hill ...? What in Hell's name ... ? Known since the early 20th century. This expression enrols the name of Sam Hill, a 19th-century American politician, to avoid having to say the worst. 'Characters [in 1936 production] are given to Will Rogerisms like "What in Sam Hills is the matter with her?" and

"Creeping Jesus!" (which got them into hot water with the censors)' – Simon Callow, *Orson Welles: The Road to Xanadu* (1995); 'What the Sam Hill you yelling for, George?' – film soundtrack, *It's a Wonderful Life* (US 1946).

what the dickens! What the devil! Exclamation of incredulity, since the 16th century. 'Dickens' has nothing to do with the novelist but is perhaps a watered down version of 'devilkin' (though this is not certain). Shakespeare has 'I cannot tell what the dickens his name is' in *The Merry Wives of Windsor* (1601), III.ii.16. See also under OLD NICK.

(a) whatnot / whatsit / whatyoucallit / whatyoumaycallit Anything you don't know how to describe or don't wish to, explicitly. 'So I went round to the whatyoucall it everything was whatyoucallit ... and if he was married he'd do it to me' – James Joyce, *Ulysses* (1922); 'By the time I was fourteen I'd been a court witness in an indecent exposure case after an Indian doctor had been caught flashing his whatnot at me in an Adventure Playground' – Hamblett and Deverson (eds), *Generation X* (1964); 'Musically, I have to admit, Moby Dick is outstandingly unmemorable, which is a bit of a drawback for a musical. The idiom is rock and ballad, with the odd touch of spoof blues and whatnot' – *The Sunday Times* (22 March 1992).

(a) wheelchair user / person in a wheelchair A cripple, someone who is 'confined to a wheelchair' / 'wheelchair-bound'. A PC euphemism, the point being that 'wheelchairs liberate rather confine' and it is unlikely that anybody spends all day in one, anyway. **Wheelchair accessible** is positive in this connection, and therefore PC acceptable. 'I am fortunate enough not to be wheelchair-bound' *Daily Mail* (17 June 1981); 'As a person in a wheelchair, I read with interest the article on physicist Stephen Hawking and his severe disability. I was disappointed, however, to see you refer to him as "confined to a wheelchair, a virtual prisoner in his own body". The expression "confined to a wheelchair", though common, is misleading and insulting. Wheelchairs are tools that enable us to get around.

They are liberating, not confining. As for his being a "prisoner in his own body", who is not?' – letter to *Time* Magazine (29 February 1988).

'They are each progressive. They are each gay. They are each so politically correct that their literature assures readers that their campaign headquarters are "wheelchair accessible"' – *The Washington Post* (11 September 1991); 'If you are reporting the difficulties confronting a disabled individual or group, do not merely focus on the individual's physical or mental impairments, but upon the broader social causes of the problems, e.g. the inaccessible social environment for wheelchair users ... Do not write "confined to a wheelchair". Instead describe a person as a "wheelchair user". From their point of view (which is the important one) a wheelchair is an aid to mobility, not a restriction' – Briefing Note, The Royal Association for Disability and Rehabilitation (May 1992).

when are you going to finish off that dress? Your dress is very revealing. Addressed to a woman with low *décolletage*, a cliché used in chatting up, flirting. Tom Jones can be heard so addressing a member of the audience on the record album *Tom Jones – Live at Caesar's Palace, Las Vegas* (1971).

(a) whistle-blower A person within an organization or company who alerts the outside world to malpractice. Of American origin, since the 1960s.

(a) white elephant Something which turns out to be of no value or an expensive mistake. Known by 1851. From Siam/Thailand where elephants were sacred. The king would bestow one on awkward courtiers who then had the bother of its upkeep.

(to) whitewash To excuse (a misdemeanour), to cover up. The expression perhaps originated in Matthew 24:27 when Jesus said: 'Woe unto you, lawyers and Pharisees, hypocrites! for ye are like unto whited sepulchres, which indeed appear beautiful outward, but are within full of dead men's bones, and of uncleanness.' 'There can be no whitewash at the White House' – President

Nixon, TV address (30 April 1973), quoted in Carl Bernstein and Bob Woodward, *All the President's Men* (1974); 'No one can say that the official report on the Darlington psychiatric unit is a whitewash' – *Northern Echo* (14 May 1976).

(a) whoopsie A lump of excrement. Probably of nursery origin and popularized by the BBC TV comedy show *Some Mothers Do 'Ave 'Em*. In Episode 6 of the 2nd Series (December 1973), Frank Spencer (Michael Crawford) said: 'I threw it at a dog. He was doing a whoopsie in the dahlias.' This was thereafter more usually rendered by impressionists as 'The dog's done a whoopsie on the carpet'.

wide-eyed and legless Too drunk to stand – a phrase from the song with this title, written and performed by Andy Fairweather-Low (1976). There is no suggestion of any love interest anywhere in the lyrics. The phrase 'the rhythm of the glass' quite clearly indicates that the song is about the excessive consumption of alcohol and the inability to control such consumption. Paul Beale commented (1998): '"Legless" was certainly the popular in-word during my last army posting 1972–4 – but Andy Fairweather-Low might have added the "wide-eyed" to make it more colourful/emphatic. It sounds like a bimbo who's been plied with gin (aka leg-opener).'

(a/the) willy A/the penis. By 1900. Originally from children's usage, though as 'will' it was much punned upon by Will Shakespeare in the late 16th century. A peculiarly British affectation, barely known in the US. 'Jokey gifts are speechlessly embarrassing; this season's dud is a woolly willy-warmer' – *The Observer* (7 December 1975); 'The real reason ... why women are loath to describe their private parts must surely be that there is no acceptable word ... There is no female equivalent of the unthreatening, used-by-all "willy"' – *The Guardian* (9 July 1992).

(to) wipe out (1) To kill, massacre. By the 16th century. (2) To make bankrupt.

with a mature figure Fat. Also **with surplus weight**. Both from the second half of the 20th century.

with child Pregnant. Since the 12th century. '[Mary] was found with child of the Holy Ghost' – Matthew 1:18.

with Jesus Dead. 'Overheard in a Natural History museum – Child: "Ooh! Mummy, is that wolf real?" Mother: "No, dear, he's – er – he's gone to be with Jesus"' – quoted in my book *Say No More* (1987); '"At rest with Jesus … Asleep with Mary" – on the adjacent tombstones of a husband and wife, Myrtle Beach, South Carolina' – *Epitaphs* (1993).

(a) withdrawal of goodwill A disruption of work through inflexibility in order to draw attention to a grievance, usually about pay. In British trades union parlance, 1970s/80s. A term which the Manchester branch of the National Union of Journalists, in reference to a dispute at the *Daily Mail* at that time, explained as 'members always taking their breaks at the agreed time'.

(a) withdrawal of labour A strike. In British trades union parlance from approximately the mid-1950s, though the term is an old one: 'The Withdrawal of Labour Committee advised the men to adopt the "stay-in" strike' – *Political Science Quarterly* (May 1915).

(a) withdrawal to prepared positions A (military) retreat. A familiar euphemism in army communiqués in the early part of the Second World War, intended to allay anxiety about Allied reverses.

(a) wolf A lecher, a sexually aggressive male. By 1847 (Thackeray).

(a) woman of easy virtue / of pleasure A prostitute. 'Easy' here means 'immoral'. Both by the 18th century. John Cleland's *Memoirs of a Woman of Pleasure* (1748–9) was the original title of what is now usually referred to as *Fanny Hill*. Also **(a) woman of the town** – the dating of its use can be found in a memorandum written by Lady Susan O'Brien (1745–1823) on 'changes between 1760–1818': 'Language has always been changing, & it has been said, as morals grow worse language grows more refined ... "fair Cyprians," & "tender" or "interesting connexions," have succeeded to "women on the town," & "kept mistresses".'

James Boswell, writing at the beginning of the period of change, uses a range of euphemism that is hard to measure in terms of refinement: 'free-hearted ladies', 'splendid Madam', 'civil nymph' (diary entry for 13 December 1762); 'As we walked along the Strand tonight, arm in arm, a woman of the town came enticingly near us. "No," said Mr. Johnson, "no, my girl, it won't do"' (28 July 1763). Compare under LADY OF THE NIGHT.

(a) woman's operation A hysterectomy. Remembered from the 1950s. 'I'm going into the Northern Hospital.' 'What for, Mum?' 'A woman's operation.'

(a) word from our sponsor An advertisement on American TV and radio (chiefly). 'Now, here is a word from our sponsor.' One of the various ways of getting into a commercial break, taken from American radio and television and much employed in British parodies of same in the 1950s and 60s – though never used in earnest in the UK (for the simple reason that sponsored TV of any type was not permitted until much later). Sometimes abbreviated to **a / this word**: 'We'll be right back after this word.'

(a) work to rule A disruption of work, restricted activity. In British trades union parlance, by the 1940s. 'That conductor was working to rule. All passengers must be seated before moving off; no overtaking of other buses; and no efforts to make up lost time' – *News Chronicle* (13 March 1952).

(the) workers / workmen The common people, labourers, the LOWER ORDERS. Since the mid-19th century, particularly when seen in social economic terms as 'producers of wealth' as opposed to the 'capitalist bosses'.

(the) workforce Labourers. By the 1960s. 'They were non-unionised because "that is the wish of the majority of the work force"' – *The Daily Telegraph* (18 November 1982); 'Any immediate strike would now be an act of mass professional suicide, yet the drivers took this perilous decision at a short, emotional meeting attended by a third of the workforce' – *The Guardian* (29 April 1995).

(a) working girl A prostitute. American origin, by the 1960s. 'They call themselves "working girls" ... Their work is a "business", or even a "social service"' – *The New York Times* (9 August 1971).

workplace See BUSINESS

(a) worrier about health A hypochondriac. Since the 19th century.

(to be) written out of the script To be dropped, removed, killed, disposed of. From the practice of deleting characters from long-running radio, television and film series. Since the 1950s? Frank Marcus's play *The Killing of Sister George* (1965; filmed UK 1968) is about a soap-opera actress who is treated in this way.

(to) wrong To seduce. Since the 17th century. 'Wronged' is a word beloved of 19th-century novelists, always used in the past tense – 'She had been wronged' – and never to indicate a future intention (such as, 'He set out to wrong her').

XYZ

you-know-what A taboo subject or thing. By the 1930s. 'Since neither I nor Mr Hurt flashed you-know-what before the cameras ... we might by modern standards be considered old-fashioned' – Quentin Crisp, *How To Become a Virgin* (1981), ch. 6.

you know where to go! Go to hell! 20th-century oath modifier.

(a) young lady A girl, a young woman. Since the 19th century in this euphemistic sense. *OED* (first edition, by 1928) commented: 'This expression is now avoided in polite use, except among some old-fashioned speakers and jocularly. Various particular applications formerly existed; thus, from the 17th to the early 19th cent. a young woman or a girl waited upon by a maid-servant was called "her young lady"; until late in the 19th cent. girls at boarding schools were spoken of and addressed as young ladies. At the present day, the term is freq. applied, with the intention of avoiding the supposed derogatory implication of *young woman*, to female shop assistants or clerks of good appearance and manners.' See also LADY.

young offender See OFFENDER

(one's) youthful indiscretions One's sexual (usually) history. By the mid-19th century. 'Perhaps there is no schooling so good for an author as his own youthful indiscretions' – J.R. Lowell, *Among My Books*, Series I (1873).